"[This book] offers a sound argument for helping doctoral students achieve high performance levels in the research and writing of their dissertations by providing clear and explicit performance expectations.

The author clearly states that providing . . . explicit expectations should not replace the critical role of the advisor but should enhance the advising relationship between student and faculty member by providing a means for effective formative evaluation. This text is certainly one I wish I had had while writing my own dissertation. In addition to Lovitts' excellent rationales, she gives the reader detailed tables and rubrics that clearly outline the components and characteristics of different quality levels in dissertations.

This book is an excellent resource for graduate students beginning the dissertation phase, for faculty who serve on dissertation committees or as dissertation advisors, and for faculty who may teach dissertation process courses. The text is also a valuable resource for academic departments who may want or need to develop dissertation standards from the ground up or to revamp their existing standards and expectations. The strength of Lovitts' book lies in the practical usefulness of the text . . . and its functionality for different academic disciplines.

Students and faculty alike will benefit from this practical and useful resource."

—*The Review of Higher Education*

D0149004

MAKING THE IMPLICIT EXPLICIT

# MAKING THE

# IMPLICIT EXPLICIT

## Creating Performance Expectations
## for the Dissertation

*Barbara E. Lovitts*

STERLING, VIRGINIA

Sty/us

COPYRIGHT © 2007 BY
STYLUS PUBLISHING, LLC.

Published by Stylus Publishing, LLC
22883 Quicksilver Drive
Sterling, Virginia 20166-2102

**Library of Congress Cataloging-in-Publication-Data**
Lovitts, Barbara E., 1960-
  Making the implicit explicit : creating performance
expectations for the dissertation / Barbara E. Lovitts.
      p. cm.
    Includes bibliographical references and index.
    ISBN 1-57922-180-7 (cloth : alk. paper) —
    ISBN 1-57922-181-5 (pbk. : alk. paper)
    1. Dissertations, Academic.    I. Title.
  LB2369.L685    2007
  378.2'42—dc22                                    2006031897

ISBN: 1-57922-180-7 (cloth) / 13-digit ISBN: 978-1-57922-180-5
ISBN: 1-57922-181-5 (paper) / 13-digit ISBN: 978-1-57922-181-2

Printed in Canada

All first editions printed on acid free paper
that meets the American National Standards Institute
Z39-48 Standard.

Bulk Purchases

Quantity discounts are available for use in workshops
and for staff development.
Call 1-800-232-0223

First Edition, 2007

10   9   8   7   6   5   4   3   2

# CONTENTS

LIST OF TABLES                                              *vii*

PREFACE                                                      *xi*

ACKNOWLEDGMENTS                                            *xvii*


**PART ONE: THE DISSERTATION AND ITS ASSESSMENT**

1. JUDGING DISSERTATIONS                                      *3*

2. ACHIEVING EXCELLENCE                                      *19*

3. UNIVERSAL QUALITIES OF A DISSERTATION                     *27*

4. DISCIPLINARY APPROACHES TO DOCTORAL TRAINING
   AND THE DEVELOPMENT OF A DISSERTATION                     *59*

5. CONVERTING PERFORMANCE EXPECTATIONS INTO
   RUBRICS                                                   *97*

6. CONCLUSIONS, IMPLICATIONS, AND
   RECOMMENDATIONS                                          *113*


**PART TWO: THE DISCIPLINES**

7. THE BIOLOGY DISSERTATION                                 *121*

8. THE PHYSICS DISSERTATION                                 *145*

9. THE ELECTRICAL AND COMPUTER ENGINEERING
   DISSERTATION                                             *167*

10. THE MATHEMATICS DISSERTATION                            *195*

11. THE ECONOMICS DISSERTATION                              *219*

12. THE PSYCHOLOGY DISSERTATION                             *247*

13. THE SOCIOLOGY DISSERTATION                              *271*

14. THE ENGLISH DISSERTATION                                *301*

*v*

15. THE HISTORY DISSERTATION     *327*

16. THE PHILOSOPHY DISSERTATION     *359*

APPENDIX A: LIST OF PARTICIPATING UNIVERSITIES, DEANS, COORDINATORS, AND FACILITATORS     *385*

APPENDIX B: DETAILS ON THE STUDY'S METHODOLOGY     *387*

REFERENCES     *395*

INDEX     *403*

# TABLES

1.1.  Characteristics of Good/Passing and Poor/Failing Dissertations  *9*

1.2.  Matrix of Components of the Dissertation Used for Different Disciplines  *13*

1.3.  Background Information on Faculty Who Participated in Focus Groups by Discipline  *15*

3.1.  The Purpose of a Dissertation  *29*

3.2.  The Nature of an Original Contribution  *31*

3.3.  The Nature of a Significant Contribution  *34*

3.4.  The Characteristics of Different Quality Dissertations  *36*

3.A.  The Components of a Dissertation and Their Characteristics at Different Quality Levels  *53*

5.1.  The Basic Components of a Rubric  *98*

5.2.  Some Dimensions of the Different Components of the Generic Dissertation  *100*

5.3.  Sample Rubric for the Introduction to a Dissertation  *101*

5.4.  Literature Review Scoring Rubric  *103*

5.5.  A Metarubric for Evaluating the Overall Quality of a Rubric  *107*

7.1.  The Purpose of a Biology Dissertation  *122*

7.2.  The Nature of an Original Contribution in Biology  *123*

7.3.  The Nature of a Significant Contribution in Biology  *124*

7.4.  The Characteristics of Different Quality Dissertations in Biology  *127*

7.A.  The Components of a Biology Dissertation and Their Characteristics at Different Quality Levels  *139*

8.1.  The Purpose of a Physics Dissertation  *146*

8.2.  The Nature of an Original Contribution in Physics  *147*

8.3.  The Nature of a Significant Contribution in Physics  *148*

8.4.  The Characteristics of Different Quality Dissertations in Physics  *151*

8.A.  The Components of a Physics Dissertation and Their Characteristics at Different Quality Levels  *162*

9.1.  The Purpose of an Engineering Dissertation  *168*

9.2.   The Nature of an Original Contribution in Engineering    *170*

9.3.   The Nature of a Significant Contribution in Engineering    *172*

9.4.   The Characteristics of Different Quality Dissertations in Engineering    *175*

9.A.   The Components of an Engineering Dissertation and Their Characteristics at Different Quality Levels    *190*

10.1.   The Purpose of a Mathematics Dissertation    *196*

10.2.   The Nature of an Original Contribution in Mathematics    *198*

10.3.   The Nature of a Significant Contribution in Mathematics    *201*

10.4.   The Characteristics of Different Quality Dissertations in Mathematics    *203*

10.A.   The Components of a Mathematics Dissertation and Their Characteristics at Different Quality Levels    *216*

11.1.   The Purpose of an Economics Dissertation    *220*

11.2.   The Nature of an Original Contribution in Economics    *221*

11.3.   The Nature of a Significant Contribution in Economics    *223*

11.4.   The Characteristics of Different Quality Dissertations in Economics    *226*

11.A.   The Components of an Economics Dissertation and Their Characteristics at Different Quality Levels    *241*

12.1.   The Purpose of a Psychology Dissertation    *248*

12.2.   The Nature of an Original Contribution in Psychology    *249*

12.3.   The Nature of a Significant Contribution in Psychology    *251*

12.4.   The Characteristics of Different Quality Dissertations in Psychology    *253*

12.A.   The Components of a Psychology Dissertation and Their Characteristics at Different Quality Levels    *265*

13.1.   The Purpose of a Sociology Dissertation    *272*

13.2.   The Nature of an Original Contribution in Sociology    *274*

13.3.   The Nature of a Significant Contribution in Sociology    *275*

13.4.   The Characteristics of Different Quality Dissertations in Sociology    *279*

13.A.   The Components of a Sociology Dissertation and Their Characteristics at Different Quality Levels    *295*

14.1.   The Purpose of an English Dissertation    *302*

14.2.   The Nature of an Original Contribution in English    *304*

14.3.   The Nature of a Significant Contribution in English    *306*

14.4.   The Characteristics of Different Quality Dissertations in English    *308*

14.A.   The Components of an English Dissertation and Their
        Characteristics at Different Quality Levels                    *321*

15.1.   The Purpose of a History Dissertation                          *328*

15.2.   The Nature of an Original Contribution in History              *329*

15.3.   The Nature of a Significant Contribution in History            *332*

15.4.   The Characteristics of Different Quality Dissertations in History   *335*

15.A.   The Components of a History Dissertation and Their
        Characteristics at Different Quality Levels                    *353*

16.1.   The Purpose of a Philosophy Dissertation                       *360*

16.2.   The Nature of an Original Contribution in Philosophy           *362*

16.3.   The Nature of a Significant Contribution in Philosophy         *364*

16.4.   The Characteristics of Different Quality Dissertations in
        Philosophy                                                     *367*

16.A.   The Components of a Philosophy Dissertation and Their
        Characteristics at Different Quality Levels                    *379*

B.1.    Shell for Analyzing the Data                                   *393*

# PREFACE

Too often success in education—kindergarten through doctoral—is a function of "guess my rule." Students who can "psyche out" tests and other assignments or who are socialized into the culture of the assignment and its performance expectations by teachers/professors and/or peers, not only tend to succeed but tend to excel. Even with written feedback, the rest are often left wondering about that special something that they were missing and continue to produce work that could have been better had they known the rule.

This book and the study it is based on is about making the implicit "rules" for the assessment of the final of all final educational products—the dissertation—explicit to doctoral students. The goal of explicating the rules (performance expectations) is *not* to rate or grade dissertations or individual components of dissertations and provide a summary score. Rather, the goal is to make the expectations for the dissertation more transparent to graduate students while they are in the process of researching and writing their dissertations, thereby helping them achieve higher levels. In the language of assessment, performance expectations for the dissertation should be used *formatively*, not summatively, with graduate students to support, not substitute for, the advising process.

This study, like my last one on graduate student attrition (Lovitts, 2001), while addressed to faculty and administrative stakeholders (department chairs, deans of graduate schools, leaders of professional associations, disciplinary associations, national organizations, federal and private agencies, and foundations), is written from a student advocacy perspective. Like my last study, it too fits within a broader context of concern about the quality of doctoral education and the need for reform.

Much of the national discussion about reform has focused on what competencies (knowledge, skills, and experience) graduate students should develop, how they gain such competencies during their graduate education, and whether and how they are appropriately prepared for careers inside and outside academe (Austin, 2002). Since 1990, several national program-level initiatives have been launched to address these and other concerns. These initiatives include the Graduate Education Initiative (Andrew W. Mellon Foundation), Preparing Future Faculty (Association of American Colleges and Universities and the Council of Graduate Schools with funds from the Pew Charitable Trusts, National Science Foundation, and Atlantic Philanthropies), Re-envisioning the Ph.D. (University of Washington with funds from the Pew Charitable Trusts), The Responsive Ph.D. (Woodrow Wilson National Fellowship Foundation), and the Carnegie Initiative on the Doctorate (Carnegie Foundation for the Advancement of Teaching). Two national student-level studies have also been part of this conversation: Golde and Dore's (2001) *At Cross Purposes: What the Experiences of Today's Doctoral Students Reveal About Doctoral Education*, and the National Association of Graduate-Professional Students' (2001) *The 2000 National Doctoral Program Survey*.

Missing from these initiatives and other reports (Association of American Universities 1998; Council of Graduate Schools, 1997, 2004; Committee on Science, Engineering, and Public Policy, 1995) is a discussion of the role of the dissertation in doctoral education and criteria for its quality, though these were topics of discussion in the early decades of American doctoral education (see chapter 2). Also missing is a discussion of the learning goals of doctoral education, the quality of the educational experience doctoral students are receiving, and how that education prepares students to research and write a high-quality dissertation.

Assessment, which has been a major focus of efforts in the past decade to improve undergraduate education and which is part of some of the above-mentioned initiatives, is beginning to receive increased attention at the doctoral level (Borkowski, 2006). Regional accrediting agencies are starting to look more closely at the outcomes of graduate education (Southern Association of Colleges and Schools, 2001). The National Research Council (NRC) (Ostriker & Kuh, 2003) has revised its methods for assessing doctoral programs. And students and taxpayers are demanding greater accountability and demonstrated performance (Borkowski, 2006; Nyquist, 2002).

Although virtually all of the assessments of doctoral education are at the program level, none of the assessments provide formal, systematic, evidenced-based assessment of the quality of doctoral programs (Golde, Jones, Conklin Bueschel, & Walker, 2006). Indeed, the NRC report (Ostriker & Kuh, 2003) states that past measures of educational effectiveness relied on a question that confounded research reputation and educational quality. The new NRC survey of research-doctoral programs (see www7 .nationalacademies.org/resdoc/index.html) seeks, as measures of program quality, information on completion rates, time to degree, placement, profession development opportunities, and so on, but collects no information on the actual educational quality or learning outcomes of the programs.

The Making the Implicit Explicit (MIE) study provides a blueprint for assessing the outcomes of doctoral education at both the individual and program level. As the reader will see, the MIE study found surprising consistency in faculty's characterization of the dissertation and components of the dissertation at the four quality levels they were asked to describe. This consistency suggests that standards can be created for doctoral education writ large and for individual disciplines. Because dissertations reflect the training received, the technical skills, and the analytic and writing abilities developed in a doctoral program (Isaac, Quinlan, & Walker, 1992), such standards would provide stakeholders with a valid and reliable, criterion-referenced measure of student learning outcomes and educational effectiveness.

Having authored another book, I will readily admit that this one was an odd one to write. Each of the ten disciplinary chapters say essentially the same thing. Indeed, the focus-group faculty across universities and disciplines often used the same words and phrases to describe dissertations and components of dissertations at the different quality levels. Therein lies this study's strength. It is only by demonstrating how similar faculty's standards or criteria for evaluating dissertations are in disciplines as dissimilar as engineering and English or physics and philosophy that faculty and administrators across the knowledge spectrum will come to accept the possibility of agreed upon expectations/criteria that approach universal standards. This is not to say that there are not disciplinary differences. There are. English students do not invent devices. Engineers do not analyze and critique texts. These differences should be explored more fully for their disciplinary and transdisciplinary implications. Yet, when it comes to assessing quality, it is safe to conclude that faculty, regardless of university or discipline, do so in very similar terms.

## Origins of This Study

The MIE study has its origins in another study funded by the Alfred P. Sloan Foundation I was (and still am) pursuing. That study, The Critical

Transition: From Coursetaker to Independent Researcher (Some Make It, Some Don't) focuses on the disconnect between the criteria by which students are admitted to doctoral programs—being good course takers—and the criteria by which they are awarded the Ph.D.—making an original contribution to knowledge (see Lovitts, 2005). In thinking about the outcomes of doctoral education, I recognized that not all students achieve the goal of originality to the same degree or produce dissertations of equal quality, and that I needed to know more about what it meant to make an original contribution and about how faculty judge dissertations. I combined that need with my basic knowledge of how rubrics are developed for evaluating student performance on high-stakes assessments such as K–12 statewide examinations, the Advanced Placement tests, and the writing component of the Graduate Record Examination, and realized that I could make a contribution to graduate students and graduate education by developing rubrics of performance expectations for the dissertation and its components using a process in which faculty are asked to make explicit their implicit standards or criteria for evaluating the dissertation.

Around the time that I was submitting a proposal for a planning grant for the Critical Transition study to the Sloan Foundation, Chris Golde, senior scholar at the Carnegie Foundation for the Advancement of Teaching, asked me to participate in a panel she was putting together on assessing the outcomes of doctoral education for the 2002 Association for the Study of Higher Education (ASHE) Annual Conference (see http://www.carnegie foundation.org/CID/ashe/index.htm). I fortuitously had an idea in hand, which I turned into a "conceptual approach" paper (see Lovitts, 2002).

In April 2003, at the Council of Graduate Schools' Ph.D. Completion Project Workshop, my program officer, Ted Greenwood, told me how much he liked that paper and encouraged me to come in with a grant proposal to implement the approach. At that time, I had an affiliation with the University of Maryland and was living solely off the $45,000 planning grant for the Critical Transition and hoping to get a full proposal for that project funded. Fearing a lapse in salary and benefits while the Critical Transition proposal wended its way (unsuccessfully) through review at the National Science Foundation, I decided to pursue the MIE study with a Sloan Foundation Officer's Grant, which goes through review much more quickly than a regular grant. However, Officer's Grants are limited to $45,000 of which about half was available to me for salary and benefits over a six-month period.

Yes, this project was done for $45,000 and a lot of sweat equity, as funds ran out in March 2004 leaving me unemployed and job hunting for several months. I was fortunate to be offered a 60%-time position at the National Academy of Engineering. The initial part-time nature of the position gave me the opportunity to complete the analysis and write this project's results at home two days a week, but without additional compensation.

While working on this and the Critical Transition project, I often scratched my head and wondered why I was underwriting the reform of graduate education with my bank account—and still do. However, there have been a number of priceless intangibles. First and foremost, has been the ability to pursue my own interests in my own time and in my own way. I derive far more pleasure from working on my own projects for my own ends than I do from working on other people's projects for other people's ends. Second, despite the financial hardship, which was considerable, at the end of my life I will not rub my wrists and spirit sore from the shackles of golden handcuffs and regret never having taken a risk. The risk did not pay off as I had hoped, but there is great satisfaction in knowing that work that otherwise would not have been done has and will contribute to a national dialogue and large-scale change. Third, as a single, adoptive mom to a child who was between the ages of two and four during my "quest for independence" (sometimes referred to as "Barbara's folly"), I was able to respond to morning requests of "Read a book" or "Cuddle a few more minutes," because I was in control of my work schedule. I also did not have to kiss and run when I dropped my daughter off at daycare in the morning. I could leave work early and run child-free errands on the way home. And I could take off whenever I wanted to attend an event in my daughter's class. You simply cannot put a price on the benefits we both derived from my being there for my daughter during these formative years—and I'd do it again in a heartbeat.

# ACKNOWLEDGMENTS

This project owes a large debt to many individuals. I would like to thank them in roughly chronological order of their contributions. First comes Ted Greenwood, my program officer at the Alfred P. Sloan Foundation, for his never-ending encouragement and support—both moral and financial. Next comes William Falk, chair of the Department of Sociology at the University of Maryland, for giving me a place to hang my hat and work for over two years. He and the department's office staff—Patty Bernales, Wanda Towles, Gerry Todd, and Joey Irizarry—helped me in many ways large and small. Les Sims, senior scholar in residence at the Council of Graduate Schools, helped identify deans to invite to participate in the study and allowed me to use his name in letters of invitation.

The following faculty: Jane Donawerth, Department of English; James Henretta, Department of History; Christopher Morris, Department of Philosophy; and Jonathan Rosenberg, Department of Mathematics, at University of Maryland all met with me and helped work out the components of dissertations in their disciplines that were used in this study. However, the persistent flaws in the components reside with me, because as experienced practitioners, some of whom are also directors of graduate study, they cautioned me that the components we arrived at were oversimplifications and they did not necessarily fully agree with them. Along these lines, thanks go to Karen Klomparens, dean of the Graduate School at Michigan State University for helping "verify" the components with directors of graduate study at MSU, and for otherwise being an early and committed supporter of the project.

Many thanks go to the deans, coordinators, and facilitators (who were not paid enough) at the participating universities for the time and effort they put into making this study a success. Please see Appendix A for their names and affiliations at the time of the study. Extra special thanks go to Candice L. Miller, director of research and information, who was the coordinator at the University of Colorado site. Candice was an unabashedly enthusiastic supporter of the project with whom I exchanged many, many personal and professional E-mails during the course of the project and beyond. Candice (Miller, 2006) wrote about the impact of the MIE project at the University of Colorado from an administrator's perspective. Thanks also go to the 276 faculty who generously gave their time to participate in focus groups—I learned a lot from you!

Then there is Jeannie Brown Leonard, my always happy and cheerful graduate research assistant, who has become a good friend. Jeannie did a fabulous job editing and coding transcripts, reducing data—and, yes, listening to and correcting many of the unfortunately very poorly transcribed transcripts. Jeannie also managed to find time in her very busy life as a graduate student, graduate assistant, wife, and mother to do an uncompensated supplementary study that involved getting dissertators' perspectives on the dissertation and its evaluation as well as their reactions to their discipline's MIE performance expectations (see Brown Leonard, 2006).

Special thanks go to Peggy Maki, higher education assessment consultant, for her enthusiastic support of the MIE concept, which she talks about in her travels, and for encouraging me (and Candice, Jeannie, and facilitator Tom Cyr at the University of Colorado) to make a presentation at the American Association of Higher Education's Assessment Conference in Denver in June 2004, for inviting us to contribute chapters to her volume *The Assessment of Doctoral Education: Emerging Criteria and New Models for Improving Outcomes* (2006), for helping me find a publisher for this book, and for advising on revisions.

Susan T. Hill, director of the Doctorate Data Project at the National Science Foundation, discussed with me and provided much of the background data that leads off the disciplinary chapters. Andrew Mary at the National Center for Education Statistics talked with me about and provided the data on graduate student enrollment. A number of people in the disciplinary professional associations supplied background data as well including Michael Gibbons, American Society of Engineering Education; Carla Howrey, American Sociological Association; Jessica Kohout, American Psychological Association; James Maxwell, American Mathematical Society; John Siegfried, American Economics Association; and Doug Steward, Modern Language Association.

During the summer of 2005, John von Knorring, publisher of Stylus Publishing, and I sent copies of the draft manuscript for external review to the MIE deans, coordinators, and facilitators; as well as to assessment and higher education researchers; and to the executive director or director of education at relevant disciplinary associations. I would like to thank those who provided feedback for their thoughtful comments: Matthew deTemple, Stony Brook; Ronald Ehrenberg, Cornell University; Chris Golde, Carnegie Foundation for the Advancement of Teaching; Jack Hehn, American Institute for Physics; Phillip Katz, formerly of the American Historical Association; Karen Klomparens, Michigan State University; James Maxwell, American Mathematical Society; Candice Miller, University of Colorado; Paul Nelson, American Psychological Association; Rita Nolan, Stony Brook University; Michael Pearson, Mathematical Association of America; Terry Russell, Association for Institutional Research; John Seigfried, American Economics Association; and Andrea Stith, Howard Hughes Medical Institute. The Sloan Foundation also conducted an external review during the summer of 2005. I appreciate the valuable comments from the four Sloan reviewers, one of whom disclosed his identity: Louis Sherman, Purdue University.

The upshot of the external review was that the manuscript needed to be restructured and revised. I am grateful to the Sloan Foundation for providing financial support for the revision process, which included funds for an advisory committee composed of Chris Golde, Karen Klomparens, Terry Russell, and Louis Sherman. The book would not be what it is without their sage advice and moral support.

Not to be forgotten is my editor and publisher, John von Knorring. John offered me a book contract during our initial phone conversation in September 2004, and provided continuous support and advice ever since.

I am grateful to Serena Mann, vice president and general manager of the University of Maryland's television station, whose office was across the hall from mine, for being such a great friend and listening to me vent about project snags and job-hunting woes.

Last but not least, thanks and love go to my mother, Hannah Lovitts, for helping me out financially during my period of unemployment. Similar thanks and love go to my good friends Bob and Joanne Berger for generously watching my daughter on federal holidays, thereby allowing me to get back on track when stomach bugs knocked me off my strict writing schedule, and to my dear friend Chip Cecil for helping out with life in general.

# PART ONE

## THE DISSERTATION AND ITS ASSESSMENT

# I

# JUDGING DISSERTATIONS

The Ph.D. dissertation is the final product of years of study and independent research. Successful completion of the dissertation and award of the Ph.D. certifies that the degree recipient has the capabilities and training necessary for independent scholarly work (Council of Graduate Schools, 2004; Isaac et al., 1992). Yet, the standards for evaluating the dissertation are largely unexplicated and mysterious (Holbrook, 2002b; Johnston, 1997). Graduate students are frequently exhorted to make an "original" or "significant contribution" to knowledge. Indeed, this is the most commonly, and often the only, explicitly stated criteria for the award of the Ph.D. (Tinkler & Jackson, 2000; Winter, Griffiths, & Green, 2000). But what "original" and "significant" mean do not appear to have ever been operationalized or objectively defined for graduate students.[1]

Dissertations reflect the training received, the technical skills, and the analytic and writing abilities developed in a doctoral program (Isaac et al., 1992). Thus, knowing the standards faculty use to judge dissertations could lead to the development of informed measures of learning outcomes. These measures would constitute powerful indicators of the success of research training (Holbrook & Bourke, 2002), provide evaluation standards for Ph.D. programs, and allow more objective comparison among them. Such standards would also make dissertation evaluation more valid and reliable across candidates in a department or field. In addition, having explicit standards would enhance faculty supervision and student research performance.

The only "quality" rating of dissertations currently available at most American universities is the recommendation of the dissertation committee.[2] This recommendation is typically to pass or to fail the dissertation, though the dissertation may be passed with a variety of stipulations (e.g., revise, revise and defend again). These stipulations vary by university. However, it is not clear how well these categories align with the actual quality of the dissertation (e.g., outstanding, very good, acceptable, unacceptable). For instance, one could imagine an outstanding dissertation being passed provided corrections or additions are made because it needed only minor revisions, such as correcting typographical errors, or because a faculty member requested that an interesting finding be explained in greater detail or a novel position on an issue be expounded on further. By contrast, one could imagine an acceptable dissertation being passed without revision because the candidate had accepted a job and was leaving the area or because the dissertation committee found no technical errors and did not feel that further revision would improve the quality of the work. Indeed, evidence suggests that poor-quality dissertations are often passed. Adams and White (1994), in a study that looked at dissertation abstracts, found that a significant number of dissertations that had passed had obvious and sometimes fatal flaws. Johnston (1997) and Mullins and Kiley (2002) found that external examiners of Australian dissertations were reluctant to fail poor-quality dissertations. Thus the question arises: How do faculty judge dissertations? What standards do they apply and how do they discriminate among dissertations of different quality?

## Research on Standards and Criteria for Judging Dissertations

Virtually no research exists in the United States on the standards used by faculty to judge dissertations, most likely because dissertation assessment is viewed as a private affair conducted by a committee of experts, and the issue of quality and standards has not attracted the attention of policy makers. However, two studies have some bearing on the issue.

Isaac et al. (1992) surveyed graduate faculty in 10 fields at a large research university to tap their views on the role and function of the doctoral dissertation. Isaac et al. determined that the three major purposes of the dissertation were: (a) a demonstration of the student's research skills, (b) the development (training) of these skills, and (c) making a contribution to the knowledge base of the field. Isaac et al. are careful to point out that "demonstrate" and "train" tended to be mutually exclusive and that the responses came from faculty in fields with different research traditions. "Demonstrate" was most frequently cited by faculty in fields in which solitary research is the norm. It implies that the skills were acquired during graduate training. By contrast, "training" was most frequently cited by faculty in fields where team research and/or laboratory bench research is common. This suggests that the dissertation may be the first experience or part of a continuing training experience.

The faculty were also asked to rate the importance of six characteristics of a doctoral dissertation: independent contribution, originality, significance, substantial time commitment, length of document, and publishable or source of publishable material. Faculty identified independent contribution as the most important characteristic (4.5 on a 5-point scale). "Originality" and "publishability" tied for second place (4.3). Virtually all disciplinary groups indicated that "independence" and originality were essential characteristics of a dissertation. However, Isaac et al. note that it is not clear whether there would be agreement across disciplines on the meaning of these terms.

Adams and White (1994) reviewed dissertation abstracts in public administration, management, planning, criminology, social work, and women's studies to determine the quality of research in public administration relative to cognate fields. They used several indicators to assess quality: existence of a framework of some kind to guide the research, obvious flaws in the research, relevance of the findings to theory or practice, importance of the topic, and an overall indicator of quality. Based on the description of the dissertation presented in the abstract, they concluded that the majority of dissertations either had no framework or might have had a framework but it had to be inferred. The majority of dissertations also either had or probably had obvious flaws, such as a sample that was egregiously too small from which to draw reasonable conclusions, generalizations of findings from a single case study, the use of an obviously inappropriate statistic, the use of a clearly inappropriate research design given the problem or question addressed, blatant errors in logic, or the serious misapplication of some theory to the research problem. Given their assumption that dissertation research should contribute to theory development, Adams and White asked: Was the research relevant to theory? Again they found that the majority of dissertations contributed little, if anything, to the development of knowledge.

Adams and White further ranked the importance of the dissertation topic from "unimportant" to "very important" and found few that addressed a very important topic. More dissertations addressed a topic of "average importance" than an "important topic." Overall, Adams and White's study calls into question the nature and quality of the standards faculty apply when they review and pass dissertations, as well as the quality of the training doctoral students are receiving if such gross flaws in scholarship can be identified on the basis of the dissertation abstract alone.

## The Components of a Dissertation

No studies have been done on faculty's expectations for the different components or tasks of a dissertation (e.g., introduction/problem statement, literature review, theory, methods, results/analysis, discussion/conclusion). However, a very small body of literature exists on the nature, but not quality, of research article introductions (see Swales & Najjar, 1987). And a small but growing body of literature has emerged on students' understanding of and experiences with dissertation literature reviews (Bruce, 1994, 2001) as well as its assessment (Boote & Beile, 2004, 2005; Hart, 1998).

According to Boote and Beile (2004, pp. 6–7), "The dirty little secret known by those of us who sit on dissertation committees is that literature reviews are often (if not usually) inadequate, poorly conceptualized and written, and boring." Using a 12-item scoring rubric, Boote and Beile assessed four randomly selected education dissertations from each of three universities. They found large differences in the quality of literature reviews within and between universities. The best were thorough, critical examinations of the state of the field, while the worst were disjointed summaries of prior research and broad surveys of a haphazard collection of literature. They speculate that these shortcomings stem from insufficient preparation in doctoral programs. Indeed, in a study by Zaprozhetz (cited in Boote & Beile, 2005) faculty ranked the literature review chapter of lowest importance relative to the other chapters of a dissertation, and expected students to complete it alone with little help from faculty.

## A View from Abroad

A small body of research exists on how evaluators assess the quality of dissertations in Australia and Britain, countries where dissertations are sent to and read by examiners external to the university (Anderson, 2002; Bourke, 2002; Delamont, Atkinson, & Parry, 2002; Holbrook, 2002a, 2002b; Holbrook & Bourke, 2002; Johnston, 1997; Lovat, 2002; Mullins & Kiley, 2002; Simpkins, 1987; Winter, Griffiths, & Green, 2000). This research has been motivated by policy concerns about the quality and contribution of research degrees to the national economy, and the effectiveness of the process of pre-paring researchers (Holbrook, 2002a). The majority of studies have tried to infer examiners' standards for judging dissertations by analyzing the content of their written reports, the language used, and the proportion of space (number of lines of text) devoted to a content category, though interviews and surveys have also been conducted.

Two major themes have emerged from these studies. One is that external examiners' criteria for evaluating dissertations include a variety of technical and indeterminate qualities. The other is that the dissertation must demon-strate originality and make a contribution. Below we explore these themes in greater detail.

## Technical and Indeterminate Qualities

Studies that have analyzed external examiners' reports as well as those that have asked examiners about the criteria they use to judge dissertations typi-cally agree that examiners look for a mixture of technical and indeterminate qualities. The technical qualities operate on two levels. On one level are the technical details that reflect the technical knowledge and skill of the candi-date. These are things that can be formally taught and objectively assessed, such as command over subject matter and application of appropriate re-search and analytic methods (Delamont et al., 2002). The other level is more administrative and reflects attention to detail. It has to do with the disserta-tion's formal structure and presentation, such as appropriate style, clarity of presentation, absence of typographical errors and grammatical mistakes, ac-curate calculations, and correct referencing and citation (Delamont et al., 2002; Winter et al., 2000).

Indeterminate qualities, by contrast, are qualities that examiners can rec-ognize but not itemize or articulate precisely. Such knowledge is personal and tacit, and as such defies translation into techniques, skills, and formulas (Delamont et al., 2002). These qualities include such things as intellectual grasp, coherence, and critical thinking. They are things that are believed to be "caught" rather than "taught." In other words, possession and display of appropriate indeterminate qualities are part of the candidates' cultural capital and reflect their tacit knowledge of disciplinary and academic culture. This knowledge is acquired through personal experience and interaction with members of the departmental, disciplinary, and university community.

Although the criteria for success or failure of a dissertation cannot and should not be reduced to a set of written rules, Delamont et al. (2002) note that while the "technicalities must be correct, the real role of the examiner is to judge whether the student has mastered appropriate indeterminate skills and displayed the right indeterminate qualities" (p. 41). Indeed, Mullins and Kiley (2002) found that examiners took a holistic approach toward judging dissertations. They considered the dissertation as a whole and the way that the quality of various parts related to one another. Similarly, Winter et al. (2000) noted that no single dissertation would (or could) be described by all the positive statements provided by the examiners they surveyed. However, they argue that the dissertation should ideally be free of the weaknesses the examiners described, though one or two weaknesses could be compensated for by a wide range of positive features.

## *Faculty's Standards for Judging Dissertations*

The greatest insight into the standards faculty use to judge dissertations come from a variety of studies that either asked examiners about their standards for an acceptable dissertation or attempted to infer standards from their written reports. Winter et al. (2000) surveyed staff at nine institutions in England and received responses from 31 faculty in 21 different disciplines. Respondents were asked to discuss how they differentiated between a passing and failing dissertation. Mullins and Kiley (2002) interviewed 30 experienced examiners in Australia to gain an understanding of what was an acceptable dissertation and the context in which they developed their conceptions. Johnston (1997), by contrast, analyzed 51 examiners' reports on 16 Australian dissertations in a variety of liberal arts and professional fields to learn about examiners' explicit and implicit criteria for judging theses.

The results of these studies are quite consistent. Table 1.1 displays the categories Winter et al. (2000) and Mullins and Kiley (2002) used to organize the commonly identified features of good/passing and poor/failing dissertations. The table presents the terminology used by the authors. However, the order of presentation has been changed in order to align analogous concepts, where possible. Johnston's (1997) findings on good quality dissertations are similar to those of Winter et al. (2000) and Mullins and Kiley (2002).

According to Johnston, the studies that examiners praised:

- were well designed
- were insightful

**TABLE 1.1.**
### Characteristics of Good/Passing and Poor/Failing Dissertations

| Winter, Griffiths, and Green, 2000 | Mullins and Kiley, 2002 |
|---|---|
| **Characteristics of good-quality or passing dissertations** | |
| Coherence | Cohesiveness and clarity |
| Intellectual grasp | Critical reflection |
| Originality | Originality of presentation |
| Presentation | Professionalism (mature comments, accuracy of logic) |
| Engagement with the literature | Well-structured arguments |
| Grasp of methodology | |
| **Characteristics of poor-quality or failing dissertations** | |
| Lack of coherence | Lack of coherence |
| Lack of originality | Work that is not original |
| Methodological weaknesses | Mixed or confused theoretical and methodological perspectives |
| Lack of intellectual grasp | Lack of confidence |
| Poor engagement with the literature | Researching the wrong problem |
| Lack of generalizability | Not being able to explain at the end of the thesis what had actually been done |
| Poor presentation | |

*Note.* The data in column 1 are from "The 'Academic' Qualities of Practice: What Are the Criteria for a Practiced-based PhD?" by R. Winter, M. Griffiths, and K. Green, 2000, *Studies in Higher Education, 25*(1), pp. 32–34. The data in column 2 are from "'It's a PhD, Not a Nobel Prize': How Experienced Examiners Assess Research Theses" by G. Mullins and M. Kiley, 2002, *Studies in Higher Education, 27*(4), pp. 378–379.

- were well conceptualized
- were carried out competently
- did what they set out to do
- were thoroughly analyzed
- demonstrated a comprehensive knowledge of the literature
- made a significant contribution to the field

Johnston also presents a list of verbatim comments from examiners about their standards for a dissertation. Some of their comments include the following standards:

- Theoretical justification
- Novel concepts, frameworks, or theory
- Innovative or original approach
- Scholarly analysis of foundation concepts
- Suitable for publication

Mullins and Kiley (2002) went one step further than other researchers and asked interviewees what separated a "good" from a "passable" or "standard" dissertation, or, in other words, what made an outstanding dissertation. The one theme that unified interviewees' responses was the use of an artistic metaphor. The metaphor included such terms as "elan," "passion," "excitement," "sparkle," and "elegance." These dissertations were described as having elegant designs and being creative and well sculpted.

## Original and Significant Contribution

What counts as an original or a significant contribution to knowledge has not been explicated or codified. Studies that have assessed examiners' reports typically find statements that say that the dissertation is original and has made a significant contribution. A few commentators (Delamont et al., 2002; Isaac et al., 1992) note that what counts as "original" and as a "contribution to knowledge" is discipline specific, but no study has analyzed these concepts along disciplinary lines.

Three studies (Johnston, 1997; Simpkins, 1987; Winter et al., 2000) address the meaning of "original." For Johnston (1997), originality is demonstrated by "the discovery of new facts" or by "the exercise of critical thinking." Simpkins's (1987) study of examiners' reports of education administration dissertations is devoted to an analysis of the way examiners assess critical thinking. Simpkins found "originality" to be a component of critical thinking. The examiners expected dissertations to show originality in two ways: taking an independent line and taking an imaginative approach. Taking an independent line means that doctoral candidates are:

- Making up their own minds when they review ideas and practice
- Identifying trends and issues
- Drawing their own conclusions when assessing the value of a conceptual model, research method, or research material
- Arguing a position (p. 252)

Taking an imaginative approach means that doctoral candidates are:

- Taking a fresh look at questions, issues, and trends
- Being enterprising in interpreting evidence
- Moving beyond the clearly established to the speculative
- Supplementing logic with the intuitive and imaginative, as long as the "intuitively reasonable" is acknowledged as such (p. 252)

Finally, Winter et al. (2000) asked survey respondents who used the term "original" to elaborate on what it "looks like" in the dissertations they examined. Winter et al. provide a long list of their respondents' verbatim comments. They conclude that "originality" refers to such indeterminate qualities as inspiration, responsibility, cognitive excitement, personal synthesis, and to the candidate's "wrestling" or being "adventurous" with the method.

In sum, the existing research on faculty's standards and criteria for judging dissertations is very limited. Few organize respondents' comments into overarching categories, and when they do, the content of the categories remains largely unanalyzed. Further, no study has analyzed examiners' standards or criteria by discipline or component of the dissertation, nor has any study done a fine-grained analysis of the examiners' standards for dissertations of varying quality other than "pass," "fail," and, in the case of Mullins and Kiley (2002), "outstanding." Finally, no study on examiners' standards or criteria has been conducted in the United States where dissertations are assessed by several faculty in the same and related departments who can and do discuss the dissertation and the candidate. Under such conditions, tacit norms for judging dissertations may have emerged.

This book provides the results of a study in which U.S. faculty were asked to make explicit their implicit standards or criteria for evaluating dissertations. The overarching goal of the study, and the process it describes, is for departments, disciplines, and universities to develop objective standards for the outcomes of doctoral training—the dissertation—and use those standards in a *formative* way to improve graduate education and training, make it more transparent to students, and help them achieve to higher levels. Below is an overview of the study's methods and the structure of the book.

## Making the Implicit Explicit

During the academic year 2003–04, 276 faculty in 74 departments across 10 disciplines (*sciences*: biology, electrical and computer engineering, physics/physics and astronomy, mathematics; *social sciences*: economics, psychology, sociology; *humanities*: English, history, philosophy) at 9 Doctoral/Research Universities-Extensive[3] participated in focus groups in which they were asked to characterize dissertations and components (essential tasks) of dissertations tailored to their discipline (see Table 1.2) at four different quality levels—outstanding, very good, acceptable, and unacceptable. They were also asked what it meant to make an original and significant contribution in their discipline, and what the purpose of the dissertation was. (See Appendix B for the focus group protocol.)

Each university hired a facilitator to coordinate and conduct the focus groups, though some universities assigned an administrator to coordinate them. Faculty were selected and invited to participate in focus groups on the basis of their being high Ph.D. productive; that is, they had advised many doctoral students and served on many dissertation committees. It should be noted that Lovitts (2001) found that high producers have different, more positive attitudes and beliefs about graduate students and graduate education and are more academically and socially engaged with graduate students than their low-productive counterparts. Consequently, the comments made by the focus group faculty do not necessarily reflect the views, experiences, or expectations of all faculty.

Most focus groups had three or four participants, a few ran with only two, and one had eight. The faculty were asked to provide background data on the number of years they had been a professor and their experience with dissertations both as an advisor and as a committee member. Many faculty did not know exactly how many dissertations they had advised and virtually none knew how many dissertation committees they had served on. Consequently, they were asked to estimate. When the faculty provided a range (e.g., 25–30), the average of that range rounded to the nearest whole number

## TABLE 1.2.
### Matrix of Components of the Dissertation Used for Different Disciplines

| Disciplines | Components | | | | | |
|---|---|---|---|---|---|---|
| | Introduction | Literature review | Theory | Methods | Results/data analysis | Discussion and conclusion |
| Biology, physics, engineering, economics, psychology, sociology | Introduction | Literature review | Theory | Methods | Results/data analysis | Discussion and conclusion |
| Mathematics | Introduction/problem statement | Discussion of the literature | Statement of results/theorems | Approach to the problem (techniques) | Proof of results | Conclusion/future directions |
| English | Introduction (of problem or concept) | Review of sources | Approach to analysis | Justification of chosen texts | Analysis of texts | Conclusion |
| History | Introduction | Historiographic review | Sources/methods | Exposition/analysis | Conclusion | |
| Philosophy | Introduction/statement and clarification of the problem | Demonstration of knowledge of the literature | Development/defense of the thesis(es) | Recognition and response to possible objections | Conclusion | |
| Outstanding | | | | | | |
| Very good | | | | | | |
| Acceptable | | | | | | |
| Unacceptable/failing | | | | | | |

was used. Table 1.3 provides background information on the 74 departments and the 272 focus group faculty who provided background data by discipline. Overall, these faculty had 6,129 years of experience, had chaired an estimated 3,470 dissertations, and had sat on a estimated 9,890 dissertation committees. The average focus group participant had been a professor for 22 years, had chaired 13 dissertations, and had served on 36 dissertation committees.

Each focus group session was tape-recorded and the tapes were sent directly to a business services company for transcription. Although each participant's utterances were transcribed separately, no effort was made to link participants individually with their responses. Thus the identity of the speaker is not recoverable from the transcript, neither in most cases is the speaker's gender. (Data on participants' gender and race/ethnicity were not collected.) Consequently, given the national demographics of senior faculty, the overwhelming majority of whom are male, the participants are referred to as "he," unless I listened to that passage and heard a female voice or there is evidence in the transcript that the respondent is female. In most instances where a focus group dialogue is presented in the text in part two, the speakers are referred to as Participant 1, Participant 2, and so on. In a few instances, participants have been given pseudonyms to make the dialogue easier to follow.

Focus group discussion transcripts were edited so that potentially identifying information, such as names, locations, specialty areas, and the like, was altered, taken to a higher level of generality, or deleted. For readability, common but distracting components of speech such as "ah," "um," "you know," "I mean," "I think," and "sort of" were deleted from the quotations that appear in the text unless they were particularly meaningful. Discrepancies in grammar were not corrected. False sentence starts were frequently deleted, as was the word "and" when it linked sentences, as it often does in spoken language. In most instances, ellipses (. . .) are not used to indicate these deletions.

The transcripts were coded by protocol item and component cell. The coded transcripts were entered into N6, a qualitative data analysis software program (QSR, 2002), by discipline for sorting. After each node or item report was printed, each discipline's data were further reduced through a four-stage winnowing process. In stage one, each node report was read, and relevant information was highlighted. The highlighted information was then cut and pasted into an initial summary table by university. In stage two, each

## TABLE 1.3.
### Background Information on Faculty Who Participated in Focus Groups by Discipline

| Department | Number of departments | Number of focus group participants | Total number of years as a professor | Average number of years as a professor | Total number of dissertations advised | Average number of dissertations advised | Total number of dissertation committees participated on | Average number of dissertation committees participated on |
|---|---|---|---|---|---|---|---|---|
| Biology | 6 | 21 | 467 | 22 | 243 | 12 | 979 | 47 |
| Mathematics | 9 | 31 | 758[a] | 25[a] | 272[a] | 9[a] | 887[a] | 30[a] |
| Physics | 7 | 25 | 520 | 21 | 290 | 12 | 790 | 32 |
| Engineering | 6 | 24 | 450 | 19 | 350 | 15 | 1099 | 46 |
| Economics | 7 | 33 | 621 | 19 | 417 | 13 | 905 | 27 |
| Psychology | 7 | 28 | 690 | 25 | 454 | 16 | 1432 | 51 |
| Sociology | 7 | 25 | 567 | 23 | 336 | 13 | 1016 | 41 |
| English | 7 | 24 | 499 | 21 | 419 | 17 | 829 | 35 |
| History | 9 | 33 | 694[b] | 22[b] | 364[b] | 12[b] | 1045[b] | 34[b] |
| Philosophy | 9 | 32 | 863[c] | 28[c] | 325[c] | 10[c] | 908[c] | 29[c] |
| Total/Average | 74 | 276 | 6129[d] | 22[d] | 3470[d] | 13[d] | 9890[d] | 36[d] |

*Note.* All averages were rounded to the nearest whole number.

[a] Totals and averages are based on the 30 focus group participants who provided data.
[b] Totals and averages are based on the 31 focus group participants who provided data.
[c] Totals and averages are based on the 31 focus group participants who provided data.
[d] Totals and averages are based on the 272 focus group participants who provided data.

initial summary table was read, and the characteristics for that item were extracted and placed in a reduced summary table. In stage three, the characteristics of each item were synthesized across universities into discipline-based summary tables. These summaries, which appear in tables in the individual disciplinary chapters in part two of this book, stay as close to the faculty's actual language as possible. Because of page-length considerations, the characteristics in these tables are not bulleted as they are in Table 1.3 but rather separated by semicolons (;). In the few instances where a matrix cell is empty, it is because that cell either was not discussed in any focus group or the focus groups that discussed a protocol item or a matrix cell did not provide information that was relevant for creating performance expectations. Finally, in stage four, characteristics that appeared in many of the discipline-based summary tables were extracted and synthesized into an overall or "universal" summary for that item. These tables—with bulleted characteristics—appear in chapter 3. The text in chapter 3 and in the disciplinary chapters typically does not repeat what is in the tables, rather the text summarizes faculty's extended and supplementary discussion of the item.

It should be noted that the focus group protocol was initially developed as part of another study and was implemented exclusive of the matrix of components in seven departments (*sciences*: biology, electrical and computer engineering, physics/physics and astronomy; *social sciences*: economics, psychology; *humanities*: English, history) at each of two research universities.[4] Data from these focus groups are not included in the summary tables, though an occasional quote from those focus groups is included in the text when it contributes something important or different from what was contributed by members of this study's focus groups. Those universities cannot be identified, but will be referred to in the text as Public or Private University when one of their faculty members is quoted.

The remainder of part one of this book focuses on the big picture issues. Before presenting the interdisciplinary or synthetic results on faculty's standards and expectations for the dissertation (chapter 3), chapter 2 introduces and explores the concepts of performance expectations, outcomes and performance assessments, and evaluation ethics. It discusses why faculty, administrators, and other relevant stakeholders should care about them. Chapter 4 explores disciplinary differences in doctoral student training and how these approaches contribute to the development of a dissertation that makes an original contribution to knowledge. Chapter 5 provides advice on how to translate performance expectations into rubrics for formatively assessing a dissertation and for summatively assessing a graduate program. Finally, chapter 6 discusses the study's practical and research implications for different stakeholders (faculty, departments, universities, disciplinary associations, accrediting organizations). It includes caveats about the (mis)use of rubrics when applied to the dissertation.

Part two presents faculty's performance expectations for each of the 10 disciplines in the study. The chapters in this part are organized by domain of knowledge (sciences, social sciences, and humanities) and alphabetically within the domain of knowledge, except for the sciences. Within the science domains, the empirical disciplines are presented before mathematics, a nonempirical discipline. Within the empirical disciplines, the sciences (biology, physics) come before engineering. Each chapter starts with contextual data on graduate education in that discipline.[5]

Readers are encouraged to read their discipline's chapter or the chapter most closely related to their discipline. They are also encouraged to skim some chapters in each of the three domains of knowledge to get a sense of the similarities and differences across domains and disciplines. (There are more similarities than differences.) They are further encouraged to skim other disciplines' chapters because things may be said in other chapters that are true of one's discipline but just happen not to have come up in that discipline's focus groups.

## Notes

1. The nature of "original" and "significant" are addressed in a 1997 Council of Graduate Schools (CGS) report. However, this report is rarely cited and does not seem to have had much influence on graduate education. The report mentions that Berelson (1960) addresses these concepts. Although Berelson is widely cited for his work on student attrition and retention, his work on "original" and "significant" has not made it into contemporary discussions about graduate education.

2. In a search of 25 university Web sites for their policies on evaluating dissertations, I found only 3 that required readers to submit a quality rating or a report on the quality of the dissertation.

3. Doctoral/Research Universities-Extensive, according to the Carnegie Classification of Institutes of Higher Education, are institutions that have a wide range of baccalaureate programs and are committed to the doctorate. They award 50 or more doctoral degrees per year across at least 15 disciplines. From http://www.carnegie

foundation.org/Classification/CIHE2000/def/Notes/Definitions.htm (last accessed October 3, 2005, but link is now defunct). The universities that participated in this study are Duke University, Michigan State University, Northwestern University, State University of New York at Stony Brook, Syracuse University, University of Colorado, University of Illinois, University of Kansas, and University of Southern California.

4. Overall, 55 faculty participated in focus groups in this study; 53 provided background data. These faculty had an average of 25 years of experience, advised an average of 15 dissertations, and sat on an average of 36 dissertation committees.

5. The data are ballpark estimates that are based on eyeballing the last few years of available information on graduate and doctoral education. Estimates are provided in order to give the reader a sense of the magnitude of the enterprise rather than precise numbers because the numbers vary from year to year and become dated quickly. The data come from several sources. The data on the number of Ph.D. programs come from Webcaspar (National Science Foundation [NSF], special run, June 2005). The data on the number of subfields in the sciences and social sciences come from the National Opinion Research Center (2004) *2003 Summary Report of the Survey of Earned Doctorates*, as do the data on the annual number of new Ph.D.s. The data on graduate enrollments in the disciplines come from National Center for Education Statistics (NCES) (n.d.), *Digest of Educational Statistics, 2003*, Table 216. The data on the median time to degree come from a special tabulation of the NSF Survey of Earned Doctorates. The data on postdoctoral education come from Hill, Hoffer, and Golladay (2004), *Plans for Postdoctoral Research Appointments Among Recent U.S. Doctorate Recipients*. Some data were supplied or verified by individuals at the disciplinary professional associations. See notes in the disciplinary chapters.

# 2

## ACHIEVING EXCELLENCE

Since the first three Ph.D.s in the United States were awarded in 1861 by Yale University's Sheffield School of Science (Storr, 1953, 1973), the demand for excellence—originality, independence, methodological expertise, substantive contribution, intellectual rigor, textual clarity, and publication[1]—have been forthright. In 1878, Johns Hopkins University President Daniel Coit Gilman, in his annual report to the trustees, wrote that the doctoral candidate should demonstrate "mastery of his subject, his powers in independent thought as well as careful research and his ability to express, in a clear and systematic order, and in appropriate language, the results of his study" (as cited in Goodchild & Miller, 1997, p. 23). Similarly, in a paper titled "The Doctoral Dissertation" by Wilhelm Gardner Hale that was presented at the third annual conference of the Association of American Universities in Chicago in February 1902, Hale asserted that the dissertation must demonstrate the candidate's "power of originating for himself," that the subject matter "be of such scope that it can be treated exhaustively," and that the presentation be organic, clear, and not "*un*literary" (as cited in Nerad & Miller, 1997, p. 76). Remarks about the quality of the dissertation by Princeton Dean Andrew F. West in 1908 (Storr, 1973) indicate that many dissertations deviated from the standards held by early leaders:

> It [the doctor's dissertation] too often exhibits merely the patiently wrought results of a large quantity of mediocre work. . . . It is too often written under the spur of seeking to find something original. This is apt to result in finding something either unimportant or fictitious. . . . Too many theses exhibit merely or mainly power to arrange, classify, and tabulate; too few dissertations show the power to discover, appropriate, and use only

what is valuable, and to develop a given subject analytically and construc-
tively. . . . In conclusion, I feel that the question of the Doctor's dissertation is a question of quality—the quality of a man's general liberal
education—the quality of his subsequent graduate work, and above all his
own personal quality as a man of bright, deep, sensible, definite intellectual
character. (p. 55)

A perusal of the Council of Graduate Schools' (1997, 2004) policy statements
on the purpose and nature of the dissertation and the doctor of philosophy
degree indicate that the expectations for the dissertation have not changed
much in the intervening years. (See Geiger, 1986, 1993; and Veysey, 1965, for
a more detailed history of American doctoral education.)

Despite the early and consistent demand for excellence, doctoral programs have rarely, if ever, been assessed in terms of the quality of the dissertations departments produce. Yet, dissertations provide the most powerful,
objective measure of the success of a department's doctoral program, because, as noted in chapter 1, they reflect the training received, the technical
skills, and the analytic and writing abilities developed in a doctoral program.
Indeed, assessment, when done properly, can help departments achieve excellence by providing insight into a program's strengths and weaknesses.

This chapter focuses on the relationship between assessment and excellence. It describes how the means of assessing quality have changed over time
from a focus on inputs and processes to a focus on outcomes, and explores
the implications of this change for doctoral education. It then examines the
dissertation as an authentic performance, a true test of the goals of doctoral
education. Next it discusses the benefits to students, faculty, departments,
and institutions of specifying performance expectations for the dissertation.
It concludes with a discussion of evaluation ethics.

## Assessing Excellence

Because of the stakes involved, various parties have a vested interest in the
assessment of doctoral programs. Prospective graduate students want to know
where they can get the "best" education. Faculty want to affiliate with "high-
quality" programs. Department chairs and deans of graduate schools want
their departments and universities to be "highly ranked" so they can attract
the "best and brightest" students and faculty (Golde, Jones, et al., 2006).

Yet, excellence in doctoral education has been traditionally defined in terms of easily quantifiable student, faculty, and department inputs and processes. At the student level, these measures include such inputs as enrolled students' undergraduate Grade Point Averages (GPAs) and Graduate Record Examination (GRE) scores. At the faculty level, these measures include the numbers of hours spent on teaching, number of grants, number of publications, and number of faculty awards. At the department level, these measures include curriculum offerings, credit hours, pass rates on qualifying exams, attrition/retention rates, and time to degree. However, these inputs and process variables are only indirectly related to educational quality and do not guarantee excellence.

In recent years, the public and concerned internal and external stakeholder groups have placed greater emphasis on educational and institutional effectiveness and accountability in higher education (Borkowski, 2006). Concomitantly, attention has shifted from a focus on inputs and processes to a focus on outcomes. Accrediting agencies now stress the importance of articulating observable, measurable learning outcomes for graduating students and of meeting specified outcomes-based standards. Indeed, in 1997 the New England Education Association of Schools and Colleges' Commission on Institutions of Higher Education (Maki, 1998, p. 28) set forth the following expectations in its Student Outcomes Assessment Plan:

> The Commission expects each institution as a means of its dedication to institutional improvement, to monitor its effectiveness in achieving its mission and purposes. Accordingly, the institution collects and analyzes relevant data and uses this information in the institutional planning process as a basis for sustaining quality and self-improvement. Thus, assessment functions as a tool for the encouragement of such improvement as well as a basis for quality assurance.

## Outcomes Assessment

Outcomes assessment is a formal, systematic method for collecting evidence about the quality of a program that, in turn, can help faculty and other relevant stakeholders improve the quality of the learning enterprise. It involves specifying the desired learning outcomes (knowledge, skills, attitudes) that are expected to result from the learning experience, assessing the degree to which those outcomes have been achieved, and then making adjustments to the instructional program based on the evidence.

There are two primary forms of outcomes assessment: formative and summative. Formative assessment is for internal use, either to provide feedback to an individual student on his or her progress and performance in a course, program, or on the dissertation, or to provide feedback to the department for the sake of program review and improvement. Summative assessment is for external evaluation and accountability. It is usually done as part of a program evaluation by the administration or an accrediting agency and often results in judgments about the quality of a program, which, in turn, may be tied to resource allocation decisions. Faculty and departments that engage in formative assessment and use the results to improve their programs are likely to receive better reviews when subject to external evaluation.

Although most of the focus on outcomes assessment has been at the primary, secondary, and undergraduate levels, serious attention is starting to be paid to the role of assessment in doctoral education, to the learning outcomes that should be assessed, and to how those outcomes might be assessed (see Borkowski, 2006; Maki & Borkowski, 2006). This attention to outcomes is part of a larger discussion in doctoral education about how best to prepare doctoral students for their professional (academic and nonacademic) destinations (Austin, 2002; Nyquist, 2002). And much of this discussion has focused on the expected outcomes of doctoral education—the competencies graduate students should develop—and the processes that engender them—how they should gain such knowledge, understanding, and experience in their doctoral programs.

At the same time, numerous calls have been made for faculty and departments to specify and make transparent to graduate students their expectations about aspects of doctoral education such as selection criteria, progress expectations, time to degree, completion rates, and placement success (Golde & Dore, 2001; Lovitts, 2001; Nyquist & Woodford, 2000). However, there has been little, if any, discussion about making faculty's, departments', and/or disciplines' expectations for the primary outcome of doctoral education—the dissertation—transparent to students (or, for that matter, transparent to themselves). Nor has there been much discussion about how specifying the expectations for the dissertation could help reveal the competencies stakeholders expect doctoral programs to develop in students or about how these expectations could serve as the benchmarks for formative and summative assessment of program quality, and, in turn, contribute to the achievement of excellence.

## The Dissertation as a True Test of Doctoral Education

While doctoral education may be a latecomer in the outcomes assessment movement, it is ahead of the curve in some respects. Unlike other levels of education that have been struggling to specify what students should know and be able to do as a result of their educational experience and devise authentic or true tests of that knowledge and those skills, doctoral education has a true test—the dissertation.

Like other authentic assessments (e.g., science fair projects, musical or artistic competitions, Olympic figure skating), the dissertation instantiates the performances, challenges, standards, and habits required of professionals, and reveals a range of achievements that are not easily quantified, compared, or ranked, such as posing, tackling, and solving ill-structured problems and marshaling arguments and evidence to address them (Wiggins, 1989). As such, the dissertation allows the direct evaluation of a program's learning expectations and outcomes.

The assessment of the dissertation, like the assessment of other authentic performances, requires and uses human judges (the dissertation committee) because an authentic performance cannot be reduced to a set of rules that results in a single, supposedly unambiguous numerical score, like the GRE. Authentic assessments also require dialogue between the assessors and the assessee (the oral defense), so that the assessee can clarify questions asked and answers given (Wiggins, 1989). Indeed, as Wiggins points out, the "root of the word *assessment* reminds us that an assessor should 'sit with' a learner" (p. 708) so that the assessor can ascertain whether the student has truly mastered the task at hand. Thus, while graduate education has, and has always had, a true test of the educational experience, the challenge remains for graduate faculty and administrators to make explicit the many and varied performances embodied in the dissertation and specify their standards for assessing them.

## Benefits of an Outcomes Approach

The development and specification of performance expectations for the dissertation (and other aspects of doctoral education) serves the interests of everyone involved in or concerned about doctoral education. When students know the performances that are expected of them and the standards they will be judged on, they become more engaged in their intellectual and skill development, are better able to self-assess and correct deficiencies, and are better able to demonstrate what they know and can do. Clear expectations and clear performance data also improve communication and strengthen the relationship between students and their advisors (Cyr & Muth, 2006).

Working together to specify program outcomes and standards stimulates and revitalizes faculty. It also improves communication between and among faculty and enhances collegiality. Using performance expectations to assess student work allows faculty to see how effective they are and provides them with information they can use to improve curriculum, instruction, and advising (American Productivity and Quality Center, 1998).

When departments and universities have objective, evidence-based measures of student performance, they can make better administrative decisions about their programs that result in stronger programs and better learning. They are also better able to demonstrate effectiveness and accountability to external evaluators and accreditation boards.

## Evaluation Ethics

At the level of doctoral education, more so than other educational levels, faculty often develop close professional relationships with their students. Indeed, by the time they complete their degree, differences in power and status that characterized the initial relationship between students and their advisors has typically decreased to the point where students often emerge as colleagues and friends with their advisors and other faculty. However, because this type of relationship entails affection, mutual esteem, symmetry, and loyalty, it can create an ethical dilemma for faculty when it comes to evaluating student work in a fair, truthful, and equitable manner (Sabar, 2002), especially when the quality of the student's work is not as good as the advisor expects and the student believes. The question becomes: Should the evaluation focus exclusively on the product or should knowledge about the person and the process be factored into the equation?

Unlike other educational performances, no grade or quality rating is assigned to the dissertation.[2] Dissertations either pass or fail. Still, advisors and committee members typically provide verbal feedback on the dissertation after the oral defense and write letters of recommendation that usually include a discussion of the student's dissertation. In situations where the student's performance and the student's (and often the faculty's) expectations about the performance do not match, committee members may find themselves in a quandary. Sabar (2002) has identified four conflicts that faculty may need to resolve: (a) between care and compassion for the student and the need to judge him or her honestly, even if this may hurt the student; (b) between the faculty member's own (often implicit) evaluation criteria and that of other members of the dissertation committee; (c) between rewarding the range of student qualities and fulfilling the faculty's responsibility to uphold academic excellence; and (d) between the desire to adapt the evaluation criteria to the individual student and the obligation to produce a reliable evaluation that fairly and accurately represents the student's abilities to potential employers.

Sabar (2002) notes the almost total absence of evaluation of standards and evaluation guidelines both for the evaluator and the evaluatee in higher education, as well as the fact that "in most academic institutions, instructors are not trained in what is expected of them as evaluators."[3] In order to be fair to students and accountable to the wider community, according to Ramphele, doctoral programs need to develop unambiguous measures of excellence as well as clear-cut methods of assessment so that what constitutes a high-quality dissertation can be measured reliably (as cited in Sabar, 2002). These standards and methods need to be shared with students during the guidance process, and rigorous feedback needs to be provided in order to raise standards and attain excellence.

## Conclusion

Developing and articulating performance expectations for the dissertation (and other aspects of doctoral education) is not just about excellence, it is also about fairness and accountability. Without performance expectations and allied standards, students do not have a clear target to aim toward, and if they do not have a clear target, it is more difficult for them to take the corrective actions necessary to hit the bull's-eye of excellence. Similarly, in the absence of performance expectations and standards, faculty, departments, and universities have no way of knowing whether they are truly hitting the mark, or, for that matter, how often they are hitting the mark and how far from the mark the "misses" are. Without such performance data, faculty, departments, and universities cannot identify and remedy weaknesses or exploit strengths, much less make informed decisions about actions necessary to achieve excellence in all facets of their programs.

By contrast, faculty, departments, and universities that claim assessment as their "property" will be better able to make assessment work for them rather than against them (Linkon, 2005). Those that adopt a performance-expectations, outcomes-based approach may be better able to move up in the rankings because they will offer a higher-quality educational program and produce higher-quality graduates. They should also be better able to attract the "best" students and the "best" faculty because they will have objective, evidence-based data to support their claims of excellence. And they will be able to use these data to respond to internal and external demands for accountability. The next three chapters provide faculty and administrators with information necessary to adopt a performance-expectations, outcomes-based approach to doctoral education.

## Notes

1. The early founders of doctoral education in America believed that truth must not only be discovered, it must be made known (Storr, 1973). Consequently, starting in the 19th century, graduate students were expected to publish—and pay for the cost of publishing—their dissertation before the degree would be conferred (Tebbel, 1987). Indeed, this publishing requirement contributed to the emergence of the university press (Bowen, 1971).

2. At some universities, the dissertation committee submits a quality rating to the graduate school. However, it is not clear what, if anything, this rating is used for.

3. One notable exception is Michigan State University, where as part of an 18-month-long graduate handbooks project, departments were asked to be more explicit about their expectations for comprehensive exams, dissertations, and so on. The results have been incorporated into individual departments' graduate handbooks and mentoring guides (see http://grad.msu.edu).

# 3

# UNIVERSAL QUALITIES
# OF A DISSERTATION

D espite the importance of the dissertation for obtaining the Ph.D.,
the mystique in which it is typically shrouded, and the weightiness
of the task of completing one, the purpose of a dissertation in doctoral education, what it means to make an original and a significant contribution, and faculty's standards or expectations for quality are rarely made
explicit to graduate students. Indeed, here is a sample of questions from
David and Parker's study (as cited in Katz, 1997) that graduate students often
ask and the answers they often receive:

Question: What are the quality standards?
Answer: High!

Question: How long should a dissertation be?
Answer: Long enough to cover the topic.

Question: How exhaustive should the literature review be?
Answer: Exhaustive. (p. 11)

Since 1920, when the Doctorate Records File databank was created, over
1.5 million people have earned Ph.D.s at U.S. universities.[1] Although over
1,700 U.S. colleges and universities enroll more than 2.5 million graduate
students in master's, doctoral, and first-professional programs, only about a
fourth of these institutions award the Ph.D[2] and only 14% of these students
(less than 400,000) are in doctoral programs[3] (Choy & Cataldi, 2006).
These institutions graduate roughly 40,000 new Ph.D.s each year in over
300 fields or disciplines. The median time to degree for all fields is 8.5 years.

Roughly 30% of new Ph.D.s go on to postdoctoral positions,[4] though the percents vary widely by discipline and domain of knowledge.

Despite the long history of the dissertation and the demands and expectations for quality, the nature of those expectations have been largely tacit and undefined. This chapter synthesizes the results of the focus group discussions across the 10 disciplines in the study and extracts what may be considered the universal or transdisciplinary characteristics of dissertations of different quality. Where relevant, it also highlights disciplinary differences.

Although the content and training in the disciplines are unique to each discipline, readers may be simultaneously surprised and not surprised to learn that across disciplines faculty have common views of quality and excellence. Indeed, one theme that emerged during the analysis of this study's data is that when you strip away content and focus on quality, the disciplines are very similar. This is most likely because faculty are united in a common enterprise (producing independent scholars and researchers), and this enterprise requires a common product (a dissertation) that has common tasks and fulfills requirements that transcend individual disciplines. It is also probably because people's understandings of what outstanding, very good, acceptable, and unacceptable mean transcend the content these qualities are attached to.

Before presenting the results of the study, a couple of caveats are in order. First, it needs to be made clear that faculty were not asked about their standards for the dissertation per se. Rather, they were asked about the characteristics of dissertations and components (tasks) of dissertations at different quality levels. Consequently, it would not be correct to say that faculty hold students to the standards depicted in the tables or even that they have standards for evaluating dissertations. Indeed, they asserted that they make holistic judgments about the quality of a dissertation after they have read it. In other words, they do not have a mental checklist of items to assess a dissertation. However, the results below demonstrate that faculty do make quality judgments about dissertations and that they can (and did) make those judgments explicit. Second, the items in the tables represent the different ways that dissertations are determined to be of a certain quality. However, no dissertation does or can do all of the individual things presented. Indeed, taken together, some of the items are self-contradictory.

As mentioned in chapter 1, the discussion that follows represents the collective judgments of 276 faculty from 10 disciplines (*sciences*: biology, physics, engineering, mathematics; *social sciences*: economics, psychology, sociology; and *humanities*: English, history, philosophy) at 9 research universities. Combined, these faculty had 6,129 years of experience, had chaired an estimated 3,470 dissertations, and had sat on a estimated 9,890 dissertation committees. On average, they had been professors for 22 years, had chaired 13 dissertations, and had sat on 36 dissertation committees.

## The Purpose of a Dissertation

The dissertation is often a stumbling block for many otherwise able graduate students. Its structure, content, and its very existence is, and has periodically been, a topic of debate among faculty, administrators, and policy makers, not to mention a source of much grousing among students who are writing one. Consequently, the focus group faculty were asked what the purpose of the dissertation is; why it is a requirement of doctoral education.

Faculty in many focus groups initially had a hard time explaining the purpose of the dissertation. Yet, they ultimately came up with many purposes (see Table 3.1), and in the process they discussed the role it plays in doctoral training.

Overall, the faculty's discussion of the purpose of a dissertation indicates that they see it as both a process and a product. The faculty identified three

**TABLE 3.1.**
**The Purpose of a Dissertation**

- To train student to be professionals in the discipline
- To learn how to and demonstrate the ability to:
  - conduct independent, original, and significant research—identify/define problems and generate questions, review the literature, apply appropriate methods, analyze data/text, discuss findings, produce publishable results
  - engage in a sustained piece of research or argument
  - think and write critically and coherently
  - be a professional in and contribute to the discipline
- To show mastery of the field
- To prepare for a career and get a job
- It is a capstone on the graduate education and research experience, a rite of passage from student to professional, a union card or credential for admission to the profession

basic processes. The first two are *to train* the student in, and for the student *to learn*, the knowledge, skills, and thought processes necessary to engage in independent research and be a professional in the discipline. The third is *to demonstrate* that the student has mastered the discipline's knowledge base, acquired its professional skills and competencies, and is capable of doing independent research in the future. One goal of these processes is to produce a product that can be published.

As a product, the dissertation serves as a union card or credential for admission to the profession. Despite this, the faculty saw the dissertation as a first exercise or a first statement, the platform from which students would make subsequent, more important contributions. Indeed, an English professor said that he tells students that the first purpose of the dissertation is "to be done . . . to be written" and that the second purpose is "to get yourself a job."

One of the more interesting paradoxes of this study is that across focus groups and disciplines, the faculty said that the purpose of the dissertation is to make an original and significant contribution. This purpose aligns well with most universities' stated criteria for the award of the Ph.D.[5] Yet, in their discussion of what it means to make an original and a significant contribution (see the following sections), the faculty often said that they did not expect graduate students to make such contributions. This is particularly striking because the questions about the meaning of an original and a significant contribution preceded the question about the purpose of a dissertation in the focus group discussions. One explanation for this apparent contradiction is that when discussing "original" and "significant" the faculty may have been focusing more on their meaning with respect to the field/discipline than with respect to the dissertation, and the wording of the question may have contributed to it. Even so, in their later discussion of the unacceptable or failing dissertation, the faculty said that they will not accept a dissertation that does not make an original contribution.

Faculty in a number of fields noted that the dissertation is a rite of passage from student to professional/colleague. Faculty in mathematics and economics talked about the way the dissertation transforms people. They said those who complete it emerge with a new sense of who they are and with a new confidence in their ability to do original, independent research (see chapters 10 and 11).

## The Nature of an Original Contribution

The faculty in all disciplines defined "original contribution" with respect to its newness (see Table 3.2). The contribution can be made in almost any component of the dissertation—question, argument, theory, data, data source, method, analysis, results—by thinking, saying, or doing something that has not been thought, said, or done before.[6] The novelty can originate wholly or in part from the student, or the student may borrow an existing contribution from another field or discipline and apply it to his or her field or discipline for the first time.

### TABLE 3.2.
### The Nature of an Original Contribution

- Something that has not been done, found, known, proved, said, or seen before that results from:
  - Asking or identifying new questions, topics, or areas of exploration
  - Applying new ideas, methods, approaches, or analyses to an old question, problem, issue, idea, source, thinker, or text
  - Developing or applying new theories, theorems, theoretical descriptions, or theoretical frameworks
  - Inventing, developing, or applying new methods, approaches, computations, techniques, or technologies
  - Creating, finding, or using new data, data sets, archives, information, materials, or sources
  - Applying old ideas, methods, approaches, or analyses to new data, material, or sources
  - Developing or applying new analyses, analytic approaches, frameworks, techniques, models, or statistical procedures
  - Coming up with new ideas, connections, inferences, insights, interpretations, observations, perspectives
  - Producing new conclusions, answers, findings, or proofs
  - Combining or synthesizing things (experiments, facts, knowledge, models of inquiry, problems, sources, technologies, theoretical constructs) from other fields or disciplines
- Is publishable
- Adds to knowledge
- Changes the way people think
- Moves the field forward/advances the state of the art

There were some disciplinary differences about the nature of originality. Even though they were able to say what it meant to make an original contribution, many of the English faculty emphatically and categorically rejected the notion of originality (see chapter 14). They said that their discipline is recursive, not progressive, and asserted that people in their discipline do not make original contributions, rather, they join conversations. Indeed, O'Brien (1995) notes that recent discussions of "authorial authority" across the arts, humanities, and social sciences have undermined the "romantic notion" of creative individualism and sparked debates about the meaning of an "original contribution to knowledge" (p. 12) in these disciplines.

Although the philosophers did not reject the notion of originality, they noted that it was difficult to do something completely new and different in a field that has been around for 2,500 years (see chapter 16). The mathematicians, by contrast, noted that there is a debate within their field over whether mathematics is discovered or invented/composed (see chapter 10).

The student's role in making an original contribution is more problematic in the experimental, teamwork-oriented disciplines where students tend to work on their advisor's funded research projects than in nonexperimental ones where students typically work on independently conceived research projects in their advisor's field of expertise broadly defined. Although asked by a psychologist, the following question could have come from faculty in any number of experimental disciplines:

> How many of us . . . allow students to do dissertations that are outside of the lines of research that are our own? If the answer is none, then the answer implies we don't produce any original dissertations.

In these disciplines and situations, the more the ideas originate with the student and the more the work diverges from the advisor's, the more original it is deemed.

Faculty across the disciplines noted that there were levels or degrees of originality.[7] The lowest level of originality typically involves applying old methods to new data, materials, sources, or the like, and results in a small, incremental addition to the knowledge base that is of little consequence. At the higher levels, making an original contribution typically involves asking new questions or applying new methods to old or new problems and achieving results that have consequence, that is, they are publishable, often in the highest-quality journals, and they advance the field. At the very highest level, the contribution has the potential to change the field. The faculty noted that it was rare for a graduate student to make a contribution at the highest level, and that doing so involved creativity.[8]

The standards for originality are vague and vary across advisors. Students are often held to different standards based on their advisor's assessment of their capabilities. Indeed, the Ph.D. can be awarded for pure perseverance and technical accuracy rather than for originality (see the section "Accept-able" below). An economics professor at Public University summed it up nicely:

> There are some students who have the ability to do very original re-search—to start with an idea that's original, important, interesting, and to carry it through. And for those students, we won't let them get away with the dissertation like the [lowest] kind [just mentioned], period, because we know that they can do better. Then there are students that you realize somewhere along the way that . . . the standards you're going to hold them to are just going to be different. They're going to be lower. So, the amount of originality in their dissertation may be far lower than another student's, and you're still willing to sign the dotted line at the end of the day.

Another participant at Public University made an interesting distinction between "original" and "contribution," suggesting that something could be original but not make a contribution. Given that original simply means new, it is not difficult to do something original, "it" just has to have not been said or done before. However, contribution is another matter. What is considered a contribution and the degree to which a dissertation makes a contribution is based on community judgment and shades into the next topic: what it means to make a significant contribution. The two concepts, as we shall see, are closely related.

## The Nature of a Significant Contribution

The key distinguishing feature of a significant contribution is that it has con-sequence. The contribution has to be of interest and importance to the com-munity and has to influence the field by changing the way people think (see Table 3.3). While judgments of significance are often highly subjective—in the eye of the beholder—significance is typically determined by community,

## TABLE 3.3.
### The Nature of a Significant Contribution

- A nontrivial to very important, original breakthrough at the empirical, conceptual, theoretical, or policy level
- Is useful and will have impact
- Is publishable in top-tier journals
- Is of interest to people inside and possibly outside the community and causes them to see things differently
- Influences the conversation and peoples' research and teaching
- Has implications for and advances the field, the discipline, other disciplines, and/or society

not individual, judgment, and the judgment is often made retrospectively, sometimes many years after the fact.

The faculty's discussion of what it means to make a significant contribution demonstrates a close relationship between originality and significance. They noted that something could be original without being significant, yet many questioned whether something could be significant without also being original. Although they did not propose levels of significance, the faculty implied that in order for a contribution to be significant it had to be at the higher end of the original continuum. The timing of the contribution also appears to be important. Significant contributions seem easier to make in "hot" fields or trendy areas than in more stable or conservative ones. However, the most significant contributions are the ones that initiate a new trend or destabilize a conservative area, thus creating new questions and new research agendas.

Although significance is frequently stated as a requirement for the Ph.D.,[9] faculty do not expect graduate students to make significant contributions. Indeed, they noted that graduate students rarely made them. Instead, faculty look for evidence that the student has the ability to make a significant contribution in the future.

## The Quality of the Dissertation

As the final product of doctoral education the dissertation embodies the performance goals and objectives of doctoral training. What those goals are and how well they have been achieved are incorporated in faculty's implicit standards for judging dissertations of different quality. To get at those goals and objectives, the focus group faculty were asked to think about dissertations they had read that were outstanding, very good, acceptable, and unacceptable. They were asked to describe what made those dissertations of that quality and what distinguished them from dissertations at the next higher-quality level. Table 3.4 illustrates the quality distinctions or performance expectations for the dissertation as a whole that emerged from the focus group discussions. Chapter 5 discusses how they can be converted into rubrics.

Before discussing the quality of the dissertation, it is worth noting that contemporary dissertations come in a variety of forms, and these forms vary within and across disciplines. Paltridge (2002) has identified four main types of dissertations: (a) the simple-traditional dissertation reports on a single study and has a typical macrostructure of introduction, literature review, materials and methods, results, discussion and conclusion; (b) the complex-traditional dissertation reports on more than one study. Like the simple-traditional dissertation, it starts with introduction and literature review, and has a general methods chapter that is followed by a series of chapters that report on each individual study, and ends with an overall conclusion; (c) the topic-based dissertation also typically starts with an introductory chapter, which is followed by a series of chapters that address subtopics of the main topic under investigation, and ends with an overall conclusion; and (d) the compilation-of-publishable-research-articles dissertation, is, as its name suggests, a compilation of publishable or published articles. It typically has introductory, transitional, and concluding sections, though the review of the literature usually occurs within each of the articles. It may have appendixes that provide more detailed material on history, methods, and results than would normally be found in published journal articles (Council of Graduate Schools, 2004). This type of dissertation is now common in the sciences in the United States and is starting to become acceptable in other disciplines and in other parts of the world (Paltridge, 2002). Even though dissertations may come in different forms, judgments about the quality of a dissertation, as we shall see, are independent of its form.

## Outstanding

When asked to characterize outstanding dissertations, the faculty often said that they defied explication, that there was no single feature or set of defining

**TABLE 3.4.**
**The Characteristics of Different Quality Dissertations**

| Quality | Characteristics |
|---|---|
| **Outstanding** | • Original and significant, and also ambitious, brilliant, clear, clever, coherent, compelling, concise, creative, elegant, engaging, exciting, interesting, insightful, persuasive, sophisticated, surprising, and thoughtful<br>• Very well written and very well organized<br>• Synthetic and interdisciplinary<br>• Components are connected in a seamless way<br>• Exhibits mature, independent thinking<br>• Has a point of view and a strong, confident, independent, and authoritative voice<br>• Asks new questions or addresses an important question or problem<br>• Clearly states the problem and why it is important<br>• Displays a deep understanding of a massive amount of complicated literature<br>• Exhibits command and authority over the material<br>• Argument is focused, logical, rigorous, and sustained<br>• Is theoretically sophisticated and shows a deep understanding of theory<br>• Has a brilliant research design<br>• Uses or develops new tools, methods, approaches, or new types of analyses<br>• Is thoroughly researched<br>• Data are rich and come from multiple sources<br>• Analysis is comprehensive, complete, sophisticated, and convincing<br>• Results are significant<br>• Conclusion ties the whole thing together<br>• Is publishable in top-tier journals<br>• Is of interest to a larger community and changes the way people think<br>• Pushes the discipline's boundaries and opens new areas for research |
| **Very good** | • Solid<br>• Well written and well organized<br>• Has some original ideas, insights, and observations, but is less original, significant, ambitious, interesting, and exciting than outstanding |

| Quality | Characteristics |
|---|---|
| **Very good** | • Has a good question or problem that tends to be small and traditional<br>• Is the next step in a research program (good normal science)<br>• Shows understanding and mastery of the subject matter<br>• Argument is strong, comprehensive, and coherent<br>• Research is well executed<br>• Demonstrates (technical) competence<br>• Uses appropriate, standard theory, methods, and techniques<br>• Obtains solid, expected results/answers<br>• Misses opportunities to completely explore interesting issues and connections<br>• Makes a modest contribution to the field but does not open it up |
| **Acceptable** | • Workmanlike<br>• Demonstrates (technical) competence<br>• Shows the ability to do research<br>• Is not very original or significant<br>• Is not interesting, exciting, or surprising<br>• Displays little creativity, imagination, or insight<br>• Writing is pedestrian and plodding<br>• Structure and organization are weak<br>• Project is narrow in scope<br>• Question or problem is not exciting—is often highly derivative or an extension of advisor's work<br>• Displays a narrow understanding of the field<br>• Literature review is adequate—knows the literature but is not critical of it or does not discuss what is important<br>• Can sustain an argument, but argument is not imaginative, complex, or convincing<br>• Theory is understood at a simple level and is minimally to competently applied to the problem<br>• Uses standard methods<br>• Analysis is unsophisticated—does not explore all possibilities and misses connections<br>• Results are predictable and not exciting<br>• Makes a small contribution |
| **Unacceptable** | • Is poorly written<br>• Has spelling and grammatical errors |

*(continues)*

**TABLE 3.4.**
**Continued**

| Quality | Characteristics |
|---|---|
| **Unacceptable** | • Presentation is sloppy<br>• Contains errors or mistakes<br>• Plagiarizes or deliberately misreads or misuses sources<br>• Does not understand basic concepts, processes, or conventions of the discipline<br>• Lacks careful thought<br>• Question or problem is trivial, weak, unoriginal, or already solved<br>• Does not understand or misses relevant literature<br>• Argument is weak, inconsistent, self-contradictory, unconvincing, or invalid<br>• Theory is missing, wrong, or not handled well<br>• Methods are inappropriate or incorrect<br>• Data are flawed, wrong, false, fudged, or misinterpreted<br>• Analysis is wrong, inappropriate, incoherent, or confused<br>• Results are obvious, already known, unexplained, or misinterpreted<br>• Interpretation is unsupported or exaggerated<br>• Does not make a contribution |

features—"You know it when you see it." Even though outstanding dissertations are rare—they come along once or twice a decade, if that often—the faculty liked talking about this quality more than any other, and were able to provide a very consistent set of descriptors.

Outstanding dissertations are characterized by originality, high-quality writing, and compelling consequences. They display a richness of thought and insight, and make an important breakthrough. The body of work in outstanding dissertations is deep and thorough. Each individual component of the dissertation is outstanding and the components are integrated throughout the dissertation in a seamless way. The writing is clear and persuasive and provides a glimpse into the mind of the author—you can see how the student is thinking. Not only are outstanding dissertations a pleasure to read, they are "page-turners." They surprise and edify the reader. When they read outstanding dissertations, faculty say, "Wow! Why didn't I think of that?" Everything is anticipated; all the reader's questions are answered. The results or conclusions push the discipline's boundaries, and are publishable in the top-tier journals. Faculty in sociology and the humanities noted that outstanding dissertations have a strong, independent, and authoritative voice.

Students who produce outstanding dissertations are very creative and intellectually adventurous. They love, and are passionate about, what they are doing, and display intense curiosity and drive. They are willing to leap into new territory and transfer ideas from place to place. While they often have great advisors with whom they have rich and satisfying intellectual exchanges, outstanding students typically think and work independently of their advisor and of the educational process they have just been through. At the same time, an outstanding dissertation can also be a function of luck. The student may simply be in the right place at the right time.

## Very Good

The focus group faculty, who it should be reiterated were at highly ranked universities, indicated that the majority of the dissertations they see are "very good," and that this is the level they expect of most graduate students. Consequently, for them, very good dissertations are the prototype for comparison of all the other quality levels. As such, the faculty had less to say about very good dissertations (and very good components of dissertations) than about the other quality levels.

Although very good dissertations are solid and well written, they are distinguished by being "less"—less original, less significant, less ambitious, less exiting, and/or less interesting than outstanding dissertations. They display mastery of the field, address the next question or problem in a research program, and are executed competently and confidently. The work expands rather than alters the thinking of a field and, thus, has less consequence than that of outstanding dissertations. Very good dissertations contain material for two or three papers that could get published in good journals.

Students who produce very good dissertations show drive and ability. They have good technical skills, but may not be in control of all the elements of the dissertation. Indeed, one or more components of the dissertation may not be as strong as the others. According to the participants, sometimes what might have been an outstanding dissertation ends up being "only" very good because the student did not have or take the time to develop his or her ideas. Sometimes it is because the student ran out of time or money, had a job waiting, or simply wanted to get on with life. In experimental disciplines,

the dissertation may be very good rather than outstanding because the experiments did not work out as planned or the results were not as crisp and clear
as expected.

## *Acceptable*

In discussing the acceptable dissertation, faculty in many focus groups distinguished between acceptable dissertations and marginally acceptable ones,
though their discussion of the two was often blurred. Acceptable dissertations meet the criteria for the award of the Ph.D., whereas marginally acceptable ones are just barely over the threshold of acceptability—they pass the
"gag test."

Acceptable dissertations are rather pedestrian and are distinguished by
being "not very"—not very original, significant, exciting, or interesting.
They contain an acceptable amount of solid work that demonstrates that the
student can do research. The work is often a highly derivative, small extension of someone else's work. The writing is good enough, but the dissertation
is a chore to read. In the humanities disciplines, where the dissertation is
premised on an argument, the argument is weak and not convincing. The
acceptable dissertation adds little to the field and lacks consequence. It may
result in some conference papers, but has little in the way of publishable
material, and what is publishable would get published in lower-tier journals.

Most students who produce acceptable dissertations were said to be
functioning close to their capabilities. While most are bright, they are missing "a certain quality of mind"—they lack intellectual power and the ability
to think like a researcher. They also often lack independence and initiative,
and thus require a lot of coaching and hand-holding. Their advisors (or at
least high-Ph.D.-productive advisors) often give them their topics or problems, feed them ideas, and spend a lot of time writing and copyediting their
work.

Faculty do not expect these students to get—and these students often
realize that they are not capable of getting—tenure-track positions at research universities, though they may qualify for teaching jobs at state, liberal
arts, and community colleges or for jobs in directed research at research institutions, government agencies, and the like.

Sometimes acceptable dissertations are a function of circumstance or bad
luck. In some cases, the students are not in residence and, consequently,

have not gotten the advice and guidance they need to produce a better-quality dissertation. More commonly, the students have rushed their dissertations because they have accepted a job or a postdoc, run out of funds, have a family to support, or have simply run out of energy. In experimental disciplines, otherwise good dissertations are considered acceptable when the experiment or experiments do not work out and students get null or negative results.

Advisors and dissertation committees adjust their standards and expectations for students who produce acceptable and marginally acceptable dissertations. The primary consideration is that the student fulfilled the contract. That is, the student worked hard, did what he or she said he or she was going to do in the dissertation proposal, and demonstrated competence. The faculty also take into consideration such "extraneous" factors as their judgments about the person and the type of career the student is planning. Indeed, faculty in a few focus groups debated whether the Ph.D. should be awarded solely on the basis of the quality of the product (the dissertation) or whether their feelings about the person and their knowledge of the process the student had been through should play a role in their decision to award the degree (see "Evaluation Ethics" in chapter 2, p. 24). Ultimately, the "hidden criteria" for the award of the Ph.D. is that the student will not embarrass or harm the reputation of the advisor, the committee members, the department, or the university.

## Unacceptable

When asked about the unacceptable dissertation, the faculty balked. They asserted that they rarely, if ever, failed a dissertation, that dissertations of unacceptable quality were seldom allowed to come before a dissertation committee, that students who produced unacceptable dissertations would probably drop out of the program before advancing to a defense, and that it was the advisor's responsibility to prevent unacceptable dissertations from advancing. The faculty noted that when they did see an unacceptable dissertation, it was usually the advisor's fault; the student had not been given the opportunity to do well.

It is worth noting that very few of the focus group faculty had ever been on a committee that failed a dissertation. Those who had had the experience, with few exceptions, said that it had not happened in their department, but rather in another department or at another university where they were serving as the outside committee member. The faculty's characterization of the unacceptable dissertation is thus based primarily on their experience with unacceptable drafts.

Unacceptable dissertations are poorly written and full of errors and mistakes. They are distinguished by "not"—not original, not thoughtful, not well done. They do not have a good or clearly defined question or problem. They exhibit a poor grasp of the field and either do not use proper methods or use them inappropriately. Unacceptable dissertations do not yield new or relevant results, and the results they yield are often misinterpreted or oversold. In short, they are of no consequence and contain no publishable material.

Students produce unacceptable dissertations for a variety of reasons, though most are not able to master professional standards and do not have what it takes to be a researcher. Some should not have been admitted into the program in the first place or should have been stopped before advancing to candidacy. (This, of course, raises questions about why they were allowed to continue.) Others are not capable of handling a big project; they do not understand what needs to be done. Many cannot or will not take their advisor's advice and criticism into account, and, consequently, produce one bad revision after another. Still others are capable of producing acceptable dissertations, but fail to do so because they have taken jobs or otherwise left the university and have not kept up with the research in their area, resulting in an unoriginal or out-of-date product. Sometimes students fail because they push for the defense even though their advisors have told them they were not ready to defend.

Rather than proactively terminating students whose work is unacceptable, many advisors simply wait for students to get discouraged and leave. Some try to disassociate themselves from such students by sending signals or by telling them to find another advisor. Others use the defense to get rid of the student.

In rare instances when an unacceptable dissertation makes it to defense, the dissertation committee seeks excuses to pass it. Committee members will take into consideration such things as their feelings about the person rather than the objective document. In the end, most defer to the advisor, hold their noses, and vote to pass.

## The Quality of the Components of a Dissertation

After discussing the different quality levels of the dissertation as a whole, the focus group faculty were given a matrix of components, or *essential tasks*, of dissertations in their field (see Table 1.2) and asked to characterize each component at each of the four different quality levels. In general, the faculty did not like having to discuss the individual components of the dissertation (see the disciplinary chapters in part two for the faculty's sometimes caustic comments)—and some facilitators did not like having to ask faculty to discuss them. Indeed, 18 focus groups did not discuss them at all, and across the focus groups that did, a total of 10 cells in the matrix (mostly those at the very good level) were not discussed by any focus group.

Regardless of whether or not the components match the chapter structure of the dissertation, the focus group faculty generally agreed that all dissertations in their discipline would (and should) have all the components they were asked to discuss. This section focuses on the common themes in six components that are found in most but not all disciplines—introduction/problem statement, literature review, theory, methods, results/analysis, and discussion and conclusion (see Table 3.A in the appendix of this chapter). Components that are specific to individual disciplines (e.g., statement of results/theorems in mathematics, recognition and response to possible objections in philosophy) are discussed in that discipline's chapter in part two.

### *Introduction*

In all disciplines, the introduction states the problem. It should motivate and provide context for the work. It should lay out the research question(s) and the general strategy. As a distinct chapter, the introduction often includes the literature review and theory, and provides an overview of the entire dissertation. The introduction is often written (or rewritten) after the conclusion. In some disciplines, the sciences in particular, the introduction functions (or should function) as an executive summary. The faculty had mixed feelings about the importance of the introduction, and noted that the quality of the introduction was not critical to their assessment of the dissertation.

Outstanding introductions have a hook, an element of surprise that draws people in and makes them want to read the dissertation. They provide a clear statement of the problem, identify the contribution up front, and address its importance and significance.[10] They are written with authority, and show insight into and command over the argument/material. They also provide a chapter-by-chapter road map of the dissertation.

Very good introductions lack the "Wow!" factor. They pose a clear research question or problem, but are less interesting and less well motivated than outstanding ones. Acceptable introductions do the things that an introduction needs to do. They state, "This is a study of . . ." but do not convince the reader that the question/problem is interesting or important. Unacceptable introductions are poorly written. The problem is not well stated or well motivated. They often contain a lot of extraneous material. After reading the unacceptable introduction, the reader does not know what the dissertation is about and does not know (or care) where it is going.

## Literature Review

While it may or may not be a distinct chapter, all disciplines require some sort of review of the literature. The review provides context for and connects the question/problem to past and contemporary thought and research on the question/problem.[11] Boote and Beile (2005) argue that a good literature review is "a precondition to doing substantive, thorough, sophisticated research" (p. 3). They assert that researchers "cannot perform significant research without first understanding the literature in the field" (p. 3).

In history, the literature review is commonly called a historiographic review and is a review of other interpretations of history or the history of the problem. Faculty in physics and engineering view the literature review as a teaching document for the next student in their laboratory. A few faculty in a few disciplines said that they did not like literature reviews and did not read them. Others thought they were a very important part of the dissertation.

An outstanding literature review is important, relevant, analytical, and insightful. It reads like a good review article and educates the reader. Students who write outstanding literature reviews display a deep and sweeping grasp of the literature, often drawing on literatures from other fields. At the same time, they are selective, including only the most relevant and important works. They use the literature to show what is missing, why their project needs to be done, and how their research is going to advance the field. Faculty in the humanities noted that students who write outstanding literature reviews are generous to their sources. While critical, they show empathy for and appreciation of others' work.

Very good literature reviews are critical and comprehensive. They help the reader understand the area under investigation. Acceptable literature reviews tend to discuss everything that has been written on the topic, though they may also miss some relevant parts of the literature. Students who write acceptable literature reviews often take the literature they have read at face value and do not (or cannot) discriminate between good papers and bad ones. Their literature reviews are descriptive summaries, "so-and-so and so-and-so said," that make obvious points. Similarly, unacceptable literature reviews lack an organizing intelligence. Students who write them typically have not read enough. They fail to cite important papers, cite papers they have not read, and do not seem to understand their sources. Sometimes they even plagiarize their sources.

## Theory

Faculty in mathematics and the humanities were not asked about theory per se and thus are not represented in Table 3.A or in the following discussion. Faculty in the disciplines that were asked about theory noted that it is typically part of the introduction, though theory and methods are often intermingled as well. A study's research question(s) should be linked to theory and students should use theory to help select appropriate methods. Faculty in economics and sociology noted that dissertations in their disciplines had to have theory.

The outstanding theory component is elegant and insightful. Students who use theory in an outstanding way have a deep understanding of it and employ it creatively, often developing a new theory, or revising or synthesizing existing theories. At the very good level, the theory is appropriate for the problem. Students use it correctly and build on the work of others. At the acceptable level, theory is used appropriately, but is not articulated well and there is no value added. At the unacceptable level, there is no theory, the theory is wrong, or it does not relate to the research question or the research methods. Students who function at this level do not understand theory and cannot explain it.

## Methods/Approach

The data in Table 3.A and the following discussion derive primarily from faculty in the empirical sciences and the social sciences. The English faculty were asked about "approach to analysis," which is the theory or method behind the analysis, and are only minimally represented here. The historians were asked about "sources/methods." Their responses focused more on sources than on methods, and, thus, they too are only minimally represented here. Faculty in philosophy were not asked about methods per se.

Across disciplines and focus groups, there was some blurring in the discussions between the methods used to conduct the research and the actual write-up of the methods section. The social sciences faculty made few general remarks about the nature or role of the methods component in a dissertation, whereas the science faculty indicated that the methods section had to provide sufficient detail to allow replication. Some science faculty do not pay much attention to the methods section, others read it very carefully.

Outstanding methods are simple, elegant, and creative and often at the cutting edge. They derive from and are closely integrated with theory. Students whose methods are outstanding often use multiple methods and attack their problem from all sides. Their write-ups are thorough and include justifications for each method as well as a discussion of its pros and cons, strengths and weaknesses.

Very good methods are appropriate for the problem, but less novel and less interesting than outstanding methods. Students at this level embrace challenges when things do not work out. In their write-ups, they justify their methods and discuss their advantages and disadvantages. At the acceptable level, students apply standard methods competently without considering whether they are the best methods for the problem. When things do not turn out as planned, they do not know what to do. Their write-ups provide sufficient detail to allow replication. At the unacceptable level, the methods are either wrong or fatally flawed. The write-ups contain insufficient detail.

## Results/Data Analysis

Like methods, the faculty across disciplines made few general remarks about the nature or role of results/analysis in a dissertation. The science faculty noted that there were "few degrees of freedom" for this component. The English and history faculty said that this was the most important part of the dissertation, though their discussion of this component is less well represented in this section than that of the sciences and social sciences. The philosophers were not asked about analysis per se and are thus not included in Table 3.A or the discussion that follows.

Outstanding analyses are elegant, insightful, and sophisticated. Students who do them iteratively explore questions raised by their analyses. They see complex patterns in their data and provide plausible interpretations of them. Very good analyses are clear and to the point but are less robust than outstanding ones. Although the analysis is thorough, students at this level often do not engage in supplementary analyses. However, they do make a plausible, convincing case for their results/analyses.

At the acceptable level, the analyses are routine and correct, though not particularly meaningful. Students at this level require a lot of hand-holding. They do not ask penetrating questions of their data and the important insights may come from the advisor not the student. At the unacceptable level, the analysis or presentation of results is wrong or inappropriate. Students need a lot of help from their advisors. They cannot interpret their results and they cannot answer the "So what?" question.

### Discussion and Conclusion

The discussion and conclusion is typically the last chapter of a dissertation. Some faculty drew a distinction between the discussion and the conclusion. They said that the conclusion summarizes and wraps things up, whereas the discussion, which is more important, should tie to the introduction and put the work in a larger perspective. A number of faculty thought that the discussion/conclusion chapter was a difficult one for graduate students to write, in part, because at this point in their careers most students have an insufficient perspective on the field to really draw things together and address their implications, and also because by the time they get to this chapter, students are tired and just want to be done. Faculty within and across focus groups disagreed about the importance of this component. Some thought that it was the least important part of the dissertation, others thought that it was very important. Similarly, the faculty in the sciences did not agree on the need for, or relevance of, a discussion of future directions.

The outstanding discussion and conclusion (hereafter referred to as "conclusion") is stimulating and insightful. It places the work in context, draws out its importance, significance, and implications, and identifies new questions or next steps. The very good conclusion is a solid summary. It identifies some implications and future directions. The acceptable conclusion restates what has been accomplished, but does not address the significance or implications of the work. Students often write acceptable rather than higher-quality conclusions because they have run out of steam. The unacceptable conclusion is completely missing or otherwise insufficient. Students who write unacceptable conclusions do not tie things up or draw out the study's meaning, often because the student does not understand what he or she has done.

## The Quality of the Writing

Many themes emerged in the focus group discussions that space precludes addressing. However, one theme—the quality of students' writing—came up so frequently that it deserves special mention. Faculty in 20 (or 30%) of the focus groups had something to say about it—and it was not complimentary.

Across the board, the faculty commented that the quality of students' writing is more of a problem now than in the past. They attributed the decline to the failure of high schools and colleges in the United States to require students to write. They noted that while some graduate students have problems with grammar and tense, many have problems with basic structure and basic rhetoric. One physicist summed up the general problem nicely:

> They really don't know how to form an argument . . . take it all the way from the sentence level all the way up to the entire dissertation level. If they don't know how to form an argument, they usually don't know how to write a sentence. They usually don't know how to write a theme for a paragraph and develop that theme in the paragraph. They don't know how to write a section and develop a theme for a section.

In some cases, poor-quality writing was attributed to poor-quality thinking. According to one participant, "If you're muddy up here [in your head], it's going to come up even muddier on paper." One psychologist averred, "I think clear thinkers probably make better scientists."

Regardless of how brilliant the ideas and how outstanding the research, if students cannot convey their ideas in a clear and concise way, faculty downgrade the quality of a dissertation—"It can't be an outstanding dissertation" if the writing is not good. And it is "just not acceptable if it's not understandable." Some faculty went further and argued that it is not possible to be a good researcher if one is not a good writer, because a researcher has to be able to explain and communicate what he or she has done.

Faculty in a number of focus groups talked about the time and effort they put into helping students write and into copyediting their work. Some even do the writing for them. This stands in contrast to a sociologist's observation that good writing frees up the advisor "to really work on what should be the most important part of the dissertation"—the ideas.

Finally, in addition to the decline in graduate students' writing skills, one historian lamented the decline in graduate students' reading skills. He noted that graduate students' vocabularies are smaller and their syntax weaker than they used to be and, as a result, they have a harder time grasping historical materials. He talked about how he used to assign, and how undergraduates used to read, William Bradford's *Of Plymouth Plantation* "with pleasure," and how he could not ask today's graduate students to read it unless they were specialists in the field.

## Conclusion

As the discussion throughout this chapter demonstrates, faculty are not only keenly aware of and able to articulate differences between dissertations and components of dissertations of different quality, they are also able to identify differences in the characteristics of students who produce them as well as characteristics of situations and circumstances that may affect them. However, until they came together for the focus group discussion, most faculty had never thought about these issues or discussed them with colleagues, who, many were surprised to discover, had similar, if not identical, views and standards. Indeed, faculty in a few focus groups even expressed the desire to have a copy of their focus group's transcript so they could share the results of their discussion with their students.

The next step is for faculty in departments throughout the country (and the world) to come together and agree upon performance outcomes for the dissertation and its components, and develop rubrics (see chapter 5) to communicate these standards and expectations to their graduate students. Once they articulate their standards, faculty should start to see patterns in students' work that will help them reflect upon ways in which they could improve their practice and their program to help more students meet higher standards. They should also start to see more better-quality dissertations that are executed more independently because students will now know what is expected of them and know what they need to do to meet the standard—and if they do not know what they need to do, faculty should be better equipped to help them figure it out and mentor them toward the goal. In addition, faculty and departments that develop and articulate their standards and expectations for the dissertation should be better able to more kindly and compassionately counsel out students earlier in their doctoral careers who do not and cannot meet minimum expectations, thus saving the student, the faculty, the department, and the university time, effort, and money, not to mention pain, stress, and anxiety.

In short, through the simple act of having faculty make explicit their implicit standards and expectations for the dissertation, everyone—students, faculty, departments, and universities—wins. Everyone is provided with information they need to move up a notch or two or more on the road toward excellence. And if students cannot move forward on that road, and if faculty are unwilling and/or unable to help students achieve to their fullest, they (students and faculty) will have a better understanding of why they should travel down another road.

## Notes

1. Thurgood, Golladay, and Hill (2006) state that more than 1.35 million Ph.D. degrees were awarded between 1920 and 1999. The "over 1.5 million" figure cited in the text is an extrapolation to 2005 based on the assumption of approximately 40,000 Ph.D.s per year between 2000 and 2005.

2. The number of doctoral-degree-granting institutions vary depending upon whether education and clinical degrees are counted.

3. Choy and Cataldi (2006) note that only half of the approximately 392,000 doctoral students enrolled in 2003–04 were enrolled full-time for the full year.

4. For information on the source of these data, see chapter 1, note 5. Data on first-year enrollment is from Syverson (n.d.), *Graduate Enrollment and Degrees: 1986 to 2001.* http://www.cgsnet.org/pdf/ged2001.pdf

5. In summer 2002, I searched the Web sites of 25 major public and private universities for a statement of the nature or purpose of a dissertation or what the universities required of a dissertation. The statements turned up in a variety of places: graduate student handbooks, university by-laws, degree requirements, among others. I could not find a statement for four universities, though this does not mean that those universities did not have a statement, only that it was not contained in a document that could be located on their Web site. The most frequently cited requirement (10 universities) was that the dissertation exhibit independent research or, more commonly, demonstrate that the candidate had the ability to conduct independent research or function as an independent scholar. Seven universities required

the dissertation to demonstrate originality; show knowledge or mastery of the subject area, research techniques, resources, or methods; or demonstrate scholarship. Five universities required that the dissertation make a significant contribution to knowledge. Five universities required that the dissertation be at an advanced level and demonstrate high achievement or high attainment. Five universities had requirements that addressed the structure or presentation of material in the dissertation—the "ability to organize and present the findings and results of research effectively," and demonstrate "a high degree of literary skill." Two universities addressed research in a general way, that is, that the dissertation be the result of significant and sustained research. Two universities addressed the problem undertaken by the dissertation; they noted that the dissertation should demonstrate the "ability to select an important problem for investigation and deal with it competently." The other stated that the dissertation should be an "original investigation of a significant problem." Finally, two universities indicated that the dissertation should be either "worthy of publication" or "should provide the basis for a publishable contribution to the research literature in a major field."

6. According to a paper by Hale, a doctoral student could demonstrate originality in the dissertation in three ways: (a) by discovery, that is "the announcement and proof of something not known before"; (b) by adjudication, that is the "establishment of one or two or more conflicting views already held upon a matter of doubt"; and (c) by disproof of an existing view, "held upon evidence which had appeared to be of weight" (as cited in Nerad & Miller, 1997, p. 76).

7. Although an attempt has been made in the tables here and in the disciplinary chapters to order the data from the lowest to the highest level of originality by component, the presentation does not represent a strict hierarchy. Such an ordering requires additional input from faculty.

8. The concept of originality is very similar to the concept of creativity. Sternberg (2003) has identified eight types of creative contributions that are divided into three major categories. The degrees of originality discussed above bear a strong resemblance to Sternberg's three major categories: (a) types of creativity that accept current paradigms and attempt to extend them, (b) types of creativity that reject current paradigms and replace them, and (c) types of creativity that seek to integrate existing paradigms.

9. According to O'Brien (1995), when the word "significant" appears as a requirement for a dissertation, students tend to "conceive of the dissertation in terms of a magnum opus, grande thèse, or habilitationschrift" (p. 13).

10. Bender, Katz, Palmer, and the Committee on Graduate Education of the American Historical Association (2004) note that massive anecdotal evidence indicates that far too many history doctoral students cannot explain the context and significance of their research. This is probably true for students in other disciplines as well.

11. According to Boote and Beile (2004, p. 4), a dissertation literature review should accomplish several important objectives: It should set the broad context of

the study, clearly demarcate what is and what is not within the scope of the study and justify those decisions, situate the study in a broader scholarly and historical context, and not only report the claims made in the existing literature but also examine critically the research methods used to better understand whether the claims are warranted.

# Appendix

## TABLE 3.A.
### The Components of a Dissertation and Their Characteristics at Different Quality Levels

| Components | Quality levels | | | |
| --- | --- | --- | --- | --- |
| | Outstanding | Very good | Acceptable | Unacceptable |
| **Introduction** | • Well written<br>• Brief, interesting, and compelling<br>• Motivates the work<br>• Has a hook<br>• Provides a clear statement of the problem<br>• Explains why the problem is important and significant<br>• Places the problem in context<br>• Presents an overview of the theory, methods, results, and conclusions<br>• Lays out the study's implications<br>• Provides a road map of the dissertation | • Well written but less eloquent<br>• Is less interesting; has less breadth, depth, and insight<br>• Motivates the work but less well<br>• Poses a good question or problem<br>• Explains why the problem is important and significant<br>• Provides an overview of the dissertation | • Not well written or well organized<br>• Lacks or provides minimal motivation for the work<br>• Makes a case for a small problem<br>• Does not do a good job of explaining why the problem is important<br>• Provides minimum or poor context for the problem<br>• Presents minimal overview of the work | • Poorly written and organized<br>• Provides no motivation for the problem<br>• Problem is not stated, is wrong, or trivial<br>• Does not make the case for the importance of the problem<br>• Does not provide or does not put problem in a clear context<br>• Does not present an outline or overview of the research<br>• Contains extraneous material |

*(continues)*

**TABLE 3.A.**
Continued

| Components | Quality levels | | | |
|---|---|---|---|---|
| | Outstanding | Very good | Acceptable | Unacceptable |
| Literature review | • Comprehensive, thorough, complete, coherent, concise, and up to date<br>• Shows critical and analytical thinking about the literature<br>• Synthesizes the literature<br>• Integrates literature from other fields<br>• Displays understanding of the history and context of the problem<br>• Identifies problems and limitations<br>• Is selective—discriminates between important and unimportant works<br>• Identifies and organizes analysis around themes or conceptual categories<br>• Adds own insights<br>• Uses the literature to build an argument and advance the field<br>• Is like a good review article<br>• Makes reader look at the literature differently | • Comprehensive but not exhaustive<br>• Provides a thoughtful, accurate critique of the literature<br>• Shows understanding of and command over the most relevant literature<br>• Selects literature wisely and judiciously<br>• Sets the problem in context<br>• Uses literature to build a case for the research | • Provides adequate coverage of the literature<br>• Demonstrates that student has read and understood the literature<br>• Lacks critical analysis and synthesis<br>• Is not selective—does not distinguish between more- and less-relevant works<br>• Misses some important works<br>• Cites some works that are not relevant<br>• Is an undifferentiated list, "This person said this, this person said that"<br>• Does not put problem in context | • Missing, inadequate, or incomplete<br>• Has not read enough and does not cite enough sources<br>• Misinterprets or does not understand the literature<br>• Misses, omits, or ignores important studies, whole areas or literature of people who have done the same thing<br>• Cites sources student has not read or has only read the abstract<br>• Cites articles that are out of date<br>• Does not provide a context for the research |

| Components | Quality levels | | | |
|---|---|---|---|---|
| | Outstanding | Very good | Acceptable | Unacceptable |
| **Theory** | • Original, creative, insightful, and innovative<br>• Simple and elegant<br>• Well conceived, logically consistent, and internally coherent<br>• Identifies and critically analyzes strengths and weaknesses<br>• Uses more than one theory<br>• Compares or tests competing theories<br>• Advances concepts<br>• Develops, adds to, revises, or synthesizes theory(ies)<br>• Aligns with research question, methods, and observations<br>• Has broad applicability | • Complete and correct<br>• Uses existing theory well<br>• Informs the research question and measures<br>• Identifies where it works and where it does not work | • Understands theory<br>• Uses theory appropriately<br>• Does not specify or critically analyze the theory's underlying assumptions | • Is absent, omitted, or wrong<br>• Is misunderstood or misinterpreted<br>• Cannot explain it or why it is being used<br>• Uses inappropriately<br>• Does not align with research question, literature review, or methods |

(continues)

**TABLE 3.A.**
Continued

| Components | Quality levels | | | |
| --- | --- | --- | --- | --- |
| | Outstanding | Very good | Acceptable | Unacceptable |
| **Methods/ approach** | • Original, clear, creative, and innovative<br>• Provides thorough and comprehensive description<br>• Identifies strengths and weakness/advantages and disadvantages<br>• Flows from question and theory<br>• Uses state-of-the-art tools, techniques, or approaches<br>• Applies or develops new methods, approaches, techniques, tools, devices, or instruments<br>• Uses multiple methods | • Appropriate for the problem<br>• Uses existing methods, techniques, or approaches in correct and creative ways<br>• Discusses why method was chosen<br>• Describes advantages and disadvantages | • Appropriate for the problem<br>• Uses standard or less sophisticated methods correctly<br>• Provides minimum or sufficient documentation<br>• Shows basic competence | • Lacks a method<br>• Uses wrong method for the problem<br>• Uses method incorrectly<br>• Methods do not relate to question or theory<br>• Is fatally flawed or has major confound<br>• Does not describe or describes poorly (insufficient detail) |

| Components | Quality levels | | | |
|---|---|---|---|---|
| | Outstanding | Very good | Acceptable | Unacceptable |
| **Results/data analysis** | • Original, insightful<br>• Uses advanced, powerful, cutting-edge techniques<br>• Analysis is sophisticated, robust, and precise<br>• Is aligned with question and theory<br>• Sees complex patterns in the data<br>• Iteratively explores questions raised by analyses<br>• Results are usable, meaningful, and unambiguous<br>• Presents data clearly and cleverly<br>• Makes proper inferences<br>• Provides plausible interpretations<br>• Discusses limitations<br>• Refutes or disproves prior theories or findings | • Analysis is thorough, appropriate, and correct<br>• Uses standard methods<br>• Produces rich, high-quality data<br>• Links results to question and theory<br>• Substantiates the results<br>• Provides plausible arguments and explanations | • Analysis is objective, routine, and correct<br>• Aligns with question and theory<br>• Produces small amount of thin data<br>• Results are correct but not robust<br>• Includes extraneous information and material<br>• Has difficulty making sense of data<br>• Interpretation is too simplistic | • Analysis is wrong, inappropriate, or incompetent<br>• Data are wrong, insufficient, fudged, fabricated, or falsified<br>• Data or evidence do not support the theory or argument<br>• Data do not answer the question<br>• Cannot distinguish between good data and bad data<br>• Cannot discern what is important or explain the results<br>• Interpretation is not objective, cogent, or correct<br>• Makes improper inferences<br>• Overstates the results |

*(continues)*

**TABLE 3.A.**
Continued

| Components | Quality levels | | | |
| --- | --- | --- | --- | --- |
| | Outstanding | Very good | Acceptable | Unacceptable |
| **Discussion and conclusion** | • Short, clear, and concise<br>• Interesting, surprising, and insightful<br>• Summarizes the work<br>• Refers back to the introduction<br>• Ties everything together<br>• Explains what has been accomplished<br>• Underscores and explains major points and findings<br>• Discusses strengths, weaknesses, and limitations<br>• Identifies contributions, implications, applications, and significance<br>• Places the work in wider context<br>• Raises new questions and discusses future directions | • Provides a good summary of the results<br>• Refers back to the introduction<br>• States what has been done<br>• Ties everything together<br>• States its contribution<br>• Identifies possible implications<br>• Discusses limitations<br>• Identifies some future directions | • Summarizes what has been accomplished<br>• Repeats or recasts the results or major points<br>• Does not address the significance or implications of the research<br>• Does not place the work in context<br>• Identifies a few, nonspecific next steps | • Inadequate or missing<br>• Summarizes what has already been said<br>• Repeats the introduction<br>• Does not tie things up<br>• Does not understand the results or what has been done<br>• Claims to have proved or accomplished things that have not been proved or accomplished<br>• Does not draw conclusions |

# 4

# DISCIPLINARY APPROACHES TO DOCTORAL TRAINING AND THE DEVELOPMENT OF A DISSERTATION

E ven though faculty across disciplines have very similar standards for dissertations of different quality, there is great variation among disciplines and domains of knowledge in their approach to doctoral training. These differences are rooted in the epistemological attributes of the disciplines and in the social and cultural organization of the individual disciplinary communities and that of their subfields, as well as in each discipline's funding and reward structures (Becher, 1989; Becher & Trowler, 2001). Yet, despite these differences doctoral training in each discipline ends with the production of a dissertation and the acceptance of the student into the community as disciplinary professional/scholar.

This chapter explores differences in disciplinary approaches to doctoral training and how they contribute to the development of a dissertation that makes an original contribution to knowledge. It starts with a general overview of the differences in structure and organization of the disciplines. It then touches on four broad areas of the training process: the process of graduate education from course work to candidacy, the process of selecting a dissertation topic, the process of conducting dissertation research, and the process of writing and completing the dissertation. It also explores the expected next steps for the dissertation manuscript and the role or influence of the dissertation on new Ph.D.s' early career paths.

Before exploring these issues, it is important to note that the focus group faculty were not asked directly about any of the six topics that are discussed in this chapter. Consequently, the discussion is premised on comments the faculty made about these topic areas in the process of responding to focus group questions about purpose, originality, significance, and quality. Thus, not all topic areas were discussed by faculty in each and every discipline and only broad generalizations can be made about the disciplines in which they were mentioned. Where possible, these generalizations are supported by relevant literature.[1] It is also important to reiterate that the focus group faculty were high-Ph.D.-productive faculty, consequently their views on graduate education, graduate students, and the manner in which they train and interact with students do not necessarily reflect that of all faculty.

## Disciplinary Differences

Research that has explored disciplinary differences (e.g., Becher, 1989; Becher & Trowler, 2001; Biglan, 1973a, 1973b) has focused on the cognitive and social aspects of the disciplines and has found a relationship between forms of knowledge (concepts, methods, and fundamental aims) and their associated knowledge communities (social groupings, reward systems, communication systems). This research characterizes disciplines along a number of dimensions including hard/soft, pure/applied, and paradigmatic/nonparadigmatic. The sciences tend to fall at one end of the scale, humanities at the other, with the social sciences straddling the middle, though they are more often grouped with the humanities than with the sciences.

The hard/soft and pure/applied dimensions, while distinct, are often combined into four domains. These domains and the disciplines in the MIE study that fall within them are as follows: hard pure (biology, physics, mathematics), hard applied (engineering), soft pure (economics, psychology, sociology, English, history, philosophy), and soft applied (no MIE disciplines, though the domain includes such disciplines as education, law, and social work). The following summary of the disciplines is derived from Becher (1989), Becher and Trowler (2001), and Biglan (1973a, 1973b.)

Pure disciplines deal with theoretical knowledge, applied disciplines with practical and theoretical knowledge. Applied disciplines are more amenable to trial and error approaches than pure ones. The hard applied disciplines focus on mastering the physical world. Their primary outcomes are products and techniques. The soft applied disciplines focus on enhancing the quality of personal and social life.

Hard pure disciplines are concerned with universals and they search for causal explanations. They have clearly defined boundaries and clear criteria for establishing or refuting knowledge claims. Knowledge growth is steady and cumulative. Hard disciplines are organized around paradigms all members subscribe to. The shared paradigm provides agreement on where the frontiers of knowledge are and on what questions to pursue. The paradigm also promotes consensus about content and method, and available methods determine problem choice. The high degree of consensus about problems, theory, content, and method within the discipline facilitates teamwork. It also allows much background information to be taken for granted, which permits research to be communicated in an abbreviated form using standardized and esoteric symbols. Research in hard disciplines increasingly involves teams of diverse specialists to work on transdisciplinary, applications-oriented problems. Hard disciplines produce a greater number of multiauthor journal articles that are often circulated informally before publication in order to establish priority. Commonly used terms of appraisal such as "elegant," "economical," "productive," and "powerful" indicate a concern with structural simplicity and with reducing explanations to essentials.

Although the social sciences strive for a paradigm, the soft disciplines are nonparadigmatic. They are concerned with particulars and they search for empathetic understanding. They have less well-defined boundaries than hard disciplines, and the borders with neighboring areas are more permeable. Soft disciplines lack a clear consensus about what constitutes an authentic contribution. Rather, they apply a diversity of criteria to knowledge claims. Knowledge growth is recursive or reiterative. Members explore ground already traversed by others. Contributions take the form of interpretations that lead to enhanced understanding of or insight into familiar objects of knowledge. Problem choice determines method or approach, and content and method in these disciplines tend to be idiosyncratic. Consequently, members must describe and justify their assumptions and clearly state their method or approach to the problem. This typically requires longer, more elaborate forms of communication. Indeed, soft disciplines produce more single-author books or monograph-length publications than hard disciplines. Commonly used terms of appraisal in the social sciences, such as "persuasive," "thought provoking," and "stimulating," suggest a concern with the quality of analysis. Whereas such terms of appraisal as "masterly" and "good crafts-manship" in the humanities suggest an emphasis on producing an aestheti-cally pleasing, purposeful, and well-articulated product.

Different fields within each discipline may fall along what Becher (1989) calls the urban/rural dimension. The urban/rural dimension characterizes differences in specialist fields within disciplines. These fields differ in the na-ture and scale of the problems their members are engaged in, patterns of communications, and opportunities members have for securing research funds. The urban specialties typically involve a large number of people who are clustered around a few salient topics and discrete problems. Questions are addressed relatively quickly by a group of colleagues, though competition between groups may be intense, even cutthroat. Groups tend to be secretive and race to publication to ensure priority. Rural specialties, by contrast, in-volve fewer people who span a broader stretch of intellectual territory. The problems they address are not sharply demarcated or delineated, but rather are spread out thinly over a wide range of themes. Questions may take years to resolve and are typically pursued by individuals not groups because it is less likely that there will be a close overlap with others. Funding agencies are more likely to support urban groups than rural ones because they have a higher profile and make larger claims for support.

## Course Work to Candidacy

Graduate education can be divided into two stages, a dependent and an inde-pendent stage (Lovitts, 2005). During the dependent course-work-to-candidacy stage students are immersed in mastering the knowledge base of their disci-plines and specialty areas, learning their discipline's theories and methods, and establishing relationships with peers, faculty, and their advisor. In some disciplines, the dependent stage focuses exclusively on course taking, in other disciplines, the sciences in particular, the dependent stage involves a combi-nation of course taking and closely supervised or managed research. The stage ends when students are admitted to candidacy. Below we explore the disciplines' approaches to course work, comprehensive exams, and the disser-tation proposal.

### Course Work

The first two or three years of most graduate programs involve taking a com-bination of required and elective courses. Elective courses are generally taken in areas students plan to specialize in and they determine which qualifying or comprehensive examinations students will take. Areas of specialization are key to the selection of a dissertation topic as well as the selection of a dissertation advisor. During the course-work phase of their education students are expected to learn a vast array of facts, principles, concepts, theories, paradigms, attitudes, and opinions toward various issues in the domain, techniques, and methods of solving problems, and aesthetic criteria for judging others' contributions.

With the exception of mathematics, focus group faculty in the sciences did not discuss course work. Although some mathematics doctoral programs have some common course requirements, students typically have the freedom to select courses that most interest them (Golde, Walker, & Associates, 2006). Graduate mathematics courses focus on the results of the subject, though according to faculty they also try to teach students about the "big new theories" and give them "some new techniques."

Like most other disciplines, students in economics spend their first two years taking courses. However, economics is unique among disciplines in that almost all economics Ph.D. programs require the same first-year course sequence—microeconomic theory, macroeconomic theory, econometrics, and mathematical economics. Economics students do not take courses on research methods because research methods are interwoven in other courses. Indeed, one focus group participant said, "Everything we teach is how to do research in economics."

The course-work phase of psychology and sociology doctoral programs were not discussed, though these programs typically require students to take statistics and methodology courses in addition to specialized subject-area courses. In psychology, "theoretical knowledge is gained through coursework and seminars," whereas sociology programs typically have required courses in classical and contemporary theory.[2] According to a psychology focus group participant, the American Psychological Association "tells" clinical psychology programs what they must do. Clinical psychology students are required to take more courses than other psychology students and, according to one clinical psychologist, the faculty "have very little leeway as to what they can do within their class structure."

Many English programs have some type of introduction to graduate study course, which one focus group participant characterized as "the boot camp for beginning graduate students." The course introduces students to research and it is here that students often define what will eventually become their dissertation. According to one participant, because of the time-limited nature of courses and seminars English students "do not get very far into archives, to theory, and to critical books on their subject." They can only do what was described as "very curtailed artificial projects." These projects allow students to do a little research and practice formulating arguments and coordinating other people's arguments. However, these projects are typically too short to allow students to set "text against text and critic against critic," which is common and expected in many dissertations. English students also commonly take courses on specific historical fields or topics that correspond with the time period of the literature they will be exploring in their dissertation.

When they enter their doctoral programs, history faculty expect students to be ready to move from *learning* history to learning to theorize and write *about* history. This represents a special challenge to history programs because only about half of history doctoral students majored in history as undergraduates. History programs typically require students to take 14 courses, some of which may be in other disciplines. History seminars are small, often composed of two to three students and a faculty member. These seminars usually focus on historiographic (interpretive) readings of a topic in a specialized area (Golde, Walker, et al., 2006).

## Comprehensive Exams

Graduate students are usually required to demonstrate that they have acquired a broad and deep knowledge of their discipline before being admitted to candidacy or the independent research stage of their education. They may demonstrate this knowledge in one or more of the following ways: formal course work, proficiency examinations in language and/or other research tools, comprehensive (or general) written and/or oral examinations, and one or more research papers showing evidence of the ability to do original work (Council of Graduate Schools, 2004).

The comprehensive exam is probably the most common qualifying mechanism. Universities, departments, and programs determine the structure of and the process for the exam. Consequently, there is much variation within and across disciplines. Students are typically examined in two to four specialty areas. The written and/or oral exams may be administered on campus under controlled conditions over one or more days and each exam may last anywhere from two to six hours. Some comprehensive exams are given as take-home examinations.

In some science departments, the comprehensive exam is "more or less the thesis proposal." A physicist characterized his department's comprehensive exam as a paper that summarizes "the work" (presumably the research project the student has been working on), and demonstrates understanding of the knowledge and context of the field. In some engineering departments, students may prepare for their exams, in part, by making presentations to their research group. This process helps other students "see what it takes to prepare for the comprehensive exam."

The mathematics comprehensive exam does not demand a high level of knowledge of "basic stuff." Rather, it involves solving problems that are "more unexpected, not routine." Many students find this type of exam very difficult, and, according to one focus group participant, "half don't pass."

The comprehensive exam in history typically covers one major field and from one to three minor fields. The minor fields represent the fields the student is preparing to teach. The major field is in the area in which the student intends to do research (Golde, Walker, et al., 2006). The American Historical Association (Bender et al., 2004), has become concerned that the focus of the comprehensive exam has tilted too far in the direction of the student's research interests and dissertation field at the expensive of the development of intellectual breadth and a wider sense of the discipline.

Although the purpose of the comprehensive exam is for students to demonstrate that they have mastered and integrated the vast edifice of formal knowledge they have studied over the previous two or three years, passing these exams does not guarantee that graduate students have a sophisticated or deep understanding of the knowledge base of their discipline or specialty area(s). According to Bargar and Duncan (1982), "Ph.D. students, despite having passed their general examinations, often have a naïve understanding of their subject of inquiry and the methods employed for studying it . . . , more often than not, [they] have failed to grasp some of the deeper meanings, implications, and more subtle nuances of the theoretical formulations in their subject of inquiry" (p. 24). In short, their knowledge may be inert (Whitehead, 1929); the information may not be stored in ways that allow them to use it productively or innovatively, in part, because they may never have been asked to do so.

Indeed, over 30 years ago, Katz and Hartnett (Katz, 1976; Katz & Hartnett, 1976) voiced concern that the structure of graduate education could lead to trained incapacity. They argued that "the requirements set down for the sake of having students master some of the 'body' of their discipline" could "stifl[e] individuality" (Katz, 1976, p. 116) and create students "who remain passive vis-à-vis their field's subject matter" and "who look to being told (or follow fashion) about what to write their thesis on" (Katz & Hartnett, 1976, p. 269). They go on to note that "the habit of originality does not develop after a period of obedience" (p. 269). Further, while some experts in the field of creativity say that it is not possible to have too much knowledge about a problem area or task domain (Amabile, 1988), others caution that a large amount of knowledge about a specific field can lead to rigid mind-sets that are unreceptive to innovation and to entrenched thinking—the inability to think about problems differently, the inability to move beyond the established bounds of a field, or the inability to engage in original thinking (Runco & Sakamoto, 1999; Sternberg, 1988; Sternberg & Lubart, 1995, 1999; Weisberg, 1999; Williams & Yang, 1999).

A survey of graduate students (Golde & Dore, 2001) enrolled in their third year of graduate school raises additional concerns about the preparation for independent research/scholarship that students receive during the dependent phase of their education. The survey found that 35% of respondents did not believe that their graduate course work laid a good foundation for doing independent research.[3] According to C. M. Golde (personal communication, February 2002), the percentage of graduate students who felt this way was significantly higher in the sciences (biological sciences 40%, physical sciences 42%) than in other fields (social sciences 31%, humanities 29%, other disciplines 25%).

## The Dissertation Proposal

There is much variation in the timing and nature of the dissertation proposal across disciplines and even in departments within disciplines. The proposal may come before, be part of, or come after the comprehensive exam. It may be a formal or informal document, which may take the form of a 15-page "grant" proposal or it may be what is essentially the first three chapters of the dissertation. In most but not all cases, the student submits a research proposal or prospectus to his or her dissertation committee, which, in turn, critiques, provides advice, and ultimately approves the student's research plan. Approval of the proposal—the topic, method, and scope—serves as a kind of contract, which, if fulfilled, almost always guarantees that the student will be awarded the Ph.D.

As indicated above, the dissertation proposal is or is part of the comprehensive exam in many science departments. In biology in particular, the proposal often takes the form of a mock grant proposal, which helps socialize students to the process for formal grant writing. In the other sciences, the proposal was described as more of an informal document, one that says, "I will do this," "These are my directions." When it is part of the comprehensive exam, the proposal is an outline that is "not that detailed." It identifies the area in which the student will work and "what they will try to do."

In engineering, faculty often request that students have "journal papers by the time they write a proposal." Thus the proposal can be "a staple of papers." A mathematics professor noted that "it takes a long time to formulate well the proposal for your dissertation." This is because mathematics students first have to have "incredibly strong knowledge" of a research area before they feel comfortable discussing it.

In the social sciences and professional disciplines (e.g., education), the dissertation proposal is often the first three chapters of the dissertation. These chapters are or contain the following components: the problem statement, literature review, theory, and methods. The economics faculty noted that they ask students to identify a logical or empirical gap in the literature in theory or data and "convince us . . . that they have an idea about how to fill the gap and are capable of executing the research." They also look for students' ability to frame significant questions, questions that are "not just technically of interest" but are also "of social science significance."

The dissertation proposal in psychology is usually based on some pilot work. Students rarely write a dissertation proposal until some experiments have been completed or partially completed and they have found something. The starting point for the proposal is thus the finding, and the "proposal is about investigating the finding." This process is designed to "zero out a bunch of problems in advance" and establish that the measure(s) the students plan to use will work. Psychology students typically defend their proposal before their dissertation committee. The committee's role is to "catch the confounds" and "make sure the methodology is correct." Once the committee approves the student's experimental plan, the student "can get the degree no matter how it turns out."

In the humanities, the proposal is often referred to as a "prospectus," which suggests more of a summary or outline than a detailed plan. Indeed, the humanities faculty typically expect that the final product will be very different from what the student initially proposed.

According to the English faculty, the proposal process is about "figuring out what the question is." It also involves defining "the list" of the 50 to 100 works the student has command of and that will form the intellectual foundation of the dissertation (Golde, Walker, et al., 2006). The English faculty noted that the students who have the most problems at this stage tend to be students "who don't have a question, just a set of interests." Although they view the prospectus as a "trivial stage of writing a relatively short document in the area they have been studying," the English faculty noted that many students "have to face their demons" and they "get blocked" at this juncture. The blockage was attributed to "psychological fear," "fear of sending it [their work] out."

The history prospectus identifies "a legitimate and appropriate question to investigate." The prospectus has to explain where the work fits in the literature, explicitly lay out the methodology, and provide some evidence about how the student will go about answering the question.

The philosophy proposal is typically 15 pages long, though sometimes it is the opening chapter or the basis of the opening chapter of the dissertation. It presents a problem and often includes a table of contents and a hypothetical outline of the shape of the dissertation. According to one philosophy faculty member, the role of the prospectus is to help the candidate "get a clearer sense of what the project is." The philosophers noted that having a manageable issue, one that goes to the "core of the problem" was "extremely important for the future success of the dissertation," and that students' proposals often tend to be "far too broad." Consequently, during the "proposal exam," the committee may say, "Not yet well formed. Too much. Too little. Alternative perspectives need to be considered."

## Topic Selection

The method of choosing a dissertation topic varies markedly among disciplines and subfields as well as among institutions. In general, the harder and more paradigm-driven the discipline, the less opportunity there is for negotiation over the dissertation topic.[4] Conversely, the softer and less paradigmatic the discipline, the greater the freedom candidates are granted over topic choice (Becher, 1989). Becher has identified two related reasons for the constraints placed on topic choice in hard disciplines. One, graduate students in hard disciplines are typically taken on and supported as junior members of their advisor's research team and are thus expected to work on problems or projects that are a part of their advisor's funded research. Two, as novice researchers who are "relatively unfamiliar with the field," students in hard disciplines are not usually "in a good position to judge which problems or parts of problems are both relevant to current developments and at least in principle amenable to solution within the time-span of a doctoral programme" (p. 110). The focus group faculty's remarks on topic selection support this contention.

Physics and engineering are among the hardest pure and applied disciplines, and students are given the least amount of choice, though there seems to be a bit more flexibility in physics than in engineering. As one participant said, in engineering, "in 80 to 90% of the cases there is a significant correlation between funding and the dissertation," because nearly all engineering students are research assistants for most of their dissertation work. Consequently, according to more than one focus group faculty member, engineering students are "assigned" a subtopic of their advisor's funded research project. Similarly, in physics, most graduate students start out as research assistants and work on externally funded projects. Physics faculty feel that it is their "responsibility to suggest" or to "try to identify" a research topic for their students that is likely to succeed and be worthy of publication in a top-tier journal. One physicist thus described the constraints imposed on topic choice by externally funded research :

> I'm on a fairly tight schedule. I've got three years as a typical grant cycle, that's not the lifetime of a graduate student. So that's a real difficulty that we are constantly facing. . . . My field moves pretty quickly in that what's hot in one three-year period is not necessarily what's hot in another three-year period. That is also very difficult for graduate students, in that you try to get them going on direction. I try not to be too specific about the project that they are going to work on. I want them heading in a general direction that we could eventually get the work done that I promised in the grant.

Despite the constraints of externally funded research, another physicist commented that he usually had a "couple of different things that a student could pursue." He felt that what "works happiest is if the student has a couple of things they can look into and then they pick." The physicists also noted that theory students are less constrained in their choice of topic than experimental students.

Although most research in biology and mathematics is externally funded, focus group faculty in these disciplines did not relate topic choice to grant funds, though the biologists noted that the "laboratory is funded to conduct a certain level of investigation," and that students have "more freedom" if they have their own funds. "Ideally," the biology and mathematics faculty like students to come up with their own ideas and find their own problems. Faculty in both disciplines discussed the process of topic selection.

In biology, the problem the student works on is typically related to what is "available in the lab," though the faculty noted that in some fields (e.g., ecology), students have "a little more freedom." When they enter a lab, faculty often give students two or three projects to "get them started," and then they have to select one and develop it further. However, some students come in with fixed projects in mind, about which one participant commented, "such students should be encouraged unless the idea is patently foolish." Other students, "don't have a specific group or audience or don't have a specific theory they wish to test," and thus need some help and advice. Although biology faculty sometimes feed students their topic, many do not like to:

> We have students pretty regularly failing out because they are not capable of identifying a research question in a broad field. And you can do whatever—background reading, talk about science. They are smart students, students [who] come in with NSF fellowships and ace all classes. Then they get to that stage where they can work on proposals and they can't come up with anything. I and I think most of my colleagues, we just let them play out. We don't tell them what to do.

In mathematics, students work on "open problems," problems that have not yet been solved. The top students in mathematics either find their own problems, often by going to journals and reading about open problems, or they work out ideas that are not their advisor's ideas. However, most mathematics graduate students do not have an adequate perspective on "what's solved and what's not solved, what's important, what's publishable, and what's worth it to me." Consequently, mathematics faculty usually refer students to a problem and direct their reading. Giving students a problem is "the hardest and most important thing faculty do." The problem has to "match the students' abilities" and be "interesting and doable," not "routine and trivial." Some faculty have a set of problems that are part of their research program, so they give their students a problem from the set as well as some possible techniques. Other faculty have a problem in mind and go to conferences or visit with colleagues and say, "Hey, do you know anybody or are your students working on this problem, because I'm thinking of my students doing this."

The method of topic choice in economics and psychology resembles that of the hard disciplines more so than does sociology. Indeed, an economist's description of the problem space in economics resembles Becher's (1989) description of that of the hard disciplines:

> In economics, we do, as a community of scholars, have a really coherent sense of what are the important or pressing questions for the discipline, because as a field it stresses the ways of quantifying the value of different kinds of things. So there's a certain amount of collective consensus in any moment in time about what are the important kinds of questions, both at the policy and empirical level, and also theoretical level.

Every thesis in economics has to identify a gap of one kind or another. The gap can be a small point that is difficult to fill and needs to be retooled, or it could be much broader and involve reconceptualization. Although one participant noted that some economics faculty believe in "the chemistry model," where students only work on things their advisor is working on "so you don't blow yourself up in the lab," ideally, the economists want students to come up with topics by themselves. However, they expressed concern about allowing students to work on topics they believe would make it "incredibly difficult" for them to continue in a research career. One common type of economics dissertation involves students taking an existing theory, one that faculty in their department may be working on, and extending it some way. The faculty noted that most economics graduate students are not well equipped to go from a general area of interest to a specific operational statement of what the dissertation is going to do. They thus require a lot of hand-holding to lay the topic out appropriately.

Topic selection in lab-based fields of psychology also resembles that of the hard disciplines. Psychology students are relatively tightly tied to the general area of the lab, and their dissertations are outgrowths of the research they have been doing since they joined the lab. Some dissertations are "carved out" of the advisor's funded project. Most are in an area in which the advisor works. Indeed, one participant said, "Most of my dissertations are variations of some theme that I've done." Even though most psychology dissertations are wrap-ups or syntheses of pilot work, one participant described the process of topic selection students go through with their advisors as, "They float a lot of ideas past us and then we go, 'Nah, nah,' and then they come up with whatever you help them come up with." In other fields of psychology, students may raise and address significant social problems, though the faculty noted that there are studies that would be too politically sensitive for students to do at that point in their careers.

In contrast to economics and psychology, sociology is less driven by large research grants. The discipline does not stress the idea of the student "latching on" to the advisor's project, nor is most work in the field "amenable to being a direct spin-off of the advisor's work." Some students enter their programs with, or quickly identify, a particular problem they are interested in studying and are able to obtain funding on their own. Others develop their topics based on their research assistantships. Although sociology graduate students usually work in their advisor's general area, they are expected to generate, with varying degrees of help, their own research project. No topic is too small for a dissertation in sociology. Indeed, the discipline has a long history of the sociology of everyday life, and research has been done on laundromats and carpools.

Not only is topic selection in English very different from that in the sciences and some of the social sciences, the current method of topic choice is "very different from the way the profession used to be run." "Decades and decades ago," the dissertation topic was assigned. The advisor would say, "Here, you're doing an edition of this medieval [text] that's never been done before." Now it is the student who decides on and defines the dissertation project. The dissertation project in English is independent and separate from the advisor's research, and it is not uncommon for English faculty to know relatively little about the student's topic. Indeed, English faculty feel that it is the student's job "to teach us the field." Some students define what eventually becomes their dissertation in their introductory research course. Some go into their comprehensive exam or their master's with a very clear idea of what they want to do for their dissertation and just work toward it. But most do not. Most develop it along the way. Many English faculty feel that doctoral students in English choose their topics for psychological reasons. One participant described students' deep psychological relationship with their dissertation as follows:

> You're working out something in yourself and maturing and growing as an individual as you are working intellectually on this particular intellectual project. People who don't finish are the ones who haven't taken that time to look at themselves through the lens of their project.

History is similar to English in that faculty do not give students their topics, and history students may work on something that their advisor knows very little about, though there are some advisors who do not want students to "fall too far from the tree." Some students enter their programs with preconceived ideas about what they want to do their dissertations on, and some older "mature scholars" even enter with "a suitcase full of Xeroxed documents." Most students know the general field they want to work in but have to search around for a topic. One participant noted that it can be hard to choose because "you are surrounded by topics that everybody thinks are hot right now." Other students do not have any idea of what they are going to do and say they are "going to fill a gap in the literature." History faculty do not like this approach to topic selection. They noted that there are usually good reasons why there is a gap. It may be that the topic is not very important or it may be that nobody has been able to find any evidence that can really fill the gap. When history students select a topic they are "actually posing a problem." The problem can be of several types. It can be finding an incompatibility in the existing literature or there may be some disagreement about how to interpret a set of documents. It may be finding a historical inconsistency or an apparent inconsistency that a previous historian putatively reconciled. One participant gave the following example of a good historical problem: "Why did a nation with this background experience and tradition want to behave in this way because it seems contradictory?" For the historians, a manageable topic is a story with a beginning, a middle, and an end.

Students' interest in and enthusiasm for their research topics/problems is an important determinant of whether they will actually finish their research and their dissertations and of the nature and quality of the contribution they make. Research shows that people who are allowed to pursue their interests and choose their own research topics or problems are more internally motivated and exhibit higher levels of originality and creative performance than people whose activities (research topics or problems) have been chosen for them by others (Amabile, 1996; Nickerson, 1999; Sternberg & Lubart, 1995). Katz (1976) has observed that "Many dissertations are poor and many others are never written because the problems that the students were inquiring into did not mean that much to them. They did not care to know" (p. 123). This may be particularly true for women and racial and ethnic minorities because they are often discouraged from pursuing topics related to gender or their minority status that they have an inherent interest in (Ibarra, 2001; Magner, 1989). Further, according to Perlmutter (2006) students in the social sciences (and probably those in other disciplines as well) who complete "dead-end dissertations" (dissertations that are extensions of their advisor's work) often struggle to earn tenure as assistant professors. They may only be able to get one paper out of their dissertation or may not want to ever look at their dissertation again, let alone publish from it.

## Dissertation Research

During the independent or dissertation stage of doctoral education, students' relationship with knowledge changes from learning what others know and how they know it (Katz, 1976) to conducting original research and creating knowledge. Depending on the discipline and subfield, students are expected to be or become autonomous and either work independently or demonstrate that they are capable of doing independent research/scholarship in the future. Many faculty, particularly those in the sciences and laboratory-based social sciences, acknowledge that this transition is hard for many students (Lovitts, 2001; 2004). Indeed, numerous studies estimate that 15% to 25% of graduate students who advance to candidacy never complete the Ph.D. (Benkin, 1984; Bowen & Rudenstine, 1992; Moore, 1985; Nerad & Cerny, 1991).

Below we explore the process of dissertation research in the different disciplines. Where relevant and where information from the focus groups is available, the discussion includes the nature of financial and social support students receive during this stage of their education, the sources of data/material/text—who collects it and how, the expected duration of the project, and who decides when it is done, as well as the discipline's concern with being "scooped" and its handling of negative results.

## The Sciences

In the sciences more so than in other domains of knowledge, with the possible exception of psychology, dissertation research often begins early in the first year when the student joins a research laboratory. Some students join labs upon entry as part of their research assistantship, others rotate through several labs to become familiar with different techniques and possibilities and select a lab by the end of the first year.

In another focus-group-based study I conducted about the transition to independent research (Lovitts, 2004), faculty in the laboratory-based disciplines were asked about the differences between the research students do when they first join a lab and the research they do for the dissertation. The early research experience was viewed as a training phase, one where students focus on learning the tools of the trade. It was described as being more directive and less independent than dissertation research. Students are given a problem that is more manageable and focused than a dissertation problem or project. The faculty indicated that they did a lot of "hand-holding" with beginning students because they are "sort of nebulous as to what they're doing" and tend to "flounder" in the first year or two because "they do not know how to approach the research." Much of what beginning students learn comes from other, more advanced students, postdocs, and technicians. These people help beginning-stage students with "mundane, day-to-day things like how to run the program, how to do certain kinds of analyses." Dissertation research, by contrast, was described as much more independent and open ended. Students take on more responsibility for the project and work on more sophisticated "stuff." In short, the structure and process of the research science graduate students do at the beginning of their doctoral training, while laying the foundation for their dissertation research, is very different in structure and process from their dissertation research. Next we look at the process in the individual disciplines as described by faculty in the MIE focus groups.

### Biology

In biology, students work under the direction of someone who has a laboratory of ongoing research projects. Advisors are typically in the lab every day, and some have lab meetings as often as twice a week. Some are intimately involved with their students' research projects. Contributions to the biology dissertation often extend beyond that of the individual student. Indeed, the biology dissertation was described as a "combination of contributions" from the student, the mentor, and the other members of the laboratory. According to a participant, the process of doing dissertation research in biology involves:

> Learning how to evaluate a large body of empirical data and judge it as the evidence. Learning how to critically analyze [the data], to extract a meaningful hypothesis, how to test it, how to look at results and say, "What can I meaningfully conclude from these results or are there alternative explanations or hypotheses?"

According to one focus group participant, this involves a huge amount of practice and skill that, for the most part, students have not previously been engaged in.

Negative results are not viewed positively in biology, though they may be begrudgingly accepted. The faculty noted that hypotheses and experiments should be set up in such a way that whether you reject or accept the hypotheses, you get interesting data that can be published. One participant averred that a failed experiment is one that "doesn't yield data to provide the answer 'yes' or 'no.'" Another felt that everyone should do experiments that initially do not work so that they can figure out how to "get them right." However, he noted, "You don't show failed experiments."

*Physics*

Virtually all physics graduate students are supported by research grants or by external fellowships, and they commence work that will lead to their dissertation when they join a lab, usually by the end of the summer of their first year. Most of the physics focus group discussions centered on experimental physics, though it was noted that theoretical physics was much less collaborative, mainly just the advisor and the student working together. The physics faculty commented that in the past, in the ideal case in experimental physics, the student would plan an experiment, design it, collect data, and analyze it in a year. By contrast, experiments today in fields like particle, nuclear, and high-energy physics can involve collaborations with hundreds of scientists in research groups throughout the world and can take 10 to 20 years to complete. As a result, students in these fields can only work on stages of experiments and be responsible for "one particular part of a detector, one particular subassembly, one particular piece of analysis software looking at the data for a particular reaction to take place."

Physics faculty get students started by having them read previous students' dissertations because these dissertations provide a good introduction to the field as well as detailed information about exactly how the technique was done, how the analysis was done, and how the data were analyzed. The advisor has a "big hand" in the direction the student takes:

> You have weekly or maybe daily meetings with the graduate students where both of you move the process along together. In the end, the advisor has put a lot of himself [*sic*] into the thesis and sometimes helped write it. Sometimes [the advisor has] programmed the program underlying it. . . . In most cases [the advisor] help[ed] do the measurements, because it is teamwork more than anything.

The thesis is thus a record of the collaborative effort of the student and the advisor; the contribution is viewed as mutual.

Because of the fast-paced nature of much experimental work in physics, students can get scooped in the three- to six-year time period it takes to do a dissertation project. Faculty guard against this possibility by getting students trained on the equipment and by making sure they are very knowledgeable so that if they need to drop their project, they can jump on something quickly before someone else does. Dissertation research is considered "done" when the student's advisor and mentors feel the student is ready to finish and move on. This judgment is based on the amount of work the student has completed, and faculty's appraisal of whether the student has developed the skills, maturity, and ability to do independent research projects.

> I'm looking for persons who demonstrate that they can be an original thinker . . . where they don't come to me to be asking questions. . . . When I can see that they are beginning to troubleshoot their own problems in the lab or in doing any kind of theoretical analysis or explaining, then I know they are starting to mature as a researcher. I want someone who has a Ph.D. from [our university] to able to stand on their feet, be able to be given a new problem and just have a mechanism within themselves for being able to address a new problem.

*Engineering*

As in physics, nearly all engineering students are research assistants for their dissertation research and work with a faculty member who has external funding. As noted earlier, the advisor gives the student a broad topic and then steers the student along. Once students have a topic, they have to define a problem, propose a solution, and discuss the efficiency of the solution—why something works better or works in a different way. One participant noted that defining what the problem is and what you are trying to solve was the most difficult part of the dissertation process.

Solving a problem in engineering often means having to build something before an experiment can be run. Consequently, even though the student may know exactly what experiment needs to be run on exactly what system, the student may "disappear for two years" to build the system. One participant commented that because engineering tends to place "too much emphasis on system building and not enough emphasis on what you are trying to test," that is, what the system is an example of, "students think they can get a Ph.D. for writing code, when, in fact, the code is being written as a vehicle for running controlled experiments to get a theory to test a hypothesis."

Dissertation-related work takes about three years, and in many fields of engineering requires a lot of teamwork. Faculty have weekly meetings with their graduate students where the students present their work to each other. Although advisors play a large role in their students' dissertation—one participant said, "Seventy to eighty percent of the dissertation goes back to the advisor"—faculty "don't usually get their hands dirty." It is the students who write the code or build the equipment.

In engineering, it is every student's "nightmare" to pick up a journal and see that his or her dissertation research has been published by someone else. If that happens and the students cannot start over, advisors try to help them figure out how their work is "just a little bit different." Engineers value the outcome more than the process and, consequently, do not typically award the Ph.D. for negative results or for disproving the hypothesis. When experiments fail, students usually take what they have learned, change the process to correct the flaw, and rerun the experiment. Faculty decide that students are ready to graduate when they feel that students are ready to go out and be independent; that is, when they have an idea of what their next problem might be and have the skills to do it on their own.

## Mathematics

The goal of mathematical research is to obtain a new result. Thus, every dissertation has to have theorems that were not known before. However, unlike the empirical sciences, results in mathematics are not obtained through experiments. Rather, the mathematical ideal is a statement of fact and a deductive logical proof of that fact. Though, according to one participant, in reality mathematics is "not 100% deductive until after the fact." A lot of mathematics involves "doing experiments and little computations" on a scratch sheet, seeing what is going on, and then writing down deductive proofs.

In the classical model of graduate education in mathematics, "the advisor gives a problem to the student and then the student comes back two years later with the solution." This does not happen anymore because mathematics is more complicated than it was 30 years ago—students have to start at a much higher level and understand a much greater amount of technically complex material. For most mathematics graduate students, the dissertation is the first piece of original research they have ever done because contemporary research in mathematics is not something that is accessible to an undergraduate or a beginning graduate student. Indeed, many graduate students have to be "weaned away from just sitting in class and absorbing information" and be taught to "start thinking on their own, asking themselves questions."

Advisors often start students out by giving them proofs they know can be done in order to give students a sense of confidence at the beginning. They may suggest that students try a method or give students a "crude simple generalization" to work on. Each time the student produces something, the conversation gets vaguer until the student reaches the point where he or she can think of a problem to work on alone.

The nature of dissertation research in mathematics and the amount of collaboration between advisor and student is not the same in different areas of mathematics. In some areas, students work on a single problem that is looked at in great depth. In other areas, students work on several problems that are only tenuously, if at all, related and solve them separately. In pure mathematics, students work on open problems relatively independently. The first approach to the problem is "usually boring," because it is difficult to solve problems in a beautiful way. "The beauty comes much later." By contrast, applied mathematics involves the formulation of new problems and sometimes the development of new techniques. Research is carried out in large groups, similar to those found in the empirical sciences, where a lot of graduate students and postdocs work on different aspects of a large research problem.

In mathematics, it is impossible to know for a fact that a theorem has never been proved before. One participant said that he had "heard of people who have worked on something and proved a theorem and then they find out that somebody else has published it and possibly by a different argument." When this happens to a graduate student, "the burden falls on the supervisor, not the candidate." The people on the dissertation committee have to determine whether "something in this direction has already been done." If the results are really simultaneous, "the supervisor will vouch for the work," that it had essentially been done before the other result was presented or published.

Unlike the empirical sciences, a mathematics dissertation cannot be based on "I tried all these and none of these worked." There has to be a result and the result has to be right. When students are finished with their research varies with the faculty's assessment of the students' abilities. They "make the very good ones continue to work on it to make it better and prove how good they are." But, by and large, before they allow students to graduate, faculty want students to be doing things that they themselves had not thought of.

## The Social Sciences

There is much variation within and across the social sciences with respect to when students commence their dissertation research and how it is conducted. Fewer students have research assistantships and their dissertation projects are less often tied to their advisor's funded research than students in the sciences. Students in the social sciences are also less likely to work as part of a team than students in the sciences.

### Economics

Even though economics is not a laboratory or an exact science, economists think of economics as being "perhaps the most scientific of the social sciences." They put a lot of emphasis on theory and methodological approach and on making an empirical or theoretical contribution, usually in the form of a mathematical model of some segment of the economy. Graduate students are expected to learn how to use the tools of the trade appropriately.

The dissertation thus demonstrates, "Here's the kinds of things I can do. If you hire me, here's what you get." However, students should be able to do more than "very technical stuff" in their dissertations; they should be able to understand and interpret what is important about their results.

Although there is a "premium" in the profession for people who have outstanding data collection skills, original data collection is unusual in economics. Graduate students and professional economists typically work with large data sets or tables that governments or funding agencies have developed and made available for public use. According to one participant, if each graduate student or researcher collected his or her own data, we would "wind up with a whole bunch of poorly constructed data sets." However, there are fields in economics where individual data collection is common. For instance, faculty in the field of development economics often require their students to go to, and collect data in, the country they are studying.

## Psychology

In psychology, newly admitted students identify a faculty advisor and typically work as a research assistant to that advisor for several years. Even though it may not be a formal requirement, most doctoral students get a master's degree along the way. The master's thesis serves as an intermediate step, "a prelude to the dissertation by demonstrating a certain degree of mastery over methodology and technical matters." After they complete their master's, psychology graduate students are at the "advanced level in the apprenticeship mode" for two or three more years. As noted earlier, the dissertation project is based on experiments students have been doing with their advisors over a number of years. However, the students are now expected to independently conceive and conduct their research project—"have their hands in every single aspect of the study," "take the lead in making decisions"—though faculty may offer suggestions to consider.

Most psychology dissertations are empirical and students are expected to collect their own data. Most empirical dissertations are experimental, hypothesis-driven attempts to distinguish among alternative or competing hypotheses. Other empirical dissertations are premised on survey research. Still other dissertations in psychology are based on the analysis of secondary or archival public-use data sets. Faculty expect more of students who do not collect their own data.

Because most dissertation research projects in psychology are replications and extensions of pilot work, it is rare for students' experiments or research studies to produce negative results. Most departments will award the degree for experiments that do not yield statistically significant results, though faculty in some of the harder areas of psychology, like neuroscience, will not accept a dissertation without statistical significance. One participant felt that requiring students to have significant results, "invites bad science." He went on to say, "And, God forbid, it's fraud, if you make the results to be a contingency for earning a degree."

## Sociology

According to the sociology faculty, the strength of sociology is that it is a very flexible, undisciplined discipline, one where the cutting edge is not as well defined as it is in other disciplines. "We have the luxury and the misery of being able to study everything in any way possible." Many students go into sociology because "they want to have a public impact, they want to change the world," but the training focuses more on what is "significant within academia within the discipline of sociology."

Although there is no reigning theoretical orthodoxy in sociology, and theory testing is rare, most dissertations are expected to be theory driven. Students are expected to apply specific theoretical frameworks to specific topics and contexts using unique data. According to one participant, it is the theoretical analysis that "makes work significant and interesting in quantitative and qualitative [sociology]."

Sociology graduate students may collect their own data through a variety of means, including ethnography, participant-observation, interviews, focus groups, surveys, and/or document analysis. Others may do secondary analyses of public-use data sets. Because research in sociology is so context specific, it is a discipline in which it is particularly hard to get scooped. One participant noted that although it is conceivable, it is very unlikely that two students would ask exactly the same question from the same theoretical perspective and use the exact same data.

## The Humanities

Most graduate students in the humanities do not start their dissertation research until they have advanced to candidacy. The teaching assistantship is a more common source of financial support for humanities students than the research assistantship during the dissertation phase of their education. Dissertation research is done independently, and students have less frequent interaction with their advisors than students in the sciences.

## English

Graduate students in English usually select their dissertation advisors after having taken several classes with them, and they may be more expert in their topic area than their advisor. The conditions under which students write dissertations in English are "not created equal." According to the focus group participants, by the time they get to the dissertation, most English graduate students have run out of funds and are scrambling to support themselves. Students who have fellowship funding have a very different experience than those who "have to teach five classes to survive."

Because many English graduate students "have a lot of insecurities" the advisor/advisee relationship is one that needs to be "cultivated" by a regular set of exchanges. Indeed, the focus group faculty felt that the dissertation should be "very hands-on between student and advisor," that there should be "a lot of interacting," and that you "shouldn't see your student [only] once a year." They described the advisor/advisee relationship as a close, intense pedagogical relationship:

> You gauge and you have to adjust to what the student is doing, what they're experiencing, a kind of psychology about what causes them to have a blank page or that they might have their planning or fear, and all kinds of things. It's a really very personal engagement as well. It's not just anything else.

Some of English graduate students' insecurities and fears appear to stem from the "romantic ideal" that "we write for ourselves . . . [in] an idealist intellectual space beyond consumerism," that "you write in a narcissistic fashion where you think you're the only one that's going to read it." Problems arise when students do not feel ready to and will not share their work with their advisors and the larger community.

Dissertation research in English is an individualized process that requires sustained engagement. One participant characterized it as "a marathon not a sprint." It involves thinking through the questions and stating an argument, then engaging in conversations, organizing time, gaining confidence, and wielding authority. Students often write "things" before they realize that they had "a different question than they thought." One important part of the process is learning "to find their own voice," their own distinct perspective on the topic, though students "often have to be pushed to put in their own voice."

It is during the process of doing dissertation research that English students acquire the tools of basic research and learn what research is. English faculty feel strongly about the importance of the dissertation in doctoral education. Without the dissertation,

> you'd get somebody who has read a bunch of books and can speak for two hours about them, but not somebody who has put together their own argument in writing and can synthesize it, and map out their own territory, and become an active participant in this ongoing conversation.

Indeed, the "hardest job" of the English dissertation is achieving a "broad synthesis," and a lot of dissertations "stop at analysis."

The English faculty talked about when dissertations are complete and also about dissertations that never are finished. Dissertations are considered final when the advisor senses that the student has done all he or she can, that revising it one more time is not going to offer the student "anything additional," and when the advisor feels the student can continue the revision process more meaningfully at the "next stage." Dissertations do not get completed when the "topic doesn't come to life" or when students "don't have some sense of the standard that they need to meet," or feel they cannot meet it.

> What defeats students more than anything else—it's very sad when it happens—they have a sense of a standard that they must meet and a feeling that they can't get there, and no matter how hard they try, they can't. Then it's always incomplete. The work is never finished. The deadlines are always missed for these people.

### History

Getting a Ph.D. in history is a "big sacrifice." History graduate students tend to be somewhat older than graduate students in other disciplines and many have returned to school after they have been out working. Many are married and have families. While the better graduate schools have more money and can support the students they accept, many students are "teaching heavily" at the same time they are working on their dissertations. "They have no other financial support. They have obligations at home. They're going deeper and deeper into debt."

According to the history faculty, the only way to get to know what history is, is by doing it, and the dissertation is the only way to develop the skills necessary to be a historian. In history, the student is apprenticed to the craft of history not to the advisor. The process is very self-directed and self-disciplined. During the apprenticeship, students are supposed to master the art of doing historical research—how to "put archival sources into play"— how to find them, how to use them, how to read them, how to ask questions of material, how to draw the evidence together, how to synthesize and interpret the evidence and put it into the broader context of the field, and how to write a long, coherent narrative.

Different fields of history have different requirements. In fields like cultural studies, students may focus on a single text and do a very complex, multifaceted reading of the text with additional context. However, most history graduate students do archival research. Indeed, going into archives and getting out a fresh batch of sources "is really quite crucial for the history Ph.D." Faculty like students to start working with sources that are available while they are taking courses and writing seminar papers to give them a sense of what they will be looking for when they enter the archives. Students who go abroad may need to know as many as three or four languages. And it often takes six months to prepare to spend one year abroad. Despite the heavy emphasis on new sources and archival research in history, "Nobody shows you how to go into the archives, how to react to your primary sources, how to figure out handwriting from the 18th century or the 17th century." Succeeding at this task "is a sign that you are initiated."

A good predictor of success is how much reformulation of the dissertation is going on in the process of researching it. Students need to be "confident enough and flexible enough to allow themselves to change the topic with the sources without completely panicking." If after conducting their research, students "come back with exactly the same question they left with, that usually suggests there is a round peg in a square hole thing going on." According to the faculty, the best students digest the materials in the course of doing research and keep adjusting, adapting, and updating their outline while they are doing their research. The "worst" students "just bring stuff back."

Because of the emphasis on new sources and the interpretive nature of history, it is highly unlikely that a graduate student will get scooped. However, students who take an excessive amount of time to complete their dissertations may find that the field has overtaken their work.

## Philosophy

The business of philosophy is argument, and according to one faculty member, the goal is "to discover some conceptual distinction or connection or some novel line of argument that has a significant bearing upon the truth or falsity of a major philosophical issue or problem." Philosophy dissertations thus involve positing something and putting forth a set of views about a philosophical issue. Philosophy faculty are more interested in the force of the argument than in the truth of the conclusions.

There are several kinds of dissertations in philosophy. The main types are historical, comparative, and analytical. Also different types of arguments vary by area (e.g., theory of knowledge, philosophy of science, theory of value, moral philosophy, ethics). In some areas the argument is more straightforward and logical in character than in others. There is also a branch of philosophy known as continental philosophy that involves working with foreign language texts and that requires knowledge and skill in foreign languages. It sometimes involves translating "not necessarily the words, but the ideas, the concepts, the approach, [and] the attitudes, into an English language idiom and making that idiom accessible."

Like history, philosophy graduate students are apprenticed to the craft of philosophy. During the apprenticeship they are learning "philosophicalese." Mastering philosophy involves learning a certain vocabulary and a certain way of talking and thinking. Although philosophy graduate students work with their committees, their advisors in particular, to develop the dissertation, the dissertation research and writing is an individual task. The advisor's role is to teach the student "how to make the moves" and also help the student keep the dissertation narrow.

The process of doing dissertation research in philosophy involves ingesting and understanding a large body of literature and finding "questions you have to address in order to address the other questions you want to address." Students have to present a thesis, raise objections to it, and then draw final conclusions. Along the way, they have to develop arguments in defense of whatever it is that they are arguing.

During the course of dissertation research, philosophy students some-times find something in the literature and say to their advisor, "Someone has already done this! I'm halfway through my dissertation and now I've got to start all over again." In most cases, it was not done in the way the student is approaching it, and "there are always ways to bring out other aspects of a concern or a topic in a way that hasn't yet been done."

Despite the importance of research in doctoral education, Golde and Dore (2001) found that 35% of third-year students who were planning an academic career did not feel that their program prepared them to conduct research and that 28% were not very confident in their ability to do so. The percentages of students who felt like this were significantly different across disciplines: *not prepared to conduct research*—26% biological sciences, 37% physical sci-ences, 32% social sciences, 43% humanities, and 54% other disciplines; *not very confident in their ability to conduct research*—23% biological sciences, 40% physical sciences, 24% social sciences, 30% humanities, and 30% other disciplines (C. M. Golde, personal communication, May 24, 2006). Further, only half of all the students reported having the opportunity to take a pro-gressively responsible role in research projects (Golde & Dore, 2001). Not surprisingly, students in experimental disciplines (psychology and the sci-ences) were the most likely to report having had such opportunities, with students in the humanities least likely to report having had them (51% biological sciences, 51% physical sciences, 48% social sciences, 25% hu-manities, and 43% other disciplines) (C. M. Golde, May 25, 2006, personal communication).

## Writing the Dissertation

The relationship between the process of conducting dissertation research and the process of writing the dissertation varies across the disciplines. In the sciences, the knowledge is created before students write their dissertation, whereas in the humanities, knowledge is created through the act of writing. The process of writing was not discussed in any of the social sciences focus groups, though one would expect the process in the experimental and quan-titative disciplines and fields to resemble that of the sciences, and the process in the qualitative disciplines or fields to resemble that of the humanities.

Below we explore what some of the science and humanities faculty had to say about the process of writing the dissertation and their role in it.

In the sciences, writing is generally done after the fact. As one physicist said, "First there is the work and material, then there is the document." The hardest and biggest part of the thinking and most of the insights come while students are conducting their research. After students have completed a series of experiments, it is not uncommon for faculty to say, "OK, you've got a thesis. Write it up." While the research may take two to three years to conduct, science dissertations can be written in six months or less, especially if students have already written conference papers or journal articles on their work. The engineers noted that most engineering students have not been trained to write extensively and that engineering students "almost by definition are not good at being able to tell someone else what you have done." Because writing is "organizing in your head what you're doing," one engineer felt that better writing skills would help students do their research.

In physics, the advisor sometimes helps students write the dissertation. Indeed, one physicist said, "We really put [in] a lot of time helping them and writing *for* them" [italics added]. Similarly, in mathematics, the advisor plays an active role in writing the dissertation:

> [The presentation of the mathematics] is an area in which the advisor can contribute greatly to the development of the student and really has the responsibility to do so. It makes a big difference in how other people who might read it if it is presented well. It is important for the advisor to convey to the student how to put together [the] mathematics, how to present, what order to do things in.

In the humanities, you "don't do your reading and then write the dissertation." As one philosopher said, "The writing out of the dissertation is the data analysis. . . . fused together are the preliminary research, the data collection or the method, the procedure, and then the results." To be successful, humanities students need to be writing and thinking about themes that are emerging while they are doing their research. They also need to be constantly reformulating their problem and constantly revising their writing. The English faculty made the following two comments about how knowledge in the humanities is constructed through the process of writing:

You don't know what you are saying until you've said it. You don't know what your thought process is and what your argument is until you've worked your way through it, which is why it takes so long.

One often discovers the point, the thesis statement of the dissertation, only upon finishing it. So finishing it usually means that you understand what it is about.

Humanities faculty are very concerned with the prose and writing style of the dissertation. More so than other disciplines, they want the writing to be elegant. They also want students to find and express their own voice in the process of writing their dissertations.

## The Next Steps for the Dissertation

Publication is critical not only to the research process, but it is also important in defining and shaping many doctoral students' careers. Different disciplines have different expectations for the public presentation dissertation of research both in the pre- and postdefense stages of students' careers. The expectations are, in large part, a function of the reward structure of the discipline, the competitive pressures in the discipline's academic job market, and the discipline's requirements for tenure. Below we explore the disciplines' expectations for the nature and timing of the publication of students' dissertation research.

Science has become a "hurried affair" and the bottom line in the science disciplines is that students are expected to produce papers "all along" and get at least one published or in the publication pipeline before they graduate. Indeed, science students have to show a publication record in order to be invited to job interviews. As noted previously, science students are often encouraged to add an introduction and a conclusion to three published or publishable papers and call the compilation a dissertation. The main exception is in mathematics. Although there is a trend in mathematics for students to submit papers for publication before they get their degree, only about half of mathematics doctorates are published and only 25% publish after they complete the dissertation.

The pressure for rapid publication has become especially great in contemporary physics. In the 1950s and 1960s, the typical doctoral student was expected to modify his or her dissertation slightly into a 40-page paper with a footnote saying that it was a dissertation and submit it to *Physical Review*. Now, by the time they defend, many physics graduate students have, as part of their research group, been coauthor on "a minimum of three and sometimes as many as ten already published papers," and have been a primary author on one publication. The acceptable length for these publications has shrunk to 10 to 15 pages. Although physics has several kinds of publications—very concentrated letter publications, broader journal articles that allow authors to expand on experimental techniques, and review articles on broad topics—since the late 1970s, the physics community has been sharing information electronically to the point where most physicists agree that traditional journals "don't have a long-term future." Papers and dissertations, which are usually a compilation of papers, are now available on bulletin boards and on what is known as "the archive" (see http://www.arXiv.org[5]). Research results and preprints are uploaded on the archive, receive a time stamp to establish priority, and are made available to the community instantaneously. The archive, which is supervised but not refereed, allows for revisions and keeps track of prior versions so authors "can't hide dramatic changes." The archive has made physics

> feel even more competitive because people get cited because they published a paper [on the archive] which is two weeks before a competing group published their paper [in a journal(?)] and the late group doesn't get credit. . . . The publication date is now completely irrelevant. The relevant date is submission to the archive.

Although there seems to be less pressure for publication before the defense in the social sciences than in the sciences, given the nature of the academic job market, "people are making the calculation that publishing along the way is an important part of the process." However, graduate students in economics who are going into business or consulting and psychology students who are going into clinical practice often publish little or nothing because publishing is not as valued in nonacademic settings. The sociologists noted that there is a book sociology and an article sociology, with the more qualitative and humanistic fields leaning toward books. Qualitative faculty want their students to think of their dissertation as a book, and noted that the closer the dissertation is to a book at the time of the defense, the faster the student will be able to revise it and approach a publisher.

The book is the structural model for the humanities dissertation because most humanities graduate students go on to academic positions, which typically require faculty to have published a book in order to get tenure. According to one English professor,

> These days anyone who does not think of the dissertation as potentially their first book is crazy. It's career suicide because you can't get a job. . . . It's very, very difficult to start a new job and start a completely new project, which will be your first book.

The humanities view the dissertation as the end of a technical stage rather than an end product. Faculty see the dissertation as the "beginning of a series of engagements with the field on that subject," as a work that is "on its way to being a book." Because academic presses no longer publish dissertations, the dissertation has to be thoroughly revised before it can be published. Indeed, during the dissertation defense, humanities faculty provide students with advice about how to revise their dissertation for publication. At the same time, humanities students are encouraged to mine their dissertation for publications, to publish chapters from their dissertations in different places, and to use a chapter for a job talk. Yet, they are also cautioned against publishing all their chapters as articles, because publishers "want your book."

Despite the critical role publication plays in many doctoral students' early career paths, Golde and Dore (2001) found that less than half (43%) of the doctoral students in the sample who were planning an academic career felt that their program prepared them to publish their research findings, and that only slightly more than half (52%) felt confident and comfortable doing so. The percentage of students who felt like this was significantly different across disciplines, with science students feeling more prepared than students in other disciplines to publish their research, but not necessarily more confident and comfortable in their ability to do so: *felt prepared to publish their research findings*—60% biological sciences, 48% physical sciences, 42% social sciences, 30% humanities, and 46% other disciplines; *felt confident and comfortable publishing their research findings*—70% biological sciences, 50%

physical sciences, 52% social sciences, 44% humanities, and 73% other disciplines (C. M. Golde, personal communication, May 24, 2006).

## The Influence of the Dissertation on the New Ph.D.'s Career Path

There are three primary markets for new Ph.D.s—postdoctoral positions in academe and industry; business, industry, and government; and academe. Even though faculty expect and/or encourage students to publish part or all of their dissertations and stress its importance in getting a job, the focus groups faculty's remarks suggest that the dissertation itself plays a minimal role in most new doctorates' careers in all three markets, the one exception being humanities Ph.D.s in academe.

In the sciences and psychology, more and more entry-level positions for both academe and industry are postdoctoral positions, in part because research in these disciplines has a long learning curve and in part because these disciplines have produced more Ph.D.s than there are academic jobs available for them. Although the dissertation signifies that "this person can do original research," new Ph.D.s are often selected for their postdoctoral positions more by who they worked with and the type of skills they acquired in their doctoral training than for the work they produced for the dissertation. During the postdoc, new Ph.D.s often make a clean break from their dissertation research, acquire new skills, and become truly independent researchers/scholars, though some hold a journeyman status, a status somewhere between an apprentice and a master.

Many students in the sciences and the experimental and quantitative social sciences take positions in business, industry, and government. Industrial employers are less interested in what potential employees did their dissertations on, than whether "they are dedicated and smart and stubborn enough to go through the project" and have "the qualities of somebody who can solve hard problems." The same can probably be said for business and government, where new doctorates need to demonstrate that they have the skills to function in a highly quantitative way or engage in sophisticated policy analysis and evaluate rather than produce original research.

While new Ph.D.s from all disciplines seek and acquire academic positions, the dissertation appears to be most critical in the early career of humanities students. At job interviews, it is "extremely important" that job candidates be able to summarize their dissertation research succinctly and discuss what it means in an intelligible way. The humanities faculty in particular noted that although job candidates can talk about their dissertations, many cannot stand back and discuss the larger implications. Once hired, new humanities professors may use the dissertation as their professional identity for the first few years of their professional life and as the basis of the book that they hope will earn them tenure, but in reality, at many colleges and universities, being a humanities professor means being a teacher and a scholar rather than a publishing researcher.

After all the time and effort doctoral students devote to researching and writing their dissertations, at first blush it seems surprising that the dissertation does not play a larger role in most new Ph.D.s' career paths. However, if we return to the faculty's discussion of the purpose of the dissertation, we see that the dissertation has in fact fulfilled its purpose. It has both provided the new Ph.D. with and allowed the new Ph.D. to demonstrate that he or she has acquired the knowledge, skills, and thought processes necessary to be hired into positions that require those competencies and to engage in independent research/scholarship. The dissertation is, as the faculty said, a first exercise or a first statement, one that provides the foundation necessary for new Ph.D.s to make subsequent, more important, and perhaps even different kinds of contributions in their professional lives. And thus it is not surprising that most Ph.D.s quickly move on to other projects.

## Conclusion

The foregoing discussion of disciplinary approaches to doctoral training and the development of the dissertation reveals a number of similarities and differences across the disciplines. The similarities lie primarily in the macrostructure of the process—course work, qualifying exams, dissertation proposal, and researching and writing a dissertation. The differences lie in the microstructure of the individual requirements and processes—the nature of the course work, the nature and style of the qualifying examination and dissertation proposal, when and how dissertations topics are selected, as well as the nature of financial support and how it relates to research training and dissertation research, method of advisor selection, when and how dissertation or dissertation-related research begins, how research is conducted and how knowledge is created, the nature and frequency of interaction with the advisor during the dissertation stage, and so on. These differences raise more questions than they answer about the relationship between the process of doctoral training and the quality of the dissertation because, despite the differences, students in each discipline produce dissertations across the range of quality levels. Among the unanswered questions are: What features of those processes and what characteristics of the participants in the processes—the student, the advisor/faculty, and their interaction—lead to the production of very good and outstanding dissertations? And where could interventions be made to reduce or eliminate the production of acceptable, marginally acceptable, and unacceptable dissertations? Let's review what we know and what would be useful to know.

We know the transition from course taker (consumer of knowledge) to independent researcher/scholar (producer of knowledge) is hard for many students and a significant number of students leave their programs at this juncture. We know that a sizable percentage of students across disciplines do not feel that their course work laid a good foundation for doing independent research, do not feel that their programs prepared them to conduct research, and do not feel their programs gave them the opportunity to take a progressively responsible role in a research project. Clearly, it would be important to know why some students feel this way about their programs and others do not, whether there are actual differences in the training these groups of students receive and, if so, what those differences are and whether these perceptions and these experiences result in different performance outcomes for satisfied and dissatisfied students.

We know that interest in and enthusiasm for one's research project is an important determinant of the nature and quality of the contribution. We know that students have more freedom of choice in some disciplines than others, that there is variation among advisors in the freedom they allow students to choose their topics, and that there is variation among students in their ability to identify a good question or problem. How do these factors interact? What are the differences between students who arrive at their own questions/problems and those who do not or cannot? Can students be taught to ask good questions or identify good problems? If so, how? What happens to highly capable and creative students who are denied the opportunity to pursue their research interests? And what are the characteristics of advisors who deny their students this opportunity?

We know that there is variation in the capabilities of students who are admitted to doctoral programs and who are admitted to candidacy—both in analytic and creative ability. We know that GPAs and GRE scores are not good predictors of success, and that highly creative people do not always do well in course work and may not look like good bets on paper. Are doctoral programs admitting the right students? Are there better ways to identify talent? Can doctoral programs do a better job of nurturing quality and creative performance in the students they admit?

We know that there is variation among advisors. We know that some produce many Ph.D.s over the course of their careers and others produce few or none. We know that some advisors are more willing to hold students' hands and coach them through the process than others. We know that some advisors adjust their standards based on their assessment of students' capabilities and others do not. What are the characteristics of advisors and their approach to doctoral education that lead to more and less successful outcomes? Can advisors and the advising process be changed to increase and enhance student outcomes?

There is much we do not know and much to learn about how the process of doctoral education within and across disciplines interacts with the characteristics of the people who provide the training and the characteristics of the people who receive that training to produce the wide range of outcomes that currently prevail. However, one thing we do know is that when people are provided with the normative criteria for success, they are more likely to succeed. The next chapter provides guidance on how to translate performance expectations for the dissertation into a tool that can be used with graduate students to help them meet those expectations and that can be used by departments and programs to identify strengths and weakness in the educational process.

## Notes

1. When I started this study, I intended to write a chapter about similarities across disciplines and a separate chapter on disciplinary differences in how faculty assess the quality of a dissertation. However, the similarities were so great and the differences so small that a chapter on disciplinary differences seemed baseless. Yet, there was a clarion call for a chapter on disciplinary differences from the individuals who reviewed the first draft of the manuscript. Consequently, I reread the transcripts for each discipline with an eye toward what members of that discipline were saying (e.g.,

words, phases, structures, processes, values) that was not being said, and often could not be said, by members of other disciplines or domains of knowledge (e.g., hypothesis, mechanisms, text, archives). I compiled a list of issues/themes that emerged from this rereading (few of which directly related to differences in perceptions of quality) and shared it with my advisory committee. By the time we got to the discussion of the disciplinary differences chapter at the advisory committee meeting, the committee had become sold on the idea that when you strip away content, the disciplines are similar with respect to their assessment of quality, and, much to my amusement, they started to argue among themselves that there was no need for a chapter on disciplinary differences. We ultimately resolved that I should write a chapter on disciplinary approaches to doctoral training *"as described by the focus groups,"* and that given the nature of the data I was working with (emergent as opposed to targeted), that I make "broad generalizations" about the disciplines.

2. Except for the statement about theoretical knowledge in psychology, these characterizations derive from my experience as a doctoral student in psychology and sociology programs.

3. The statistic in Golde and Dore (2001) is incorrect and has been updated in the tables at http://www.phd-survey.org.

4. There is a body of literature on topic or problem choice that focuses primarily on how researchers in the sciences select their topics. See, for example, Zuckerman. (1978).

5. In addition to providing open access to e-prints in physics, the archive, which is based at Cornell University, provides access to e-prints in three other very highly competitive, fast-paced disciplines: mathematics, computer science, and quantitative biology.

# 5

# CONVERTING PERFORMANCE EXPECTATIONS INTO RUBRICS

T he tables in chapter 3 and in each of the disciplinary chapters in part two can best be described as faculty's performance expectations for the dissertation and its various components. Making faculty's implicit standards for judging dissertations explicit and available to students is an important step in helping students understand faculty's expectations, in socializing them in the discipline and its standards, and in helping them perform at higher levels. However, while the performance expectations contained in this book are a good start, they are an imperfect guide, primarily because many of the characteristics of the dissertation or the components of a dissertation were not discussed or described at each and every quality level. The next step or challenge for faculty is to convert their performance expectations into rubrics (see following sections).

This chapter is designed to encourage thinking about standards and criteria for the dissertation and about the underlying concepts and principles of pedagogy that lead to those ends. The chapter starts by defining what a rubric is and describing its parts. It provides an overview of methods for developing rubrics and discusses how to use them with students as well as the benefits of rubrics for students and for faculty. It concludes with a discussion of how departments/institutions can use rubrics to self-assess and improve the quality of their programs.

## What Is a Rubric?

A rubric is a set of criteria that identify the expected dimensions of a complex product or performance (in this case, the dissertation) along with detailed descriptions of what constitutes different levels of accomplishment for each of those dimensions (Huba & Freed, 2000; Maki, 2004; Moskal, 2000; Moskal & Leydens, 2000; Simon & Forgette-Giroux, 2001; Stevens & Levi, 2004). The criteria are laid out in a grid or template composed of three basic parts:

1. A scale that identifies levels of achievement or mastery
2. The dimensions or tasks that constitute the product or performance
3. A description of what constitutes each level of achievement

Some rubrics have a fourth part, a task description (Huba, Schuh, & Shelly, 2006; Stevens & Levi, 2004). Stripped down to its basic elements a rubric would look like Table 5.1.

The scale of a rubric typically has three to five levels. The MIE study used four—outstanding, very good, acceptable, unacceptable—though many faculty discussed a fifth level: marginally acceptable. Other common scale descriptors (Maki, 2004; Stevens & Levi, 2004) for each of the quality levels include:

- *Outstanding*—excellent, exemplary, exceptional, expert, proficient, strong, superior
- *Very good*—commendable, competent, good, intermediate, satisfactory

**TABLE 5.1.**
**The Basic Components of a Rubric**

| Task description: | | | | |
|---|---|---|---|---|
| | **Scale** | | | |
| **Dimensions of the task** | **Level 1** | **Level 2** | **Level 3** | **Level 4** |
| **Dimension 1** | description | description | description | description |
| **Dimension 2** | description | description | description | description |
| **Dimension 3** | description | description | description | description |
| **Dimension 4** | description | description | description | description |

- *Acceptable*—apprentice, beginning, developing, marginal, needs improvement
- *Unacceptable*—not yet competent, novice, unsatisfactory, weak

The dimensions, sometimes called criteria, are the fine-grain elements of the larger task or component. For instance, some of the dimensions that emerged from the focus group faculty's discussion of the components of a dissertation are listed in Table 5.2. The task for faculty is to identify the most important components and dimensions of the dissertation (and even other important aspects of doctoral training such as teaching and oral presentation) and provide descriptions of the dimensions at each quality level. Part of that task may involve identifying components that differ from those used in the MIE study or that differ by the type of dissertation a student is doing. For instance, in some disciplines students may do experimental, theoretical, or historical dissertations, do basic or applied research, or use quantitative or qualitative methods.

Table 5.3 is a sample rubric for the introduction to a dissertation based on the results of the MIE study. It is a work in progress and should be refined by those who have experience evaluating dissertations, perhaps with some assistance from those experienced in rubric development. By contrast, Table 5.4 is an example of a high-quality rubric developed by experts for the literature review (Boote & Beile, 2005). The Web site http://www.educ.iastate .edu/elps/elpsrubrics.htm has high-quality rubrics developed for doctoral students in an Education Leadership and Policy Studies program on a variety of other aspects of doctoral training, such as research skills, oral presentation, written communication, and inter- and intrapersonal skills.

## Developing Rubrics

There is no one right way to develop a rubric. Rubrics can be developed based on an analysis of existing products or by reflecting on the objectives of learning tasks. The MIE process is a modified hybrid. The strategy used in the MIE study emerged from my basic understanding of how rubrics are created for scoring essays and other complex products written or created for K–12 statewide examinations, the Advanced Placement examination, and the writing section of the Graduate Record Examination (GRE). For these and other similar examinations, a group of experts are each given copies of a large

**TABLE 5.2.**
**Some Dimensions of the Different Components of the Generic Dissertation**

| Introduction | Literature review | Theory | Methods | Results/analysis | Discussion/conclusion |
|---|---|---|---|---|---|
| • Problem statement<br>• Research question<br>• Motivation<br>• Context<br>• Summary<br>• Importance<br>• Road map | • Comprehensive<br>• Up to date<br>• Command of the literature<br>• Contextualization of problem<br>• Selective<br>• Synthetic<br>• Analytic<br>• Thematic | • Appropriate<br>• Logical<br>• Understood<br>• Alignment with question and methods<br>• Strengths and limitations | • Appropriate<br>• Detailed<br>• Alignment with question and theory<br>• How used<br>• Advantages and disadvantages | • Appropriate<br>• Alignment with question (and hypotheses)<br>• Sophistication<br>• Iterative<br>• Amount and quality of data/information<br>• Presentation<br>• Interpretation<br>• Insights<br>• Limitations | • Summary<br>• Refers back to introduction<br>• Ties everything together<br>• Larger perspective<br>• Strengths and weaknesses<br>• Implications and applications<br>• Future directions |

**TABLE 5.3.**

**Sample Rubric for the Introduction to a Dissertation**

**Introduction:** Introduces the work to a nonspecialist and sets the stage for the entire dissertation

| *Dimensions of the task* | Scale | | | |
|---|---|---|---|---|
| | **Outstanding** | **Very good** | **Acceptable** | **Unacceptable** |
| Problem statement | Presents a very interesting and compelling problem | Poses a good problem but is less interesting and less compelling | Orients the reader to the problem, but the problem is not very interesting or compelling | Does not state a problem or the problem statement is wrong or trivial |
| Research question | Sets up and articulates an interesting question | Poses a clear research question | Presents a small, narrow research question | Does not lay out the research question or the research question does not follow from the problem statement |
| Motivation | Is well motivated and has a compelling hook | Has a hook but is less well motivated | Has a marginal hook and is not compelling | Provides no motivation for the problem |

**TABLE 5.3.**
Continued

| Dimensions of the task | Scale | | | |
| | Outstanding | Very good | Acceptable | Unacceptable |
| --- | --- | --- | --- | --- |
| Context | Provides a historical overview and a clear description of the cutting edge<br><br>Positions the work in relation to other work on the topic | Places the work in context | Provides minimal context.<br><br>Does not make it clear why the research needs to be done | Does not provide a context for the problem or the context is not clear |
| Summary | Provides a clear and concise summary of the methods, data, results, and conclusions | Discusses the methods, data, results, and conclusions | Provides minimal description of the methods, results, and conclusions | Does not provide a summary of the work |
| Importance | Explains why the problem/work is important and significant | Indicates the importance and significance of the work | Does not convince the reader that the problem is important | Does not make a case for the importance of the topic |
| Road map | Provides a road map of the dissertation | Provides a good overview of the dissertation | Provides a minimal overview of the work | Does not present an outline or overview of the work |

## TABLE 5.4.
## Literature Review Scoring Rubric

| Category | Criterion | 1 | 2 | 3 | 4 |
|---|---|---|---|---|---|
| 1. Coverage | A. Justified criteria for inclusion and exclusion from review. | Did not discuss the criteria inclusion or exclusion | Discussed the literature included and excluded | Justified inclusion and exclusion of literature | |
| 2. Synthesis | B. Distinguished what has been done in the field from what needs to be done. | Did not distinguish what has and has not been done | Discussed what has and has not been done | Critically examined the state of the field | |
| | C. Placed the topic or problem in the broader scholarly literature | Topic not placed in broader scholarly literature | Some discussion of broader scholarly literature | Topic clearly situated in broader scholarly literature | |
| | D. Placed the research in the historical context of the field. | History of topic not discussed | Some mention of history of topic | Critically examined history of topic | |
| | E. Acquired and enhanced the subject vocabulary. | Key vocabulary not discussed | Key vocabulary defined | Discussed and resolved ambiguities in definitions | |
| | F. Articulated important variables and phenomena relevant to the topic. | Key variables and phenomena not discussed | Reviewed relationships among key variables and phenomena | Noted ambiguities in literature and proposed new relationships | |
| | G. Synthesized and gained a new perspective on the literature. | Accepted literature at face value | Some critique of literature | Offered new perspective | |

**TABLE 5.4.**
**Continued**

| Category | Criterion | 1 | 2 | 3 | 4 |
|---|---|---|---|---|---|
| 3. Methodology | H. Identified the main methodologies and research techniques that have been used in the field, and their advantages and disadvantages. | Research methods not discussed | Some discussion of research methods used to produce claims | Critiqued research methods | Introduced new methods to address problems with predominant methods |
| | I. Related ideas and theories in the field to research methodologies. | Research methods not discussed | Some discussion of appropriateness of research methods to warrant claims | Critiqued appropriateness of research methods to warrant claims | |
| 4. Significance | J. Rationalized the practical significance of the research problem. | Practical significance of research not discussed | Practical significance discussed | Critiqued practical significance of research | |
| | K. Rationalized the scholarly significance of the research problem. | Scholarly significance of research not discussed | Scholarly significance discussed | Critiqued scholarly significance of research | |
| 5. Rhetoric | L. Was written with a coherent, clear structure that supported the review. | Poorly conceptualized, haphazard | Some coherent structure | Well developed, coherent | |

*Note:* The column-head numbers represent scores for rating dissertation literature reviews on 3-point and 4-point scales. Reprinted with permission of Boote & Beile, 2005. Adapted from *Doing a Literature Review: Releasing the Social Science Research Imagination* (p. 27), by Christopher Hart, 1999, London, SAGE Publications. Copyright 1999 by SAGE Publications. Adapted with permission.

sample of the product and asked to individually review and sort them into piles corresponding to the identified quality (scale) levels. The experts then come together, compare results, and discuss and categorize products that were not completely agreed upon until they achieve consensus. The experts then go through the products in each pile and identify and describe the dimensions and the distinguishing characteristics of the dimension at each quality level. The length of the typical dissertation makes this process prohibitive. The MIE study thus chose to rely on high-Ph.D.-productive faculty's recollections of different-quality dissertations.

Stevens and Levi (2004), describe a four-stage process for developing rubrics for course assignments based on reflection. The first stage involves reflecting on performance outcomes, what faculty want from students. The MIE questions about the purpose of the dissertation and what it means to make an original and a significant contribution were designed to make the goals or performance outcomes of the dissertation explicit. Focus group faculty also often spontaneously identified the performance outcomes (purpose, nature, role, goal) of the individual components. The second stage involves identifying and listing the particular details of the task and the learning goals. This stage corresponds to MIE's four-stage data reduction process described in chapter 1. The third stage, grouping and labeling, involves organizing the reflections into component skills, which then become the dimensions of the rubric. Finally, the fourth stage, application, involves transferring the lists and groupings to the rubric grid, and filling in descriptions for each dimension at each quality level. Rubric developers typically start with the highest and lowest levels, and then fill in the intermediary level(s). The lowest performance descriptions are often the negation of the exemplary description as well as a list of common mistakes (Stevens & Levi, 2004).

The descriptions should be as concrete as possible. It is best to avoid indeterminate or undefined terms such as "brilliant," "solid," "trivial," and value-laden terms such as "excellent" or "poor" (Huba & Freed, 2000), as the goal is to provide students with detailed information about how well they have achieved the criteria and how they can improve their work. For example, a description like, "The statistical analysis contains no errors," is preferable over "The statistical analysis is good."

For universities, departments, or disciplinary associations wishing to develop rubrics of performance expectations for the dissertation, I recommend a somewhat more streamlined approach than the one used in the MIE study.

Instead of starting completely from scratch, faculty could begin by analyzing, discussing, and modifying the tables in chapter 3 and/or any of the disciplinary chapters. Shells for developing rubrics based on MIE are available at http://www.styluspubs.com/.

Rather than analyzing transcripts of group discussions,[1] the process could be enhanced by recording individual participants' characterizations of a quality of a dimension on a blackboard, flip chart, overhead projector, or by another method that allows for visualization of the proposed characterizations. Such a strategy has several advantages. First, because spoken language is often imprecise (see discussion of the word "good" in Appendix B), and because discussions often digress and otherwise jump around, it helps guarantee that the characteristic being discussed is assigned to the right dimension and quality level. Second, it allows participants to discuss and debate the location and merits of the proposed characteristics and tack toward a consensus. Third, it allows participants to *see* the descriptions of each quality level juxtaposed against each other. The latter two advantages should lead to more refined and higher-quality descriptions. Fourth, it allows rubrics to be created and refined much more quickly. This process, or some variation of the ones described above, could also be used to create rubrics for course assignments, seminar papers, master's theses, qualifying examinations, dissertation proposals, and even oral presentations. After a rubric has been developed, faculty may wish to use a "metarubric" to assess the quality of the rubric (Stevens & Levi, 2004). Table 5.5 is an example of a metarubric.

## Rubrics and Students

The literature on rubrics typically refers to them as *scoring rubrics* because they are usually developed and used to score and grade students' products and performances. I have eschewed the word "scoring," because as I have said and will say elsewhere in this book, rubrics for dissertations should be used *formatively*, to provide feedback to and educate students while they are in the process of researching and writing the dissertation; *not summatively*, after the fact to rate a student's dissertation or individual components of the dissertation and provide the student with a summary score. Indeed, a summary score diminishes the rubric's ability to provide detailed and meaningful information about the quality of the work (Simon & Forgette-Giroux, 2001)

**TABLE 5.5.**
## A Metarubric for Evaluating the Overall Quality of a Rubric

| Rubric part | Evaluation criteria | Yes | No |
|---|---|---|---|
| The dimensions | Does each dimension cover important parts of the final student performance? | ___ | ___ |
| | Does the dimension capture some key themes in your teaching? | ___ | ___ |
| | Are the dimensions clear? | ___ | ___ |
| | Are the dimensions distinctly different from each other? | ___ | ___ |
| | Do the dimensions represent skills that the student knows something about already (e.g., organization, analysis, using conventions?) | ___ | ___ |
| The descriptions | Do the descriptions match the dimensions? | ___ | ___ |
| | Are the descriptions clear and different from each other? | ___ | ___ |
| | If you used points, is there a clear basis for assigning points for each dimension? | ___ | ___ |
| | If using a three-to-five-level rubric, are the descriptions appropriately and equally weighted across the three to five levels? | ___ | ___ |
| The scale | Do the descriptors under each level truly represent that level of performance? | ___ | ___ |
| | Are the scale labels (e.g., exemplary, competent, beginning) encouraging and still quite informative without being negative and discouraging? | ___ | ___ |
| | Does the rubric have a reasonable number of levels for the age of the student and the complexity of the assignment? | ___ | ___ |
| The overall rubric | Does the rubric clearly connect to the outcomes that it is designed to measure? | ___ | ___ |
| | Can the rubric be understood by external audiences (avoids jargon and technical language)? | ___ | ___ |
| | Does it reflect teachable skills? | ___ | ___ |
| | Does the rubric reward or penalize students based on skills unrelated to the outcome being measured that you have not taught? | ___ | ___ |
| | Have all students had an equal opportunity to learn the content and skills necessary to be successful on the assignment? | ___ | ___ |
| | Is the rubric appropriate for the conditions under which the assignment was completed? | ___ | ___ |

*(continues)*

**TABLE 5.5.**
**Continued**

| Rubric part | Evaluation criteria | Yes | No |
|---|---|---|---|
| The overall rubric | Does the rubric include the assignment description or title? | ___ | ___ |
| | Does the rubric address the student's performance as a developmental task? | ___ | ___ |
| | Does the rubric inform the student about the evaluation procedures when the student's work is scored? | ___ | ___ |
| | Does the rubric emphasize the appraisal of individual or group performance and indicate ways to improve? | ___ | ___ |
| Fairness and sensibility | Does it look like the rubric will be fair to all students and free of bias? | ___ | ___ |
| | Does it look like it will be useful to students as performance feedback? | ___ | ___ |
| | Is the rubric practical, given the kind of assignment? | ___ | ___ |
| | Does the rubric make sense to the reader? | ___ | ___ |

*Source:* Reprinted with permission from D. D. Stevens & A. Levi (2004), p. 94.

and thus defeats the educational purpose of creating it and using it with students.

Ideally, rubrics should be given to and discussed with students at the beginning of the course or program in which they will be used. For the dissertation, optimal times may be during orientation or the proseminar and again in a dissertation preparation course, if the program has such courses. Focus group faculty and doctoral students (Miller, 2006) expressed interest in putting performance expectations in graduate student handbooks and on department Web sites.

Early provision of rubrics can educate students in a variety of ways (Huba & Freed, 2000). They help inform students about the discipline's and/or profession's expectations and standards of excellence for research and communication. They provide students with benchmarks they can use to judge and revise their work, thus not only enhancing students' ability to assess and correct their own work and that of their peers (and, consequently, reduce the amount of work advisors and committee members have to do), but also increasing the likelihood that those students who pursue academic careers will use them with their students. They create opportunities for students and faculty to discuss the discipline's standards and the students' progress toward those standards. Indeed, rubrics should be used to enhance and support the advising process, not substitute for it. In short, the more time departments and faculty spend up front explaining and discussing the criteria in rubrics with students, the smoother and easier the process should be for everyone.

In addition to talking to students about the expectations contained in a rubric, advisors and committee members can and should use it to provide feedback to students on dissertation proposals and chapter drafts. As they read a proposal or draft, faculty can check or circle the demonstrated level of performance on each dimension and return the rubric to the student with the draft. Over and above reducing (but not eliminating) the extent of the comments an advisor or committee member may need to write on the draft, the rubric will help students see how their work differs from the target level and will provide them with information about what they need to do to progress toward the target (Huba & Freed, 2000). In most cases the target for the dissertation should be very good (proficient) and not outstanding (exemplary), as very good is the level most faculty expect of most graduate students (see chapters 3 and 6). Again, the rubric should be used to open and support discussion about disciplinary and professional standards of excellence, performance goals, and how to meet them.

While using rubrics will not eliminate ideological differences among committee members, they should increase the likelihood that committee members' assessment of the quality of the dissertation is consistent. Indeed, as noted earlier, the faculty in many focus groups were surprised to discover how similar their standards were. This is consistent with the literature on rubrics, which indicates that when colleagues share rubrics or develop them together they are often startled to discover that they are looking for the same qualities in their students' work (Huba & Freed, 2000; Stevens & Levi, 2004).

## Rubrics and Programs

Faculty, departments, and universities have typically used course evaluations, exit interviews, alumni surveys, and other indirect measures of student satisfaction to assess the quality of their programs. However, these forms of assessment do not provide direct or objective evidence of what was learned and how well it was learned or whether intended learning goals were achieved, as is now beginning to be demanded by accrediting agencies and other stakeholder groups (Borkowski, 2006). Further, graduate faculty know that graduate students do not do equally well on all aspects of their graduate programs (Murphy & Gerst, 1996).

Because rubrics provide a rich record of student achievement, departments, disciplines, and universities can use them to register the *aggregate* performance outcomes for dissertations for a department, for program or specialty areas, for individual advisors, or for types of dissertations (e.g., quantitative, qualitative, historical, theoretical, empirical). As dissertations come up for defense, the advisor, all committee members, or the dean's representative (outside committee member) could be asked to check or circle the demonstrated level of performance of each dimension on a rubric. (Committees should produce a single, common rubric.) The performance on the different dimensions of the dissertation would then be transferred to a master rubric in the form of checks or tally marks. After the results of a set of dissertations have been recorded on the master rubric, patterns of student performance should become evident. For example, the master rubric might indicate that most students' methodology and analytic techniques fall in the very good range but that fewer students do a good job aligning theory with methods, or that students who took statistics with Professor X do better statistical and analytical work than students who took statistics with Professor Y. These patterns should help individual advisors, departments, and universities (as well as accrediting boards) identify strengths and weaknesses in pedagogy; instructional design; curricular and cocurricular design; institutional programs and services that support, complement, and advance student learning; educational resources and tools; educational opportunities; and advising (Maki, 2004). This information can then be used to build on strengths and adjust or modify weak aspects of graduate programs.

In sum, the development of rubrics can lead to spirited discussions among faculty about common expectations, collective educational practices, and curricular design, as well as about ways to prepare students to achieve the intended learning goals. In turn, the existence of rubrics should make it easier for faculty to provide focused feedback to students by giving them a document that they can point to and discuss with students at various stages of their doctoral education. Similarly, the existence of rubrics provides more opportunities for students to learn about, practice, and receive feedback on their progress toward the discipline's and profession's standards of excellence. Finally, in the aggregate, rubrics can provide students, faculty, departments, and other stakeholders with formal, systematic, evidenced-based information about the quality of a doctoral program.

## Notes

1. Tape-recording group discussions has both advantages and disadvantages. The advantages include having a complete record of the discussion, which will likely include other interesting insights and observations about the dissertation process, students, and advising. The disadvantages include the high cost of transcription. Further, relying solely on tapes and transcripts for the analysis increases the risk that information is lost because it is inaudible as well as the risk that participants' intentions are not clearly understood.

# 6

# CONCLUSIONS, IMPLICATIONS, AND RECOMMENDATIONS

The overarching goal of eliciting faculty's implicit standards for judging dissertations and codifying performance expectations for doctoral students is to help faculty, departments, disciplines, and universities identify the learning outcomes for doctoral education, improve the doctoral education process, and make it more transparent to students. This study was the first step in what I hope will be a multiyear project for graduate education, one that stimulates local discussions that are national in scope, yet point to local resolutions.

While I have compiled what can best be described as performance expectations for the dissertation and its component parts, it is up to faculty and administrators to develop them for their local circumstances and translate them into rubrics that can be used *formatively*, not summatively, to support, not substitute for, the advising process. That is, they should be used to help doctoral students understand the goals of doctoral training, identify strengths and weaknesses, and identify what needs to be revised, why, and how, *while* the students are in the process of conducting their research and writing their dissertation so that improvements can be made along the way. The result of applying these rubrics to the doctoral training and dissertation research and writing process should be better-quality research and dissertations as well as better-quality researchers and scholars.

## Practical Implications and Important Caveats

I agree with Mullins and Kiley (2002) that *rubrics of performance expectations should* not *be used to rate dissertations or individual components of the dissertation, total the results, and declare a dissertation passed or failed, or of such and such quality.* A dissertation is an extended argument and should be viewed and judged as such. Indeed, the focus group faculty were adamant that their judgments of the dissertation were holistic, not compartmentalized. The purpose of establishing performance expectations for the dissertation and for the component parts of a dissertation is to clarify the learning goals of the enterprise and its individual components (e.g., literature review, theory, methods, analysis), thereby strengthening each piece of the whole while at the same time strengthening the whole.

Despite my call to create performance expectations and bring greater clarity and objectivity to the evaluation of the dissertation, many of the "standards" are indeterminate qualities that faculty can recognize but not articulate precisely (e.g., compelling, elegant, surprising) (see Delamont et al., 2002). Indeed, it was not uncommon for faculty to respond to a protocol item by saying, "You know it when you see it," or "It's like pornography. You know it when you see it." Although these qualities may remain relatively undefined, faculty should at least be able to agree that they are or are not important outcomes of graduate training and are or are not found in the dissertation. These qualities are and should be conveyed to students through the advising and other professional socialization processes and appropriate exemplars.

Another reason why the rubrics should not be used for summative assessment is because, as the faculty noted, there are many kinds of dissertations and they serve many different purposes. The focus group faculty were high-Ph.D.-productive faculty, and like the high producers in my previous study (Lovitts, 2001), many commented that they, but not all their colleagues, held their students to different standards based on the students' needs and capabilities. Not all graduate students can produce outstanding dissertations nor should they be expected to. Indeed, the ability to produce an outstanding dissertation, one that says something totally new or opens up a new field is often a function of the state of the field at the time the student is in graduate school. Some fields are ripe for analysis and criticism that will take them in new directions, most are in a state of what Kuhn (1962) calls "normal science," where the bulk of the work is "mopping up operations" or expanding what is known within the dominant paradigm. Further, setting the bar at outstanding (or even very good for some students) could result in at least two unintended consequences. One, it could increase time to degree as students may spend extra time striving to achieve what is often an unrealistic goal. Two, it could increase attrition by causing otherwise excellent or very good students to make inappropriate, negative self-assessments of their capabilities. For instance, straight-A students whose dissertations are very good, may associate very good with a B and deem a B unacceptable, when in fact, very good corresponds with an A, and outstanding is super or über A. Finally, as is stated on the title page of virtually every dissertation, the dissertation is submitted "in partial fulfillment of the requirements for the degree of doctor of philosophy." Thus the fulfillment of the other "requirements" should play a role in the decision to award the degree.

A common saying about the dissertation is, "Done is better than perfect." Graduate school is the beginning, not the end, of a career. Thus the goal should be to use rubrics of performance expectations in a formative way to help doctoral students understand the learning goals of their discipline; help them to achieve the highest level possible given their needs, capabilities, and professional goals; and to get them out of graduate school and into their careers.

## Recommendations for Developing Performance Expectations

Further research designed to elicit faculty's implicit standards for evaluating dissertations can and should occur at several different levels—institutional, university, discipline, department. Each has different implications for graduate education. At the highest level, institutional, several focused discussions could be conducted with faculty in each of many disciplines across a variety of universities and the results analyzed for universal themes in a manner similar to this study. A group of graduate school deans could be brought together to discuss the findings and then issue a statement of performance expectations for doctoral education writ large. The performance expectations contained in the statement would then provide an objective standard for training doctoral students and for evaluating Ph.D. programs across disciplines and universities. Indeed, universal standards would facilitate training and assessment of research that is conducted at the interface of two or more disciplines.

At the university level, the graduate school dean could strongly encourage all Ph.D.-granting departments to convene discussion groups and create clearly defined performance standards for their graduate students. The resulting standards could then be analyzed for cross-disciplinary themes, and the university could then compose its own performance standards, much the way universities currently have statements about the nature or purpose of the dissertation. The existence of such standards would allow universities to more easily arbitrate student claims that they are not receiving the training they came to the university to receive or that their dissertation had not been judged fairly. The existence of such standards would also facilitate the termination of students who cannot meet the standard, provide these students with objective reasons for their termination, and reduce the probability of (successful) litigation from disgruntled graduate students.

At the disciplinary level, professional organizations could convene one or more discussion groups with leaders in the field to define the performance standards for their discipline and its subfields. The existence of such standards would allow for more consistent training and objective comparison across programs. They would also provide another measure for accreditation boards to use in determining whether departments are providing doctoral students with the expected level of education and training.

Finally, the creation of performance standards in individual departments would make the training process and its goals more transparent to faculty and students, thus enhancing faculty supervision and student research performance. Having codified standards should also lead to more valid and reliable judgments of quality across candidates in a department or field.

Over and above creating rubrics of performance expectations of the dissertation, faculty, departments, and universities should consider creating them for seminar papers, master's theses, qualifying or comprehensive exams (both written and oral), dissertation proposals, and even individual course assignments and oral presentations.

## Recommendations for Research and Discussion

The MIE focus group discussions raise many practical and policy-relevant questions. First are questions related to implementation. When and how should rubrics and performance expectations be used with students? Does their use improve communication between students and advisors and dissertation committee members? Does their use reduce the amount of time and effort faculty have to spend providing high-quality feedback on dissertation drafts? Does their use lead to more higher-quality dissertations?

Other questions relate to how faculty judge dissertations. Some faculty said they evaluated only the dissertation, some said they took the person into consideration. Should faculty's judgments be limited to the product (the dissertation) or is it OK to consider the person and the process?

Along these lines, it was not uncommon for faculty to say that they held students to different standards based on their assessment of the students' capabilities and career goals. At the same time, the focus group faculty (who were high-Ph.D.-productive faculty) often noted that some of their colleagues did not vary their standards. This raises questions not only about standards and whether they should be varied, but also about differences among faculty. Who varies their standards? Who does not, and why? Do high-Ph.D.-productive faculty and low-Ph.D.-productive faculty have different standards? If so, what are they? Are high-Ph.D.-productive faculty more likely to vary their standards than low-Ph.D.-productive faculty? Are there differences in the way high- and low-Ph.D.-productive faculty train and interact with their doctoral students? If so, how does this affect the quality of the dissertation? Do new assistant professors, associate professors, and full professors have different standards? How do faculty develop their standards?

The focus group faculty who commented that they were in lower-ranked departments frequently compared their department's standards with the standards at Harvard and other Ivy League or more highly ranked universities, suggesting that their standards were lower. The question is, do faculty's standards for the different quality levels really differ across types of universities or is it just that faculty in lower-ranked departments at lower-ranked institutions are more willing to accept lower-quality dissertations? And should they?

This study also shed some light on the "hidden criteria" for passing the dissertation and the politics and social dynamics of dissertation committees, including how faculty handle marginal dissertations and how they typically defer to the advisor, often against their better judgment. These are clearly ripe and open areas for further investigation, as is faculty's failure to terminate failing students when they recognize (often long before the dissertation stage) that the student does not have what it takes to do research and write an acceptable dissertation.

# PART TWO

---

# THE DISCIPLINES

# 7

# THE BIOLOGY DISSERTATION

O ver 250 Ph.D. programs in the biological sciences in the United States award degrees in 28 subfields that are tracked by various organizations; these programs also confer degrees in several other untracked subfields. Graduate biology programs enroll roughly 60,000 students (master's and doctoral), and graduate roughly 5,700 new Ph.D.s annually. The median time to degree is 6.7 years. Roughly 75% of new biology Ph.D.s go on to postdoctoral education.[1]

Twenty-one biology faculty at six universities participated in the focus groups. They represent such diverse fields as anatomical sciences, botany, cell and molecular biology, developmental biology, ecology, evolution, genetics, population biology, and systematics. Overall, these faculty had 467 years of experience, had chaired an estimated 243 dissertations, and had sat on an estimated 979 dissertation committees. The average biology focus group participant had been a professor for 22 years, had chaired 12 dissertations, and had sat on 47 dissertation committees. Below is a summary of the biology focus groups' discussions. Their performance expectations for the dissertation are displayed in the tables. Their supporting discussion is recounted in the text.

## The Purpose of a Biology Dissertation

Biology, like most of the other science disciplines, is in the "midst of a real revolution in terms of just what the meaning of a dissertation is in universities all over the country." It is "changing rapidly," because "science has become such a hurried affair." The biology dissertation in many fields and departments is becoming a compilation of two or three papers that have been accepted for publication and "thrown together," plus a review that covers the background material. While one participant asserted that the contemporary dissertation was an exercise for the committee that did not have much value, his colleague countered that it was only the format of the presentation of results that had changed, not the process. It still involved "training a lot of scientists to learn how to do science."

The biology faculty saw the dissertation as having many purposes (see Table 7.1). Most of the biology faculty felt that the dissertation was an educational experience. They saw it as an opportunity for students to catch up on and demonstrate knowledge of the literature as well as an opportunity for students to bring together everything they had done and speculate on where they might go with their research. Some noted that the dissertation was a good record for other investigators, especially the next person in the lab. The faculty did not expect the dissertation to be the biggest thing the student ever did. Rather, they saw the dissertation as "the first major exercise in demonstrating expertise in science," "a chance for students to show what they had learned," an opportunity to demonstrate that they were "an authority in a little niche that they carved out for themselves" and "can do all the things expected of a researcher."

Unlike faculty in most of the other disciplines, the biology faculty did not say that the purpose of the dissertation was to become an independent researcher or to help the student get a job. This may be because the vast majority of new biology Ph.D.s go on to postdoctoral education (Committee on Science, Engineering, and Public Policy, 2000; Hill, Hoffer, & Golladay, 2004). Indeed, one participant noted that "it's routine to then go on to postdoc and get several more years training, because . . . learning how to do

### TABLE 7.1.
### The Purpose of a Biology Dissertation

To train students to do science and prepare them for a career in science; to make an original and significant contribution; to learn how to do science/scientific research—how to identify scientific problems, how to approach problems (methods), how to critically analyze and evaluate a large body of empirical data and judge the evidence, how to write coherently and argue a point in writing; to demonstrate that they can do scientific research and be an authority in their niche—have knowledge of the field, the ability to generate hypotheses, the discipline to collect data and the resourcefulness to organize and analyze it, the ability to put their work in broader context of what is happening in the field, and the ability to write up and publish their work.

research in the sciences [has] a long learning curve." Faculty in this focus group did not interpret finishing the dissertation to mean "that you are a scientist."

## Original Contribution

The biology faculty identified many ways to make an original contribution (see Table 7.2). Like other disciplines, an original contribution was something that had not been done before, which one faculty member said was "a pretty minimal requirement." One participant noted that what it means to make an original contribution in biology can vary by field. He went on to note that in experimental fields, it usually involves generating novel information or data. By contrast, in theoretical fields, like computational biology, he noted it could be a new idea or algorithm. Another participant commented that an original contribution was "something no one else has published," implying that originality resides more in the act of publishing (making the result known) than in the act of discovery, as unpublished discoveries typically do not contribute to the advancement of science.

The faculty indicated that originality derives from the intellectual endeavor of the individual and, for the dissertation, it has to come from the student. However, given the funded-research, mentor-driven, team-oriented nature of modern biological research, the locus of originality is not always clear. Indeed, one participant stated:

> The dissertations I am involved in, the projects . . . are not totally original because almost always [the students] are working under the direction of someone who has a laboratory of ongoing research programs. So, every one I have been on, the doctoral student has taken on part of the mentor's overall program. Usually at the beginning they don't know enough about

### TABLE 7.2.
### The Nature of an Original Contribution in Biology

Something that has not been done or found before; new questions, theory, methods, techniques, technologies, observations, data, information, inferences, or analytical approaches; applying a new method or analysis to an old question or problem; new answers to an old question; combining a problem and a technology that had not been combined before; something that moves the field forward the research to make a highly original contribution. I haven't seen, in the ones I have been involved in . . . novel idea[s] in students.

Original contributions can range from trivial to significant. Dissertations can be "disappointing" or lack significance because the results turned out to be largely negative. Though, in many faculty's minds, original and significant are linked: "I saw questions 1 [original] and 2 [significant] being so closely tied together that I couldn't distinguish between them. . . . Original is something that almost has to be also significant to me. When I tie the label 'novel' or 'original' to work, it's also significant work."

In addition to characterizing what an original contribution is, the biology faculty discussed what it is not:

> If, for example, an original observation is made with animal A and you do the same experiment on animal B and find the same thing, then, yes, it is new because it's not been done in animal B, but [it] is not an original [contribution] because it's [already] been observed in a different animal.

A participant in another focus group who gave a very similar example said, "They're just following a recipe. They've got to improvise a little." Similarly, while confirming a known result may be a very important step in the development of a particular field, repeating something that has already been done is generally not acceptable for a dissertation.

## Significant Contribution

The key characteristics for a significant contribution in biology are its importance and relevance to the field and its publishability (see Table 7.3). The faculty in half the focus groups noted that significance is a community judgment, a "post facto decision based on how research actually affects the field."

### TABLE 7.3.
#### The Nature of a Significant Contribution in Biology

A very important contribution that is publishable or published in top journals; increases understanding of an underlying mechanism; answers a very important question; disproves prior work; is a discovery of a new biological process; influences or changes the field; moves the field forward; opens up a new field

Unlike faculty in some of the other disciplines, no biology faculty member said that he or she did not expect graduate students to make a significant contribution. However, one biologist said that he did not insist that the dissertation be "unusually" significant.

The biology faculty implicitly rather than explicitly indicated that there were degrees of significance. They expressed it in terms of how forward moving the contribution is—the more forward moving, the more significant—and in terms of the type of journal the research could get published in—the higher ranked the journal, the more significant the work. On the subject of journals, one participant, playing the "role of the devil's advocate," countered, "Some damn fine significant contributions in biology have been published, but not in the top journals." This same biologist also drew a distinction between a meaningful contribution and a significant one in terms of the difference between descriptive studies and tests of hypotheses. In his opinion, meaningful contributions could be made by describing phenomena or by describing the developmental course of some process. By contrast, significant contributions are derived from a group of focused hypothesis-driven experiments. An ecologist in another focus group indicated that his colleagues in other fields of biology (e.g., genetics) might have a different perspective on what it means to make a significant contribution, "The next 600 base pairs might be what it's all about."

Finally, one participant shared some advice about significance he received when he was a graduate student:

> One of my committee members suggested to me as a career strategy to try to only be two to three years ahead of the curve, because if you're eight years ahead of the curve, no one will be able to see around the corner what you are doing. . . . That's a very interesting question,—how far in front of the field can you be and still survive?

Both he and one of his colleagues gave examples of significant work that "fell flat" and on "deaf ears" when they were first published.

## The Dissertation as a Whole

Students in biology may submit a "traditional" dissertation, one based on a single, extended line of thought or, as indicated above, students may submit two or three journal articles that have been submitted or accepted for publication and are tied together by an introduction. Indeed, some universities do not require students to write a dissertation if they have published two or three substantive articles in good-quality journals. Below we explore the characteristics of different quality traditional and "essay" biology dissertations (see Table 7.4) and what the biology faculty had to say about them.

## Outstanding

Although it is "hard to boil it into a formula," the two things that contribute most to making biology dissertations outstanding are the ideas and the quality of the writing. Outstanding dissertations either express significant, independent ideas or expand upon influential ideas; they demonstrate that a question can be solved or that an approach works. The writing is not only clear and convincing, but fun to read. Outstanding dissertations also show deep knowledge of the literature and the field, are well designed and well executed, show understanding of the contributions they are making, and tie the whole project together. Outstanding dissertations are rare and are "connected in some way to [question] 1 and [question] 2"—original and significant.

Members of one focus group had differing positions on the characteristics of an outstanding essay dissertation. One participant asserted that the papers had to "fit together," to which his colleagues responded that they did not care whether the papers fit with each other. They commented, "There have been some excellent theses where the three chapters are essentially unrelated to each other, each one significant," and, "What happens if you have one nugget and you tie together two really boring pieces of work, what have you really accomplished?"

The best dissertations were described as coming from the best graduate students, students who enjoyed science and who came to see themselves as independent scientists:

*Participant:* You get some of these students who are really excited about what they are doing. They have a "can-do" attitude. They are confident. They love coming in each day and doing research. And, of course, it's a good thesis. It just sort of happens.

*Participant:* The best graduate students are the ones who really make the transition to seeing themselves as an independent scientist during the tenure of their graduate work. When they come in, the majority of them look

**TABLE 7.4.**
**The Characteristics of Different Quality Dissertations in Biology**

| Quality | Characteristics |
|---|---|
| **Outstanding** | Very organized and well written; the writing is clear, concise, critical, persuasive, and compelling; is focused, coherent, and organized around a major theme or question; is original and significant; expresses new and independent ideas; addresses a very important issue or answers a long-standing question; shows a deep understanding of the literature and the gaps in the field; is hypothesis driven; has well-planned and well-performed experiments; uses or develops new tools, methods, approaches, or new types of analyses; the experiments are brief and very well described; has a large quantity of high-quality data; the data are extremely clear; has a very significant new discovery; the conclusion ties the whole thing together; has an impact on theory; opens up a new area for research; will move the field in a new direction |
| **Very good** | Solid, yeomanlike work; has an argument; is well written, well organized, and broad in scope; is original and significant but less so; the quality of the science is good; demonstrates understanding of all aspects of the subject; has a novel, timely question or may look at an old question with a new approach or a new analytical method; makes a prediction; uses appropriate techniques and analyses; has all the right controls; the data are very well done; provides solid answers; may confirm an already known answer; will not necessarily have a huge impact on the field |
| **Acceptable** | Workmanlike; student has done a significant amount of solid work reasonably well; well written, well organized but is a chore to read; is original but not very original and not very exciting; has a few innovative things but little in the way of publishable data; the science is acceptable but is not particularly good science; the concepts are derivative; sets up a problem and answers the question, but the question is not exciting; the literature review is adequate, shows acquaintance with the key papers but does not really discuss what is important about them; is technically adequate; uses good scientific methods; the experiments are reasonably well done; has all the right controls; produces some novel data; adds data to an existing hypothesis; the results are useful but not exciting; may confirm what is already known; is not a particularly meaningful contribution; is not going to have a great impact on the field |

*(continues)*

**TABLE 7.4.**
**Continued**

| Quality | Characteristics |
|---------|-----------------|
| **Unacceptable** | The quality of the science is not good; shows a lack of depth of understanding of the project; does not make an original contribution; the writing is bad, has no storyline or argument, has spelling and grammatical errors; does not have a good question; the experiments are poorly done and poorly analyzed; the quality of the data collection and statistical analyses is poor; may have engaged in unethical behavior; the data are false or fudged; the data are not interpreted well; makes too much of the results; draws invalid conclusions from the data; does not (cannot) explain what has been done or what it all means |

to you as the expert. . . . If they could actually figure out . . . by the end of their graduate work that they know more about this topic than anyone else, they're creating the knowledge that will ultimately go into textbooks. That self-taught knowledge is the most valuable form of learning. They produce the best thesis.

In keeping with the idea of the student becoming the expert, the faculty characterized outstanding dissertations as ones from which they "learned some new stuff," and as ones that cause them to think, "Well, why didn't I think of that, because that is going to really change the way people think about this."

Outstanding dissertations may also be a function of luck. A student might be in a new field at the right time or might stumble on a very significant new discovery. One participant cautioned about the need to distinguish between the body of work and the actual document. He noted that a student can have a middle-of-the-road dissertation but do very outstanding work, or a student can have an outstanding dissertation that is based on work that is not as outstanding.

Although outstanding dissertations typically contain major discoveries and lead to papers that "stand the test of time" and "define what we now recognize as a field five or ten years later," students who write outstanding dissertations do not always fare as well. One participant asserted that "there is no correlation between that document and the success of the student." Another participant in a different focus group observed:

It's almost [like] you've exhausted the student's abilities and resources in that effort. . . . I've had a couple of students who I really thought, based on their dissertation research, had the potential of becoming leaders in the field, and I think they squandered that opportunity. . . . I don't know whether it's our fault that somehow extinguished their passion, but they've never risen back up to that level again. It's just been a kind of downward spiral.

Finally, one participant defined outstanding dissertations with respect to the impact they had on his receipt of grants. "The three most outstanding from my lab, each of them almost singularly was responsible for me to get a new grant. . . . They were really pace setting and opened up a new area for research. . . . In each of these cases . . . [it] gave me fuel for another grant."

## Very Good

The very good dissertation is the most common dissertation. The quality of the science can be described with the same descriptors as the outstanding dissertation. It is just less original and less significant. One participant noted, "It's probably more a reflection of the project . . . than the actual document." It "is something that other people have worked on and there's something known, but they still make an original advance on it." In other words, the science is good normal science. The results can be published in a good journal. The article(s) will be read by a number of people and cited in a moderate way.

## Acceptable

The acceptable dissertation is "sufficient" for the award of the Ph.D. It contains a few innovative things, but, in general, it has a paucity of publishable data. The research may confirm that what happens in one organism happens in another. It may be a "fishing expedition," as illustrated in the following example:

You might grow some neurons in a dish, throw in a hundred different growth factors and do a lot of work and say that some work and some don't. There is no hypothesis about mechanism, but you've produced a large amount of novel data. That would not be a particularly meaningful contribution, but it would get you a thesis.

Students who produce acceptable dissertations have proven themselves capable of independent thought and endeavor, and can write and speak. However, the dissertation often displays little enthusiasm for the field, and is often a chore for the student to write and for the committee to read. Readers tend to feel a little uncomfortable about the dissertation, "Is this really enough here? Is this analyzed sufficiently?" They tend to pass it with "more relief than excitement."

One participant opined that the difference between an outstanding and acceptable dissertation is a function of how the student thinks: "It's all in their intellectual abilities." By contrast, faculty in another focus group indicated that "a lot of times the student is not necessarily at fault." The student may have had "bad mentorship," "bad luck," a "bad" or "very difficult" project, or a project that gets "all negative results."

One focus group found the acceptable category to be "a tricky one," one that borders on "whether we sign off on it." The following remarks provide insight into the politics and social dynamics of dissertation committees:

> My choice of whether to rank a piece of work as acceptable or not can be highly influenced by my colleagues in that room. There are probably a couple borderline theses where my gut was telling me this is not work that I would want to sign off on. But when we start going around the table at the end of the defense, and people say "It's not the best I've seen, but this person has a position in a community college or something," and they're going ahead, it talks me into saying, "OK, check off on it." Things enter into my decision other than just the quality of the work. The environment in which the decision was made has, in the past, a couple of times, influenced my decision.

### Unacceptable

Unacceptable dissertations, like outstanding ones, are rare. Students who produce unacceptable work are typically stopped or "weeded out" before they get to the dissertation phase of their education, usually with qualifying exams. According to the faculty, mechanisms are in place to prevent unacceptable dissertations from coming to defense, and, in rare instances where they do come to defense, the faculty typically blame the advisor and/or the committee:

> A student should be showing the thesis to the people on the committee [while he or she is working on it], and if it is unacceptable in some way—

and the committee is doing its job—they give feedback to that student so that the student knows it is not ready to be defended and cannot be defended successfully. So, essentially you don't let an unacceptable thesis come to a meeting. . . . If you have a thesis that fails at the meeting, then you have an advisory committee that hasn't done its job.

Sometimes a dissertation fails because the student refuses to listen to his or her committee:

> His major professor had been telling him all along that he needed to do some things differently and he needed to talk to his committee, neither of which he did. . . . He wrote some chapters and we were saying, "This is not good enough. . . . You need to go back and get more information."

Sometimes students produce unacceptable dissertations because they run "out of steam," or do not have the "perseverance," "understanding," or "personality" that it "takes to be a researcher." In very rare and unfortunate situations, a dissertation becomes unacceptable because some other research group comes out with a paper that "blows away the assumptions on which that work was based."

Faculty in one focus group discussed the difference between bad writing and bad science:

> If someone is a really poor writer but has [an] awesome grasp of methods and results and data analysis, what do you do? [Do] you say, "You've got to write this all over"? Or do you say, "Well, this is acceptable even though the writing is poor"?

To which his colleague responded, "Usually the advisor rewrites it for them. . . . That's usually what happens."

Committees do not like to fail dissertations, and in borderline cases they appear to seek excuses to pass them. Said one faculty member, "I have been on thesis committees where the committee has sort of looked around at each other and I asked, 'How far are we are willing to compromise our integrity?'" Faculty also take factors other than the actual product before them into consideration:

> *Participant*: We just had a woman, her husband had been in Europe for a year. . . . She had hoped to finish six months ago, and we persuaded her

to extend it to a year to make a better thesis. It still wasn't perfect, but our feeling was that was about as far as we could push, and the best product for the effort. To make it better would have taken longer. These other human-aspect factors figure into it.

*Participant*: I think it is fair to say that a substantial part of the judgment about a dissertation is based on the committees' actual feeling about this person as a scientist rather than on the objective document.

## The Components of a Biology Dissertation

The biology faculty did not particularly like having to discuss the quality of individual components of the dissertation, and one focus group did not discuss them. In general, the biology faculty did not conceive of dissertations in terms of the components presented in the matrix (see Table 1.2). They asserted that dissertations were not constructed in such a linear way. And they said that they did not evaluate each component individually. One participant, who seemed to be thinking about the essay dissertation noted, "In a way, each chapter is going to have methods, results, theory, literature reviews. The introduction, title, and the discussion and conclusion wrap it up." On the positive side, one participant who was critical of the matrix said, "I think what we talk about in terms of components of these things have important aspects that have to be containable. The more you do the right thing the right way and analyze it correctly, et cetera, et cetera, the better your chances of having a very good to outstanding thesis." Despite their dislike for the matrix, as a group, the biology faculty managed to discuss all but three cells in the matrix: very good introduction, theory, and discussion and conclusion. Below we explore the characteristics of the components of the biology dissertation (see Table 7.A in the appendix of this chapter) and what the faculty said about them.

### Introduction

The introduction to a biology dissertation should set the stage for the research and tie the whole thing together. It should state the problem, provide a context for and lay out the research questions, indicate the importance of the study, and provide a road map for the rest of the dissertation. The introduction is often written after the discussion and conclusion because it "evolves depending on how the dissertation matures." One participant indicated that he read introductions to bring himself "up to what is the question," and was not usually critical of them.

For one participant, an outstanding introduction displayed "an uncommon feeling in people so young for the history of the topic and what's an important question and why is it important." Another said that if it's really well written one would think, " 'Why didn't I think of that? Why didn't I formulate these questions? Because they are so obviously the next questions that need to be asked." By contrast, one participant did not think that there was much difference between an outstanding and a very good introduction; rather, for him, what made the dissertation outstanding, very good, or even acceptable was the quality of the work in the middle chapters.

Acceptable introductions were characterized by one participant as not showing "any depth beyond here's what I'm going to work on from the lab I'm working in." Faculty in another focus group attributed the quality of an acceptable introduction to the student's intellectual abilities:

> *Participant*: An acceptable student can't move from a very good introduction to an outstanding introduction because they don't have the intellectual capacity to put the thoughts together where describing makes it a pleasure to read through their thoughts.

> *Participant*: It's acceptable at that point because you recognize the student as a highly capable student, but not one with that stroke of intellectual originality that allows them to identify that field in the introduction. Maybe they are not capable of putting that statement of the boundaries of the field into the introduction unless the committee tells them what that is and writes it in for them.

## Literature Review

In the traditional biology dissertation, the literature review is typically part of the introductory chapter. In the essay dissertation, each substantive chapter starts with an introduction and literature review. The literature review should not just be a summary of the literature, rather it should connect the literature to the problem being developed and provide a context for the problem by synthesizing the history and controversies of the field and build a story that leads to the hypotheses.

The quality of the literature review is defined less by the quantity of the literature cited than by the quality. As one participant put it, "You could cover everything that's been published, mention every paper published in the field, but the difference between outstanding and unacceptable is your ability to know which [papers] are important and relevant."

An outstanding literature review, said one participant, reads like a good review article and causes the reader to say, "My God, this is a good review article. It should be published." One participant noted that outstanding literature reviews should sometimes include literature from outside the English language. He lamented, "I'm amazed, somehow we've lost the sense that work published in a foreign language is valuable."

For the outstanding and very good literature reviews, faculty rarely have to recommend that the student read something. Whereas on the first draft of an acceptable dissertation proposal, there are a lot of places where faculty write, "You need to read so and so." Students who write acceptable literature reviews were characterized as not being able to discriminate between a good paper and a bad one, and as taking the literature at face value. "If it's published it must be true." By contrast, students who write unacceptable literature reviews often lack an appreciation "that there are two hundred years of scientists thinking about this subject." They also fail to cite important papers, about which one participant commented, "And that is a strike whether they knew about it or not. They should have known about it. If they did know about it, they should have looked at it."

## *Theory*

Some fields of biology are more theory driven than others. Indeed, the field of cell biology was described as not having a theory about how the cell worked. Theories in biology can range from narrative to mathematical or statistical expression of ideas. When theory is present as a driving force in a dissertation, it may be included as part of the introduction. It should be linked to the research question(s) and help the student select appropriate methods. A theory-driven dissertation will test things rather than just describe them.

One participant described theory as "that ethereal level of thinking that takes the observations way beyond the actual observations." However, another participant noted that, "A lot of students in biology pick some theory . . . and test it," and commented that that approach "is not outstanding." Some students fail to realize that there is a theory undergirding their work, about which a participant remarked, "You can see by their methods that they just picked what was in the cookbook. They really don't understand what they're doing. They can push a button and get the results, but they can't explain why they are doing it, and it's not really connected to the predictions of what they think they are studying." Another participant felt that, in most cases when the theory component is unacceptable, it is usually not the theory that is the problem, rather it is either the quality of the writing or the students have misinterpreted theory papers they have read. About the latter, one of his colleagues responded, "If it happens, it's the mentor's fault."

## Methods

In their discussion of the methods component, there was some blurring between the methods students used to do their research and how students wrote about them. Even though one participant stated that "in science, methods are extremely important because the results often depend on how you did it," for the most part, the faculty did not see much distinction between an outstanding, very good, or acceptable methods component because there are "fewer degrees of freedom" across these levels.

The biology faculty defined the purpose of the methods component as allowing someone "to replicate exactly what you did." As long as students explained their methods in sufficient detail so that someone else could figure out exactly what they did, the faculty were satisfied. In fact, as the following comments indicate, biology faculty typically do not pay much, if any, attention to the methods component: "I don't pay much attention to the methods section." "I often . . . flip over through the methods, but not necessarily pour over each section. . . . It's not that important." "I read the methods section for my own students just to make sure they haven't made a mistake. But students from other labs, I usually skip the methods section." "I read it looking for holes, for things they've omitted." "Unless it's a new method, the ones I read, the methods are cookbook."

Although the faculty said there was not much difference between outstanding and acceptable methods, they did provide additional insight into outstanding methods. First, the outstanding student, unlike the acceptable one, really understands the methods, and it shows. For instance, "There are a lot of methods that students use. They [can] run a machine and they really don't understand [how it works]. The really outstanding student can give you the pros and cons about how much to trust the data, with precision and accuracy." Second, the best ones attack the problem from all sides. For instance, in cell or developmental biology the student might approach the problem by genetic, chemical, and molecular means. Third, the student might develop a new technique or new way of doing something that leads to a breakthrough. However, another participant in this focus group raised the point that students could come up with a totally brand new method based on ideas that weren't their own, but rather their mentor's. They "just had the tenacity and the careful hands to get it to work out."

## Data Analysis/Results

Data analysis and results involve taking raw material and trying to make sense out of it. Like methods, the biology faculty did not see a great degree of variation between outstanding and acceptable data analysis and results, because, as they said, the analysis and results are "correctable." Indeed, a participant in another focus group stated, "theses might not look so much different than if I'm giving them lots and lots of input [because] that ultimately leads to the same end product."

Despite the limited degree of variability between the passing levels, the faculty did identify ways in which they were different. The main difference between outstanding and the other levels was described as follows: "It's the proactive students who are outstanding because they are taking an active, hands-on approach to looking at the data, noticing things, organizing it into patterns, and thinking about what that means." The very good students were described as being able to do the results or data analysis as well as the mentor but were also characterized (along with acceptable students) as being less independent and having more advisor involvement:

> They come to me and say, "How should I do this?" I'm spending a relatively larger amount of time sitting down at the microscope with them and saying, "You might think about this or you might do it this way, or you might do it like this." So the end product might be very much the same, the difference is that I've contributed a lot more in some cases than others.

Acceptable students were further described as requiring lots of "handholding." The novel insights of their dissertations were said to "have come from the mentor or someone else."

By contrast, unacceptable students were characterized as very passive, as coming to the advisor about once a week and asking, "How do you think I should do this?" about which other participants in that focus group commented, if the student needs that much help from the mentor, he or she is not "going to be able to make it as an independent scientist," "you can see they are not ever going to be able to acquire that skill." Other faculty gave examples of inappropriate analyses or presentation of results:

> *Participant:* Their data are not distributed normally, but they use parametric statistics. You have to say, "Stop. Your data don't fit the assumptions underlying this statistical test. . . . You have to go back and see that your data are not normally distributed. Either transform them or if they can't be transformed, then use a different type of symbol system.

> *Participant:* I saw a graph once that had two points and they commented [that] it was a straight-line relationship.

The faculty also discussed dissertations that were "data dumps," and ones where students reported on failed experiments or presented "figure after figure" without providing any context.

### Discussion and Conclusion

Unlike the earlier parts of the dissertation where the advisor was often described as making a big contribution to the dissertation, the discussion and conclusion component was characterized as the creative part, the place where the student has a chance to draw independent conclusions about the project and show what it means in the larger perspective of science. The faculty felt that it was "very difficult for young people" to understand the importance of what they had done, and that doing so was one of the "key things to making outstanding dissertations."

Outstanding conclusions were characterized as displaying a depth of understanding that goes beyond the advisor's. One participant summed up the outstanding discussion and conclusion as follows:

> One that is truly outstanding is one that after reporting on whether the hypotheses were accepted or rejected, it provides new insight into what was being studied. And furthermore, it may go a further step to say now what we have to do is the following. They tell you which path to go down or which hypotheses should be tested next. So there is a person who is directing the field and providing really new insight, not just yes or no, I accept my hypotheses or I reject them.

Students often end up writing acceptable or unacceptable conclusions because they have "run out of steam," are "tired" or "burned out." Their advisors often have to remind them go back to the discussion in the introduction about the significance of the research and tell the reader about the extent to which their results "bear upon these." Students may also write poor-quality conclusions because of time constraints that result from having taken a postdoctoral position before finishing their dissertation. Another reason for poor-quality conclusions has to do with mentoring:

> There are some mentors that never let their students go, they're always there. And because . . . it was never demanded upon them to think for themselves, when finally asked to [come up with conclusions], they don't have any, because they weren't mentored to do that.

## Notes

1. For information on the source of these data, see chapter 1, note 5.

# Appendix

## TABLE 7.A.

### The Components of a Biology Dissertation and Their Characteristics at Different Quality Levels

| Components | Quality levels | | | |
|---|---|---|---|---|
| | Outstanding | Very good | Acceptable | Unacceptable |
| Introduction | Thorough, interesting, well written in an engaging style; expresses independent ideas; identifies an important problem in the field; demonstrates good knowledge of relevant literature; creates a context for the question; provides a historical overview and a clear description of the cutting edge of the field; develops a compelling rationale for why the question is important; makes clear how the research fits in with what has happened before and how it will push the boundary; leads the reader directly to the hypotheses; lays out implications of the research in a clear and compelling fashion; ties everything together; lays out a road map for the rest of the dissertation | — | Shows some evidence that student knows what he or she is supposed to be doing; makes a case for the problem and justifies the work but lacks depth; does not put the problem in proper context; does not fully comprehend the nuances of the various arguments and controversies that shaped the field; lacks perspective on the field; does not establish the boundaries of the field; does not build the case for the hypotheses; has not told the reader what he or she needs to know | Hastily prepared and poorly written; bad grammar; confusing; no argument, just a bunch of paragraphs strung together; does not express any independent ideas; does not show sufficient knowledge of the area; student does not really understand why student is doing what student said he or she is doing |

*(continues)*

**TABLE 7.A.**
Continued

| Components | Quality levels | | | |
| --- | --- | --- | --- | --- |
| | Outstanding | Very good | Acceptable | Unacceptable |
| **Literature review** | Comprehensive; thorough; up to date; shows superior, discriminating, evaluative knowledge of the literature; synthesizes the field; brings the literature together like a good review article; adds own insights; cites only important, relevant information, knows what to put in and what to leave out; makes it clear that student is widely read and has read things that are not cited; deeply historical, covers the history of the concept and the controversies; connects the literature to the theme that is being developed in the dissertation; explains why the work is important and where it comes from; helps build the argument leading up to the hypotheses; may include papers the advisor has not seen or read; may include papers not written in English | Knows what the problem is and what has been done; discriminates between important and informative papers and unimportant and uninformative ones | Not in full command of the literature; cites all the right papers but does put them in the right context; misses important papers or includes a lot of irrelevant ones; ne-judgment or discrimination between key papers and poor papers, treats all papers as equal; discusses every paper in succession; does not really understand the question the paper was asking; does not use the literature to push boundaries | Not thorough, less synthetic, and limited in scope; nebulous and confused; lacks knowledge of the literature; does not cover all the different points of the field; neglects half the field; misses key papers; does not seem to understand what the questions are and what is important and what is not; does not credit or appreciate the history that went before it; incomplete survey of the literature, or the survey is adequate to thorough but there is no clear statement of the bounds of the field; just description, almost a listing of the literature |

| Components | Quality levels | | | |
|---|---|---|---|---|
| | Outstanding | Very good | Acceptable | Unacceptable |
| Theory | Superior presentation of how the theory relates to the problem; links the question with the theory; explains why the research is going in one direction and not another; is innovative, comes up with new concepts or new mathematical or statistical applications, invents theoretical representations of the data; takes the observations way beyond the actual observations; has implications that go beyond the specific situation; makes a contribution to theory; develops or adds to existing theory, revises or comes up with a new variation of a theory; is insightful; is completely inventive or original; changes the way people will do research and approach data | — | Understands theory; uses theory properly and correctly but may need guidance | Is absent; student is unaware of it; misinterprets it; does not understand it; gets it wrong; cannot explain why he or she is using it; methods do not flow from it; student leaps to generalizations based on limited observations |

(continues)

## TABLE 7.A.
### Continued

| Components | Quality levels | | | |
| --- | --- | --- | --- | --- |
| | Outstanding | Very good | Acceptable | Unacceptable |
| **Methods** | Appropriate, inventive, clear; connected to the predictions; laid out in excruciating detail; precisely describes how data were handled; has a lot of detail and attention to detail; provides pros and cons about how much to trust the data with precision and accuracy; applies new methods; comes up with a new method or technique | Complete; comes up with novel ways to use existing techniques | Appropriate to the study; used correctly; explained in sufficient detail so someone can figure out exactly what was done | Leaves things out; not enough detail; misapplied, not used correctly; did not do things that should have been done |

| Components | Quality levels | | | |
| --- | --- | --- | --- | --- |
| | Outstanding | Very good | Acceptable | Unacceptable |
| **Results/data analysis** | Novel insights; notices things and organizes them into patterns; sees things the advisor did not see; connected to and aligned with the hypotheses being tested and other parts of the study; done rigorously and with good controls; has a very strong statistical foundation for the analysis; creative, innovative analytical methods; sophisticated analysis of the data; gets as much out of the data as possible as opposed to just the obvious; sticks to statistically relevant interpretations; unambiguous and clearly presented; good figures and graphs | Analysis is appropriate and done well at a sophisticated level; uses a relatively new analytical technique; results are associated with the problem; writing goes beyond the data in the tables and is not cluttered with extraneous data | Uses the right procedures; analyzes the data correctly in a clear-cut fashion; produces a small amount of modest data; has difficulty making sense of the data; novel insights come from the mentor or someone else | No results; results are ambiguous with respect to the hypotheses; results do not reflect the methods; results come from failed experiments; results are not presented in a succinct and informative way; data dumping; insufficient data; data do not answer the question asked; unable to distinguish between good and bad data and between important and unimportant data; student sees too much in the data; inappropriate or incompetent analysis of the data, data do not fit the assumptions underlying the statistical test; unable to justify the statistical test; analyses are wrong; obvious things are not analyzed; flat out reporting with no context; mentor tells student how to interpret the data |

*(continues)*

**TABLE 7.A.**
Continued

| Components | Quality levels | | | |
| --- | --- | --- | --- | --- |
| | Outstanding | Very good | Acceptable | Unacceptable |
| **Discussion and conclusion** | Creative; flawless writing; brings everything together; student really sees what the data are saying; provides new insights on what was studied and extrapolates on it; identifies new problems and asks more questions; discusses future directions, which path to go down, which hypotheses should be tested next; realizes the importance, significance, and implications of the work and the contribution made; shows what it all means in the larger perspective of science; puts it in a context that goes beyond the science, discusses the broader impacts, says something about the societal importance or what it means to the world at large; opens up a whole new way of thinking about the problem; pushes the discipline further | — | Simple; workmanlike; technical; summarizes the dissertation, draws it all together; simply says whether the hypothesis was accepted or rejected; repeats or recasts the results; conclusions are consistent with the results; does not address the significance or implications of the research; no next steps or suggestions for other kinds of research that might continue this line of reasoning | Inadequate; does not have any conclusions; just a summary of what was already said; student does not have a clue about what he or she did; does not understand the results; does not understand or put results in the broader context; does not know its impact or thinks its impact was far greater than it actually was; does not discuss the implications of the work to the extent that is warranted |

# 8

# THE PHYSICS DISSERTATION

There are 185 Ph.D. programs in physics in the United States that, depending upon the system of classification, award degrees in 9 to 27 subfields that are tracked by various organizations; these programs also confer degrees in several other untracked subfields. Graduate physics programs enroll over 10,000 graduate students (master's and doctoral), and graduate roughly 1,200 new Ph.D.s annually. The median time to degree is 6.9 years. Roughly 60% of new physics Ph.D.s go on to postdoctoral education.[1]

Twenty-five physics faculty at seven universities participated in the focus groups. Five of the departments were Departments of Physics and Astronomy. While most of the participants were physicists, some astronomers participated in two universities' focus groups. (All focus group participants will be referred to as physicists.) The physicists represent a mix of theoretical and experimental programs. Overall, the physics faculty had 520 years of experience, had chaired an estimated 290 dissertations, and had sat on an estimated 790 dissertation committees. The average physics focus group participant had been a professor for 21 years, had chaired 12 dissertations, and had sat on 32 dissertation committees. Below is a summary of the physics focus groups' discussions. Their performance expectations for the dissertation are displayed in the tables. Their supporting discussion is recounted in the text.

## The Purpose of a Physics Dissertation

The physics faculty saw the dissertation as having many purposes (see Table 8.1). They said that the dissertation was only part of the graduate education process and that the Ph.D. program was an important tool for the discipline. One saw the process as an "amplifier":

## TABLE 8.1.
### The Purpose of a Physics Dissertation

To obtain professional training for the future; to learn and to demonstrate the ability to conduct projects independently; to learn how the field functions; to demonstrate expertise in student's area, mastery of the subject matter, and the ability think critically and put student's project work in the context of the field; to convince the committee that the student is able to do certain things independently; to demonstrate the completion of formal academic requirements; is a capstone on the student's research project and training; an opportunity to provide a coherent presentation of the body of work the student has done as a graduate student; a union card to become a member of the research community

> There's only so many hours in my day. If I can have an apprenticeship system, from maybe undergraduates to graduate students, to graduate students doing their dissertation, on to postdocs, the ideas I have and the data I might have access to, bring in a bigger team. So it's an amplifier, it's an amplifier of the research ideas.

Another participant commented, "I think the faculty in our department, probably most, would not be at all . . . interested in having a Ph.D. program if it would not serve their research and the possibility to get grants to make progress in an area."

Some faculty felt that the dissertation was a formality, one that demonstrated that the student had satisfied academic requirements, that "your advisor and your mentors feel you are ready to finish and go on." Indeed, one participant said, "The moment we find the student start having the ability to be able to do independent projects, that's about the time . . . this student can graduate." Another said, "Being able . . . to do [research] without being babied by the advisor is the real goal." A physics professor in Private University's focus group, who felt strongly about the dissertation, highlights the difference between being ABD (all but dissertation) and completing the Ph.D.:

> What I think is a real misperception [is] when you will hear people say, "Well, I have an ABD, 'all but dissertation.'" It seems to me they've missed the real point of the dissertation, which, in my mind, is this demonstration that you can do something coherent, and that you can persevere, schedule, write it up, and in the end get the degree. I think that's what it's

demonstrating as much as the originality, [it's] demonstrating just the ability to stay with this process.

While the physics faculty emphasized the role of the dissertation in becoming an independent researcher, they noted that Ph.D. students typically go on to postdoctoral positions where they "will really try to become truly independent." Like the biology faculty, the physics faculty did not say the purpose of the dissertation was to help the student get a job, though they did see it as a union card for entry into the research community.

## Original Contribution

The physics faculty identified many ways to make an original contribution (see Table 8.2). They agreed that original means "new," but that it does not have to be "significant," "earth shattering," or "change the whole science like Einstein's relativity." One participant noted that "even if it's an original contribution, it could mean you solved a problem and you have told people, 'Just don't go this way anymore because this is just the wrong direction.'" While many felt that the contribution should be "worthy of publication," they recognized that "publishable" does not define "original," but rather sets the standard for it. Others noted that the contribution can be "original and stupid" or "garbage."

Making an original contribution, according to the physicists, is usually

### TABLE 8.2.
### The Nature of an Original Contribution in Physics

Something new in the state of the art of the field that is worthy of publication in the top-ranked journals; something that has not been solved, done, seen, or known before; coming up with new ways of thinking about old ideas; inventing or developing new techniques, computations, statistical procedures, or theoretical descriptions; improving mathematical formulations; pushing the frontier in sensitivity and accuracy of the theory being tested; building something new, such as a small apparatus or a more complex one; making new forms of matter; making measurements that lead to an unexpected answer; closing off an unproductive or incorrect line of research; tying together different experiments or facts in one experiment a function of talent and "requires some determination and intensity and creativity of the student," though sometimes it is a function of "luck." The faculty also noted that students cannot always come up with an original idea. One participant discussed how he got his students started on original research and the problems he has encountered:

> When it comes to original research, the idea is that I've already tried to pick something original when I wrote the grant, so I'm hoping that they are working on an original project. . . . I really try to push the students to really time it themselves, what is original research, [and] not to let the committee decide whether their research was original, but have them demonstrate through their own digging in the literature and defending in their thesis that they have done something that is original. Not leaving it up to the committee to decide whether or not it's original. That's been really tough. Students nowadays seem to think that if it exists on the Web, then it exists. If it doesn't exist [on the Web], then it doesn't. Really getting them to go into the literature and really be familiar with what is out there so that they can really defend that their own work as original has been getting more and more difficult as time goes on.

## Significant Contribution

A significant contribution in physics is an original contribution that advances the understanding of the field (see Table 8.3). Most of the time it is a new idea and "very seldom" an "incredible discovery," though it could be a new tool like a machine or a computer program "from which then someone else would get a Nobel Prize." One participant was not sure a contribution had to be original in order to be considered significant. He said that "if there is an important experiment—like . . . you went and actually just repeated

**TABLE 8.3.**
**The Nature of a Significant Contribution in Physics**

A nontrivial, original, publishable contribution; advances the understanding of the field; raises questions about current knowledge; makes predictions; answers existing questions; explains experimental facts; points to new directions for research; is of interest to people outside the community; has an impact on other people's research almost exactly the same thing, that might still be considered significant even though it is not original." However, he may have been talking about physics research in general and not dissertation research in particular, as faculty typically said that a pure replication was not acceptable for a dissertation; students had to do something original. Another participant extended the issue by stating, "It may be original and significant, but then the question is whether it's correct." Cold fusion comes to mind.

Significance is determined by the community and the impact the work has on it. As one participant stated:

> To be significant, I can't decide that, and I don't think the department can decide that. I think it has to be my subdiscipline within the field that really has to say that this is a hot topic. Or even through conferences. It doesn't really have to be through the journals. . . . It's when the outside community is interested in that person's work, that's when I know it's risen to the ideal.

He also stated that because all the graduate students in his department work on faculty's sponsored research projects, "By definition . . . if the advisor has gotten that funding, it has the stamp of significance."

Timescale plays an important role in the community's assessment of significance. An idea can be "too early." "Something could be significant 50 years from now or 30 years from now and something can be significant five months from now." One physicist noted that in fields like particle physics and nuclear physics that have collaborations of 300 to 400 people and "wrap-up" times of 10 to 15 years, the meaning of original and significant for Ph.D. work "just [isn't] the same . . . as what we usually associate with physics research." He went on to say:

> there is other research involved in what kind of techniques work to make a certain device perform at the level that . . . is required to do the science. So as you go along, you have to redefine your goals . . . for a Ph.D. One cannot make a general statement that it has to lead to a publishable result in the research area . . . For that reason, often we require that one has to publish in the instrumentation journals and compare some instruments and methods. . . . That is also not a measure for how successful you are. People can generate internal memos to the collaboration that have much more impact than a publication in an instrumentation journal.

One participant discussed what people needed to know and do in order to advance the understanding of the field:

> To answer what is significant in the field, first you have to understand what are the outstanding questions. Or it could be that the work actually raises questions that were not there before. So you have to understand what is the understanding of what is the state of the field and you have to advance it beyond that by either raising questions about the current knowledge, or answering questions that exist, or pointing into new directions of research that haven't been considered before.

Finally, the physics faculty noted that there are levels of significance, but they did not elaborate on them.

## The Dissertation as a Whole

Students in some physics programs may submit an "essay" dissertation, which consists of three papers that have been submitted or accepted for publication along with a "binder" chapter. However, the majority of physics dissertations conform to the traditional, extended-argument style. Physics dissertations are generally either experimental or theoretical. Physics faculty typically view the experimental dissertation as a manual for the next graduate student in the laboratory. Consequently, it is expected to contain details about techniques, apparatus, methods, and analysis that would not usually be found in a journal article. Below we explore the characteristics of different quality traditional and essay physics dissertations (see Table 8.4) and what the physics faculty had to say about them.

### Outstanding

Outstanding physics dissertations are rare and contain some element of "breakthrough." They are based on outstanding research and thought processes, and have "a great body of work," about which one participant stated was a "necessary condition to writing an excellent dissertation." Outstanding dissertations show mastery of the subject matter and contain ideas that are original and significant. The quality and care put into the measurement techniques, the analyses, and the statistical methods instill confidence in the results. The results are useful, that is, they open up something new or advance a field or subfield. Outstanding dissertations are "beautifully" written,

## TABLE 8.4.
### The Characteristics of Different Quality Dissertations in Physics

| Quality | Characteristics |
| --- | --- |
| **Outstanding** | Is based on outstanding research; written beautifully and coherently; ideas flow at a high level of sophistication; puts things in context; addresses a scientific audience that is broader than the student's narrow discipline; exhibits very mature, high-quality, original, independent thinking; explains something everybody knows in a very insightful way; opens new vistas for understanding some element of the subject matter; uses a method from a different area; provides a good incremental solution or makes significant progress on a problem; solves a problem; contains some element of a breakthrough such as a new discovery or a new technique for collecting or analyzing data; develops a model that explains the data; synthesizes two or more separate things; makes connections to, or contains ideas or predictions that are transferable to other areas; makes a contribution to and advances the field or subfield |
| **Very good** | A large body of solid work with a lot of very nice results; is original, but does not contain a real breakthrough or open up the field; writing is organized and flows nicely; has a coherent argument; displays mastery of the subject matter but puts it in a less clear perspective; the style needs some polishing; may use a lot of buzz words or terms that are not directly related to the project; student may not understand all the possible connections and may not explain the most important ones as well as possible |
| **Acceptable** | Acceptable amount of solid work that does not go much beyond what is required but shows that the student has mastered his or her apprentice-physicist role; uninteresting and uninspiring; exhibits very little originality or imagination; presented clearly, but style and content may be far apart; the English is sometimes very bad; demonstrates that they can take data, analyze them, and do calculations using the same techniques that have been used before; results are solid but not exciting; lacks broad understanding of the field; student has not made all the connections he or she could; marginally advances the field |
| **Unacceptable** | The body of work is inadequate and not of sufficient quality to be publishable; just stapling papers together without providing background; the problem is not original; completely misunderstands some very fundamental physics; arguments are wrong; uses the same methods to redo an experiment; the results are wrong, substandard, or already well known; does not advance the field |

which, according to one participant, is "more than just a writing skill." They provide the reader with "the background of what has been done, why it is important, and explain it in a way so that an advanced graduate student in the field should be able to understand it." In reading the dissertation,

> you basically have a glimpse into the mind of the author. You can see how this person is thinking. They just basically go from one step to the other explaining what you need to know in order to understand the work that they've done. It's like reading a good novel.

The faculty said that "excellent people make excellent dissertations" and felt that it was very hard to separate excellent dissertations from excellent students. Excellent students were described as being "very mature," as being "almost at the level with the professor—thinking independently and talking about it and explaining it." They are people who, when they meet a problem, can make significant progress on it.

One participant felt that his "opinion" on an outstanding dissertation was "totally useless because the thesis results from a collaborative effort between the advisor and the grad student," implying that the advisor's and the student's contributions could not be separated. By contrast, another participant characterized a specific dissertation he advised as outstanding "for the simple reason that he got out of it as much or more than what I put into it."

Outstanding dissertations may also derive from "fortunate circumstances." "Somebody can get lucky." They could "just happen to hit at the right time while taking data."

### Very Good

The very good dissertation is "what we try to achieve." It is "what you should really expect of . . . students." This expectation includes the student having analyzed the problem, reflected on it, considered other possibilities, as well as having good results. The student also has to present a coherent argument. "It is not sufficient just to do the work, because if you cannot communicate at some level then, sorry." In addition, the very good dissertation "could be and should be submitted to journals."

### Acceptable

The acceptable dissertation is "not earth shaking." The research is "not terribly exciting, but, hey, it was not terrible." It is something faculty look at and say, "Boy, they could have done a lot more with that" or "there was so much more that they could have explored." Sometimes a dissertation ends up being acceptable because the experiment "just doesn't work." But in the end, "it's not wrong and it's not stolen." The work can be published, but it will have little to no impact on the field.

One participant thought that a lot of dissertations were acceptable. Other participants distinguished between what most would consider solidly acceptable and "barely acceptable." Barely acceptable was defined as "epsilon over the threshold." It is work that "no one will go through the pain of using . . . and it's not interesting."

Faculty in one focus group said that acceptable "almost never has to do with the writing of the thesis." They said that if the writing is substandard, "It's very common to say, 'This needs to be rewritten.' Then we will provisionally pass it on the assumption that it is satisfactory."

Most students who write acceptable dissertations were said to be functioning close to their capabilities, "but their capabilities are really not that high." They are often "spoon fed." Their advisors spend a huge amount of time and effort trying to get them to "come up to speed." Ultimately, "everyone is tired." The faculty's attitude is, "They've spent their time. They've done something. They've provided a service. So, it is Ph.D. work in that sense." The faculty noted that people in the "acceptable' category sometimes do "okay," not necessarily as physicists, "but they find they can have a contribution in the field."

Some students who write acceptable dissertations are capable of writing excellent dissertations, but get waylaid by the "pressure at the end" or funding issues. Others "see their future someplace else," or get a job in industry "nine-tenths of the way through" and say, "Fuck the degree."

## Unacceptable

Unacceptable dissertations "should not, cannot, must not happen." Usually unacceptable means that "you should develop something a little bit more." Though a less charitable participant said if it is not acceptable, "It's not a thesis. . . . It's in the trash."

When confronted with an unacceptable dissertation, the focus group faculty either blame the advisor or defer to him. They said that it was "irresponsible" for an advisor to allow a student to be in a doctoral program for three or more years and then to decide that "there is no way you can cross the threshold of becoming acceptable." If this happens, "the advisor is unacceptable." Alternatively, if the dissertation has "passed the judgment of the advisor" and if the advisor is "deemed to go to bat for the thesis," then the faculty on the student's committee will pass the student.

In rare cases where a student fails, it is either because the student does not really understand what he or she has done or because the student ignores his or her advisor's advice. Lack of understanding was characterized as not being able to "explain in a little breadth" to committee members what the dissertation meant. One participant gave an example of a case where "the advisor had been working with the student for months trying to get him to read this or that to try to correct his arguments and the student just said he didn't understand those things, but he still was trying to make the arguments."

Two faculty gave examples of students who ignored their advisor's advice. One said, "I would make my . . . corrections and the student would refuse to put the corrections in." Another said, "This happened where the supervisor and Ph.D. student had a different idea about the dissertation, and the Ph.D. student said 'I'm ignoring your advice, I'm going to do this thesis and I'm going to take my chances.'"

Finally, the physicists noted that unlike the humanities and the social sciences, where occasionally a student may fail because the student and the advisor have an intellectual disagreement over a controversial theory, this "virtually does not happen" in physics. This is because most physics students are working on projects that have defined goals that do not encourage the development of controversy.

## The Components of a Physics Dissertation

The matrix of components of the physics dissertation (see Table 1.2) was far less objectionable to the physics faculty than it was to faculty in other disciplines. "In general," the physicists found the matrix to be "a pretty good framework for a physics dissertation." They "didn't see any components that should be missing from this" or "things [that] should be there." However, faculty in several focus groups noted that the structure of the theory dissertation was different from an experimental one. In particular, they said that in the theory dissertation, theory and methods are combined. One focus group had a brief discussion about how the template "of what our thing looks like" differs from subfield to subfield, and from student to student. However, they agreed that "you do need an introduction, a conclusion, and a couple of middle chapters."

Despite the general concordance on the matrix, there were some objections. One participant did not like the rigid quality categories. He and a colleague said that quality was a "matter of degree," almost like a "continuous scale." Another participant did like not the idea of putting "this format around the whole thing and saying, 'OK, to be good it has to have X, Y, and Z, and make a formula.'" A third participant objected to the focus on the "written part." He said, "The written document makes me think higher or lower of the person, but it's only a piece of the evaluation of the document. It's an element."

Three focus groups did not discuss the components of the physics dissertation. The ones that did, managed to say something about all but four cells of the matrix: very good introduction, theory, and methods, and unacceptable discussion and conclusion. Below we explore the characteristics of the components of the physics dissertation (see Table 8.A in the appendix to this chapter) and what the faculty said about them.

## Introduction

The introduction to a physics dissertation motivates the work, explains the research, puts it in perspective, and tells why it is important or significant. It typically includes the literature review, but it is not an introduction to the field. Rather it is "like" a summary of the thesis up front," because "if a committee member is too busy [to read the whole dissertation], the committee member could read the introduction and walk into the thesis [defense] and have a very good feeling about what is going to be presented." One participant commented that "it's extremely difficult to write a good introduction" and that he had "almost never" seen a student who could really write a good one because "it's essentially like an extended abstract." An experimentalist noted that the introduction to an experimental dissertation covers the theory. A theorist noted that he looks at the introduction of a theoretical dissertation to see whether the student understands the experimental data.

The outstanding introduction achieves the "objective of putting this body of work into the context of the field." It talks a little bit about "where the different parts of the dissertation are going to lead. Like, in chapter 3, we'll discuss this, then in chapter 4, we'll [discuss something else]." One participant said that after reading a "very compelling introduction . . . you understand the full import of why the thesis is done."

The acceptable introduction "doesn't make clear why that person's spent five years on that area."

> They don't know the background. They have heard of the background, but they don't understand the connections and they don't know how to really make/build them in a way which is strong. . . . They'll build links, sometimes to everything, even wrong results, because they feel like that's putting [it] into context.

## Literature Review

To the extent that physics dissertations have a formal literature review, it is part of the introduction. However, the literature should be "woven through-out all the chapters," as appropriate. Students should reference the specific topics under discussion and the references "must be directly related to the argument." If the reference is not "crucial" to the argument, one participant said the student should instead reference recent review articles that are. Another participant commented that "you have to cite the people you might want to get a postdoc from." One physicist shared his views on how students handled references:

> I think all students really end up with two or maybe three piles of papers of references. There's this pile that they essentially have memorized, which they know very, very well. It's usually a dozen or something like that. Then there's this other pile that's maybe four dozen or something, which they've actually read pretty carefully and they know more or less what was in them. Then there's this giant pile over here with things that are largely irrelevant, but they're part of the field. So, maybe they do end up with around fifty really good references that are of some value.

The outstanding literature review demonstrates that the student "really, really" understands the key references, where they fit, and why they are important. It is written by students, who "on their own initiative" read the relevant literature and make the effort to find out if they have an "original, unique perspective." The "best" students "study review articles carefully for their good style and also for giving that very broad view of setting their project in perspective." The outstanding literature review is very important for the next student in the lab and is one that the advisor will use as a reference. One participant described what he likes to see in an outstanding literature review:

> If they have read the literature and really understand the literature that's out there, they can come up with some very simple examples to try to create this hook into someone that doesn't have that much of a background. Then I want them to try to develop either a simple model or try to explain some other people's experiments and that is an entrée into the thesis. . . . It says here's a general way to think about the field and when you are doing that, you reference some of the more important papers that are out there that develop that point of view. . . . [They] take a very large body of literature and synthesize that into an entrée into the field.

By contrast, an unacceptable literature review is one where students cite "chapter and verse of things they don't really understand," and one in which students repeatedly cite "the same 15 to 20 papers" their advisor gave them and miss "the other thousand that they should have read a long time ago."

## Theory

Both the theoretical and the experimental physics dissertation have to have, or be informed by, theory, though faculty's expectations differ for the two types of dissertations. The standards for theory in a theoretical dissertation are much higher than for theory in an experimental dissertation. For the theoretical dissertation, the theory has to be "new and original and significant." For the experimental dissertation, it could just be "a summary of relevant theories," about which one participant remarked, "Basically, we open up the theory paper and copy out the relevant parts. Maybe you add a little bit to it, but not much more than that." The relevant parts of the theories do, however, need to be explained with respect to the experiment, "there must be some linkage."

How much theory goes into an experimental dissertation is often a function of the student's abilities. Some students are "quite confident theoretically." They "can actually do some original analysis, some original theory, and analyze their experimental results." According to one participant,

> This is where the thesis advisor has to look at the abilities of a given student and also the [student's] interest and try to make the decision about how

much theoretical work, original theoretical work and experimental [work] the student should do. The gamut ranges from no theoretical work at all . . . just showing a figure or a line, if there's one, that comes from a calculation [and] deciding it properly, all the way to actually doing/making a theoretical calculation on the student's own. I think that in the case of nuclear physics, I think the experimentalist can do a variety of amounts of theory. Some experimentalists do no theory at all. Some of them are more than half theorist.

In discussing different quality theory components, the faculty focused mainly on the experimental dissertation (see Table 8.A, p. 162). The participants in one focus group said that they could "tell whether the person is good or not" by whether the student could describe the theory behind the "experimental part." The best students know the context for the experiment and the principles behind it. They know what model has been proposed and how their experiment tests the model and answers the question. Participants in another focus group noted that in experimental dissertations, there are actually two parts to the theory, and how a student handles the second part distinguishes the outstanding dissertation:

*Participant 1*: There is explaining the theory as theory. You need to understand that. There's also another part where you take the theory and you adapt it to the actual experiment that you're doing. It's not always obvious that the theory applies to your experiment, and you have to show that it actually does. That's the part that is hardest to do. In a really outstanding thesis, you can see somebody take theory and say it doesn't exactly apply to what I'm doing, so it has to be changed slightly to make it work. This is the most critical part and [inaudible] part that very often doesn't exist.

*Participant 2*: Very, very, very few people can do that.

*Participant 3*: Yeah, very few people can actually take an existing theory and say, "Well, in my special case we have to modify it this way." That really requires command of the theory and that's going to be outstanding.

Acceptable theory is theory that is understood and used appropriately and yields correct physical information. By contrast, unacceptable is theory that is described minimally, "like a one-sentence level." Students whose theoretical work is unacceptable, show "no understanding of theory or relevance of experimental theory."

## *Methods*

The physics faculty want to see "a nice, coherent description of method," one that provides enough detail so that they can understand what the method is, but does not "go into such gory detail that I can't see the forest for the trees." Just as the biologists felt that there were few degrees of freedom for methods, similarly one physicist asserted that there was "only one acceptable [quality] level,"—the level that "an intelligent graduate student can read . . . and then carry on from." According to this participant,

> A thesis should be something that would be almost like an instruction to a beginning graduate student, a manual about how a certain type of research can be done. . . . You don't have to spell out every single step, but it should be enough that an intelligent student can fill in the blanks and figure out what/how to do things and what are the important steps that are needed to solve or attack a certain physical problem.

One participant opined that there were two criteria for outstanding: "elegance of conception" and "optimally sufficient."

> One is just what I call "elegance of conception," whether it's in theory—you have an entirely new mathematical approach to solve the problem just because you figured it out or you found that somebody had done it someplace else and you applied it to this problem—and that means a certain elegance. But there's another one, which I would call "optimally sufficient." There are a lot of students who figure out just the minimum that it takes to get something to work and then they do it. I'm always impressed with that because it means they get things done fast. And both of those I like, but they're very different types of people that do these things.

He went on to say:

> A lot of students will do something very elegantly. [They] didn't need to do it, but they just wanted to show that it could be done. Sometimes it is very impressive if they really wanted to do that. The other type does just the minimum that it takes to get the thing done and that's also sort of optimally sufficient.

Another participant noted that, "There's a definite threshold between improving something a little bit and making something that works, which is

. . . very good, but outstanding is you . . . go out and make a completely new device that really makes a quantum leap."

## Data Analysis/Results

The data analysis/results component should "bring it all together." It should have a coherent introduction and summary of the results. It should provide enough detail in between so the reader can understand the intermediate steps. In short, it should answer the question, "What has been done in this work?" One participant thought that there were not "any shades of gray" for this component, "either it is acceptable or it isn't acceptable." Another said the quality of this component was a question of "Were they able to solve tough problems? How hard is the problem they solved? How much responsibility were they able to take?"

Outstanding was described as coming up with "some very clever method" that provides "insight" into what was happening in the experiment or obtaining "better or more believable results" or getting "some new piece of information that you never thought you could." Indeed, one participant said that "cleverness" and "insight" are "something highly valuable that we look for." Students who do outstanding analyses were described as ones who say to their advisors, " 'I really would like to follow this analysis line,' and you say, 'OK, come back [when you're done].' "

At the very good level it is clear that the student put in a lot of time and effort to get a lot of high-quality data. At the same time, good students may produce results that are deemed acceptable because they were "beaten out by another experiment in the later stages," by someone who has a result that is "better or almost as significant" and "resolves the issue." More commonly, at the acceptable level, the analysis, interpretation, and discussion of the data and models applied to the data "stand some kind of basic bullshit test. If you can't look at it and say, 'This is obvious bullshit,' " then it is acceptable. Acceptable or "weaker" students often need help. They often have a hard time understanding when to present "figures that don't provoke laughter in the group or that somebody can't immediately find something wrong with it just by looking at it."

In addition to discussing the intentional falsification of data, the physics faculty also talked about unacceptable data analysis/results that stem from students unintentionally adjusting some calibration parameter such that the apparatus generated something that was incorrect, or from students using an

apparatus that cannot measure to the necessary precision or with the necessary accuracy, in which case, "you just can't do what you intended it to do,
then that's inadequate."

## Discussion and Conclusion

When it came to the discussion and conclusion, the physics faculty often
returned to the introduction. They said the conclusion has the same characteristics as the introduction, "You can repeat exactly the same thing" but
"now you just add what you have followed through" and show how the
work in the dissertation "actually added to that context." Referring to both
the introduction and the conclusion, one participant said, "[They] are an
important part of the presentation, but they are not the important part of
the work." The faculty also noted that the conclusion typically contains a
discussion of the future directions. One participant had a "real extreme
view" on that. He said, "Basically when you complete a piece of work, you
have no idea where it is going. . . . Most of these fancy conclusions are un-
justified . . . and often later turn out to be totally wrong. It's just ridiculous,
predicting the future."

The outstanding conclusion is "stimulating to somebody who's knowledgeable about the field." It is insightful in an unexpected way and adds
inspiration. When they read an outstanding conclusion, faculty say, "Oh, I
never expected that. Oh, . . . I never thought about that."

## Notes

1. For information on the source of these data, see chapter 1, note 5, as well as
the American Institute of Physics Web site at http://www.aip.org/statistics/trends
.gradtrends.html

# Appendix

## TABLE 8.A.
### The Components of a Physics Dissertation and Their Characteristics at Different Quality Levels

| Components | Quality levels | | | |
|---|---|---|---|---|
| | Outstanding | Very good | Acceptable | Unacceptable |
| Introduction | Is a microcosm of the whole thesis; motivates the work; is clearly written so that a general physicist or a scientifically literate person can understand the significance of the project; states where the problem is with respect to the field and situates it in a broader context; provides a deep understanding of the project—briefly describes what has been done before, what techniques are going to be used, where the project is headed, and what the results are; discusses the significance of the research in a very honest and direct way; builds connections to other scientific issues | — | Provides an understandable motivation for the work; does not convey a sense of excitement; provides the minimum context for the work; does not make connections to other areas | Displays clear lack of mastery; provides no motivation for the problem; does not say why the problem is important; does not provide context; student fails to cite some very important papers; is not understandable |

| | Quality levels | | | |
|---|---|---|---|---|
| **Components** | **Outstanding** | **Very good** | **Acceptable** | **Unacceptable** |
| **Literature review** | Is almost like a review article; is comprehensive and critical; picks out the important key papers and synthesizes them; shows understanding of where each reference being evaluated fits; puts the problem in perspective and conveys its importance | Comprehensive | Cites all the relevant references but student is not aware of the context; is not directly related to the exact work the student is doing | Does not cite key works; cites a limited number of articles; is unaware of the broader context; totally ignores what has been going on in the area; lacks key references |
| **Theory** | Elegant, simple, original, significant, universally applicable; is aware of the range of theories and their strengths and weaknesses; finds a problem in a theory; points out why the current understanding is wrong or irrelevant; understands that one parameter cannot be tweaked without looking at the whole; leads to a very hard experiment that yields wonderful results; adapts theory to actual experiments | — | Used appropriately; used to derive the correct physical understanding from the data; experiment demonstrates understanding of theory | Wrong; not relevant to the experiment; not understood; regurgitated; described at a nominal level |

*(continues)*

**TABLE 8.A.**
**Continued**

| Components | Quality levels | | | |
|---|---|---|---|---|
| | Outstanding | Very good | Acceptable | Unacceptable |
| **Methods** | A nice, coherent description of method; shows understanding of the advantages and disadvantages and strengths and weaknesses of the method used; elegantly conceived theoretical or new mathematical approach to a problem; new methods, techniques, instruments, or devices that make a quantum leap; developing an algorithm; codes data in a way that yields stable and efficient results | — | Student has done just enough work; provides minimum information about the method | Uses the same equipment and same methods as previous students |

| Components | Quality levels | | | |
|---|---|---|---|---|
| | Outstanding | Very good | Acceptable | Unacceptable |
| **Results/data analysis** | Provides a coherent introduction and summary of the results; has enough detail to provide understanding of intermediate steps; finds and analyzes challenging data; applies a known technique to a new context; analyzes the data in a new way and obtains better, more believable results or information thought impossible to obtain | Contains a large amount of high-quality data; thoroughly investigates almost all sources of error | Correct results; does not have obvious flaws; assesses the data objectively and with integrity; does not know when to present figures that make sense; someone else has better results | Fabricates data; student could not measure phenomenon with precision or accuracy; does not interpret data objectively; does not provide a context for the results |
| **Discussion and conclusion** | A short, clear, concise summary that refers back to the introduction; places the results in context; explains what has been done, what it means, and how it advances the field; is insightful and makes inspired connections; demonstrates the student's understanding of the broader field; discusses applications and suggests new directions for future research | Summarizes the project; refers back to the introduction, and ties everything together; makes uninspired connections; points to some possible future work | Gives the expected standard discussion without any further thought; establishes links with the introduction | — |

# 9

# THE ELECTRICAL AND COMPUTER ENGINEERING DISSERTATION

There are roughly 1,250 Ph.D. programs in engineering (all fields combined) in over 250 universities in the United States. Depending on the system of classification, these institutions award degrees in 19 to 24 subfields that are tracked by various organizations, as well as degrees in several other untracked subfields. About 184 of these Ph.D. programs fall within the subfield designation of "electrical/computer engineering," "electrical engineering," and "computer engineering." Graduate engineering and electrical engineering programs, respectively, enroll over 100,000 and 30,000 graduate students (master's and doctoral), and, respectively, graduate roughly 6,500 and 1,700 new Ph.D.s annually. The median time to degree in engineering is 7.3 years, and 7.6 years in electrical engineering. Roughly 20% of new engineering Ph.D.s go on to postdoctoral education.[1]

Twenty-four faculty in electrical and computer engineering departments (hereafter "engineering") at six universities participated in the focus groups.

Overall, these faculty had 450 years of experience, had chaired an estimated 350 dissertations, and had sat on an estimated 1,099 dissertation committees. The average engineering focus group participant had been a professor for 19 years, had chaired 15 dissertations, and had sat on 46 dissertation committees. Below we present a summary of the engineering focus groups' discussions. Their performance expectations for the dissertation are displayed in the tables. Their supporting discussion is recounted in the text.

## The Purpose of an Engineering Dissertation

The engineering faculty thought that the dissertation was "very useful" and saw it as serving many purposes. In addition to the purposes presented in Table 9.1, the faculty talked about the importance of the dissertation process. They said that the dissertation helps the student to learn to think about the research "so that he's [*sic*] not going willy-nilly looking for needles in a haystack. He's going in a systematic way with some hypothesis." They also felt it was important for students to document the research process:

> Not just results, but the process itself. What did the student go through? In what way did he or she go look at the literature" [How was it] summarized? . . . What kind of a problem did he or she define? In what ways solutions were found? And the reasons why the contributions that are claimed are original. . . . So it's the documentation of all of this process.

One participant, speaking about his own dissertation, talked about the benefits he derived from the experience: "The part on literature research forced me to look into them. . . . In fact, I had to write it and summarize it. I think it is a good exercise for students and good for their career later." Another felt that the process was useful for students because "it helps him [sic] to understand how his work fits in the context of his area." In short, the faculty said that the process taught students how to perform research and

### TABLE 9.1.
#### The Purpose of an Engineering Dissertation

To teach the student to think about process and how to write; to learn to define a problem, summarize the current state of the art and gain a little global perspective on the problem, place the problem in a broader context, propose a solution, perform research, and obtain significant results; to develop mastery of a particular area to the point where the student can contribute to the field; to demonstrate thinking and writing skills, and professional engineering competencies; to document the student's research and provide a tutorial for the next student; to provide evidence for the scholarship the student has achieved during graduate school; to communicate the student's results to his or her colleagues and the rest of the world; is an instructional tool how to report on it—skills "you use . . . for everything you do after you learn it."

The engineering faculty also talked about why "you need the dissertation" rather than "just publications." One participant noted that publications had length limitations that typically do not allow students to convey everything they have done. Another talked about how the dissertation gives students the opportunity to show they proved something in a "beautiful way" that had been previously proven in the literature in an "ugly way." He noted that reviewers will continually say, "This is kind of a sideshow. Take it out." This participant went on to say, "Those are great nuggets to have in a Ph.D. dissertation. . . . Maybe it's not significant enough [to put in a journal article], but it adds a lot of value to somebody reading it, especially a student coming upon the research, because they get to see a nice, unified writing."

The dissertation provides the dissertation committee with evidence of the scholarship that the student has achieved during his or her Ph.D. training that goes beyond just the results:

> You see that through the context that's given and the writing in the introduction and the references and this kind of thing. So part of the Ph.D. training is to develop a mastery of a particular area to the point that they can contribute. If they make a contribution but they don't have scholarship in that area, then their ability to continue to contribute is just that much more limited.

A participant in Private University's focus group talked about the value added from completing a dissertation.

> Once in your life you are actually being put in a situation where you have to come up with a reasonable problem, come up with a reasonable solution, and put the whole thing [together] and produce a reasonable body of work explaining what in hell you are doing and why. . . . Once you have done it once, you may not be afraid of doing it again.

## Original Contribution

The engineering faculty identified many ways to make an original contribution (see Table 9.2). Like other disciplines, an original contribution in engineering is something new, something that has not been done before. The

**TABLE 9.2.**
**The Nature of an Original Contribution in Engineering**

Something that has not been done before; comes from the student not the advisor; new and innovative theories, methods, or applications; solving a solved problem by a better, cheaper, or easier method; successfully solving new or existing problems; developing new algorithms, models, or computational methods; inventing new devices; creating new things; making something work better or differently; taking a method or a result from another field and applying it to an engineering problem; making a conceptual contribution; elucidating a topic; advancing the knowledge base or the state of the art

engineering faculty noted that what constitutes an original contribution depends upon the subdiscipline and that there are different types of original contributions. It may be solving a problem "in the spirit of engineering." It may be inventing new devices, or it may be developing new algorithms or new computational methods. It also may be

> a situation, and this is probably the most difficult, you try to find new applications and basically rely on some standard approaches, which when slightly modified are tuned to resolve more challenging problems. It is less likely to see original contributions where you have all these long jumps, something that is off the wall, and very well used.

One participant said he liked to see students who could "think critically and then transfer knowledge from one area to another area and successfully solve new problems." Another participant thought that the "majority of original contributions fall into that category." Regardless of subdiscipline or type of originality, the bottom line is "one would have to show that this thing the student has done is an advancement to the state of the art."

One participant separated the concept of "original" from the concept of "contribution." He said, "The original is easy, the contribution is hard. What makes it a contribution? . . . Perhaps the difficulty." Another participant commented that there is "a greater range in contribution for significance than there is for originality." Another participant in that focus group tied the degree of originality to the level of creativity and noted that "It may not be particularly creative, but it's building on a natural extension of other work. So that's something that's [original but] not particularly outstanding."

While the faculty agreed that the Ph.D. contribution should be original, they noted that in "reality the degree of originality is really not that high." One participant said that his "personal standard" of originality was "very simple":

> You are bound to do an extensive literature search and understand what is going on and understand the technical details of what is called "state-of-the-art" research and what people know how to do. Compared to that, what you come up with in the thesis should be different in some way that you can argue about. You actually are required to document that this is original. That is part of what the Ph.D. is doing, that is, to document the originality.

Faculty in one focus group commented that an original contribution looks different in engineering than in other fields because engineering has elements of invention and elements of science:

> So when you look at an engineering thesis you'll see both types. . . . In my field, plasmas and particle accelerators, for example, someone may invent a new way to accelerate particles I haven't thought of before or a way to improve the way particles are accelerated by adding a magnetic field or creating some new configuration or using some new material. On the other hand, it might be science-oriented where there's a large particle accelerator and the accelerator, after so many thousand turns, goes unstable. At that point you're acting like a scientist trying to understand the basic physical processes that are going on. You're looking at the waves and the way particles interact. In that sense, you're acting somewhat like a scientist would. . . . So that's interacting. So, engineering theses tend to look like those two things, the invention and the scientist trying to explain the phenomenon.

Another participant in that focus group commented that there is a "gray area in originality" in engineering because of the applied-science nature of engineering, where "you're trying to build something eventually." He went on to say:

> You can write a good thesis where you're basically taking a method or a result from another field, from mathematics or theoretical computer science, and apply it to a relative engineering design problem. In some sense it's not original because you're not inventing a new concept, but go and mine another field and understand a technique that engineers don't understand and show how it's relevant to a problem.

His colleague noted that it is the application that is original. Still another participant in that focus group said that engineers can make original conceptual contributions that elucidate a topic or extend understanding rather than building "a better widget."

The engineering faculty thought that the problem of "original" and "significant" is "a problem of the student and advisor together." This is particularly true for students who have research assistantships and work on their advisor's funded research projects. One participant described the problem or the process thus:

> You sit down with your faculty advisor and he or she's doing research. They already have some topics that are well defined and that will lead one to do original research. Their faculty member will guide that student in the direction that the originality will just fall out. So, from my point of view, the student hooked up with a faculty member [who] already has a plan to do original research, and the objective is to do certain things in that research that have already followed on what other people have done.

## Significant Contribution

A significant contribution in engineering is something that has an impact on the field, though when it comes to the dissertation, one participant noted that it is not the impact itself, but the "expectation of an impact. . . . You would say, 'This is a significant dissertation,' but it's just an estimate." Indeed, another participant noted that significance is subjective and "something that may not be considered significant now, but may become significant twenty years from now." (See Table 9.3 for the characteristics of a significant contribution.)

### TABLE 9.3.
#### The Nature of a Significant Contribution in Engineering

A nontrivial, useful breakthrough that will have an impact; putting a folk theorem into a solid theoretical framework; combining existing techniques; coming up with a clever solution to a very important problem; solving a long-standing problem; developing a product that gets adopted by an interested company; having implications or leading to applications in other fields and areas; stimulating further work; opening up a new field

As mentioned earlier, the engineers thought that there was a greater range in contribution for significance than for originality. They also thought that significance is "tightly related to how significant the problem you are addressing is." At the higher end of the scale, significance was described in terms of the long-term interest the field had in the problem/result, its difficulty, its ability to "cross out of electrical engineering and impact other fields," and how much it influenced further developments. At the lower end of the scale, one participant said, "People should not say, 'So what? You did this but, so what?' It should have a new result with at least some archival value." Another noted, "We . . . often [have] dissertations where most of the things are of marginal value, like little improvements here, little improvements there." One professor talked about how he advised his students and of the different ways in which something could be significant:

> What I encourage my students to do is to try and make a nice, rich conceptual contribution and also think about a connection to engineering practice, if not today then fifteen to twenty years on the horizon. How will this be useful in engineering practice? I think you see good contributions along that scale. You might have something that in hindsight isn't very mathematically elegant and in hindsight might be an obvious solution, but makes a huge impact on engineering research just by a really clever way of solving a really very important problem. That's significant. . . . Or if you just happen to figure out a way to build a better widget, that could be a significant contribution even if it's not wrapped in some beautiful mathematics or logic. At the other extreme, we might have things that people do in engineering practice already and it's just sort of a folk theorem, Do this, it works. People use it all the time. You can make a nice contribution by showing that it's the right thing to do by putting that in a solid theoretical framework.

There was some difference of opinion on whether something had to be original in order for it to be significant. One participant said, "For a doctoral dissertation, my point of view is that the originality is what is the prerequisite, the necessary condition for significance. You can't have a significant contribution without having it be original. There is no significant contribution in electrical engineering as far as the Ph.D. thesis is concerned if it is not original in the first place." A participant in another focus group felt that it was a matter of semantics and gave an example in the design automation area of something that was very significant, but of questionable originality:

> A professor was working on a topic for a long time and he got significant results. But things were not maybe clicking as they should click. Then one of his students took a course with somebody else and basically the student saw that by taking the techniques of the second professor and applying it in the area of the first professor, you can make a huge impact and, in fact, this was a breakthrough in design automation. Definitely it was significant. Now, one could argue maybe it was not very original . . . the two techniques were existing already, so the brilliance was in putting them together. Now one could argue that maybe this is not very original, but very significant.

However, his colleagues thought the contribution was original and that its originality lay in combining two techniques that had not been brought together before.

## The Dissertation as a Whole

The faculty at Public and Private Universities, where part of this study's focus group protocol was piloted, noted that the importance of the engineering dissertation as an archival document has "really diminished." They said that by the time students get to the dissertation, much of their work has already been presented at conferences and submitted or accepted for publication. Thus the dissertation is often a compilation of these papers: "You take several of the articles . . . and you staple them together and that's your thesis." The focus group faculty in this study did not make similar comments. Rather, as noted earlier, most valued the traditional dissertation. Below we explore the characteristics of different quality engineering dissertations (see Table 9.4) and what the engineering faculty had to say about them.

### *Outstanding*

The outstanding engineering dissertation was thus characterized by one participant:

> It's like as Tolstoy said in *Anna Karenina*, "Happy families are all alike and unhappy families are unhappy each in their own way."[2] The same thing with outstanding theses/dissertations. They're all well written, and they're all significant, and they all show a depth and tenacity to the research.

## TABLE 9.4.
### The Characteristics of Different Quality Dissertations in Engineering

| Quality | Characteristics |
|---|---|
| **Outstanding** | Well written; clearly states the problem and why it is new and important; writing demonstrates clear thinking; sets out ideas clearly and concisely; presents a convincing argument; includes many details; is original, significant, insightful, and creative—puts things together in unique ways; shows intellectual effort, depth, and tenacity; takes knowledge to a new level; is based on mathematical or physical science; addresses a new problem, large class of problems, or a problem that has been of great interest to the field; is thoroughly researched; invents new methods or devices; results in an elegant solution or a general model that applies to a broad class of problems; obtains results that are of interest to the larger community; results in several publications in top-ranked journals in different areas; opens new areas for research |
| **Very good** | Very solid; well written; clear, comprehensive, and coherent; original but not very significant; lacks the sparkle of elegance; is lacking in one of the key components (theory, methods, data analysis); problem is not broad, interesting, or significant; has solid theory, methods, and data analysis; data and results are described in detail; misses several opportunities; has some obvious loose ends; makes a modest contribution to the field |
| **Acceptable** | Good work but feels incomplete; demonstrates the student can do research but does not demonstrate true mastery of the area; difficult to understand; may need strong editorial work; project is narrow in scope; is original but not very significant; does not make the case for why the research is new or important; is not particularly interesting or creative; introduction is sloppy; shows lack of understanding of how referenced papers fit together; does not place the work in context; the theory and methods are marginal; the experiments are not exciting or do not work; connections are missed, not fully explored, or made in a tenuous way; has some applications; results in some conference papers; is a small, weak contribution |
| **Unacceptable** | Has big holes; poorly written, difficult to follow; is not original; problem is insignificant or has already been addressed; may be a great idea or conceptualization but the student does not have the technical skills to carry it out or has the technical skills but not |

*(continues)*

**TABLE 9.4.**
**Continued**

| Quality | Characteristics |
|---|---|
| **Unacceptable** | the conceptualization; the context is missing or the student misses the point of the context; there are big problems with the topic, theory, and/or methods; no new method or results; talks only about the mechanics of a certain engineering solution; poor presentation of correct results; the student understands what the solution does but does not know what problem it solves or how it relates to other people's problems; does not advance the state of the art or make a new contribution |

An outstanding engineering dissertation is one in which the ideas are set out very clearly and concisely such that "any graduate student in the area should be able to understand clearly what you have done." Outstanding dissertations are "very pleasurable to read"; they are like "page-turners." Indeed, the quality of the writing can affect how an outstanding piece of research is judged:

> I had a student who had very significant work. She had publications. Many chairs and I wanted to submit her thesis for a prize, but the writing wasn't very good. That's what kept it from being truly outstanding, unfortunately. So good writing is still very important; clear thinking as it shows up on the paper.

While the problems engineering students work on are often based on a faculty member's funded research proposal, the really outstanding dissertations "are the ones where the students have taken [the research] beyond [the proposal], have not just taken the problem as given, but they have been innovative in expanding it to something innovative beyond the faculty member's original concepts." When reading an outstanding dissertation, the reader gets a sense of:

> a thoroughness and a tenacity that they took to their research. You just feel it coming up off the page. They just got the tiger by the tail solving this problem and just really went after it at a level where probably you wouldn't maybe do if you weren't doing a dissertation. You'd just skim the cream

off the surface and then go on to another topic, but that comes through in a good dissertation.

Outstanding dissertations are written by the best and most creative students. These students put things together in unique ways. They transfer ideas from one place to another. They adapt their thinking to different applications that they want to do. "You can't stop them." They "come to your office and say, 'This is how it is and I will teach you why.'" Reflecting on the dissertations that he found "most appealing," one participant said:

> I think fondly of the student as being a little scholar. I think of someone who has really spent a lot of time in science or mathematics in working through that dissertation, as opposed to spending hours in the lab in front of a computer putting in time rather that putting in intellectual effort.

## Very Good

The participant who quoted Tolstoy went on to say that what makes dissertations not outstanding is that they are "missing any number of things. There's not one way in which they are outstanding." He and a participant in another focus group provided similar characterizations of the very good dissertation:

> *Participant*: It may be poor writing or it may be great writing, but just somehow the problem itself is not significant or interesting.

> *Participant*: Very good would be excellent writing and not [a] very broad problem, or [a] very good problem and bad writing.

Very good dissertations are original but less significant than outstanding ones. They are often lacking in one or more of the component parts of the dissertation. Participants in two different focus groups talked about things that get missed in a very good dissertation that would not get missed in an outstanding one:

> *Participant*: One characteristic that comes out a lot of times is . . . tenacity. Several missed opportunities. You see they've made some contribution here, but in the meantime there are some really interesting problems that have cropped up. A really truly outstanding thesis would have talked about it, documented and fully explored it.

*Participant*: [A]n outstanding one will say, "Nobody thought of looking at applying concept X to problem Y." Whereas this [very good] person has applied concept X to problem X, and did so successfully and better than has been done in the past.

## Acceptable

The acceptable dissertation should, at minimum, convey ideas and results, have some applications, lead to some conference publications, and advance the state of the art "to some extent." It cannot be just a review of what has been done before or a reworking of "things that are out there." It does not have to be extremely well written or of great interest to many people, but it must be correct and contain original material.

In discussing the acceptable dissertation, the engineering faculty talked about both solidly acceptable dissertations and marginally acceptable ones, and the characteristics of students who produce them. In both instances, students who write them were said to have reached, or were functioning, close to their potential. Those who write solidly acceptable dissertations were described as students who struggle with "the thinking process, the creative thinking process." Their work is "just the standard process," it does not hit the creativity level of outstanding or very good dissertations. By contrast, students who write marginally acceptable dissertations were described as not understanding the context of what they have done. They understand that "what they did hasn't been done before, but they don't understand why anybody would care about that, and they can't tell you exactly how unique it is relative to these other papers, or even how it's connected." However, because both types of students went through the entire process, did good work, and demonstrated that they can do research, they will receive the Ph.D., but "the committee will understand that that person isn't intended to go on and do this for a living . . . certainly shouldn't be doing this for a living."

The engineering faculty also discussed factors external to the student that result in the production of an acceptable dissertation. Sometimes experiments do not work. Sometimes a student is involved in an experiment "that's a big collaboration or perhaps requires a large infrastructure which perhaps doesn't become available in the time scale [in] which they need to finish." Consequently, "a lot of experimental students complet[e] acceptable theses which involve an elucidation of an experimental design with some theory and simulation." Sometimes the work is "rushed," "pushed," and "partially executed" because "a grant finishes and there is the prospect of not having support," or the student has accepted a job offer. In these instances, rather than asking the student to work on the project/dissertation longer and improve it, "you would accept an acceptable work."

Regardless of whether an acceptable dissertation results from factors internal or external to the student, the faculty noted that they have a "hidden criteria [*sic*] for finishing." The criterion is that "we feel good about this person wearing the label Ph.D. from our department."

## Unacceptable

An engineering dissertation is deemed unacceptable if it is missing any of the following four elements: an original solution, evidence of the merits or shortfalls of the solution, enough details so that others in the field can replicate the experiment, or a clear understanding of the state of the art. "We can't have a thesis without these four elements. It is unacceptable," said one participant.

Drafts of dissertations are frequently unacceptable in the early stages and are returned to students to be revised. A student who is "bad" will come back with another "bad" edition. "They never get any better." Advisors typically will not allow an unacceptable dissertation to go to defense. "I keep him going until he gets there or quits."

The faculty provided a number of reasons why dissertations may be unacceptable. Poor writing was mentioned by a few. Sometimes English is the barrier and sometimes it is a lack of clear thinking. One professor gave an example of the latter two, each involving nonnative English-speaking students:

> I had a Taiwanese student who was so poor in English that I almost couldn't read the thesis. I suggested that he try to get someone to help him with his English. He actually found someone to hire and that person sat down with him and translated all of his work. That person knew no science whatsoever, [had no] technical background at all. That thing read like a Rolls-Royce. I thought, "Oh, this is the solution." So then I had another student . . . the second student had a barrier with the language and was not a clear thinker, so when it got translated it still was a mishmash.

Sometimes an unacceptable dissertation is a function of advisor overload. Faculty in one focus group indicated that some faculty in their department had over twenty advisees and, consequently, could not give some students the attention they need. Indeed, some students require so much advisor help that the advisor thinks, "I can write this thesis, but am I really helping this student develop any further?" Indeed, a participant in another focus group talked about a case where a student had three journal articles, yet did not get his dissertation approved because he lacked independence in his work; the journal articles were the collaborative work of the advisor and the student.

More commonly what happens is a student is job-offer ready, has accepted a job, or decides "all of a sudden after five or six years, 'I'm going to graduate this semester.'" These students suddenly

> get serious about their research, not realizing that it takes at least a semester, if not more, to write a dissertation. They think if they get their research done by March they can graduate in April. It doesn't work that way. Those are the kinds of dissertations that just have to go back to the drawing board.

## The Components of an Electrical and Computer Engineering Dissertation

The engineers did not object to the matrix of components of the dissertation (see Table 1.2). They more implicitly than explicitly agreed that all the components listed in the matrix were a part of an engineering dissertation, though they said that the components did not constitute the chapter structure of a dissertation. The faculty noted that all engineering dissertations had introductions and conclusions, but that everything in between was "very, very different" and "varies a great deal from project to project." For example, a dissertation might have multiple chapters on different cases or assumptions that are being considered or on different algorithms being developed for the same problem. Consequently, each chapter will have theory, methods, results, and data analysis and some conclusions, with the literature review often running through each chapter. The faculty said that it was unlikely to find a dissertation with a chapter called "Theory," and another chapter called "Methods."

Although they were not necessarily comfortable talking about the different quality levels of the components, the engineers also did not overtly object to the task. All six engineering focus groups addressed most of the cells of the matrix. Only one cell was not addressed by any engineering focus group: unacceptable conclusion. Below we explore the characteristics of the components of the engineering dissertation (see Table 9.A in the appendix to this chapter) and what the faculty said about them.

## Introduction

The introduction to an engineering dissertation should be "an invitation for whoever gets the dissertation to read it." It should set the stage for and summarize the whole dissertation. It should be "an executive summary." It should also provide the context for and a little history of the problem. Indeed, a person who is not an expert in the field should be able to understand what it is about. The engineering faculty noted that it is not easy to write an introduction, and given the broad scope of the introduction, it should be the last thing students write.

Outstanding introductions "reel you in." They make readers say, "Wow, I want to read this dissertation." They provide a two- or three-page summary of what the "whole thing is about." Because the introduction and literature review typically go together, the outstanding introduction provides "an excellent tutorial on the material relative to the thesis." It does not go "astray" and teach "us something irrelevant." Indeed, one participant said that "outstanding is how well they get all that garbage out of there."

A very good introduction "doesn't have that 'wow' factor." Yet it is still clearly written, describes the problem clearly, and motivates the study, though it may be less well motivated than the outstanding one. Students who write a very good introduction often think they are "solving this little problem X, but actually it's a much broader solution and they haven't realized that."

For an introduction to be acceptable "it has to be salvageable, at least, with major corrections." At minimum it should have the "newspaper approach." It should say "how you got your results and how broadly applicable they are and exactly [what] your setup [is]," because "if all [someone does] is read the [first] four pages, that's where you have to hit the mark."

An unacceptable introduction will have all sorts of "stuff" mixed into it. It might have "16, 17, 20 pages of history without even knowing what the problem is yet." "They'll talk about . . . the history and why in 1940, why this person did this, and you don't know what the student's going to work on or has worked on." One participant said that one of the things that "drives me crazy," is lack of context. "When somebody says, 'Lot's of people have looked at this problem using these tools,' then they . . . reference 10 to 25."

The faculty noted that a dissertation should not fail because of the introduction and that a wonderful introduction will not save a failing one. "If a dissertation is failing, it doesn't matter what the introduction looks like."

## Literature Review

The literature review supports the statement of the problem and allows students to "rightfully claim" that they have made a contribution and provide evidence that "something tangible . . . was accomplished in the dissertation," for instance, proving that the state of the art has been advanced. In reviewing the literature, students have to state the limitations of the previous work. "If [others] have solved your problem, then why are you solving it? There must be some problem with those [other studies]. Why is your work better than theirs, easier, cheaper, et cetera?" One participant noted that a literature review was "an ethical process." "You don't claim what other people have already done. You have to document that."

The literature review also serves to educate the reader. In a diverse field, it teaches readers "what it is that they are reading about." For example, "Somebody may be reading about control theory, but there may be artificial intelligence in it, there may be signal processing in it, which a typical scholar in control theory may not know about. So, you really have to not only set the stage for [the work], but also educate people."

Overall, the engineering faculty felt that the literature review was an important component of an engineering dissertation and noted that some students tend to "skip" it or "slop" it off because they see the dissertation as a means to an end and not as part of the scholarly process. They also noted that many students are not in the habit of reading.

One participant provided a number of reasons why students should do a literature review:

> First of all, the student has to learn and become an expert in a certain area of research. Going back and reading the literature and finding out what's been done is an important process, a learning process. . . . Part of that learning process is reading the literature and . . . learn[ing] how to communicate in the field. So the process is not only learning what's going on, but

it's also learning how people communicate. Third then, is to . . . bring it together and organize it in a way that has some coherency. That could mean it's done right as a contribution in and of itself for people like myself that already know a lot about it, but haven't . . . updated [themselves in] the literature. I mean, I . . . read everything, but I haven't really quite synthesized it. . . . It's important for developing a person's mind-set of knowing what's going on, and also then to be able to organize and communicate. Often a student will learn something was going on, and . . . then in that process become more creative in the field. So a literature review is important.

The outstanding literature review is a teaching document. Students who write outstanding literature reviews do not just "grab" the last two or three years of conference papers or journal articles, they go back further in discussing fundamental applications. Their literature reviews do not simply say, " 'Here's what person Y did, and what person X did, and what person Z did,' but instead say, 'Here's how what person Y did relates to what person X did, and here's how person Z's relates to both of these and how all of this relates to my problem.' " In other words, they take a very critical look at the literature and show how the studies fit together, how they build on each other, and where the gaps are. An outstanding literature review also teaches the reader about new methods "in a way that's easy to understand and ties together all of the different methods that people have been suggesting" using a common notation. According to one participant, reading an outstanding dissertation from a student is "better than reading the 10 papers that he's [*sic*] writing about and referencing," because the student makes "it clear. You can understand what they're about."

To be acceptable, a literature review has to be comprehensive and show "why the problem that you are addressing has not been addressed in the past." In addition to omitting major articles or whole branches of research, plagiarizing, or citing articles that they have not read, a literature review will be unacceptable if it does not tie into the overall dissertation topic. "They're not saying how it relates to what they're doing. . . . There's a paragraph of 'This guy did this. This person did this.' But it's not done in the context of what they're doing." Sometimes literature reviews are unacceptable because the student is "underread." Sometimes a "well-read" student will assume that "every body knows this." Other students just "don't see any purpose to a literature review."

## *Theory*

The engineering focus group faculty did not provide much in the way of a general overview of the role of theory in an electrical or computer engineering dissertation. One participant said that in electrical engineering, theory and methods are "intermingled," they go "hand in hand." Faculty in one focus group said, "For us, theory equals mathematical foundation," though they indicated that the theory "doesn't have to be math" per se. One participant in that focus group said that he did not "consider a Ph.D. thesis something that just relies on simulation," though he noted that he had colleagues who did not agree with him.

The outstanding theory component was described with "some of the same words that we use for the overall dissertation. . . . The elegance of it, the insight the person used in getting to this point . . . looking at something from a different point of view that nobody has thought of." One participant defined "elegance" as providing a "nice, constructive proof" of a theorem rather than using "brute force" and proving it "using a very ugly method." Outstanding may also involve coming up with a theory, "Like, Hey! Nobody looked at the impact of time on which documents are more important. Therefore I'm going to come up with a whole model of identifying the best documents that incorporate the time factor."

A very good theory component usually builds on "something that somebody else has done." It has to be "appropriate" to the problem and "sound," "correct," and "complete," where complete "doesn't mean that it works in all cases," though the student needs "to define where it works and where it doesn't." In discussing the acceptable theory component, one participant gave examples of things he commonly sees. One is a student who knows a lot of mathematics but uses it incorrectly and incoherently. Another is the student who is "in love with mathematics" and finds a problem "which is an excuse to use this field of mathematics." One participant gave an example of a "clever" student who assumed away all the difficulties to the point where "it finally came down to solving a very, very trivial problem. That's bad theory."

In addition to the characteristics of unacceptable theory listed in Table 9.A, the faculty talked about two types of common problems or errors. One problem is not understanding the theory or phenomenon. For instance, students may include a lot of equations but use the equations and variables in a way that indicates that they do not understand what the theory is about, or they may have a lot of heuristics but no substantial deductive process, or they may have few or no equations, which indicates a lack of theory.

The other common problem or error is when there is no need for theory, but the student feels that there must be a theory and builds a theory around his or her work just to have a theory. "So you look at it and say, 'What you're really doing is just adding two numbers.' 'You expressed things in all these nice frameworks. What did you achieve with that?'" The faculty noted that there "has to be a justification for the theory and there has to be a justification for especially complex theories that you see sometimes."

## Methods

The engineering methods component was described as being the "core of the dissertation." It is where "what has been done by the student" is explained in detail. It should state what the contributions are and "warn against pitfalls." This component is essential because other people "read that chapter very carefully and probably do some future work" based on it. "Without this component it will be difficult to persuade people" of the validity of the work. One participant said that methods "are more important in the thesis proposal stage, because that's where the students have to convince the committee that they have the tools or the methods to be able to apply it" to their problem.

Outstanding methods and methods components are simple, elegant, and complete. New methods are often "seized" and applied to the problem. Outstanding dissertations typically have a "balanced use of theory, experiments, and simulations," such that the student is not just proving things, but demonstrating them through examples or simulations. In both outstanding and very good dissertations, students "really know" why they are using different methods, why those methods are appropriate for that particular study, and what the range of parameters is over which those methods are going to work. In their write-ups, students discuss "why they chose that method and why it's working for their particular experiment."

One of the things that differentiates very good from outstanding methods is that the very good student "solves a problem but uses a tool for which there's now a better one. They could have done a better job." A very good methods component discusses the advantages of the chosen method and compares it with other existing methods. By contrast, in an acceptable or "mediocre" dissertation, students often have a "different-is-better attitude" and avoid discussing alternative methods. "They just want to focus on the idea that [they are] going to find a new method to this. It's different and, therefore, it's novel."

In their discussion of acceptable methods, the faculty also talked about students who "work as if they're looking for a needle in a haystack. Although they "have a lot of energy, a lot of motivation," they have "no sequential process." Their style of research is "random," "willy-nilly," and they do not know what to do when they discover they are wrong.

Unacceptable methods are typically fundamentally flawed. The write-ups do not discuss what the students were measuring or "why they were measuring what they were measuring." In the case of user studies, students may make inappropriate generalizations. For instance, they may conduct their research using Ph.D. computer science students as subjects and generalize their results to students in grades kindergarten through 12. One participant talked about what drives him "crazy":

> You'll say, "Well, why did you assume that? [And they'll say,] "Because then I can get the close-form analysis for it." Well, that's the worst reason of all. It's OK to assume things so that you can get close-form results for the purposes of drawing qualitative conclusions, but you have to supplement that with [an] experiment or, in my field, computer simulation so you have a more realistic model. . . . A lot of times students don't have that clear thinking either, which is clearly the scientific method, deductive thinking, where you run a bunch of simulations. They try and just blind you with simulation curves and so forth, whereas you're trying to answer this question. It's experimental . . . you construct an experiment that would tell me if this is the effect that's causing it. And that's an important aspect of methods.

### Data Analysis/Results

The data analysis/results component of the engineering dissertation is a "bridge" between the theory and methods and the conclusions that allows students to establish their conclusions. In an outstanding data analysis/results component, students make the case that their numbers are not only "very reliable, very accurate, very precise," but also "have good meaning."

Outstanding results are not just statistically significant, they are also usable. One participant explained this as follows:

> Quite often if we're designing a system for people to use, we compare system A with the same users in system B. We're going to look for statistical significance, in that system A [is] statistically proven to be significantly different than system B. But that's not enough, because if you run enough trials you might find that a 1% improvement in performance is statistically significant but not [observable] to a human being. . . . So an outstanding one should be . . . observably better to the end user.

When reading an outstanding analysis, one participant said that he is so struck by the analysis that he thinks, "I'm not sure I would have gotten that myself from the data, but this person was really very intelligent in terms of how they saw things and put it together."

Very good data analysis and results components explain the correlation between the theory and the results, whereas acceptable ones typically do not even explain the results. For instance, according to another participant:

> You'll see papers where they'll say, "We simulated this. The performance is this," and there's nothing. The graph doesn't tell you. There's no conclusions. . . . Students will say, "OK, I've done it and this works better than that." OK, why does it work better than that? And will it always work better than that? Those are questions to look at that a good researcher will go into. The marginal ones won't.

Another participant described what students needed to do to make their data analysis and results better than just acceptable. He said, "You've got to explore the design space and really exercise your theory. Challenge your own assumptions with it; try to break it a little bit to show where it holds up and where it falls short."

In addition to having the problems shown in Table 9.A, unacceptable data analysis/results components were described as ones that present "page after page" of tables and data but show no understanding of "how I'm building a case here" and say nothing about analysis or contribution. At the opposite extreme are ones that draw conclusions based on very little data. In between are ones that hide data and "show the part that you like and don't show the part that you don't like." Students who produce unacceptable data analysis/results components often claim that their analysis and simulation results are the same when they have not even tried to validate them, or they will argue that the errors that cropped up in the validation are "explainable." Others were described as only caring about or wanting to "get out." They'll say, "Here's one little particular narrow scenario where this works. Yeah! I'm done."

## Discussion and Conclusion

The engineering faculty had different views on the nature and importance of the discussion and conclusion. When asked about this component, faculty in one focus group said, "Two pages. Who cares?" and also that they would rather their students write an executive summary in the introduction so that "you know what the results are in the beginning." By contrast, faculty in another focus group distinguished between the discussion and the conclusion. They noted that the discussion was much more important than the conclusion, as it is "understanding the results beyond the data of the paper." The faculty also noted that the discussion/conclusion component typically discusses future directions.

Outstanding discussions and conclusions provide a very short summary of what was done, what the dissertation's contribution is, and why it is important. They "take a step back, look at the whole field, [and] place that work within the general framework. For instance, extrapolate out of there in what ways would it extend the technology." Outstanding conclusions identify shortcomings and anticipate criticism, which is something that most students are "always very scared" to do "because in their mind . . . now they will have to graduate later." Finally, outstanding conclusions clearly show that the student has a feeling for what to do next, about which one participant said,

> That's in some sense the key difference between the student pre-Ph.D. and post-Ph.D. The student is really ready to graduate when they have an idea of what their next . . . problem might be. At that point they're really ready. So that's the key thing that you look for in this discussion and conclusion, whether they're really ready to go out and be independent and do the skills on their own and not be given the problem by their advisor anymore. That should come out of the discussion and conclusion.

## Notes

1. For information on the source of these data, see chapter 1, note 5. Michael Gibbons of the American Society for Engineering Education also provided some of the data (personal communication, May 16, 2005).

2. The actual quote is: "Happy families are all alike; every unhappy family is unhappy in its own way." Quotation retrieved from http://www.quotationspage .com/quote/27719.html, April 29, 2005.

# Appendix

## TABLE 9.A.

### The Components of an Engineering Dissertation and Their Characteristics at Different Quality Levels

| Components | Quality levels | | | |
| --- | --- | --- | --- | --- |
| | Outstanding | Very good | Acceptable | Unacceptable |
| **Introduction** | Well written; captivating; provides motivation and establishes the importance of the problem and places it in context; presents a very clear and concise statement of the problem, results, conclusions, and contributions; lays out the plan for the dissertation | Writing is good; motivates the work but does it less well and is not captivating; clearly describes what the problem is and why it is important; starts with the big picture and narrows it down to the point being made; indicates what the contributions are | Mediocre; not well written; the ideas seem to be there; is narrower in scope | Problem is not stated; includes a lot of extraneous material |

| Components | Quality levels | | | |
|---|---|---|---|---|
| | Outstanding | Very good | Acceptable | Unacceptable |
| Literature review | Complete, comprehensive, up to date, organized, and coherent; has a nice, logical structure; provides a critical look at the problem; supports the statement of the problem and the statement of the contribution; puts the work in context of what has been and is being done; shows a good understanding of the state of the art; discriminates between important and unimportant papers; identifies gaps in the literature; states limitations of previous work; simplifies and discusses very complex papers; summarizes and ties together all the different methods people have been employing, using a common notation; provides detailed examples of existing methods; is a contribution in and of itself; educates the reader | Written at the appropriate level of depth with the appropriate amount of references | Good enough; pretty comprehensive, but may be missing a few important works; shows that there are holes in the literature with respect to the problem | Inadequate or missing; does not provide a context for or relate to what the student is doing; omits a lot of important material; cites works that the student has not read; plagiarizes articles |

(continues)

**TABLE 9.A.**
Continued

| Components | Quality levels | | | |
| --- | --- | --- | --- | --- |
| | Outstanding | Very good | Acceptable | Unacceptable |
| **Theory** | Creative, insightful, elegant, significant; conceived and presented logically and correctly; takes theory beyond the literature; develops a new theory; is or provides a mathematically correct foundation for the research | Appropriate, complete, and correct; builds on existing theory; ties the project together; defines where the theory works and where it does not | Presents a lot of theory that is never used; assumes away all the difficulties | Omitted; does not understand or justify the theory; uses theory inappropriately |
| **Methods** | Provides a comprehensive description; has a simple, complete, elegant approach; exhausts all possibilities; combines theory and methods; has a balanced use of theory, experiments, and simulations; uses existing theory to develop methods for useful applications; seizes new tools and applies them to the problem; demonstrates things through examples or simulations | Compares chosen method against existing methods; discusses its advantages and disadvantages; identifies why the student chose the method; states all the assumptions; indicates the range of parameters over which the method will work; tests hypotheses experimentally or with simulations | Precise and complete enough so others can replicate; states what the student is trying to establish and how he or she will go about it; sequential process—does all combinations randomly; may require major corrections | Shoddy; lacks clear scientific deductive thinking; does not identify what is being measured or why; just a bunch of simulations; makes improper generalizations |

| Components | Outstanding | Very good | Acceptable | Unacceptable |
|---|---|---|---|---|
| **Results/data analysis** | Well written; clear, simple, and appropriate presentation of unambiguous results, contributions, applications, limitations, and impact; insightful; very repeatable; measurements have a high degree of precision; documentation supports the precision, accuracy, and reliability of the results; has statistically and observably significant usable results; results, match or support the theory; graphically displays carefully selected variables and results; draws proper conclusions and makes proper inferences | Theory and results correspond; provides an explanation for the correspondence | Sufficient; measurements, theory, and analysis align; does not justify the claim it works better than something else; needs major revisions | Data are inaccurate, fudged, or falsified; selectively presents only supporting data; has lots of tables but no analysis or discussion of the contribution; provides evidence that it works in only one little narrow situation; student does not understand the results; draws conclusions based on very little data |

(continues)

**TABLE 9.A.**
**Continued**

| Components | Quality levels | | | |
|---|---|---|---|---|
| | Outstanding | Very good | Acceptable | Unacceptable |
| **Discussion and conclusion** | Short summary that brings out major points and ties back to the introduction; contains lucid insights; places work within the context of the field; identifies contributions and applications as well as limitations and shortcomings; anticipates criticism; discusses future directions | Good summary of results; clearly states contributions, possible applications, and future directions | Not well done; provides some considerations for future work based on shortcomings of current work | — |

# 10

# THE MATHEMATICS DISSERTATION

T here are roughly 270 Ph.D. programs in the mathematical sciences (mathematics, applied mathematics, and statistics) in the United States that award degrees in 10 subfields that are tracked by various organizations as well as degrees in several other untracked subfields. Graduate mathematics programs enroll roughly 15,000 students (master's and doctoral), and graduate roughly 1,000 new Ph.D.s annually. The median time to degree is 6.9 years. About 20% of new mathematics Ph.D.s go on to post-doctoral education.[1]

Thirty-one mathematics faculty at nine universities participated in the focus groups. Most came from pure mathematics programs, though a few came from applied programs. Overall, these faculty had 758 years of experience, had chaired an estimated 272 dissertations, and had sat on an estimated 887 dissertation committees.[2] The average mathematics focus group participant had been a professor for 25 years, had chaired 9 dissertations, and had sat on 30 dissertation committees. Below is a summary of the mathematics focus groups' discussions. Their performance expectations for the dissertation are displayed in the tables. Their supporting discussion is recounted in the text.

## The Purpose of a Mathematics Dissertation

The mathematics faculty saw the dissertation as having many purposes (see Table 10.1). The training purpose of the dissertation is captured in one participant's retort to his colleague's cynical comment that the purpose of a dissertation is to "provide you with labor":

> No, it doesn't provide us with labor. They don't give us labor. We give them labor. In mathematics that's the way it goes. We're teaching them.

## TABLE 10.1.
### The Purpose of a Mathematics Dissertation

To produce a fully formed professional, independent mathematician, or mathematics researcher; to make sure students have acquired the stills necessary to learn and carry on professional activity as mathematicians; to gain some experience in solving problems; to give students practice writing papers and organizing their thoughts; to learn how to come up with good problems, do research, and write mathematics; to demonstrate that the student can do original, independent research of some significance in some area of mathematics; to certify that the person is qualified to have a Ph.D., that he or she can do certain kinds of things, is able to do research after graduate school, and get certain kinds of jobs.

> We're trying to train. . . . Part of what we're doing is . . . trying to explain ideas and get them familiar with certain techniques and able to be self-sufficient in guiding their way around and understanding the huge numbers of mathematical ideas that are out there. [We are] giving them some experience in solving problems, and, with any luck, . . . once they've had some experience they can go on and do it on their own.

Yet, another participant in a different focus group questioned whether mathematics faculty were doing a "terribly good job" of training doctoral students "these days." He noted that more and more of the entry-level positions for new mathematics Ph.D.s are postdoctoral positions, and commented that "a postdoc is someone that still hasn't quite gotten to the point where they're a completely independent researcher." The student is still in an apprenticeship position, albeit at a different, formal level of apprenticeship, where he or she is still somebody's student.

In contrast to course work, which is often "just repeating what you have been taught on the blackboard," the dissertation "should grow the student to a point where they can get some independence." Unlike other academic degrees and accomplishments, one participant stated that the dissertation is "to prove yourself academically and . . . [prove] that you could do research and . . . produce a new result." He noted, "The Ph.D. is the only degree that is not given, it's taken." Indeed, the faculty thought that master's work was completely different from the dissertation, because master's students have a set of requirements to fulfill. That "never happens" with the dissertation, "they have to do something extra." The dissertation was also defined as being different from a research paper. It is more comprehensive, it requires the problem to be explained and put in context, and it contains "all the details." One participant's reason for this difference was, "You have to make sure that, among other things, the student has mastered those techniques and really knows how to do those kinds of computations."

One participant noted that the dissertation is one of many goals of graduate education:

> I would say the goal of the graduate education is to produce a fully formed mathematician, a professional in some broad sense. That means they should understand lots of things about mathematics in general. They should be experts in a specialty, they should know how to go about research, they should know how to talk about mathematics and give talks. So, there are a lot of things that go into being a professional mathematician. . . . My point is that the document itself, and even the result, it's not the only goal.

Faculty in another focus group discussed how completing their dissertations gave them a new level of confidence and changed their lives. One participant said:

> Your life changes, I mean, my life changed; I knew I could do original work. I read a lot and you grind through all these problems that are put before you and they're in the book and you do exercises, and then someone comes to you and says, "Here is a problem that nobody knows how to do." . . . The professor says to you, "I don't know how to do this." So you get to working on it and you solve it. . . . The Red Sea parts for you. "I can do it! Yeah!" So it changed my life. It really did . . . I thought, "OK, yeah, I can be a mathematician. That's really cool. Maybe I can make the grade now."

In contrast to pure mathematicians who felt that the main purpose of the dissertation was to learn how to do future research, an applied mathematician commented that in his field this was not necessarily the case. He noted that many applied mathematics Ph.D.s are employed by industry and that industrial employers are less interested in what the prospective employee did his or her dissertation on than whether that person is smart, dedicated, and stubborn enough to work through a project.

Finally, faculty in two focus groups discussed and debated whether a person needed a Ph.D. to be a good mathematician. One participant asserted that you did. She felt that without "lots of training" there is "no way you can gather that . . . research and information." By contrast, a participant in the other focus group commented that he knew "some pretty super-outstanding mathematicians who never got the Ph.D. degree."

## Original Contribution

The mathematics faculty identified many ways to make an original contribution (see Table 10.2). They indicated that the notion of originality was different in mathematics than in other disciplines and expressed two philosophical views on it. One philosophical view is that mathematics is something that "is always there," and mathematicians discover it rather than invent it. The more frequently stated view is that mathematics is not simply the synthesis of known results and ideas, it is an art form and thus invented or composed. One participant said, "I can't think of another department except music that requires students to compose a sonata or symphony, but in mathematics, people actually compose something." Another participant said:

> Of all subjects, except for perhaps fine arts, the concept of originality in mathematics makes sense much more so than philosophy or history. It's possible to do original work in mathematics and it's a prerequisite for a thesis. . . . It's . . . like composing a symphony. You simply cannot play

### TABLE 10.2.
### The Nature of an Original Contribution in Mathematics

Something new; something not previously proved or done before; new ideas, perspectives, connections, approaches, methods, computations, theories, theorems or sections of theorems, counterexamples, proofs, or shorter proofs with more insight and motivation, results, or applications; solving a big, open problem with a known technique; a new approach to an old problem or an excellent improvement on known results; advances the body of knowledge in mathematics, including improving the presentation and understanding of how known things fit together; a publishable result, a step beyond what is currently available in the literature; extends the frontiers of the discipline

*Applied mathematics*: formulating a new problem; making connections between fields that have not been made before; new results

some well-known piece of music on an instrument and get a Ph.D. in mathematics. You have to do something new and something interesting. It must not just be new . . . it must be of interest to some other mathematicians.

Faculty in one focus group "unanimously" agreed that the work had to be new. However, a participant in another focus group thought that there was a real difference between originality and newness. He felt that there were "a lot of new results that are proved that aren't really worth proving." More than one focus group defined "new" with respect to the knowledge of the advisor or the dissertation committee: "as far as the advisor knows, [it] is believed to be original, is believed to be new," "to the best knowledge of all people involved." Cautionary remarks like these were typically not made by faculty in other disciplines. This may be because in mathematics it is impossible to prove that no other mathematician has ever considered and proved a theorem or because there is a very real possibility that others are working on the same problem or theorem.

While a participant in one focus group stated that there is "no criterion" for originality, a participant in another focus group articulated objective and subjective criteria. The objective criterion was that it be new, "not done by somebody else before." The subjective criterion was that it be interesting. He went on to state, "Those sorts of things are not very common for a Ph.D. thesis because it's tougher to do that sort of thing." Another participant defined his personal standard as, "What I want is for the graduate student to tell me something I don't know a lot about." Overall, the mathematicians felt that the minimum standard for an original contribution was having a publishable result.

In addition to characterizing what an original contribution is, the mathematics faculty discussed what it is not. An original contribution is not "add-[ing] together two really big numbers that never were added together before," which this participant felt would be "stupid." It should not be "as routine as work in a course or even a fairly advanced course." It should not be a long homework set. It should not be too easy, "just an exercise that anybody could have done." It should not be "something where the advisor sees all of the steps in advance," though the advisor may see the broad outline in advance. And it should not be following a path parallel to something the advisor has done; that is, it should not just be a different case with very similar steps.

The faculty also discussed how they got their students started on the path of original research. One said that he suggests generalizations to weak students. Another starts students with easy proofs, something "which you know can be done." He noted, "It's not maybe worth doing by most people, but it gives the student a sense of confidence as he/she begins the research." Similarly, another said:

> Very often what happens is that their thesis advisor will suggest, "Try this method or this kind of problem and see where you get." Then what the person has done is . . . work out details and see where the technicalities come and sort of put things together. . . . The less help a thesis advisor has to do of this kind, of course, the better the thesis is because you would ideally like people to be original and have their own ideas and understand for themselves a new way of looking at things, but that doesn't happen terribly often.

Finally, one participant provided a cautionary tale about the need to define what is meant by an original contribution.

> Theodore Streleski was a . . . graduate student at Stanford University, where I almost went . . . for graduate work. He was working with Karel deLeeuw. He was there for 19 years and he wasn't making the grade. Apparently nobody was really forceful enough to tell him, "Fish or cut bait." So one day he walks in with a hammer and kills Karel deLeeuw. The reason was because he wasn't given a Ph.D. Karel deLeeuw would not sign off on his thesis because he hadn't done any original work. So they said this is an extreme case of being upset because there is confusion on the definition.[3]

## Significant Contribution

As with the other disciplines, a significant contribution in mathematics is based on community judgment, its interest to others and its impact on the field, and is usually, but not always, determined many years later. Publishable was mentioned as a "sufficient condition," but it was discussed far less in the mathematics focus groups than in many others (see Table 10.3)

One participant opined that significance was harder to judge than originality because it is more subjective. Along these lines, another participant said:

## TABLE 10.3.
### The Nature of a Significant Contribution in Mathematics

Something that is of interest to others that provides a better understanding of and advances the subject, field, or science; a profound improvement in what is known; a publishable result that has depth and breadth; a new idea; a huge insight; something that is not intuitively or mathematically obvious; unexpected connections between things or fields of mathematics; doing something that other people have tried to do and failed; solving or making headway on an open problem; a unified proof of two disparate results; a new methodological approach that can be applied to other things; having implications that are of value to a wide community

> One of the reasons I went into mathematics is, unlike most other subjects, the question of right and wrong is usually not an opinion. . . . But as far as significant and nonsignificant, that's still very fuzzy. . . . That's disappointing to me because I went into mathematics partly for clarity.

For him, solving an open problem would be "a good way to prove it's significant."

The mathematicians noted that there were degrees of significance. One participant said that degree of significance was a function of the failed effort that others have put into answering a question that has been around for a long time. At the highest level, a significant contribution was typically defined as a huge insight or a profound improvement on what is known. However, the mathematicians said it was "pretty rare" for a dissertation to make a contribution of this magnitude. Indeed, one participant said, "If we were all judged by those standards, none of us would have tenure. Very few of us, anyway." One participant even felt that significant contributions "should come later when people are grown up and maybe doddering at the end of their careers," though he acknowledged that they could come earlier.

The mathematicians did not discuss the lower levels of significance per se, but they noted that "99%, 99.9% of the results in mathematics are mostly incremental improvements." They said that what they wanted Ph.D. students to do was "make some contribution in a direction that an expert would consider to be of some value to the field." Students could do this by answering a question naturally led to by the current research. "The problem may not be a major problem with broad impact, but it's the current trend. . . . I view solving this kind of problem as significant, that is, for the Ph.D. students." In short, the general feeling was that while it would be wonderful if every dissertation had surprising and unexpected results, the mathematics faculty felt it would be counterproductive to say, "We're not going to give the degree unless the thesis also meets some standard of significance." Indeed, the faculty at one university said that at places like their university (i.e., those with less strong mathematics programs), the standards for significance are "pretty low."

## The Dissertation as a Whole

The content of the mathematics dissertation varies by area. In some areas of mathematics, students focus on a single problem in great detail. In other areas, students may solve several problems that are only tenuously related, if at all. With respect to the style or structure of the dissertation, it was noted in one focus group that the mathematics dissertation is moving in the direction of a compilation of published or publishable papers. The lack of discussion of structure of the dissertation in the other mathematics focus groups suggests that most mathematics dissertations—at least at the universities in this study—still conform to the "traditional" style. Below we explore the characteristics of different quality mathematics dissertations (see Table 10.4) and what the mathematics faculty had to say about them.

### Outstanding

The outstanding dissertation goes beyond the "basic standard" of what faculty expect from students and what should be in a dissertation. All the components are of very high quality. One participant commented that "you can tell the difference fairly quickly" between "somebody who is really elegant and sharp and outstanding [and someone who is] really very good . . . from almost anywhere in the thesis." Faculty in one focus group disagreed about the quality of the exposition. One participant quoted a colleague not present at the focus group. He said, "[He] told me he thinks the importance of exposition rises inversely to the quality of the work. If the work is good enough, a correct proof, or a significant enough result, you don't care as much." To which one of his colleagues replied, "I disagree totally with what [you] just said. No, the exposition is totally crucial. If a thesis is not well exposed, it

## TABLE 10.4.
### The Characteristics of Different Quality Dissertations in Mathematics

| Quality | Characteristics |
|---|---|
| **Outstanding** | Original, significant, and hard to do; is short, simple, elegant, surprising, beautiful, and out of the ordinary; does something others have tried and failed to do with a combination of good, original, artistic ideas or clever, original arguments, and exceptional technical virtuosity; uses ideas or techniques from other areas that no one thought to use before; provides a very simple proof for a result or a conjecture thought to require a long proof; decisively solves a problem that many people have wanted to know about; develops new methods or approaches that other people will use; anticipates developments to come<br><br>*Applied mathematics*: is intellectually deep, even if it does not create new mathematics; provides new insight into and understanding of the natural sciences |
| **Very good** | A very solid, moderately significant contribution that proves the student has mastered the methods and technologies of the field and can do mathematics; well written; somewhat surprising; contains a few new ideas; is technically difficult; obtains the expected result with the expected method; uses standard methods to solve a new problem or prove a new theorem; solves a less well-known problem that fewer people have tried to solve; has a very good result; contains material for one to three papers; has a reasonable chance of having some impact |
| **Acceptable** | Has done enough work on a problem that is typically given to the student by the advisor; has mastered the literature, figured out the techniques, and can think about and solve problems, often with some hints from the advisor; usually well written, but may need better structure and organization and may contain typos and grammatical errors; the problem is not exciting; the proof is pretty standard but done correctly; result is not very interesting or surprising; has a few new approaches or ideas, but shows little original thought or creativity; tends to be narrowly focused and not technically difficult; lacks elegance—contains long, very technical calculations without a lot of insight; adds to the common literature in mathematics; extends knowledge and moves the field forward a little; will not have a significant impact on the field |

*(continues)*

**TABLE 10.4.**
**Continued**

| Quality | Characteristics |
|---|---|
| **Unacceptable** | Not original or significant; is original but too easy or trivial; has mistakes or errors; the result is already known, copies (plagiarizes) existing work or borrows parts of existing work and puts it in the student's own language; the theory or results are wrong; the proof is wrong because of technical things or the student does not understand the subject; the proof is incomplete or contains a serious gap or mistake; the proof needs to be simplified; the student missed some nontrivial details; is a very easy extension of already known work; the student did not recognize that the result could be easily proven in a few lines; is a compendium of existing examples |

should not be accepted. I think this goes without saying. What the person is learning also is . . . how to write mathematics."

Outstanding dissertations are written by outstanding students. Outstanding students were described as people who complete some very advanced studies, usually beyond the mathematics of the advisor. They are actively involved in the subject. They do not just know what has already been done, they understand the ways of thinking that lead to it and can recreate those ways of thinking for themselves. They are very independent and have original ideas. They take the initiative and work on interesting problems independently of details and advice from their advisors. They have the maturity and insight of a seasoned professional. As one participant said, "They've already achieved some potential. They've already made contributions that somebody who's been out [of school] quite awhile would be happy to have done. That's fairly rare, but it certainly has happened."

Outstanding dissertations may be a function of luck. A student might "just happen to be at the right time in the right place and have a great contribution, and then not do very much later on in their academic research life." Alternatively, a student may have a good advisor and the advisor has a great idea," about which one participant said, "That's being in the right place." To which his colleague replied, "Not necessarily, but yeah."

One participant thought that there were fundamentally two different kinds of outstanding dissertations. "One decisively solves a problem that many people have wanted to know about. It closes the door." The other kind "anticipates developments that come about. Maybe the thesis itself cannot be published in the *Annals of Mathematics*, but consequences of the thesis do get published there."

The mathematics faculty used several indeterminate terms—beauty, elegance, simplicity, surprise—to describe the outstanding dissertation, terms about which one participant commented, "are absolutely the criteria you would apply to an art form, which mathematics is." Unlike faculty in many of the other disciplines, the mathematician faculty defined these terms. "Beauty" is "seeing some important underlying principle below all the detail." "Elegance" involves cleverness and originality. "Surprise" is seeing connections between two things. And "simplicity" is providing a simple proof for a result or conjecture that others thought would require a long proof or take a lot of mathematics or work. The faculty also defined the indeterminate quality "difficultness," which they noted would not, from their perspective, apply to an art form. They said something that is difficult may not involve much elegance, but it involves a lot of work, ideas, and machinery. For example, one participant talked about a student who solved difficult problems that had been around for about 25 years. "He did a lot of work. The proofs ran 30 or 40 pages."

When faculty read outstanding mathematics dissertations, they make remarks like, "I never could have done this in a hundred years," "I would never in a million years myself have come up with that idea," and "God, I wish I'd done that. . . . Why didn't I think of that? Then you think, 'Aw, man, I'm going to have to compete with this guy for the next 10 or 20 or 30 years.' . . . It's something that you wish you'd done, that you wish you'd thought of."

In addition to defining what outstanding dissertations are, the mathematics faculty provided some insight into what they are not. Outstanding dissertations do not involve "taking some standard techniques and applying them to [a] problem," rather, as suggested above, they involve "solving interesting, hard problems with new ideas." A dissertation with a correct and original proof would also not be considered "excellent" if the student "couldn't answer questions during [the] defense or . . . cannot really handle [the] discussion around the subject."

## Very Good

The very good dissertation is the level that most mathematics faculty expect of mathematics graduate students, and the quality dissertation that most mathematics graduate students produce. While the very good dissertation shows drive and the ability to understand long techniques, it "probably would not have very new ideas [and] the approach would not be different, but it would be technically difficult and hard." It is something that "quite a number of people" could do "if they put . . . that much effort into that problem." However, faculty are "happy" when a student "does such a thing," because getting there is "a long hard road."

One participant characterized the journey as follows:

> Most of the time when you're a graduate student, you've only been doing mathematics significantly for the last two years. You have to read this some-times vast literature, absorb it, look at this problem, try to put it in context, try to find the techniques to do it, and put together various things and with some degree of difficulty. That's a significant achievement. I would say that's very good. [There] is a reasonable possibility that they'll be able to continue doing research, that they will make more significant contributions in their career.

Indeed, another participant said, "If somebody is planning to be a research mathematician, then they better have a good thesis."

Although the very good dissertation was characterized as containing material for three papers, one participant noted that those papers usually could not be written "by cutting out pieces of the thesis." To write those papers, the student would typically have to take different parts of the dissertation and finish "those strands of thought." The professor estimated that "the student might end up spending maybe six months on each of those [papers]."

## Acceptable

An acceptable dissertation is not surprising. It is one where anyone in the field would say, "Yeah," when they heard it had been done. They would be glad someone did it, but they would not be surprised that it had been done. Acceptable dissertations do not require "the specific talent of this person to make progress." If this student had not done it, "the next student down the road" would.

Students who write acceptable dissertations are typically given a problem by their advisor that the advisor usually knows how to solve. They show less initiative and require more spoon-feeding than students who write higher-quality dissertations. Indeed, they often wait for their advisor to "feed them hints and tell them where to look and [what to] read" to the point where "it's sometimes hard to separate out the contribution from the advisor and [from] the student." One participant said, the "advisor is known to sort of write the thesis for the student." According to another participant, in instances where a paper gets published from the dissertation and a colleague says, "I read an interesting paper by your student, the supervisor may make a face. . . . It's a sour look that means, 'Yeah that was one of the more unpleasant [dissertations] I have ever had to write for somebody.' Not literally, but in terms of feeding them all the important ideas." On the other hand, one participant said:

> It's still telling that they do show some promise, that they can read the literature, [and] that they can figure out how to apply certain techniques that are available to the problem. You hope that they'll do better after they get their Ph.D. . . . So acceptable just means, yes, they can read the literature. They can learn techniques. They can solve problems. They can think about problems. They can try things and if something doesn't work, they can try something else, maybe with some hints.

Students who write acceptable dissertations often do not want, realize they are not capable of, or ultimately do not seek academic careers at research institutions, and faculty will often adjust their expectations for these students accordingly, as shown by the following comments:

> *Participant:* I had a couple of students who wanted to go into industry instead of academics. So, a solid thesis is OK because they are not planning to have a research career.

> *Participant:* If you have a student who wants . . . a research career, and they're simply not capable of doing a very good thesis, then at some point you realize that the best thesis they can possibly do . . . is only acceptable. Then they can get their degree, but they won't get a research position.

> *Participant:* There are students who are separate cases. Maybe they decided they don't want to continue in academics for one reason or another, or . . . if they do want to continue in academics, they've already decided not to

continue at a research-level institution. They have done enough work for us. A thesis and the degree will help them . . . in getting a position at a teaching school. . . . So you could have cases where somebody finishes with an acceptable but not particularly strong thesis.

Even though faculty may adjust their expectations for these types of students, the faculty will not give up their standards. "A Ph.D. is not a consolation prize," said one participant. At the same time, faculty will typically not allow students who are interested in and capable of pursing a research career in a very competitive environment or at a very high-ranked university graduate with an acceptable dissertation:

> There is a certain level that you need to reach and the quality of the work that we say is enough to graduate. Some students may reach these very quickly after a year of study, and [if] the person is capable of a lot more, in that case, well, we won't call that a dissertation.

### Unacceptable

The mathematics faculty drew a distinction between unacceptable performance and unacceptable dissertations. They said unacceptable dissertations are rare because students whose performance is unacceptable are usually stopped before they can write or defend a dissertation. These students typically do not pass qualifying exams. Those who get past qualifying exams often fail to make progress on their research. Unlike the sciences, where students can be (begrudgingly) awarded a Ph.D. for negative results, in mathematics "we cannot show our dirty test tubes." Students cannot say, "This is all the ways I tried to do this problem and none of these worked in my case." These students usually "drop out" before it becomes an issue or are told to "go find another advisor because you're not going to get a degree with me."

Most faculty said that they had never seen an unacceptable or failing dissertation, but asserted that if it did happen, it would be the advisor's fault. One participant said, "I would seek the indictment of the advisor saying, 'The advisor made a mistake.'" Another participant said:

> Hypothetically, how that can happen would be, for example, if someone [on the committee] realized that a result was already known, and . . . realizes [that] the thesis advisor didn't know it, or it turns out that it was easy to prove this result, [you] can do it simply in few lines and the person didn't recognize it, or there was a serious gap, a mistake in the proof.

However, two faculty had experience with unacceptable and failing dissertations. One participant was on a committee at another university in the 1970s that voted to pass a dissertation that he thought was unacceptable. "That was kind of shocking to me . . . [The] dissertation was basically a compendium of examples; not examples that he himself derived. So, it was like a Master's thesis where it was scholarship, but not an original contribution." The other participant was on a committee, also at another university, that rejected a dissertation.

> The original thoughts were just so easy. [The] theorems, they were just real easy. . . . In this case . . . the background was that the student really wanted to graduate and the thesis advisor was telling him, "Well, you don't have enough," and the student insisted. Finally, the thesis advisor just used the committee as a way to force the student to see that he was right.

## The Components of a Mathematics Dissertation

The mathematics faculty did not particularly like having to discuss the quality of individual components of the mathematics dissertation; two focus groups did not discuss them. In general, the faculty felt "uncomfortable" doing something that they thought was "too facile." They felt that what they were being asked to do was difficult and subjective, and that focusing on the individual components trivialized the more general discussion of quality of the dissertation as a whole that they had just had. One participant said, "You take the thing as a whole. You read it and say, 'Is it eloquent? Is it correct? Is it well exposed?' and so on. The order doesn't even matter." Another, echoing the sentiments of many, said, "It's all results, that's what counts. If they're good results, the student will get the degree and it will be thought of as a good thesis."

On the positive side, one participant said, "I think the task of what we are doing here, trying to struggle with it, isn't a bad task for us." A few even defended the matrix (see Table 1.2). They felt that the "six columns belong in every thesis and in every paper" and that "this is something the student should learn how to do in writing a thesis."

There was some disagreement between two focus groups over which of the components were most important. Faculty in one focus group thought that the "heart" of the dissertation was "3" (proof of results) and "5" (statement of results/theorems). Faculty in another thought that the "only two columns" that "have any relevance at all" were the approach to the problem/ techniques (column 4) and proof of results (column 5), about which one participant noted are "80% of my judgment."

In short, the faculty's problems with the matrix appear to have less to do with what students are asked to do in a dissertation than with how faculty judge what the student has done. Despite their dislike for the matrix, as a group, the mathematics faculty managed to discuss all but one cell in the matrix: unacceptable conclusion. Below we explore the characteristics of the components of the mathematics dissertation (see Table 10.A in the appendix to this chapter) and what the faculty said about them.

## Introduction/Problem Statement

The introduction/problem statement in a mathematics dissertation is a "user-friendly" way of introducing the reader to a very complicated and difficult subject. It should put the work in context and convince the committee, and perhaps even people outside the committee who are not experts in the field, that the problem is important. It should state, "Here's the problem I want to solve. Here's why it's useful to solve the problem. . . . Here's how I want to go about solving the problem." Most of the mathematics faculty did not view the introduction as critical and said that the quality of the introduction/problem statement would not be a factor in their assessment of the quality of the dissertation as a whole: "A supergreat introduction is not going to move something from very good to outstanding or unacceptable." If it is not well done, it is "not going to change my opinion about the significance of the thesis." One participant said that he put more emphasis on teaching his students how to write "a good introduction for a paper coming out of the thesis." Faculty in another focus group noted that the introduction "doesn't occupy the same role [that] somehow I get the sense [it does in] other disciplines," about which one of his colleagues went on to say:

> I think [writing an introduction/problem statement] is such a critical discipline that we should be more serious about it. . . . I don't think we are as disciplined as a college. I don't think we spend the same amount of time that other disciplines do. Maybe because it's harder and a little more technical [in mathematics], but I don't think historically mathematicians have made a big effort in this regard, which is a shame.

The outstanding introduction is "pretty rare." The problem is formulated well mathematically and may contain an element of surprise. A participant said the student may say, "Consider this relation," and "Bang! Everything falls . . . everything follows from it." "How the hell" the student ever got that "consider this" was described as "genius" and as involving creativity.

## Discussion of the Literature

The discussion of the literature in mathematics does not seem to be quite the same as the literature review found in most other disciplines. Indeed, this difference was noted but not explained. As mentioned earlier, the discussion of the literature typically occurs in the introduction, and the mathematicians did not feel that it was a very important part of the dissertation. In fact, one participant said, "Traditionally, a student in math is not trained . . . to make a big effort to explain to other people what they are doing."

The focus group participants felt that mathematics was more accumulative than other disciplines, and that what mathematics students really have to do is "digest very thoroughly and internalize a good bit of work that has been done in mathematics [in order] to do something new." Another participant said, "We take the point of view that the reader has read and understood every other previous paper. We don't spend a lot of time discussing what others have done in their techniques." Indeed, one participant said that "mathematicians can sometimes work on things for which there is no literature." Despite this, students are supposed to find out what literature there is out there and state what literature they are going to use and where it came from in a coherent fashion.

The outstanding discussion of the literature shows maturity. The student puts his or her work in context and competently discusses how his or her work is related to existing results and how it is different. In the context of their discussion of acceptable literature reviews, one participant said:

> Hopefully they will learn to read the literature. Certainly it's nice to have literature in the dissertation, some discussion of it, and maybe bring the problem into context. You certainly want them to learn to do that so they can recognize what a good problem is and whether it's something they should work on in the future once they get their degree.

Finally, one participant discussed what he likes and does not like in students' handling of the literature:

> If [in] the text [there] should be a comment about [the literature], "See 72." Just [a] comment [about] how to find this referenced book. . . . I hate something like [when] people say, "Well, we used one of the theorems in the book of Mr. Smith." That's terrible. . . . It is better to quote the theorem, even though he rephrased it. It is needed for our own work. . . . But sometimes it is too much. . . . But this [is an] indication [of] why this particular item in the literature is useful, that might be the outstanding way of doing this.

## Statement of Results/Theorems

The statement of results/theorems is one of the most important components of a mathematics dissertation and "the main indicator" of a student's "research potential." It is where and how faculty "distinguish between outstanding and very good and acceptable." One participant said, "There should be a straight line between the beginning of the paper [the introduction] and the statement of results, [because readers] don't want to read a whole bunch of stuff. [It's] not like a novel. They want to read about your stuff before they figure out what the paper is about." The statement of results/theorems also needs to be clear, correct, and coherent.

The outstanding statement of results/theorems component was distinguished from the other quality levels by the ease with which it is understood. It is something that an "educated person can simply read" and know what the result is without too much effort. All the other levels are "just a gradation of . . . how easy and clear it is to understand." Indeed, in the unacceptable statement of results, something is usually wrong, and the notation may be "horrible." Faculty "could spend a year trying to figure out if it is correct."

## Approach to the Problem (Techniques)

The mathematics faculty's discussion of the approach to the problem (techniques) component did not include a mention of the role of this component in the dissertation. An outstanding approach to the problem was said to depend on how important the theorem is to the discipline. If the theorem is really important, then having a novel approach is less important than the fact that the theorem has been proven. Still, outstanding approaches are "far from obvious." Though the field may think, "Wow! That's a great, surprising idea to apply here," whether the approach is really outstanding depends on "whether it was really the student's idea or whether it was the supervisor's idea or somebody else's idea." In cases where the idea originates with the student, outstanding approaches make the advisor say, "I could never have done that. . . . I would never have thought of that approach."

An acceptable approach looks deep only because it is so complicated that others cannot find out that it is not really deep. The faculty said that it is usually complicated because the student did not make the effort to make it easier.

## *Proof of Results*

The proof of results component is indispensable. One participant went so far as to say, "If the proof of the result isn't outstanding, then it isn't a thesis at all." The quality of the writing is also very important at this point of the dissertation. Poor writing makes it difficult to impossible for faculty to decide whether the proof is correct or not, and faculty's assessment of the quality of the dissertation can "drift up or down" based on the quality of the writing.

The faculty also indicated that there are many techniques for doing or presenting the proof; two were described. One is a very clear presentation that decisively proves the problem, but does not provide any insight into what is going on. The other is a lot less clear and a lot harder to read, but provides better insight into what is going on.

To be considered outstanding, the dissertation has to prove that its original idea is really original and not simply a modification of ideas that are already in the literature. Outstanding proofs are also elegant and sophisticated. One participant provided insight into how he assessed elegance:

> I will sometimes distinguish elegant proof from, let us say, not elegant proof. In other words, somebody can use very simple techniques in a rather inelegant way and take the long way to get it. When you know sophisticated techniques, you can do the same proof in a nice, elegant way, a simpler way, a shorter way. So, I measure the level of what I call "elegant proof." Some say, "Proof is proof." You can always find a way to prove somehow, but the way you are proving that—the tools that you use, the techniques you use—may distinguish a more sophisticated student and the less sophisticated student.

An acceptable proof is often apparent from the style. It is introduced in a confusing manner and "goes around about." The faculty can see that the student is struggling to "put it all together." One participant discussed how, through revisions, a first draft of a proof can move from acceptable to very good:

> The proof is correct, but they bring in extraneous stuff. [They] don't get to the heart of the matter clearly. . . . The first proof is not as good as what it is later on. It should be at a stage beyond when they prove it with big, massive computations, where you say what was really crucial. They really need this generality. [You ask them], "Can you simplify it and . . . get it down to something more clear and to the point?" So, something there in clarifying and boiling down and revising in the proofs, that can be the difference between an acceptable and a very good.

Unacceptable proofs are wrong. Though one participant said, "There is no such thing as a wrong proof. You have a proof or you don't have it." Unacceptable proofs are also difficult to follow. One participant said, "You go in and put red marks all over it and say, 'Rewrite it.' And it may not be better. So there's the issue of whether it's readable [and] somebody can follow it, other than the person writing it. Sometimes they can't even follow it."

### Conclusions/Future Directions

The existence of a conclusions/future directions component of a mathematics dissertation may be a department- or university-specific requirement. Focus group participants at one university said that they required a conclusion, but "it could be a very short one," while participants at other universities said that it was not required, that "It's not even a heading. I don't think that we expect it." Participants at still another university suggested that its presence may be a function of the type of dissertation (possibly the traditional versus essay). One said, "I'm not sure the old theses actually have this section." To which his colleague replied, "It varies. There still are some."

By contrast, the mathematics faculty were almost unanimous in stating that the conclusion is the statement of the theorems. "Basically, the theorems will be the results. That's what you are leading to." "You conclude that the theorem is correct. You proved it." One participant explained, "In math more than in other disciplines, when you prove a theorem, the achievement is self-evident."

The mathematics faculty also do not expect to see a discussion of future directions. One felt that making conjectures about what may or may not be true and what may be conceivable to try to prove "would be very difficult for a new Ph.D. to think about." However, another participant felt that talking about future directions was valuable. He thought that "It is good for the student to list them so they have in mind what they can continue to do. It's also good for anybody who might read it to know what you have to do and [it] points to the new problems." With respect to quality, one participant felt that the gradation from acceptable to outstanding was a function of the student's ability to convince people and justify that the result "really does look like this [and] that this is going to lead to lots of other stuff."

## Notes

1. For information on the source of these data, see chapter 1, note 5. James Maxwell at the American Mathematical Society also provided some data (personal communication, June 1, 2005).

2. The totals and averages are based on the 30 focus group participants who provided data.

3. The Streleski case is discussed in Schmidt (2000) and Cude (2001).

# Appendix

## TABLE 10.A.
### The Components of a Mathematics Dissertation and Their Characteristics at Different Quality Levels

| Components | Quality levels | | | |
| --- | --- | --- | --- | --- |
| | Outstanding | Very good | Acceptable | Unacceptable |
| **Introduction/ problem statement** | Well written; provides motivation for the research; presents a clear, mathematically well-formulated statement of the problem; tells why the problem is important and how it fits into the world; places the problem in a historical context and connects it with the literature/previous research; indicates how the student will solve it; provides a synopsis of the main results and a road map for the rest of the dissertation | Well written, but may not clearly delineate the difference between the background and the new results; introduces the reader to the subject in a friendly way; provides an overview of the methods; states clearly what has been proved | Provides a context for the work | Problem statement is wrong or trivial, or the problem has already been solved; one paragraph that simply states "We will prove the following results"; is not put into a clear context; the background is not explained very well |

| Components | Quality levels | | | |
|---|---|---|---|---|
| | Outstanding | Very good | Acceptable | Unacceptable |
| **Discussion of the literature** | Shows an understanding of the history and context of the problem, and how this work is related to existing results and how it is different from them; uses original sources; presents the literature coherently and quotes sources correctly; shows that the student has very thoroughly digested and internalized a lot of mathematical work; indicates how it fits the problem into the greater world of mathematics | The problem is placed in context, but less clearly | Places the problem into context; provides some discussion of the literature; mentions important things | Inadequate coverage of the literature; misses a lot of very relevant things; does not harmonize the conventions used in different articles |
| **Statement of results/ theorems** | Provides a clear and correct statement of results; is self-contained and easy to understand; is surprising and of great interest | Has clearly made progress; is interesting, but not surprising | Statement is correct but not that good; student can speak the language of mathematics; is not terribly interesting; has some minor discrepancies; terms are not well defined and may cause some confusion | Incorrect, something is mathematically wrong; the notation is so bad that it is impossible to understand |

*(continues)*

**TABLE 10.A.**
Continued

| Components | Quality levels | | | |
|---|---|---|---|---|
| | Outstanding | Very good | Acceptable | Unacceptable |
| **Approach to the problem (techniques)** | Original, insightful, clear, clean, unique, innovative, brilliant, beautiful, and unquestionable; uses a completely new group of ideas; synthesizes two totally dissimilar things; improves prior work; is useful elsewhere | Stylistic not just formal; is clear what methods were used | Uses well-worn techniques; presented in a very complicated way | Unclear; the approach is wrong or so messy reader cannot tell whether it is right or wrong |
| **Proof of results** | Well written; original; has new ideas; short, slick, streamlined, precise, correct, elegant; difficult but easy to follow; unexpected—uses a theorem from another area; beautiful—as simple as can be but no simpler; shows exactly how assumptions are used; does not make any unnecessary assumptions; bridges between or synthesizes areas | Clear, correct; skillful use of sophisticated techniques; proved rigorously and mathematically; notations are clear | Has some original thinking, some new ideas, but the innovation is confusing; contains extraneous material; does not get to the heart of the matter clearly; long, boring, routine; needs work | No proof or the proof is not shown; the logical deductions are not correct; contains unnecessary assumptions; is difficult to follow |
| **Conclusion/ future directions** | Really thinks about the problem in a new way; is convincing; main result has applications and implications; makes conjectures, discusses future directions | Solid summary of results; discusses limitations, obstacles to overcome; points to new problems; specifies some possible future directions or implications | States that the theorems are true; makes some conjectures | — |

# 11

# THE ECONOMICS
# DISSERTATION

There are more than 130 Ph.D. programs in economics in the United States that award degrees in 18 major fields and dozens of subfields. Graduate economics programs enroll roughly 12,000 students (master's and doctoral), and graduate roughly 900 new Ph.D.s annually. The median time to degree is 7.4 years. Close to 6% of new economics Ph.D.s go on to postdoctoral education.[1]

Thirty-three economics faculty at seven universities participated in the focus groups. Overall, these faculty had 621 years of experience, had chaired an estimated 417 dissertations, and had sat on an estimated 905 dissertation committees. The average economics focus group participant had been a professor for 19 years, had chaired 13 dissertations, and had sat on 27 dissertation committees. Below is a summary of the economics focus groups' discussions. Their performance expectations for the dissertation are displayed in the tables. Their supporting discussion is recounted in the text.

## The Purpose of an Economics Dissertation

The economics faculty viewed the dissertation as serving many purposes (see Table 11.1). They saw it both as an "input" in the sense of training or as an "investment" in the student as well as an "output" in terms of a contribution that moves the student along in his or her career. They also saw it as the "one great chance" that a person has in their entire life to do independent research with a backup team of experts and become a serious expert on one subject.

The faculty conceived their role in the dissertation process as one of

### TABLE 11.1.
### The Purpose of an Economics Dissertation

To train students in the habits of professional economists and to be researchers who do original, creative, significant work; to learn how to do research, generate questions, apply the appropriate methods, and solve problems independently at a professional level; to demonstrate the ability to do original research, use tools appropriately, and produce an independent piece of work; to launch a career and help the student get a job; to credential the individual as a professional economist

training students to achieve originality and significance in their research and as putting a "stamp" on the Ph.D., certifying that the student has the appropriate skills to go out and do economics. The faculty were very clear that students could not demonstrate their ability to conduct independent research at a professional level without doing a dissertation:

> You can't give a test on learning how to do a thesis and then say that's enough, because the thesis requires an enormous range of different skills from being able to conceptualize questions, being able to figure out how to go through conceptualization and conduct research. Then it involves the discipline of sitting and writing and being able to communicate what you did to others. This whole variety of skills is what's being tested in the dissertation. It's the demonstration that you have all of these skills and that you can use them together to produce this nice, beautiful painting in the end. It's the difference between studying how to paint and being a painter. . . . The only way to see whether you actually [can] demonstrate all these skills is by doing it.

The faculty said that from the students' perspective the dissertation is a learning process, one that helps them think about research. After they have completed their course work, the question becomes: Can I take the next step? Can I do independent research? Indeed, according to the faculty, when a student starts a dissertation, the student does not know whether he or she can do a dissertation until it is done. In the end, students have not only learned how to do independent research,

> [they have learned] something about themselves, that they have the power to do it. . . . It's an amazing transformation that comes over people in the

process when it works right. From people who are very unsure of themselves to people [who] when we send them out [say], "I can do this now. I
have found this and this." . . . There's no other way that they can learn
that they can do it [than] by doing it. So they come out transformed people. The dissertation transforms these people.

One participant stated "crassly" that the dissertation was a "hurdle over
which people in this profession have to jump in order to get a job." Others
saw the dissertation as part of a student's portfolio, something to show
around to prospective employers, "Here's the kinds of things I can do. If
you hire me, here's what you get."

## Original Contribution

The economics faculty identified many ways to make an original contribution (see Table 11.2). Like the other disciplines, an original contribution in
economics is something new, something that has not been done before. But
unlike other disciplines, most economics faculty felt that an original contribution in economics should have some type of practical application. It
should inform policy or inform understanding of the economic behavior of
individuals, firms, markets, or systems.

While they felt that originality often implies creativity, the economics
faculty thought that "new" and creative" were slightly different. They noted
that a new idea does not have to be creative. Indeed, one participant said, "I
can think of lots of dissertation students . . . who have come to me with an

### TABLE 11.2.
#### The Nature of an Original Contribution in Economics

| |
|---|
| Something nontrivial that has not been done before; is publishable; a deviation from or a new way of thinking about an economic feature, issue, or problem; identifying a gap in the literature; redefining or reconceptualizing old problems; asking a new question; making new connections among existing data; using a new source of data or data set; constructing or amalgamating new data; applying old econometric ideas to new data; applying new econometric ideas to old data; applying, modifying, or developing a model or technique to solve a problem; proving a new result; proving a theorem using weaker assumptions; challenging existing theories or policies; advances knowledge |

idea for a paper which no one's done before, but the fact [is] that it's not terribly creative or interesting or relevant." His colleagues responded, "Just because no one's done it before, doesn't make it a good idea," and "That's exactly right . . . you'd be surprised at how many doctoral students don't understand that, really don't understand that."

Faculty at another university said that all they ask their students to do in their dissertation proposal is to identify a gap in the literature (something that is an anathema to historians). They direct their students to "think about originality in terms of logical or empirical holes" in either theory or data and convince their committee that they have an idea about how to fill the gap. The gap can be a small point that is difficult to fill and needs to be filled or it could be something that involves reconceptualization.

Faculty in still another focus group commented that "very few theses are really original." They noted that their students "are not almost encouraged to do it [be very original]." "We almost discourage somebody from [asking new questions] because of the fear it wouldn't go anywhere and because students who work on things that are really original tend not to finish promptly." Rather, the faculty "usually deem something as original if it's asking an old question using somebody else's approach, but you have a new data set that hasn't been used to answer that question before." In short, original contributions can come in "big packages and sometimes really tiny ones," but "most dissertations are in that tiny category."

Thus, while the economics faculty had never heard of a dissertation failing to be accepted for lack of originality, they noted that there has to be some advance on the existing literature that is defensible in both theoretical and empirical terms.

## Significant Contribution

The key characteristics of a significant contribution in economics are its importance to and its impact on the field (see Table 11.3). Using the language of their discipline, the economics faculty indicated that for a dissertation to be significant, its "marginal value" has to be high relative to the existing literature. The faculty also talked about the "distance" between the assumptions and the conclusions. Sometimes "it's no surprise once you read what's going on . . . what's going to be the outcome." Indeed, many faculty used

**TABLE 11.3.**
**The Nature of a Significant Contribution in Economics**

A surprising, impressive, important, useful contribution that is publishable in top-tier journals; causes people to see things in a different way and makes progress at the empirical, theoretical, or policy level; a big, useful, relevant idea; increases understanding of an economic problem; challenges existing theory or policy; advances methodology and pushes the empirical frontier; extends data or methods in a nontrivial way; provides greater validation of existing results; will have wide applicability; cuts across many fields or disciplines; will be used by other people; advances or provides greater insight into the discipline or the world

the term "surprise" to talk about significance. The bigger the surprise, the greater the significance. One participant said, it "is that 'aha!' sense of 'Why didn't I think of that?' It's so obvious once somebody else says it, but it is completely not apparent until they have that insight."

There was some disagreement within and across economics focus groups on whether something had to be original in order to be significant. Some faculty said that it was hard to think of something that was significant but did not have some measure of originality. Others had a hard time thinking of dissertations that were original but not significant, about which one participant remarked, "No, it's not hard to think of them. It's easy to think of them, but it's not easy to think of a really good dissertation that's good and creative but not a significant contribution." Another participant said he "could imagine something that was a significant contribution which some people at least would question whether it was original or not." A participant in a different focus group supplied an example:

> I was thinking of [Robert] Lucas, who's a Nobel Prize winner in economics in rational expectations. Rational expectations was not an original idea. [John] Muth, a mathematician, is attributed with the idea. Lucas is attributing it to macroeconomics in particular. It wasn't a particularly original idea, but the significance, it just totally revolutionized macroeconomics.

Significance is hard to determine until something is actually "out there" and the profession has had a chance to evaluate it. However, faculty can make judgments about potential significance because in economics we do, as a community of scholars, have a really coherent sense of what are the important or pressing questions for the discipline, because as a field it stresses the ways of quantifying the value of different kinds of things. So, there's a certain amount of collective consensus at any moment in time about what are the important kinds of questions, both [at] the policy and empirical level and also [at the] theoretical level. . . . One of the kinds of things that are front and center stage is dissertations that make progress in one of those areas. [They] are the ones that are likely to stand out as seeming like significant contributions.

The faculty indicated that there was a range in the degree of significance. "As with anything else, it's a matter of where you draw this imaginary line between what's sufficiently this or that. It's pretty arbitrary . . . something that's clearly above or clearly below. . . . That's the nature of dissertations anyway." However, the faculty did say that as a profession it does have standards.

We could line up these different degrees of quality dissertations with where it could be published and you could send the same paper off to other universities and get the same level of agreement about where it could be published. So if we can't vocalize the standards well, as a profession we know that they actually exist.

This participant went on to say that "there's not overwhelmingly strong agreement" on the standards, to which one of his colleagues replied that the disagreement is usually about the degree of importance. Reflecting on differences in standards, another participant in that focus group said:

I remember one of my professors in graduate school said if you look at all the top economics journals, he felt there were usually only three significant contributions a year. That would mean that most professors live their lives without making a significant contribution. That suggests to me that there are different standards. That speaks for the dissertation. Publishable would be pretty acceptable.

Regardless, most faculty would not consider a contribution to be significant "unless the result is so interesting that serious colleagues in other major departments are going to take notice of this."

In general, the faculty do not expect graduate students to come up with something that is very significant. "It doesn't happen here and it doesn't happen at other top schools. I think what we generally look for is a series of results that may stem from quite original ideas but generally do not." Indeed, most dissertations make incremental contributions to economics. Occasionally faculty will see something that is revolutionary, "but it's the exception rather than the rule." "Those are rare."

## The Dissertation as a Whole

Economics dissertations come in two "flavors." One flavor, which used to be the standard, is where there is one question and the student does a full analysis—"reviews the literature, does some theory, collects data or finds somebody else's data, and addresses those and reaches a conclusion." The other, more common, "flavor" is composed of two or three separate but related journal-article-type essays that are "stapled together" and can be polished and sent off to peer review journals.[2] The rise of the essay dissertation is part of a shift in the culture of economics, which favors publishing journal articles rather than books. Below we explore the characteristics of different quality traditional- and essay-style economics dissertations (see Table 11.4) and what the economics faculty had to say about them.

### *Outstanding*

The outstanding economics dissertation is insightful. It contains a new way of thinking about and measuring things. It causes the reader to feel that he or she has really learned something. It is a "page-turner." It is compelling to read and surprises the reader. According to one participant, "You say, oh my goodness, I really didn't think about that. I didn't know this tool could be used that way and I didn't know that this problem could be conceptualized that way," or "My goodness, I couldn't have seen that," or "Huh! Wow! This is a really fine piece of work." It is work that could be condensed or shipped as is to a major journal and get published.

Outstanding dissertations "illuminate an entire area." They "startle the field" and "stimulate a lot of activity in the profession." One participant noted that there are different metrics by which one could gauge an outstanding dissertation. He asked, "Outstanding to whom?" and then proceeded to supply an answer:

## TABLE 11.4.
## The Characteristics of Different Quality Dissertations in Economics

| Quality | Characteristics |
|---|---|
| **Outstanding** | Extremely well written; thoughtful, elegant, clever, compelling, and surprising; internally coherent; chapters have a lot of substance; has the beauty of simplicity; a lot of creativity, insight, originality, and independence; exhibits command and authority over the material; makes you look at something differently; addresses a very interesting question in a solid way; exhibits a deep understanding of the literature and theory; challenges the literature and strongly held traditional views; contains a very interesting theoretical component; integrates theory across fields; makes a theoretical contribution; constructs a new data set; develops or applies new tools, methods, models, or analytical techniques; exhibits incredibly good data collection and analysis skills; has a complete, comprehensive, and convincing sophisticated analysis; solves a controversy or answers questions of interest to the field; is very practically useful for a lot of people; will fundamentally and radically change things |
| **Very good** | Not quite as original, insightful, or integrated; may involve new and creative ideas and be well executed, but the problem is not that interesting; some elements are surprising; has a good question or problem, but the topic may not be of central interest to the field; good question but poor empirical execution; the question is good, but the answer is not; the answer is good, but the question is not; is an extension of someone else's work; the hypotheses have not been developed in a theoretical way, are mainly statements about how the world behaves; lacks the theory needed to conceptualize the work; uses appropriate data collection and analytic techniques; uses advanced mathematical or econometric techniques to analyze the data, but the student cannot really interpret the results; provides convincing evidence, but the analysis does not live up to the idea; has consistent results derived from well-formed assumptions but not contained in the assumptions; the outcomes are more or less predictable; does not push the frontiers; does not really make a significant contribution; contributions are not as deep as they might be; may readjust the way people think but does not fundamentally change things |
| **Acceptable** | Competent, useful, adequately organized, investigated, and communicated but not particularly clever or original; plausible but |

| Quality | Characteristics |
|---|---|
| **Acceptable** | not compelling; shows some gaps in reasoning; is directed as opposed to independent research; asks an old question; is highly derivative, is a correct, small, not exciting extension of someone else's work; synthesizes other people's work; has an interesting question that is poorly addressed; does not exhibit a broad understanding of the subfield; does not place the work in context; displays competence in applying theory to a specific problem, in collecting data, and in managing and analyzing the data; applies an existing model to new data; uses a very restrictive model to narrowly answer a question; has not really answered the question; results are believable but the conclusions are not; does not realize the depth or the significance of what he or she has done, contribution is of minimal value to the profession |
| **Unacceptable** | Trivial and poorly written; not thorough; lacks careful thought; is too ambitious or idealistic; contains errors or mistakes; is misleading; has no introduction or literature review; student does not understand the relevant literature; the question is not posed well; asks an inappropriate or unoriginal question; student does not see that the question has an obvious answer; has a series of hypotheses that are not rooted in theory; uses the wrong data set or analytic techniques; uses inappropriate or incorrect methods; uses a system of equations that does not have a solution; cannot solve the problem; the problem has already been solved; student misinterprets the data; student is unable to explain the results; results are self-contradictory; student overinterprets the results; student does not understand the implications of the results; student cannot demonstrate the conclusion |

The broader the audience, the more outstanding. We could imagine a dissertation that was very good in a particular field, but it wouldn't be outstanding from the perspective of the profession because it would just be very specific to that particular problem and that particular area. If one wants to be outstanding in economics, one wants to do something that has broad appeal and that a lot of people will be able to use your results or learn from your results. So everything else constant, the broader the appeal of the question you're asking or the answer you're giving, the more likely it is to be outstanding.

Indeed, outstanding dissertations ask and answer interesting questions. The question may be one that the advisor has not thought about before, though that is "quite rare." The dissertation may answer a question that "everybody is waiting on" or provide an answer that everybody is curious about. Outstanding dissertations also present complete and convincing analyses. "You don't look at it and think of a handful of different ways that you could try to change the analysis and perhaps find different answers. . . . You say, 'Yes, they have pretty much done everything I might have checked.'" Indeed, outstanding dissertations are outstanding in several or all components simultaneously. Although the faculty do not always acknowledge it, the rhetoric—how persuasive the dissertation is—matters.

Great dissertations often have great advisors, though the best students do not always write the best dissertations. Indeed, students get varying degrees of help from their advisors and committees in the course of writing the dissertation, though the better students do more of the work themselves. They are more capable of "doing it independently and thoughtfully and quickly, as opposed to slowly with much prodding and help." One participant said that the dissertation students write in one year by themselves "is more impressive than the ones that take three years and they [the students] are at your office all the time even if it's . . . literally the same outcome."

The better students are also never satisfied—or their advisor never lets them be satisfied—until this "thing" is analyzed as comprehensively and intensively with the best techniques possible. Finally, one participant talked about the advice that he would give to a graduate student who really wanted to write an outstanding dissertation. He said he would tell the student

> to go to *Dissertation Abstracts* from the last five years from students out of the best schools in the country and the world, students that got placed in top schools whose work is cited . . . and write [your] dissertations on the topics that you're interested in. So . . . the very first thing is to identify a topic, identify a question or issue that you're interested in.

## Very Good

The very good dissertation is similar to the outstanding one, but it is just less—less interesting, less original, less significant, less well executed. Faculty want students to produce "something" that other people would be interested in reading, and the very good dissertation may fail to live up to this standard.

One participant said that he could "think of all kinds of dissertations that might involve new and creative ideas that might be very well executed, be extremely competent, but which just no one would be interested in reading." Sometimes the work is not of interest to others because the student is working on things that are a "little out in the outfield of the discipline." At the same time, faculty worry when students come to them with "hot" or "sexy" topics, because they believe that there is a role for less hot topics and that students should be able to research exactly what they want to. However, given the "market" in North America, faculty realize that students need to work on topics that will increase their market value and enable them to continue in a research career beyond the end of their dissertation.

The faculty discussed two other situations that result in very good but not outstanding dissertations. In one situation students start out with some really good ideas but do not take the time to develop them, either because they want to get on with their lives or they have a job waiting for them. In this case, given a little more time, the dissertation could be a "great work." In the other situation students present real skills as engineers or mathematicians but not as economists. The students can use very advanced techniques to analyze data or solve a theorem, but "they really can't interpret the results. They do not really understand what the results mean in terms of economics." "And that can't be an excellent dissertation."

## Acceptable

The acceptable dissertation meets the "minimum criterion." It is "satisfactory." The original content is often "close to zero," "almost undetectable." The research question and the answer often do not "come together in the end." Faculty may not believe or agree with the conclusions or interpretations. The work is such that it does not have much of "any chance to get in a journal" or, if it does, it would be published in a "second-tier or even lower-level journal." However, the student has worked hard, gone through the process of learning how to do a research project, investigated the question, communicated the results adequately, and demonstrated competence and skill. In short, the student "did what we agreed that they were going to do," and "this is the best this person is possibly going to be able to do."

Students who write acceptable dissertations often require a lot of guidance, "they can't pick up the ball and run with it," said one participant.

Although they may be "very bright," they are people who "aren't really capable of doing it on their own and need to be . . . directed in their research." Sometimes advisors help these students by giving them what they think is a "pretty good topic," but they "prove incapable of doing something at the level you had originally intended" and the project needs to be scaled back. These students take "forever" to "work it through" and it "seems like you always have to be there helping out." Indeed, when he was in graduate school, one participant remembered one of his professors saying, "If you . . . want to get a degree, just go to your advisor each week and say, 'I didn't understand what you told me to do last week.' Just keep doing that each week. He will ultimately get tired."

Particularly "irritating" to faculty are students who "can't or won't do what you tell them to do. . . . If I say, 'OK, you need to do some sensitivity test,' . . . and then they come back a week later and I say, 'So, how did that sensitivity test go?' and, [they say,] 'Well, I didn't want to do that because . . .'"

When they have students who need to be guided through the process, the faculty look for growth "relative to what we consider capabilities" or progress. At the end, do the students still need to be guided? Or are the students "at the stage where they are in fact seeing the bigger picture, seeing how it fits in, seeing where the next question lies?"

Faculty do not want to "sign off on something that isn't very good," because "we have to put our name on it." They want to have some confidence that "the person is not going to be an embarrassment to your name or herself or, even more importantly, to the department." They do not want someone to say, "You gave this person a Ph.D. and they can't do X, Y, and Z."

In deciding to award the Ph.D., faculty think about what "this person is going to be capable of doing if we certify him as being employable as an academic." "Can that person credibly say they've developed some research skills and can go off into the marketplace and, whether inside or outside of academia, at least have a sense of what it means to do careful research?" While faculty would recommend these students for positions at "state campuses" and teaching colleges, they would not recommend them for jobs at major research universities. Indeed, students who write acceptable dissertations often end up in jobs that are in directed research at research institutions, in government agencies, or "they go off and do something else."

## *Unacceptable*

An unacceptable dissertation should never be failed because an unacceptable dissertation should never be written. According to most of the economics faculty, if a department allows a student to defend a dissertation that is unacceptable, then the faculty have not done their job. However, a few participants provided reasons why students produce unacceptable dissertations.

Sometimes students bite off more than they can chew. "They think they can do everything and persist in thinking they can do everything, and then, in the end, they can do nothing." Others run out of steam.

> People can get some distance down the track before it becomes obvious that they just don't have that [staying] power. They don't have what it takes to actually go the full distance. . . . It becomes obvious that they are not independently able to sustain this. . . . They're not in command of something. They're in command of the methodology that's required, [but] they don't properly understand the implications of the results that they're generating when they apply the methods to the data. They're engaged in something more abstract and theoretical, and they simply cannot solve the problem.

Some get job offers and say, "I've got to finish in the next four months." They put together an argument that under normal circumstances would have taken much longer, and it "just isn't together."

One participant knew students who had "flunked" their defenses. They were students who pushed for the defense. "They're usually also not in residence. They go out and have taken a job. You gave them things to do and they didn't do it."

## The Components of an Economics Dissertation

The economics faculty's comments about the matrix of components of the dissertation (see Table 1.2) were mild relative to other disciplines. One focus group did not discuss the components. The main objections were to the structure of the matrix. One participant remarked on the absence of a column that relates to data. To him, methodology and data analysis were the same thing. Another participant objected to the matrix's focus on the structural aspects of the output rather than on the scientific merit of the contribution. He said, "We don't care about the font or the binding or the introduction. What we care about is, is there a contribution there?" A third participant, who liked the idea of the focus group, did not think you could impose a structure on the quality of a dissertation. Below we explore the characteristics of the components of the economics dissertation (see Table 11.A in the appendix to this chapter) and what the faculty said about them.

## Introduction

The introduction to a traditional economics dissertation, which is typically the last thing the student writes, motivates the work. It should set up the question, frame the issue, and provide an overview of what the dissertation is going to accomplish.

The faculty had slightly different views on and experiences with introductions to the essay-style dissertation. One participant noted that he had seen essay dissertations that did not have introductions but then went on to say, "It's almost an afterthought. Someone says, 'Hey, wait a minute, we need an introduction.'" Another participant commented that in his last job, the Graduate School "bounced" an essay dissertation that did not have an introduction, saying, "It's got to be an integrated piece of work and the only way to show it's integrated is to write an introduction." Indeed, a participant at another university said, "In general, we expect people to write an introduction that somehow connects these three essays and identifies some common theme, some conclusion that comes out at the end." Still another participant described the introduction to the essay dissertation as "pretty much your dissertation abstract. 'In this dissertation I have three essays. Essay one . . .'" And then each essay has its own introduction, which sets up the question.

The outstanding introduction is well motivated. It articulates an interesting question and places it in a larger context. It displays authority and command over the argument and tells the reader everything he or she needs to know: "Why the discussion is important. What you're doing that's different from the previous literature. What your methods are. What your data are. What your results are, expressed in economics context. How important they are. And . . . that's all within two to three typewritten pages, double spaced." It also provides a road map of "where we are going and how this paper or this chapter is organized."

An outstanding introduction catches the reader's attention. "It's wow!" "It's like a[n] overture to an opera. You can play it by itself. It is incredibly penetrating and insightful." However, judgments about the quality of the introduction are dependent on the consistency of the work, if the rest of the dissertation does not live up to the promise of the introduction, then the faculty would not call the introduction outstanding or even very good.

In introductions that are less than outstanding, students typically cannot independently connect all the pieces; they need help from their advisors. One common error in lower-quality introductions is launching into the research question without putting it in context or stating what the general problem is and "where are we going from here." Indeed, one participant said:

> Writing an introduction, even to a research article, is a skill that is very difficult, and most students fail at it miserably initially. Part of it is because they become so ingrained in the minutiae of the problem. It's actually hard for them to write a two-page summary of what's really important about what they did.

Acceptable introductions often do not do a good job of convincing the reader that the problem is important or of explaining why anybody else should care about it. In some cases, this is because the introduction was written hurriedly at the end of the process. Students do not "show enough care," and only hint at what the problem really is.

Finally, the unacceptable introduction is one does not provide a clear sense of what the dissertation is going to do. After reading the introduction, the reader either does not know what the dissertation is about or the reader thinks he or she knows what it is about and is "pretty sure it's wrong." As with the acceptable introduction, the faculty attributed the lack of clarity, in part, to rushing it at the end. "They're tired. They're burning out." One participant gave an example of finding his own mistakes perpetuated in students' introductions:

> There have been times I have made mistakes. I said that paper X did this and I was wrong. I was actually thinking about paper Y and I said paper X. Then I see the mistake show up in the introduction, meaning that what they relied on was what I [said was in the paper]. They were relying on secondary sources and they never even went back and read the paper. . . . So, once in a while I'll find my own mistakes in these [introductions] and then I know it is not acceptable.

## *Literature Review*

The literature review and the introduction are typically intertwined in the economics dissertation. Many dissertations do not have literature reviews in the sense of "here is everything ever written on this topic and you cite what's wrong with it." Rather, students need to "clarify the marginal contribution of [their] work to the literature." In the essay dissertation, each essay typically includes some discussion of the literature.

Some of the focus group participants liked literature reviews, others did not. They commented, "Literature reviews don't do much for me." "Ones with literature reviews are usually very dull." "I don't read literature reviews." Despite its seeming lack of importance and faculty's general distaste for it, the focus group faculty did manage to characterize literature reviews of different quality.

The outstanding literature review is analytical and insightful. It shows "how these things interrelate and what actually can be done to improve them." It tells the reader how he or she should think about what is going on and it causes the reader to think about the problem in a different way. For instance, it may show how two seemingly disparate things turn out to be part of an integrated whole.

The outstanding literature review is also comprehensive. It covers all the important articles without going "overboard." One participant, who indicated that others might disagree with his view, said it

> has to focus like a laser on those N, which could be anywhere from three
> to a hundred papers that are most directly relevant to what's going on here.
> And every one of those papers has to be discussed pretty carefully with a
> view towards making the reader understand what's missing there and how
> this research is going to extend it.

For one participant, an outstanding literature review "is one that convinces me that if this student goes out and gives a job talk, he or she is not going to be surprised by somebody else asking about a reference that this student should know." Indeed, the outstanding literature review is close to the cutting edge. It may cite works that have been placed on Web sites or are under review.

One participant said that outstanding literature reviews were "very hard to do," because they "require a lot more experience than the typical graduate student has." Another said he had never seen an outstanding literature review in the "modern model," because "the chapters are more or less limited to article length, so the student doesn't get into great detail in the literature."

The very good literature review tells a story and helps the reader comprehend an area. Whereas, the acceptable literature review "has a lot of extra garbage" and a lot of "fluff." It typically reads, "Joe Blow says this. Somebody else said that." It is often unsophisticated about the material being used and may say, "This model follows from Reed '65, Reed-style overlapping models." Yet, the faculty do not want students to talk about Reed '65 because it is well known in the discipline. Rather, they want students to prove that they understand it. Indeed, one participant drew a distinction between "knowing the literature and where your contribution fits in, and what literature you decide to cite and actually review in your article." He noted that not everyone can draw this distinction, and, consequently, students produce 50-page literature reviews and cite papers that are not even relevant to their research question.

Unacceptable literature reviews tend to suffer from one or both of two problems. One problem is a lack of an "organizing intelligence." The student does not know what the question is. Consequently, the literature review is "just random things" that the student has read that seem to be related. It is just a list of names, "This person did that and that person did that." According to one participant, these types of literature reviews are "the most painful things to read." The other problem is failure to cite relevant articles. This is a "fatal flaw" and the "hallmark of stupid." As one participant said, "Missing . . . important [articles] is just a real good indication that the student isn't thinking along the lines of being a real scholar." However, another participant noted that "if there is something in the thesis," then "the literature review is the easiest to repair."

## Theory

There are two types of theory in economics, econometric and economic. Econometric theory is "basically high-powered statistical stuff" and falls under methods. Economic theory is "pure" theory. One participant thought that there would be differences in faculty's answers to the theory question across universities because theory-based departments require dissertations to have a strong theoretical foundation and a strong model.

While it is not clear that the faculty's responses differed by university, focus group faculty at one university did point out that many, but not all, of them were theoreticians. They noted that in the theoretical dissertation the student is setting up a model of an economy or a sector of an economy and trying to answer a question about it. Thus, in the theoretical dissertation there are no methods and the entire analysis is about the model and how it "reflects on our understanding of how the real world works." Regardless of whether the dissertation is theoretical or empirical, economic theory is essential to a good dissertation. The question being researched has to be posed in terms of theory and the ensuing analysis has to be set in terms of theory.

Outstanding theory is very hard to do. It is "an art, not a science." Outstanding theory components are written by students who have a sense of exactly how much theory they need to communicate about what they are doing. An outstanding theory component is in large part a function of the question being asked and of how well the theory answers the question without putting in a lot of very restrictive assumptions. In other words, it is being able to draw very precise conclusions from a very general theory. Outstanding is also coming up with results that are not obvious, and being able to provide good insight and understanding for those results. Outstanding theory components may involve developing more unified models, borrowing theories or techniques from other fields, or looking at a problem in reverse.

In the case of acceptable theory, there is no value added. The theory may be implicit rather than explicit. Faculty who read such a dissertation know it has a theoretical foundation, but the student has not been able to articulate it. One participant noted that "It's possible for an acceptable thesis to have a theory and an empirical part that neither alone you could imagine being published individually, neither is good enough, but when the two are combined, it makes it acceptable. . . . That's one of the things that distinguish[es] an acceptable from a very good from outstanding."

It is conceivable, but not likely, that faculty will accept an economics dissertation that does not have theory. Such a dissertation would discuss an issue in a reasonably coherent way and provide some empirical work. More typically, a dissertation will be unacceptable when the theory is wrong, does not make sense, or has elements that are mutually incompatible. Dissertations may also fail if students cannot explain their theory.

## *Methods*

The economics faculty said little about the role of methods in an economics dissertation. However, they did note that economics, unlike other social sciences, typically does not offer courses in "research methods." Rather, everyone who gets a Ph.D. in economics, no matter where he or she is trained, acquires a shared body of knowledge by taking the same sequence of courses in the first year: microeconomic theory, macroeconomic theory, econometrics, and mathematical economics. The faculty also noted that while purely theoretical dissertations are perfectly acceptable, there is a preference in the marketplace for empirical dissertations and there is a premium for people who have strong data collection skills.

Outstanding methods have two defining characteristics. One is a strong integration or correlation of theory and methods. "The survey you write or the experiments you design or the econometric technique you choose actually is closely related to the theory." The other is that it is "frontier and careful." The student is doing "something that most other people can't." He or she may use a technique that no one has ever used in economics to solve a problem or may develop a methodology that "everyone's waiting for." Indeed, the methodology may be so innovative that it can get published by itself. "Careful" was defined as, "appropriate," "sensible," and "professionally done."

> In the empirical work, the data points, every one is contestable. There's potential for error, multiple kinds. To watch a student make and justify judgments about procedures and trustworthiness of the data is to see something that is professionally done. . . . The emergence of judgment. That structuring an argument in a way that acknowledges the potential weaknesses of the argument.

Methods may be unacceptable when the student uses the wrong method or does something wrong. However, the faculty indicated that it is hard for a student to "fail in the methodology section." If students cannot do what the faculty "called acceptable" then "we sort of help them along, make them use the right methodology." Indeed, it would be "rare" to get to the final defense having used the wrong tools. On the other hand, shading into data analysis/results, the faculty noted that a lot of dissertation writers fail to look at their data and see what it actually tells them. While they may have used appropriate methods, they "don't really know what they are doing, what it means" and, consequently, they misinterpret their results.

## Data Analysis/Results

In economics, as with most social sciences, the goal is usually to infer causality from nonexperimental or correlational data. Consequently, the quality of the data analysis/results component is a function of how complete the analysis is, the techniques used, and the robustness of the results. Faculty also look to see how well aligned the results are with the research question.

The faculty noted that the thing that really distinguishes good empirical work from mediocre empirical work is that "you believe the results and . . . you are not able to offer alternative interpretations of their results that are very likely or very plausible." Indeed, there is a fine line between acceptable and unacceptable,

> You could get the four of us in a room watching somebody present an empirical analysis and two of us might think it's acceptable and two not, because with nonexperimental data people try to infer causality, and when it's pretty clear that some finding might just be spurious, often those analyses are deemed to be acceptable even though you have a data set, you don't have many controls, [and] it's not experimentally collected. So the question is, Do you throw your hands up and say, "I can't learn anything," or do you trudge ahead and have lots of people question the findings? . . . I have been in several empirical dissertations where you are not entirely convinced at the end that some sort of causal relationship has been found, but it's often deemed acceptable.

Quality is also a function of having the "maturity" to think critically and go beyond the statistical significance and assess the economic significance of the results. It is having the economic insight to interpret a coefficient from an economic perspective as opposed to just a statistical perspective. If the dissertation does not address the economic meaning of the results, if it focuses only on the statistical value, "then it's a failure. They need to do better than that." Indeed, the economics faculty gave examples of students whose work was unacceptable because they did not know what they found, could not explain variances that were "wacko," could not defend their results, could not place their results in context of the existing state of knowledge, or answer the "So what?" question.

## Discussion and Conclusion

In economics there is a strong relationship between the introduction and the discussion and conclusion. They say much the same thing in different ways. The introduction lays out the problem and the research questions and tells readers what they are going to learn by reading the dissertation. The discussion and conclusion sums it up, brings it all together, concludes the argument, and tells readers what they should have learned. "For better or worse," according to one participant, "the introduction and conclusion is [*sic*] an exercise . . . in marketing . . . you want [them] to be persuasive."

The discussion and the conclusion are often viewed as two different things. The discussion expresses the results in a concise, coherent way and brings out their implications. It is often integrated with the results rather than with the conclusion. By contrast, the conclusion, as noted above, basically just "summarizes and wraps it up." What goes into a conclusion also depends on the topic or field. If the dissertation has a "true policy," the conclusion "is the policy" and it discusses the plausibility of the analysis. In fields like health economics, "you have to have a long discussion of practical implications for practitioners."

Whether the faculty view the conclusion as important depends on the nature of the dissertation. If it's an "old-fashioned" traditional-style dissertation,

> there's a continuity, a historical development, and then a model and an analysis in relation to other applications. Then I think the conclusions are probably more important. But when, as most of our students are doing these days, writing essays, they're almost compelled to have a concluded part within each essay. As a consequence, the final conclusion at that point is not even clear. We force them to do it, but it's not even clear it's necessary.

Outstanding discussions and conclusions (hereafter "conclusions") are short, "three pages, five pages, maybe ten pages." They place the work in context, tell readers why they should care, and motivate other people to look at the issue. Outstanding conclusions show a keen understanding of the limitations of the work and what can be done to strengthen it. The results of an outstanding dissertation are, according to one participant, "OK, the door's closed. We've finished this topic. We can go on to something else. Here's an interesting set of results that raises more questions in the end than they answer. Here's a research agenda out of which other things will come."

Acceptable conclusions often oversell or overinterpret the results. Students may take an econometric or a statistical result that is barely significant and build an entire policy prescription on it. Faculty "beat on them" and they take "out one sentence at a time or . . . one glowing adjective at a time" until "finally you give up and sign the thing." By contrast, in an unacceptable conclusion, the discussion of the results is often insufficient. For instance, a student might put in "48 tables one right after another and doesn't have anything to say about them." Or the conclusion may make a big leap. The students have not "really shown anything in the body [of the dissertation] and then all of a sudden [they] say how important these conclusions are.

## Notes

1. For information on the source of these data, see chapter 1, note 5. John Siegfried at the American Economics Association also provided some data (personal communication, June 2, 2005). See also Stock & Siegfried, 2006.

2. A survey of economics graduate students who completed the Ph.D. in academic year 2001–02 (Stock & Siegfried, 2006) indicates that 61% of those students' dissertations were essay-style dissertations and that students who wrote essay-style dissertations took four months less time to write their dissertations than those who wrote traditional, single-topic dissertations.

# Appendix

## TABLE 11.A.

### The Components of an Economics Dissertation and Their Characteristics at Different Quality Levels

| Components | | Quality levels | | |
|---|---|---|---|---|
| | Outstanding | Very good | Acceptable | Unacceptable |
| **Introduction** | Well motivated, very brief, and very well written; compelling, penetrating, and insightful; motivates and prompts the reader; sets up and articulates an interesting question; provides a clear statement of the problem; identifies why the problem is important; relates this body of work to other bodies and identifies how it is different; provides an overview of the dissertation; summarizes the methods, data, and results; is like an executive summary | Well written; very clearly states what it is about; raises a question without context; clearly identifies the techniques that will be used but does not provide a good sense of the economics | Not well organized or compelling; lacks motivation; does not do a good job of explaining why the problem is important or oversells its importance; provides a general discussion of the question or issues but is insufficiently specific about the techniques and results to come; student has not pulled the pieces together | Does not or cannot lay out the question; shows a fundamental lack of understanding of the problem; fails to outline the research; overstates what was done; makes huge claims about the results |

*(continues)*

**TABLE 11.A.**
Continued

| Components | Quality levels | | | |
| --- | --- | --- | --- | --- |
| | Outstanding | Very good | Acceptable | Unacceptable |
| Literature review | Short, concise, complete, coherent, and comprehensive; focuses on the most directly relevant works; very analytical; provides new insights into the literature; insightfully synthesizes the literature; shows how the literature relates to student's question; identifies problems and limitations; shows how student's research will advance the field | Coherent, thoughtful, and accurate critique of the literature; sufficiently comprehensive to set the context for the research question; shows understanding of the literature and where student's research fits | Cites most of the key literature; may not be on top of recent literature, no new references; may cite papers that are not relevant to the question; does not sufficiently synthesize the literature; is a listing, "X found this, Y found this," puts the problem in context; identifies the student's contribution | Sloppy mind dumps; uses chronology as an organizing principle; neglects an important paper that contains the student's result; fails to cite important relevant articles; does not cite enough sources; cites sources the student has not read or has only read the abstract; shows lack of understanding of important articles; just a list of names, "this person did this and this person did that"; does not clearly relate the literature to the student's contribution |

| Components | Quality levels | | | |
|---|---|---|---|---|
| | Outstanding | Very good | Acceptable | Unacceptable |
| Theory | General, comprehensive, creative, original, simple, elegant, tidy; is logically consistent and internally coherent; has clever arguments; aligns well with the question; provides intuition for the results; identifies the assumptions under which the model works best and the internal limitations; borrows from outside the field; applies in an area where no one thought to apply it before; builds on prior theoretical models; a new, more abstract theory; a new theoretical method for solving complicated economic problems or policies; a unified model; a model that yields consistent information | Appropriate; uses existing methods or models well | Mediocre, very loose, or vacuous theory; uses or regurgitates existing theory; is not well articulated, is implicit rather than explicit; does not make predictions based on the theory; does not understand the limitations of the theory | Wrong, has errors, or is not properly adapted to the situation; student cannot explain the theory; does not convince the reader that it is cogent or logically consistent; is clearly an afterthought |

(continues)

## TABLE 11.A.
### Continued

| Components | Quality levels | | | |
|---|---|---|---|---|
| | Outstanding | Very good | Acceptable | Unacceptable |
| **Methods** | Well done; original, novel; carefully and comprehensively documented, lays out every step; indicates why the method or technique was used; is used appropriately; makes and justifies judgments about the procedures and the trustworthiness of the data; identifies limitations and potential weaknesses; flows naturally from the theory; integrates the theory and empirical work; student gathers own data; adds a new twist or application to existing methods; uses the best, state-of-the-art techniques; develops innovative new methods or estimators; introduces an estimator from another area; contributes to the theory of methodology | Is important for that problem, but does not have applications beyond that | Adequately uses the right methods for the problem; uses existing, less sophisticated, or inferior methods reasonably well; documented sufficiently so that the reader can follow and replicate the method; methods do not closely relate to the theory | Uses the wrong methodology or tools to address the problem; methods do not relate to the theory; data are not handled carefully; has mistakes |

| Components | Quality levels | | | |
|---|---|---|---|---|
| | Outstanding | Very good | Acceptable | Unacceptable |
| **Results/data analysis** | Well executed; robust, complete, meaningful, interesting, surprising; adds to knowledge; has high-quality data; student understands the data set inside and out, including the shortcomings and limitations of the data; choice of model, statistical, and/or econometric tools is convincing; uses a sophisticated or innovative technique to approach the question; analysis is multidimensional, interesting, and important; analyzes the data in different ways and explains the differences in results; develops a theory to explain anomalies; provides a very plausible interpretation of results; refutes important prior findings | Well executed, but not robust; demonstrates something believed to be true; shows good understanding of statistical and econometric methods; attempts to link theory and methods; applies established methods to a new data set; goes beyond the basic data set and makes a convincing case; points out causal relationships | Results do not seem very robust; uses a scattershot approach to statistical analysis that is not closely aligned with the theory; is not clear that a causal relationship has been found; cannot clearly state the limitations of the results | Data are wrong; is full of errors; obvious things are missing; ignores other available data; wrong, poor, or scattershot analysis; accepts incorrect data coming out of the computer at face value; magnitudes of the estimates are not convincing; results are incomplete or contradictory; results are wrong or trivial; results are not explained; counterintuitive results are not explained; results that are inconsistent with expectations are explained away or buried; makes improper statistical inferences; overstates results; empirical findings cannot be compared across chapters |

*(continues)*

**TABLE 11.A.**
Continued

| Components | Quality levels | | | |
| --- | --- | --- | --- | --- |
| | Outstanding | Very good | Acceptable | Unacceptable |
| **Discussion and conclusion** | Short and concise; completes the argument; puts the work in context; summarizes and brings the work together—sets out the problem, methods, theorems, and data; indicates what has been learned; conclusions are connected to the introduction; shows keen understanding and appreciation of the limitations of the work and what can be done to strengthen it; identifies the significance and applications for other audiences and fields; has policy ramifications; talks about future directions | Very short and well synthesized but is not as strong as it could be; ties in with the introduction and literature review; compares what was known before with what is known now; conclusions are supported by the evidence; shows an appreciation of the shortcomings of the research | Is absent or a little too thin; conclusions are not supported by the results; overinterprets or oversells the results | Does not have a discussion; simply takes the introduction and changes future tense to past tense; insufficient discussion of results; misinterprets the findings; claims to prove things that have not been proved |

# 12

# THE PSYCHOLOGY
# DISSERTATION

There are more than 900 Ph.D. and PsyD. programs in psychology in the United States that award degrees in 22 different subfields. Graduate psychology programs enroll over 50,000 graduate students (master's and doctoral) and graduate over 3,000 new Ph.D.s annually. The median time to degree is 7.2 years. Close to 40% of new psychology Ph.D.s go on to postdoctoral education.[1]

Twenty-eight faculty at seven universities participated in the focus groups. They came from both clinical and nonclinical programs. Overall, these faculty had 690 years of experience, had chaired an estimated 454 dissertations, and had sat on an estimated 1,432 dissertation committees. The average psychology focus group participant had been a professor for 25 years, had chaired 16 dissertations, and had sat on 51 dissertation committees. Below is a summary of the psychology focus groups' discussions. Their performance expectations for the dissertation are displayed in the tables. Their supporting discussion is recounted in the text.

## The Purpose of a Psychology Dissertation

The psychology dissertation was described as having three distinct functions: educational, evaluative, and societal, and as serving many purposes (see Table 12.1). The educational function is to teach students to act independently. The evaluative function is to determine whether a student has met "reasonable standards." The societal function is to train students to generate knowledge.

**TABLE 12.1.**
**The Purpose of a Psychology Dissertation**

To learn to be independent; to demonstrate the skills and the ability to independently conceive and conduct original, significant, scholarly research—develop important, researchable problems, define an experiment, generate and address hypotheses, conduct the experiment, and produce publishable results; an effective way to set high standards for the Ph.D.; a mechanism by which one is trained to be an independent researcher; a process that encourages and fosters creativity; a test of whether students can do research on their own; preparation for and launching of a career; on-the-job training; a capstone; a rite of passage; the culmination of graduate education and the movement to becoming an investigator, a transition from being a student to being an independent scholar

While the psychology faculty hope the dissertation will result in publishable papers that will make the student competitive in the job market, they saw the dissertation more as a process than a product. Indeed, they asserted that the goal is not "a dusty dissertation on a library shelf" that is only read by the committee and looked at by a mother to see "if it is dedicated to her." Rather, what is important is the experience itself.

According to the participants, when they enter the dissertation stage of their education, most students have reached the point where "we don't have anything more to teach them." The dissertation is thus an intellectual capstone, an integrative device that forces students to put together all the training they have had in theory, methods, statistics, and content, and assume the "burden of responsibility" for developing their own conceptualizations, models, and frameworks, and make a contribution to knowledge. As such, the dissertation is students' "first scholarly child," something that is theirs, not their mentor's, and "defines them in some way." "There is no way that course work would ever substitute."

The dissertation marks a transition from "studenthood" to "colleague." It answers the question: Can you go do this next year by yourself on your own with your own graduate students? Indeed, the importance of the dissertation in graduate education is captured in an exchange one participant reported he had with a graduate student. The student said, "I like everything about graduate school except the dissertation." The professor replied, "Well, maybe you shouldn't be here because that's what you're going to do for the rest of your life."

The clinical faculty had a slightly different take on the purpose of dissertation than faculty in other specialty areas. They noted that many clinical students do not intend to go on to a research career, they just want to get their "ticket punched." Consequently, "the standards for those students are a little bit different." The faculty want them to have "some scientific literacy" so that they will be scientifically oriented and responsive clinicians.

## Original Contribution

The psychology faculty identified many ways to make an original contribution (see Table 12.2). They noted that "original" is a "tough" word and that graduate students can get "hung up" on whether or not what they are doing is really original. One participant asserted that there are no new questions. He said that the "big, good, important questions in psychology have been around for a long time." Consequently, the goal for graduate students is not to come up with a brand new question that no one has ever thought of before, but rather to come up with "a new twist or a new flavor to an old question," which could be a methodological twist that allows the student to address the question in a different and more novel way.

Although they would like all their Ph.D. dissertations to be original, the psychology faculty recognized that there were degrees of originality and that the degree of originality varied among students. Some students can come up with new ideas by themselves while others cannot. Indeed, faculty gauge the degree of originality by how much original content is generated by the student and how much "was handed to him [*sic*] by the mentor." Most psychology dissertations are an outgrowth of an apprenticeship project, which is a

### TABLE 12.2.
### The Nature of an Original Contribution in Psychology

Something that has not been done, shown, or made available before that creates new knowledge and is publishable; a new question, idea, insight, perspective, theory, model, technology, method, or finding; a novel twist or approach to an old question; an empirical or theoretical advance; applying new, innovative, cutting-edge methods to existing theory; synthesizing knowledge, using or integrating something from another discipline; generating new data; analyzing existing data sets in new ways; clarifying someone else's findings; resolving issues or clearing up some confusion in the field; making an empirical and/or theoretical contribution variation on some theme of the mentor's work. Thus while there is something original it, "in another sense it is very unoriginal," because it is only an incremental advance on the apprenticeship project. Students whose work branches off from the mentor's is considered more original, though one participant characterized such work as "semi-original."

Given how closely aligned many students' dissertation projects are with their advisor's research program, one participant raised the following challenge:

> How many of us in psychology allow students to do dissertations that are outside of the lines of research that are our own? If the answer is none, then the answer implies we don't produce any original dissertations.

One of his colleagues responded:

> I am so involved in what they are doing that it is hard to separate out their contribution. . . . It's hard for me to look at that student and say, "Have you really contributed something that I would consider either original or significant?" What I have been coming to is, the answer is no, because basically I've been too much involved. . . . I really can't evaluate a student's originality if I'm right there in the picture.

## Significant Contribution

Significance in psychology depends on the "magnitude of the jump" between the baseline level of knowledge before the contribution and what exists afterward. Significance is determined by the community and plays out in the long run, usually in terms of the work's impact on future research; or in clinical areas, in terms of how people assess, treat, or prevent a mental health problem (see Table 12.3).

Faculty assess the degree of significance by the type of journal the work could get published in. The more top tier the journal, the more significant the work. However, one participant commented that an editor he knew at *Science* said that he was not willing to admit that everything the journal publishes is significant. The participant went on to say,

> So, it's impact . . . When does it get out to the public? In what format? Then, what impact does it have down the road? . . . Time tells whether the

**TABLE 12.3.**
**The Nature of a Significant Contribution in Psychology**

Something that advances knowledge and is publishable; addresses or distinguishes between competing hypotheses; influences theory development and research; leads to the modification of existing theory or hypotheses; eliminates a theory and provides support for another theory; interesting, meaningful, or counterintuitive results; has an application; is of interest to others and affects students' research; changes the discourse in the field; has an impact on future research

students, once it gets published, do they get invited by the various places to give talks? Do they get a job that's good based on the work that they have done, et cetera, et cetera?

Sometimes significance is in the graduate student's control. The student can pick a good, hard, or ambitious question. Sometimes it is outside the student's control. The student had a good idea, but it did not work out or it turned out not to be terribly useful. "So there's a little bit of luck." And, "There's a little bit of good preparation, [and] a lot of hard work."

Finally, many faculty felt that "original" and "significant" were overlapping concepts, and some had difficulty distinguishing between them. Some participants noted that work could be original but not significant. Examples include studies in which the hypotheses were wrong or the results were not statistically significant or not important or meaningful. However, the faculty said that they grant the Ph.D. for nonsignificant work. Other faculty indicated that the work could be significant but not original. Examples include work based on "your mentor's idea," or replications of a "ground-breaking study" that was done in a methodologically more sophisticated way.

## The Dissertation as a Whole

There was some variance within and across specialty areas in psychology about whether the dissertation is or should be an expansive tome or something that is more focused and closer to publication, like a series of journal articles. Some fields like biopsychology are trending toward the "essay" dissertation, in which each experiment is its own journal-article-style chapter, combined with a larger introductory chapter. Fields in which it takes a long time to complete a single experiment lean more toward the traditional "tome-style" dissertation. Below we explore the characteristics of different quality psychology dissertations (see Table 12.4) and what the psychology faculty had to say about them.

## Outstanding

Outstanding dissertations are rare. They are more ambitious and well done than the typical dissertation. They are distinguished by the quality of the thinking and writing. The logic is tight and they express independent ideas clearly and persuasively. They are theoretically and methodologically sophisticated. They shepherd the reader through complex theoretical material and complicated analyses. The gaps are laid out and everything is anticipated. "They're continually answering questions that you start raising in yourself as you're reading along." According to one participant, outstanding dissertations "advance the advisor's career."

When reading outstanding dissertations, faculty say, "Wow, I hadn't thought about that," or "Oh, that's interesting," or, "Oh, that's clever." Not only do readers feel that they have learned something from the dissertation, they know that other people will want to "take this and work from this," and that it will influence "what people do and how they approach something."

Outstanding dissertations are written by outstanding students. Outstanding students often show signs of excellence from the very beginning of their graduate careers. They are "usually driven by intense curiosity and pride in what they do" and they often work independently of their advisor. By the time they start their dissertation, they have gotten out of "student mode" and into "professional mode," and function like a colleague. Instead of saying, "What do I have to do to complete this dissertation? What are the minimum requirements?" They say, "What do I have to do to answer the question on my own?" One participant noted that outstanding students sometimes produce dissertations that have negative results. In that case he said, "You would be hard pressed to call it an outstanding dissertation." Thus, outstanding students also "have to be a little bit lucky."

## Very Good

In contrast to an outstanding dissertation, a very good dissertation is "the same," just "less of it." It is at "a threshold below which you would say, 'Eh' . . . Across the board they're not up there." Very good dissertations often

## TABLE 12.4.
### The Characteristics of Different Quality Dissertations in Psychology

| Quality | Characteristics |
|---|---|
| **Outstanding** | Scholarly; solid, clever, coherent; interesting, persuasive, exciting; counterintuitive; paradigm shifting; well organized and well written; driven by intense curiosity; has an elegant, creative, and original idea and method; identifies a gap that no one else has identified that needs to be done; builds a case in a linear, logical way; anticipates questions; very synthetic; is interdisciplinary; looks at the issue from multiple perspectives; eradicates the boundaries among the introduction, literature review, and theory, and integrates them in a seamless, fluent, articulate way; has multiple components or multiple studies; draws on diverse literatures from different disciplines; presents the literature well and shows the gaps; is theoretically sophisticated; shows depth of understanding of theory and methods; involves a set of programmatic, linear experiments; experiments are designed to falsify a hypothesis; uses very good, sound methods; develops complex stimuli; involves a new or massive data collection; has an innovative analytical strategy; has compelling data and amazing results; the general discussion ties it all together; is publishable in a top-tier journal; changes the way people think; shifts the thinking in the field; has policy implications |
| **Very good** | Novel, creative, coherent, independent but less ambitious and crisp; not highly unusual or exciting; is the obvious next step in a research program; is done confidently but lacks sparkle; technically well presented; the introduction is tight but not particularly new or different; what is original is clear and laid out persuasively; the model and hypotheses are well laid out and well tested; the methods are very good but is not conceptually exciting; explores the range with which two variables interact and affect the dependent variable; uses conventional methods and analyses; uses a new method or statistical application; the results are less crisp and clear; the experiment did not work out as planned; is publishable; does not reform the discipline |
| **Acceptable** | Yeomanlike; correct; technically competent, meets the standard, not very interesting or exciting; executes what is planned, but the research may not work out as expected; is an extension of the advisor's work or an in-depth examination of a single case; the |

*(continues)*

## TABLE 12.4.
### Continued

| Quality | Characteristics |
|---|---|
| Acceptable | questions are simple and reasonable but not exciting; lacks an introduction; has reviewed the literature and identified a gap, but the gap is not very important; is not critical of the literature and what needs to be done; hypotheses are strong enough and consistent with the proposed model; the research design is simple; uses a reasonable method to answer the question; analysis is clear and appropriate, fits the hypothesis, and answers the question; analysis does not explore all the possibilities present in the data; does not do a lot of exploratory or additional analyses to clarify the interpretation of the main analysis; results are not important; discussion does not return to the original question; restates the results; does not identify what has been learned; may not get published; will not change the way people approach the issue |
| Unacceptable | Poorly conceived, wrong, sloppy; has logical flaws; does not do what the student said he or she was going to do; says things that readers believe are false; introduction is shoddy; misses major aspects of the literature; shows little understanding of the core processes; the model and hypotheses are inconsistent; the methodological techniques are poor or flawed; fails to implement the necessary controls; data analysis and results are inappropriate, inadequately reported, unexplained, misinterpreted, or contain errors; the general discussion reiterates the major findings; explanations are not thought through clearly; jumps to conclusions; has no synthesis or big picture context; does not see the next step; requires major revisions; fails to complete the revisions |

show competence at the outstanding level, but lack the "glitter," that "extra sparkle." The research is typically the "next, logical obvious step" as opposed to, "Oh, that's very creative!" They may be parametric studies that "play around" with the variation in the environmental situation or with individual characteristics. For instance,

> We know that this drug affects a certain neural processor in learning and memory, and we know that this set of environmental conditions [have this effect] . . . and you just explore the range with which those two variables affect this thing and how they interact. All that's good and important to

know and may end up being the most applicable thing that you'll ever do, but is it going to excite the world? No, probably not.

Very good dissertations generally use conventional methods and analyses. They are "confidently done" and "technically well presented" but not necessarily "crystal clear." Sometimes everything may be "sterling," but the experiments did not work out as hoped, the results are not "crisp and clear." Other times what might have been an outstanding dissertation ends up being very good because of practical things, such as the student rushing to meet some graduate school deadline.

According to one participant, there are only two categories that you can have for a dissertation: outstanding and very good. He asserted, "You'll never get a dissertation that isn't at least very good because you meet about the proposal with your committee." Indeed, focus group faculty in most of the other disciplines, but not psychology, commented that the very good dissertation is the most common dissertation and the level they expect of most students.

## Acceptable

Acceptable dissertations are "routine," "ho-hum" and lacking in "oomph," but they meet the minimum technical requirements. The students have "done the lit review, they've identified a gap, they've developed a model, they have hypotheses that are consistent with the model that they've proposed. . . . their method is reasonable to answer the question," but they are not "going to set the world on fire."

According to one participant, the "big distinction" between acceptable and very good is in the handling of the discussion, treating it as an "afterthought."

> It's far, far too often simply a restatement of the results and far too infrequently getting back to what the original questions were, and saying, "What have we learned?" In many cases, you can completely lose sight of the original questions and what made people interested in the study in the first place. They'll get sidetracked on some peripheral thing—measurement problem or interpretational difficulty—and spend page and page and page [talking about it]. . . . Good dissertations ought to come full circle and return to whatever core question was that you began with. There's a

single error that consistently you find: underperformance in rounding things off at the end.

He attributed this "error" to "people trying to get out the door faster than the dissertation to get started on a job."

Students who write acceptable dissertations often need a lot of "hand-holding" through the "whole process," and advisors know from the very start that these students are "not going to be successful as independent scholars." In order for these students to produce a dissertation that "seems technically competent" their advisors often have to "fill in the blanks." By the time the dissertation is deemed complete, their advisors feel they have done everything they can as advisors, and that the dissertation is "not going to get any better no matter what you do." Yet, one participant commented that if "you scratch the surface a little bit . . . the student really does have the depth of understanding." So, ultimately, "Your interactions with the student and their answers to questions and their thoughtfulness and their insight determines what you think about the work, rather than [the document]."

Some students who produce acceptable dissertations may be good in research methodology but may not "get the conceptual stuff." Their dissertations are just extensions of "what they have been doing under their advisors' guidance, but they are not really able to come up with a new question with a new twist, a new tweak." Less common are students who are conceptually very good—"whose heads are in the clouds conceptually"—but who turn out to be "bad in the lab." They "change the design every three subjects. They don't follow though. They are screwing up their data."

Sometimes acceptable dissertations are a function of "bad luck." The student proposed a "very nice set of studies," but the studies did not work out or the data did not make sense, and, as a result, the dissertation is "not very useful." In the end, an acceptable dissertation is one that fulfills the contract. As long as students do what they said they were going to do in their proposal, and do a "reasonable job of writing it up," then "it's an acceptable dissertation."

### Unacceptable

It is "very, very rare" that a dissertation is unacceptable at the time of the defense. Indeed, unacceptable dissertations should not happen because the "system" has a lot of "safeguards" in place to prevent it. The proposal review committee should catch and "weed out" flaws and "zero-out" problems in advance. Both the dissertation chair and the dissertation committee should "monitor" the dissertation work "before it gets to the point of being rejected for unacceptability." Further, the advisor "should not put something up for presentation" that he or she knows "won't fly." Given the "integral" part that advisors play in what their students do, one participant wondered, "How can they possibly fail? You'd have to be really doing an awful job [of advising]."

Although unacceptable dissertations may result from "absence of strong advisor tutelage and mentoring," the focus group participants noted instances where dissertations are unacceptable because junior faculty who advise them do not have "a good model" for what the dissertation is. They also noted instances where faculty members are no longer engaged in scholarship and do not hold the student to an "appropriate standard." However, they argued that when these issues arise, the dissertation becomes a "committee responsibility" and the problems should be identified "well before the actual final oral exam." Indeed, one participant noted that when you are on a committee there is "an implicit understanding" and "a politeness thing" that if you "discover something really seriously wrong with the dissertation, that you make that note to the advisor and the student before the meeting."

Dissertations may be unacceptable because students do not work closely with their advisor or because they have taken a job and push for a defense. Members of the committee may not support the defense, but the advisor allows it; about which one participant commented, "It's not a good situation."

The main cause of "unacceptableness" in a dissertation is logical flaws. One participant who had read a few unacceptable dissertations observed:

> It's obvious the student really had no understanding of why the study even happened in the first place. . . . It's more like a master's thesis where you don't expect much; master's thesis and a student with a lot of hand-holding. You carry that forward to the dissertation level where you're expected to be independent . . . and there's no evidence there is any—that the student has very little understanding of what the core processes [are] about in the design of the study and actually expressing it in terms of research.

When the dissertation is not progressing well, advisors might ask the student "to write and rewrite and rewrite and rewrite." Even though "draconian" revisions may be required after the defense, it is rare that committee members will "refuse to sign this thing if reasonable changes are forthcoming." Some students will "get discouraged and self-end the process by saying, 'We're not getting anywhere.' . . . After years and years of hard work, they fail to complete those final revisions."

One participant made the interesting observation that dissertations were far more likely to be unacceptable and failing "to the degree that we allow our students to be original." He explained:

> If they're not so original, then they know how to model what they're doing after the standard procedures and methods used in that lab, and presumably they're working with a major professor who has some stature in their field and those methods are standard and accepted. So they know what to do because they've done it before and they've seen other people [do it]. But if they go off over here, then they have a much harder time and are more likely to make serious mistakes that the major advisor herself or himself [won't catch] because they're not exactly in that area and doesn't know enough to offer sufficient guidance.

## The Components of a Psychology Dissertation

The psychology faculty did not object to the matrix (see Table 1.2), though a few participants made some minor critical comments. Not fully understanding the purpose of the task, one participant said, "I would hate to be forced on a dissertation committee to provide the scores for an individual dissertation. We would all be sitting there scratching our heads." Another participant did not think a dissertation could be dissected "in this way." Other focus group faculty noted that the introduction, literature review, and theory were usually integrated into a single chapter. Faculty in all but one focus group discussed some or all of the individual components. Below we explore the characteristics of the components of the psychology dissertation (see Table 12.A in the appendix to this chapter) and what the faculty said about them.

### Introduction

The introduction to the psychology dissertation motivates the work and makes the case for the study. The outstanding introduction often starts with a hook, a wonderful anecdote, or opening paragraph that draws the reader in and gets them interested, "even if they are not working in that area." It shows where the students' interests are coming from and why they are excited about them. The outstanding introduction is well organized and "it narrows down to a hypotheses which must be true now that you've read it." When "you get to the end of it . . . you say, 'the study they have to do is obvious.'"

Outstanding introductions are page-turners. In reading one, "you get excited or surprised. You measure your own affect in the process of reading it. You don't say, 'Oh man, this is coherent. Oh, I can see that this is more than merely incremental.' You go, 'Ah, ah, yes!'"

Acceptable introductions survive simply on the basis of "No one's looked at this question before." The students do not tell the reader why they think it is a particularly interesting question or explain why their particular original contribution "is more interesting than any one with billions of other original questions you might choose to ask." Indeed, one participant noted that students who write acceptable introductions often gauge the importance of a question by the level of interest and activity in the field, but are themselves unable to make the case for the importance of the question:

> They'll say, "It's sufficient that a lot of people are interested in this." And I'll say, "Why the hell are you interested?" or "Why do you think so many other people are interested in this question?" And you get blank stares, and that's a bad sign. Or [you get] prose that is the equivalent of a blank stare.

### Literature Review

There was not complete agreement among focus group participants about the scope of the literature review (what is relevant to include and how comprehensive it should be) or the trend in the discipline or in various subfields about the scale of the literature review (getting more focused and shrinking versus increasing in size and scope). However, the faculty noted that, in general, they look for a certain amount of breadth and an indication that students understand where all the pieces of their hypotheses are coming from. Students also have to make a case based on prior literature that "what I'm about to do is important and really an advance." Faculty like to see literature reviews that have a theme that provides a new perspective on the literature. One participant cited the reviews in *Psychological Bulletin* as an example. He said, "In fact, those are the instructions we give them. . . . 'Do a *Psych Bulletin* kind of literature review,' so they have a model."

Outstanding literature reviews are creative and clever. They look at the literature in a new way and spend less time talking about individual studies and more time addressing the "grand scope" of the problem. They draw on more than one literature or bring in studies from a closely related field that "you didn't quite think was the same" but cause the reader to say, "This actually is an example of the same problem, but we haven't thought about it this way." Outstanding literature reviews often integrate literature that is not limited to the student's particular substantive area. For instance, "If you're looking at a clinical problem, but if you could [cite] your experimental neurocognitive kinds of literature to support it or go to the social cognition literature, if that stuff is pulled together in an integrated way, that catches your attention." Outstanding literature reviews are also scholarly. The student has gone back and read the primary literature, especially the classic papers "that get cited and cited," and makes an important new point about the study.

Acceptable literature reviews are like undergraduate term papers. They are descriptive summaries that make obvious points. There is "no critiquing of anything." They often borrow other people's critiques. Because students are not putting themselves into it and are not doing anything unique, one participant viewed these types of literature reviews as "borderline between acceptable and unacceptable."

Students who write acceptable literature reviews were characterized as not thinking broadly enough and as being "unable to think outside the little box that they're in." They cannot see possible connections with other parts of psychology or other fields. They just get their ideas from one place and do not tie them together.

### Theory

The psychology focus group faculty did not provide much in the way of an overview of the role of theory in a psychology dissertation. They did, however, mention that theory was usually part of the literature review. They also noted that often the hardest part of evaluating a dissertation is determining whether it has made a theoretical contribution.

Little was said about theory at the outstanding, very good, and unacceptable levels that is not contained in Table 12.A. At the acceptable level, students will often present a "laundry list" of different theories without relating them to their research question and jump to their hypotheses without filling in the gaps—"A miracle happens." They do not understand that "the hypotheses are supposed to be in some sense deductible logically from your theoretical premises and [that] you have to fill in the steps" or that the hypotheses should synthesize multiple theories or test competing theories. Rather, these students "throw out theories just to say, 'See, I know theories.' . . . All these are relevant to my question."

## Methods

Psychology is a diverse discipline that ranges from clinical problems to neuroscience to relationships, and as would be expected, the different fields use different methodologies. Some fields accept "very small studies" that "would never fly in other areas." The different fields also have different standards about sample size and how clean and isolated independent variables have to be. However, within areas, the research questions and the designs "can be simple to complex." In addition, faculty hold students to different standards depending on whether students are collecting their own data or are using an archival data set. For students using archival data, they expect "more out of the question that is being asked" and expect students "to show some effort somewhere else."

Outstanding methods show creativity, often in the application of "a tried-and-true method to a new question." Students whose methods are acceptable often apply a method without really thinking about whether it is the best possible way to assess the question. They proceed on the basis of "everybody uses X, so I'm going to use X." Indeed,

> You get a lot of students who have been trained to use the tool and it's like the old story with the boy with the hammer, everything needs to be hammered down. You'll find students who know how to use certain things and they'll use it even if it's not really well adapted to the problems that they're interested in.

Consequently, everything gets measured in one way or there is just one measure for each construct.

By the time they get to the dissertation stage of their education, faculty expect students "to know how best to test questions." So, "doing poor methods to answer a question wouldn't be acceptable." To be unacceptable, the methods have to be "very messed up" or "very wrong." For instance, there may be a "major confoundment" at the level of the independent variable. The students may "think they are manipulating *X*, but they really are manipulating something else instead." However, because faculty typically will not fail somebody at the defense stage whose methods they approved, faculty will accept dissertations where "in hindsight it's obvious that there's probably a flaw or a confound with it," though they are unlikely to accept a dissertation where they "immediately see something wrong" with the methods.

## Data Analysis/Results

The data analysis/results section should be written for the "general scientist." The section should tell the reader why a particular analysis is being conducted and what its limitations are. The analyses should map back onto the hypotheses and answer the research question(s). The important results should "jump out."

Outstanding data analysis/results components are "excellently organized." They tell a story. They "make a case, a theoretical argument." They "get important things out first" and communicate complicated analyses in a very clear way, which is "a very unique skill."

Outstanding analyses often involve using tools that are "different and in some ways superior to what's standard in the field."

Students who do outstanding analyses are very thorough and pay "attention to detail." They exhibit "curiosity" and are "relentless" in "digging" and "poking around." After doing the analyses outlined in their proposals, they say to their advisors, "I've been thinking about this, and I think we really need to do a different analysis" or "We need to look at this in a different way." They pursue questions that are raised by their results, about which one participant said, "The student that can do that is on the short list. They really know what's going on. They reach higher on the scale than those that just say, 'This is the correct technique A or the best hypothesis B.'"

Lower-quality dissertations do not have "that extra supplemental analysis," and the data are less thoroughly analyzed. For instance, as one participant said:

A lot of times [students] will present data and you say, "What if you do this or try this? Why don't you take out the people who have trouble with that D[ependent] V[ariable] and see what happens? Did you look at men versus women? Look at the differential dropout rates, are they significant?

Questions like that that students sometimes will not do. And no outstanding dissertation fails to nail down those loose ends. Often it's thrown away
in a footnote.

Indeed, for "routine dissertations," the most requested revision is "additional analyses." These additional analyses "may not affect the outcome.
They may not affect the interpretation. But they meet a standard of thor-
oughness or comprehensiveness."

## Discussion and Conclusion

The discussion and conclusion should be more than simply a summary. It
should talk about the implications for theory, research, or practice as well as
about future directions. It is the "one place" in the dissertation where the
student has "a lot of freedom" and where "the scholarship rises or falls."
How the component is handled tells the committee whether students "know
what to do with their data and what those data mean." According to the
psychology faculty, most students do not have a "good grasp" of what should
go into this component, and consequently it is the part of the dissertation
that students have the most difficulty with. It is also the part of the dissertation that at least one participant was "most uniformly disappointed in" and
for which "the committee will ask for most revisions."

There was some disagreement among participants about the importance
of the component. One participant felt that it was "the least important part
of the dissertation," whereas another participant thought it was "critical."

The outstanding conclusion shows that students have spent time and
energy thinking about their data, have come to see them in a new way, and
are really interested in further understanding. Whereas, acceptable conclusions are "cookie cutter." They recap the results. Students who write them,
"very seldom . . . go to the trouble to convince [the reader that] they are
sophisticated about really thinking about what they've done and all of the
implications and how that relates to a bigger picture." When they talk about
the study's limitations, they discuss "all the same limitations as every other
study that we've ever talked about and they probably got it [the limitations]
from some other dissertation." The directions for further research are very
general and do not provide structure for what the next study should be beyond saying that their sample was not heterogeneous enough, so more research is needed with people of a variety of races in different settings. One

participant attributed these deficiencies to students being "pretty tired by the time they come to the conclusions and discussion."

One participant said that he would "not sign off on an unacceptable conclusion no matter how good the rest of [the dissertation] is." In cases where the conclusion is unacceptable because it does "not adequately reflect the journey that we've been on," faculty will require students to fix it. Indeed, this type of conclusion, which was described as "revisable unacceptable," is "not entirely uncommon."

## Notes

1. For information on the source of these data, see chapter 1, note 5. Some data came for the American Psychological Association's (APA) Web site, http://research .apa.org/majorfields.html (accessed March 5, 2006), and from Jessica Kohout, director, APA Research Office (personal communication, June 6, 2005).

# Appendix

## TABLE 12.A.
### The Components of a Psychology Dissertation and Their Characteristics at Different Quality Levels

| Components | Quality levels | | | |
| --- | --- | --- | --- | --- |
| | Outstanding | Very good | Acceptable | Unacceptable |
| Introduction | Interesting, comprehensive, coherent, engaging, exciting, surprising; has a hook; draws the reader in; well organized; states the problem and shows why it is important; makes a persuasive, convincing case for the study; leads to the hypotheses; provides an overview of the answers; exhibits depth and breadth of understanding; puts forth implications | Less breadth, depth, and insight; presents well-articulated, interesting, and important questions about gaps in knowledge | Gap argument for a derivative, mundane project; has legitimate questions about gaps in knowledge, but they may not be interesting; does not try to make the case for or explain why the question is original, interesting, or the next logical step; does a poor job of connecting the question with the literature and putting it in context | No hook, poorly written, incomplete; lacks structure; approach is formulaic; does not make the case for the importance of the topic; premise fails to take into account something that is already known |

*(continues)*

**TABLE 12.A.**
Continued

| | Quality levels | | | |
|---|---|---|---|---|
| **Components** | **Outstanding** | **Very good** | **Acceptable** | **Unacceptable** |
| **Literature review** | Creative, incisive, comprehensive; sparkles; shows critical thinking about the literature; has breadth and depth; uses the primary literature, including classic papers, to make important points and generate hypotheses; has a lot of theory in it; is expansive, brings in different points of view; is not limited to the particular substantive area, integrates material from related fields; shows where all the pieces of the hypothesis come from; places the work within a larger context; makes reader look at the literature in a different way | A very critical review of the relevant literature; shows insight; has a theme or perspective; points out methodological flaws in studies; compares studies and draws connections between them; integrates things in a new way; draws conclusions; explains its relevance for the problem; demonstrates that the student can use the material, apply it to a problem, and develop hypotheses | Adequate coverage of the literature; mentions everything; talks about what others have said; student does not put himself or herself into it; is a laundry list of prior findings; lacks critical analysis and synthesis; critiques are derived from other people; makes obvious points | Incomplete; misses or omits important studies or whole areas of literature; does not go back far enough in the literature; leaves out the most recent literature; does not make clear distinctions between theory and methods, talks about them as if they were the same; the literature's relevance to the question and methods is unclear |

| Components | Quality levels | | | |
|---|---|---|---|---|
| | Outstanding | Very good | Acceptable | Unacceptable |
| **Theory** | Creative, original; has a theory; discusses and works with more than one theory or model; articulates and compares competing theories; shows how competing theories are complementary; uses competing ideas to make hypotheses and develop studies; identifies and critically analyzes key theoretical assumptions and boundary conditions; identifies the theories' implications for the student's study; advances theory | Student has a sophisticated knowledge of and ability to use relevant theories; figures out where the gaps are in the theories and extracts what is useful; uses theory to inform the research questions and measures; discusses how observations are consistent or inconsistent with prevailing theory; suggests how diverse observations can be pulled together; makes some progress | No clear theoretical framework; provides a laundry list of relevant theories; question is not integrated into a theoretical perspective; does not critically analyze the theories' underlying assumptions or boundary conditions; accepts theories at face value; hypotheses are not logical deductions from theoretical premises; hypotheses do not synthesize multiple theories or test competing theories | Has no theory; does not have a good guiding theory; theory is misunderstood, misclassified, or undeveloped; overlooks a certain body of theory; theory is unrelated to the literature review |

*(continues)*

**TABLE 12.A.**
**Continued**

| Components | Quality levels | | | |
| --- | --- | --- | --- | --- |
| | Outstanding | Very good | Acceptable | Unacceptable |
| **Methods** | High quality; a well-designed experiment with proper controls; has a level of complexity that goes beyond the obvious; has done some pilot testing to nail down the characteristics of the methods; creatively applies an existing method to a new question; uses a new method; comes up with useful measures | Applies methods in correct and creative ways; describes why they are using a particular task, what it does, and how it fits with the study; creates new tasks; uses multiple measures of the same constructs; shows interest in convergent and divergent validity issues | Shows basic level of competence; method fits the problem; follows the rules for samples, measures, and analyses; uses one measure for each construct | Uses wrong or poor methods to answer the question; has a major confound; uses an inappropriate population to test a theory; does not have appropriate controls or control groups; does not have controls |

| Components | Quality levels | | | |
| --- | --- | --- | --- | --- |
| | Outstanding | Very good | Acceptable | Unacceptable |
| **Results/data analysis** | Creative; uses proper, defensible statistical and analytical methods; uses best, most powerful, and sensitive analytic procedures to address the experimental question; uses cutting-edge techniques; takes existing commercial software and develops new models; applies newer and different models to the data set; provides information about why each analysis is being conducted; analysis is thorough and seamless; integrates among and across levels of analysis; develops new ways to look at the data and makes the most of the data; tells a story; makes a theoretical argument; analyses map back to the hypotheses and answer the questions; shows curiosity through relentless exploration of the data; iteratively explores questions raised by each analysis; pays attention to detail; communicates analyses very clearly; discusses the limitations of the analysis | Appropriate; clear; does not conduct supplemental analyses; leaves open data analysis opportunities | Meets the standard of thoroughness or comprehensiveness; has done the minimum analysis required to address the original question; results go back to the hypotheses; does not develop a meaningful story | Analyses are wrong, inappropriate, or not well matched to the research question; analyses are not reported completely enough; presents the results poorly; does not follow up on alternative interpretations allowed by the analyses |

(continues)

**TABLE 12.A.**
Continued

| Components | Quality levels | | | |
| --- | --- | --- | --- | --- |
| | Outstanding | Very good | Acceptable | Unacceptable |
| **Discussion and conclusion** | Deep, accurate, creative, enthusiastic; goes beyond summarizing the findings; draws things together; goes back to the introduction; states the hypotheses and answers each one; provides an in-depth account of the findings; develops a novel framework or explanation for unanticipated results or results that have internal contradictions; goes back to the literature and discusses the differences between student's findings and other people's findings; discusses big surprises and the strengths and limitations of the current design or research; puts the study in a larger context; says what it means for the rest of the field; identifies future directions; speculates on why and how the field might need to change; moves the field forward | Less of the same; does not close the circle, does not come back to the beginning and address the problem | Summarizes the results; provides a superficial interpretation of the findings; references to the literature simply state that the findings are consistent with other people's findings; has a rote discussion of strengths and limitations; provides some very general directions for future research that do not provide the next structure for the next study; makes wild speculations that have nothing to do with the topic | Shows lack of understanding and careful thought; the discussion and conclusion do not adequately reflect the journey; is a disconnect between data and conclusions; restates the results without providing any interpretation; misinterprets the results; interprets the results beyond what the data allow; generalizes too broadly |

# 13

# THE SOCIOLOGY
# DISSERTATION

There are 162 Ph.D. programs in sociology in the United States. Graduate sociology programs enroll roughly 10,000 students (master's and doctoral), and graduate roughly 600 new Ph.D.s annually. Although there are no formally tracked subfields, the American Sociological Association has 44 formal sections and 90 interest areas. The median time to degree is 9.2 years. Roughly 10% of new sociology Ph.D.s go on to postdoctoral education.[1]

Twenty-five faculty at seven universities participated in the focus groups. The participants included both quantitative and qualitative researchers. Overall, these faculty had 567 years of experience, had chaired an estimated 336 dissertations, and had sat on an estimated 1,016 dissertation committees. The average sociology focus group participant had been a professor for 23 years, had chaired 13 dissertations, and had sat on 41 dissertation committees. Below is a summary of the sociology focus groups' discussions. Their performance expectations for the dissertation are displayed in the tables. Their supporting discussion is recounted in the text.

## The Purpose of a Sociology Dissertation

The sociology dissertation serves many purposes (see Table 13.1). From the students' point of view (at least according to the faculty), the purpose is having the experience of independently carrying out a major original and significant piece of empirical research and seeing what is involved—all the ups and downs of living through the process, the problems and dilemmas, overcoming obstacles, and learning the value of focus. In the process students

## TABLE 13.1.
### The Purpose of a Sociology Dissertation

To train scholars to do independent research; to learn certain useful skills—how to synthesize the literature, analyze unformed data, reach conclusions, and write about them; to learn what the standard is; to demonstrate that the student can mount an original, independent research project and take it from conceptualization to completion—formulate problems or questions, review the literature, collect and analyze data, and discuss findings—on his or her own; to demonstrate that the student can do sociology, know the area at a sufficient level of depth to teach it, and be an independent, productive academic/scholar; to move the student from thinking of himself or herself as a research assistant to thinking of himself or herself as an independent researcher/sociologist; to develop independence; to do original and significant research; to put together a product that has internal logic, is coherent, and makes an innovative, significant contribution to the field; to get the Ph.D.; to have a product that can be published; to teach the student the skills to get a tenure-track job; a rite of passage; a test for establishing a person's claim to be a scholar; a certificate for admission into the profession

learn "what the standard is." Though, as one participant noted, "even though there are various standards for different students, there's a minimum standard."

From the discipline's or department's point of view, the purpose of the dissertation is for students to make a contribution to the discipline, to demonstrate that they can produce sociology. The dissertation thus serves as a "certificate for admission into the profession," one that is "jealously guarded."

From the point of view of most of the faculty, the "taken-for-granted" purpose of the dissertation is to make an original and significant contribution, though one participant thought that the dissertation was "a high-level exercise, rather than an original or significant contribution." The faculty equated making an original and significant contribution with "scholarship" and with "being an academic." "If you [don't produce original, significant scholarship], you're not a scholar. It's just the simple matter of the definition." Indeed, faculty use the dissertation for "vetting," for "establishing a person's claim of being a scholar." However, one participant noted that lots of Ph.D.s in sociology do not go into academic or research careers, they go into policy-type positions where they evaluate rather than produce original research. He went on to say,

We have a lot of discussion in many parts of the academic world about are we preparing our students only to be replicas of ourselves, who are researchers, if we're in a research university? Or, what are we doing in preparing Ph.D.s who won't be in academia?

Another "basic purpose" of the dissertation is for students to develop independence as researchers and scholars and produce a product that demonstrates their ability to contribute to the literature. One participant described his goals for his students as follows:

> I want them, when they leave, having done their dissertations, that they can start any topic in the discipline and know how to start on any new study they want to do. . . . That they know, even if it's a method they're not familiar with, they at least know the right questions to ask and where to go to figure out what that is. I always have this sort of visualization that it's giving somebody their wings to go out and now they can do this.

For many sociology faculty, qualitative researchers in particular, the purpose of the dissertation is to learn how to write or produce a book (preferably a university press book) or at least a body of work that could be developed into a book, or two or three journal articles. As such the dissertation is "an indicator, a predictor of future productivity."

## Original Contribution

Although the sociology faculty identified many ways to make an original contribution (see Table 13.2), they "worry less about originality" than faculty in science disciplines, largely because "we have the luxury and the misery of being able to study everything in any way possible." Indeed, one participant said he did not pay attention to originality.

The faculty noted that while there were degrees of originality, it is rare that they see something that "knocks you off your chair." Indeed, they do not expect students "to come up with something totally unusual, original." Because "nothing is ever totally new," sociology faculty look for incremental advances, things that build on prior research. The types of original contributions they see most frequently in dissertations involve original data collection and analysis; the reframing of existing data in a way that casts new light on

### TABLE 13.2.
#### The Nature of an Original Contribution in Sociology

Goes beyond what is known; contains new questions or contexts; opens new areas of exploration or a new angle on an old area of exploration; provides a fresh empirical focus to some key theoretical puzzle or debate in the literature; takes an important next step; brings things together in a new way; extends a debate or the current thinking on a particular topic; identifies an unanswered question that resonates with a larger theoretical issue; applies an established theory in a new context; reframes existing data and sheds new light on them theoretically, substantively, or methodologically; challenges or reinterprets existing theory or methods; develops a set of concepts or ideas, or a new theory or method; changes the way people think about a certain topic; leads to further research; is a meaningful contribution; adds to the literature

the topic theoretically, substantively, or methodologically; the bringing together of things in a new way; and the application of theory in a new context.

In addition to characterizing what an original contribution is, the sociology faculty discussed what it is not. An original contribution is not just filling in a little niche in an established paradigm or examining an idea that emerged out of someone else's work or testing or replicating something that has already been done using the same data set.

> If somebody . . . approach[ed] me with a topic like that or a project like that I would tell them that it's good for an article, maybe it's good for an empirical paper, maybe it's good for a master's thesis, but it's not what you do [for] a Ph.D. You have to dig into the literature and identify some unanswered question that resonates with some larger theoretical issue.

Further, if in reading the dissertation the faculty do not learn something new, then they do not consider it to be original. In the rare instances where the originality of a dissertation is questioned, it is usually at the very inception of a project when "some generally weak student" proposes something that looks a lot like something that has been done before.

> Students often think that having a certain topic is enough, that if it's an interesting topic, then that's enough for an original contribution. . . . A lot of the things that they want to study are already known. If you want to

study race discrimination—it's an important topic—but we know a lot about it. You have to go beyond that, but students often don't understand.

In these cases, the faculty push students in a different direction or the students "throw up their hands and leave the program."

## Significant Contribution

Sociology is a very broad discipline that is "pretty committed to the idea that most everything that [it] stud[ies] can be made significant." As long as a student takes a piece of the social world and studies it well and in depth, "there's no topic too small to do a dissertation on." However, to truly be significant, the work should not simply look at something that has never been looked at before, it should be linked to some key debate within the discipline, be associated with theoretical ideas, or be an approach that "challenges stuff in some way, turns something on its head." It should reveal the way the "social machinery functions" or have "value or weight for society." (See Table 13.3.)

Significance is also "in the eye of the beholder." It depends on who is judging or evaluating the work. "Something that is significant . . . for our department or a larger professional group might not be viewed as significant by others." Indeed, one participant said that his judgment of a candidate's work was based on his "assessment of the intrinsic worth of the work," which included whether the student had identified an important theoretical

### TABLE 13.3.
#### The Nature of a Significant Contribution in Sociology

A surprising, unexpected contribution that extends knowledge and pushes an area forward; studies something no one has studied before; contains new findings, formulations, arguments, sets of comparisons, or methods; uses a richer and more extensive data set; fills in some missing piece; unlocks a term or phase and captures people's imagination; better conceptualizes or articulates something; contains various confirmations or amendments; clarifies a point in a debate; sheds light on an issue; identifies an important theoretical puzzle; addresses an emerging social problem or question that has implications for the larger society; educates people in the field; opens up a new field puzzle or an important unanswered question and had come up with a credible answer. He also noted that there's "a tail wagging the dog kind of thing here, too. It's significant if it's published, and it's published in a refereed place. That sounds pretty crass, but it's a criterion that we're all familiar with, that we all live by." Another, participant went so far as to say that significance "isn't essentially in your work, it is somehow judged, layered on the work by others."

Timing also affects judgments of significance. The work could be on a topic that people are not ready to identify as an important social problem. One participant noted that in 1958 a major journal published an article on what we now call "date rape," but that nothing happened with it until the early 1980s.

The sociology faculty more so than faculty in other disciplines distinguished among different kinds of significance. One distinction was between public or policy significance and professional or field significance. The former relates to the "wide world" and is about having an impact on policy and society. The latter relates to the discipline itself and is about having an impact on the way future studies are done. With respect to these two types of significance, one participant discussed how graduate training and academe's reward system are at odds with doctoral students' goals.

> I think a lot of our Ph.D. students come into sociology because they want to have a public impact. They want to change the world. And then one of the frustrations with your training is we focus them more into what's significant within academia, within the discipline. . . . I try to convince my graduate students that . . . you can do both. But the way you're going to be judged, usually in terms of getting a job, and the way you're going to be judged in terms of getting tenure [is] the extent to which your work is significant within the discussions going on within your profession among other academics.

Another distinction the faculty made was about the level or degree of significance of the dissertation. A low level of significance is something that makes an incremental contribution. It pushes some fairly heavily studied area forward a little bit. It adds something potentially useful or intellectually interesting to knowledge or clarifies some point that has been debated. A high level of significance is something that might open up a whole new field, be widely referenced, become part of the basic terminology of the field, and even migrate to other fields (e.g., labeling theory, which has ended up in education and other places).

One participant described his standards for significance and how he worked with students.

> I have different standards for different students and that's the way it should be. As you meet with the person and you see how they write and how they think, you try to bring them along as far as you can to a better level of skill and analysis. But everybody doesn't go to the same level. I think a lot of the dissertations that I've done that have been absolutely excellent and have been published, I had very little to do with. It's the ones where you really spend hours and hours and hours and you try to assess where the student is and then try to push them to a level of seeing what the dissertation might be, putting it in a context that would make it significant and important and try to lead them in that direction. I have a minimum standard and then you have this kind of different way of working with different students establishing different goals.

Finally, like faculty in several other disciplines, the sociology faculty debated the relationship between "original" and "significant." Faculty in one focus group could not differentiate between the two. For them, the terms are "not precise" and are "used interchangeably." While the faculty in general felt that if something was original "it's likely to be significant"; they also recognized that something could be significant without being "totally" original, a "replication of a really important question," for example.

## The Dissertation as a Whole

Sociology dissertations tend to be large tomes. Faculty in fields where the book is the most common form of publication often tell students, especially those seeking positions at research universities, to think about their dissertations as a book from the beginning. However, there is a "disconnect" between the expected dissertation format and the format of professional publications. Thus, for "some people" the "conventional dissertation" has "lost its usefulness," and, consequently, the structure of the sociology dissertation is moving in the direction of the journal-article style for "some students." Below we explore the characteristics of different-quality sociology dissertations (see Table 13.4) and what the sociology faculty had to say about them.

## Outstanding

The hallmark of an outstanding dissertation in sociology is the quality of the writing and the richness of thought. The writing is not only engaging but seamless. It expresses the students' point of view in a voice that is "distinctly theirs." This type of writing is "rare." It is "a gift or a skill that people have," though it is a skill that students "can develop and improve on."

Outstanding dissertations are thoroughly and creatively conceptualized. They "cut to the problem," and "hone in on what is interesting." They display a coherence or consistency in quality and thought across all the components. Everything "hangs together." There is a "thread running through it and it's very tight in the sense that everything . . . comes back to bear on that thread." They are imaginative and innovative. Students who write them "think about the world in ways that somebody else really hasn't seen it."

Outstanding dissertations are intellectually engaging. They are a "fantastic learning experience," the "kind of work that anyone of us could benefit from reading." While reading an outstanding dissertation, faculty say, "Wow!" "You start sucking in your breath as you're reading it," and think, "I know this can be a book." Indeed, the outstanding dissertation is "publishable in its present form" and many "become highly visible books."

Although there is often an element of "breakthrough" in the outstanding dissertation, "sometimes the best of normal science can be outstanding:"

> I've seen some stuff which is normal science but I will put it in a brilliant category. Like . . . a piece of research that figures out how to prove a point, everybody agrees it's got to be true, but nobody had figured out how to demonstrate it . . . . They use a data set in a clever and new way, or they really have a brilliant research design that allows them to do a lot of experiment[ing] or collect[ing] data that really nails down something a lot of people have been saying. That is a great piece of work—and it's normal science.

Outstanding qualitative dissertations were also discussed. They were characterized as "deep investigations" by people who bring a "creative edge" to their work. These students do not do superficial interviews or "hang out someplace for a couple of weeks and then call it an ethnography." Rather,

**TABLE 13.4.**
## The Characteristics of Different Quality Dissertations in Sociology

| Quality | Characteristics |
|---|---|
| **Outstanding** | Well written; clear and concise; rhetorically very solid; fresh, novel, original, insightful, intellectually engaging, creative, imaginative; well crafted and well executed; coherent, has a watertight argument; the different components are connected in a seamless way; has a point of view and a distinct voice; looks at some aspect of the field in a new way; tells a story and is a good read; is grounded in a debate but goes beyond it; is a deep investigation that brings empirical focus to something hitherto unclear; shows a unique, rich, in-depth understanding of the topic that leads to the generation of an important question; is thoroughly and creatively conceptualized; theoretically sophisticated, brings together theories or concepts in a creative way; has a brilliant research design; examines the questions through the creative and innovative collection and analysis of rich data; uses several kinds of data to build the case; presents results in a convincing and articulate manner; offers a meaningful or cultural interpretation of the results; brings things together that had not been brought together before; demonstrates the student's ability to be independent; teaches the reader something; is publishable in its present form; speaks to a broader audience; has the potential to change the way people think about the problem |
| **Very good** | Solid; done correctly; follows the rules well; demonstrates technical competence; well written and well designed; thorough; has a lesser degree of originality; is not overwhelmingly brilliant; lacks a creative, broadly synthetic, innovative spark; seams are not quite as clear cut; the point of view is laid on it; does not have its own voice; may be too rhetorical; may lack a core message or sense of what is critical; addresses an important and interesting question or problem but does not produce excitement or surprise; theoretically and methodologically solid; integrates but does not advance theory; has a good data set and a good set of observations; has enough appropriately analyzed data; weaves in the data; offers useful findings; is a good, normal science contribution to the field |
| **Acceptable** | Demonstrates technical competence; all parts are there; shows student could be a professional in the field; less well written; not much originality, passion, or excitement; less thorough; usually |

*(continues)*

**TABLE 13.4.**
**Continued**

| Quality | Characteristics |
|---------|-----------------|
| **Acceptable** | small scale; not broad, focused, or integrated enough; is not well conceptualized; arguments are spongy; is consistent across sections, but has some loose ends; does not have all the subtleties and connections; literature review is very mechanistic; does not have command or grasp of the critical literature; shows poor comprehension of key areas of theory; has minimal or mundane theory; theoretical propositions are not fully worked out; does not typically involve original data collection; the data set is inadequate for the proposition; the right data are not collected; theory and data are not connected; the data are pedestrian; the student is not in command of the data; the evidence is not plausible; the quantitative analysis is very unsophisticated and elementary; has predictable results; cannot step outside of the position of participant and develop a critical, sociological perspective on the data; exhibits trouble thinking like a researcher; peters out at the end; cannot answer the "So what?" question |
| **Unacceptable** | Has major flaws; terrible writing; sloppy presentation; lacks depth of thought and coherent logic; inadequate or incorrect comprehension of basic concepts, poor conceptualization, operationalization, and methodology; pure replication of another study; does not clearly define a problem or issue; weak or no literature review; inconsistent use of references; unable to link bodies of theory to make a theoretical argument; materials were poorly chosen; problem is poorly researched; data collection is flawed; analysis is fundamentally flawed and poorly executed; uses inappropriate statistics; findings are not relevant; evidence does not support the interpretation; interpretation is exaggerated; does not link findings to the broader field |

they spend "gazillions of hours at a certain place and . . . get to know it deeply." Their interpretations of their observations offer "a meaning or a cultural understanding" that "we wouldn't normally see or the average person wouldn't see." They bring different theories or concepts together in a creative way and weave something new out of it.

Students who write outstanding dissertations love what they are doing and are engaged in the learning process. They "are able to identify a particular problem or topic that they're very interested in." They go "way beyond" what their committee members expect and beyond what the committee contributed in terms of advice and suggestions "as to how to put it together."

Sometimes an outstanding dissertation is a function of "luck" or choosing "the right thing at the right time." Sometimes it is a function of "who your chair is and who's on your committee." Indeed, the "synergy" between the advisor and student can make a difference. Faculty in one focus group had an extended discussion about how outstanding students interact with them during the process. One participant said:

> You're dealing with students more on a scholar/scholar basis instead of mentor/mentee relationship, and so you can have those intellectual exchanges that are satisfying to you . . . from the scholarship perspective and helpful to the student. So you go back to the theme of independent scholarship. They have really crossed that threshold and are actually doing it in the dissertation and that's what makes the dissertation outstanding. It's not just the product, but the process, and how they are interacting with you during the process.

Following up on a colleague's comment about the revision process and how outstanding students make major improvements with each draft, another participant said:

> I experienced the same kind of [thing] sitting with the student to talk about ideas and getting a draft back and seeing those ideas not only reflected but well executed and taking it beyond what I had suggested . . . this way of reflecting back and learn[ing] something in small capacities, which is part of what makes this a good dissertation to me also. Not so much the substance of the dissertation, but the pedagogy, the communications with students that works.

Indeed, another participant in that focus group noted that for him it was the nature of the process, not the "spectacular" product, that made some dissertations outstanding:

> There are also dissertations that a person starts and it is so bad, and then it gets to be so that you're either proud of it or if you're not, you wouldn't

be embarrassed if somebody read it. That has been some of the most, believe it or not, satisfying experiences. For me in four years in the making of
doing this and then the person comes in and you're proud that it's made. I
think that that's an outstanding dissertation of a different sort than the
spectacular. They just come back and keep doing it and doing it.

## Very Good

Very good dissertations demonstrate competence. They are good, solid contributions to the discipline but "pretty much within the confines of what
would be expected." Faculty do not learn very much from them. They are
usually good in parts that reflect the students' particular strengths. For instance, if the

> person is more methodologist, let's say that section is really good, but the
> parts that surround it are weak and not well connected. Or a person is
> really developing great ideas, but really is lost in the woods on the methods
> part, and somewhat inappropriate, and they don't know exactly how to
> link the results to the research questions.

Students who write very good dissertations often do not know what to
include and what to exclude. As one participant described it, "When you get
to the dissertation, the problem is never, 'I don't have enough data.' The
problem is always, 'I have too much data.'" Some students feel that they
have "to bring it all in," which results in a "clunky" dissertation with little
self-contained modules that do not advance the story.

## Acceptable

There are "big differences" between what faculty think of as a good dissertation and what they think of as a "passable" one. Indeed, in theory "a dissertation that is not very good would not be signed off on," so "acceptable" is
"kind of an oxymoron." However, given that acceptable dissertations do get
passed, the "operational standard" is if someone takes the dissertation off
your shelf "you wouldn't turn red." It passes the "gag test. . . . You could
show it to people and say, 'Well, it's not the best in the world, but it will
do.'"

Like faculty in several other disciplines, the sociology faculty distinguished between "acceptable" dissertations and "minimally acceptable"
ones. "Acceptable" dissertations are typically competent but very pedestrian.

"Minimally acceptable" ones are ones where "you plug your nose and push it through." They tend to be small scale. Students may not collect the right kind of data for the project, the data set may be inadequate for the proposition, or students may start with an existing data set and try "to concoct some kind of argument . . . [that] just doesn't work."

The faculty described several types of acceptable/minimally acceptable dissertations. One type is where students show that they can review the literature, use adequate methods, and report the findings adequately. Another type is where students are determined to put a theoretical architecture in place and the empirical part is thin. A third type is where students who do ethnographic or participant/observation studies fail to step outside their position as a participant and look at the data critically. Consequently, they do not develop a sociological perspective on them. Similarly, students who do gender studies or feminist research often take the idea that "the person is political and that your experience matters" too far. They think that their own life is "the most important data" and cannot "abstract themselves away from the situation."

Students who write acceptable dissertations tend to plod along. They require "an enormous amount of coaching." They need to be "redirected a lot," and "pull[ed] through the process." They may lack a critical grasp of the literature and their analyses may lack depth as well. These students often have "trouble thinking as a researcher would." According to one participant, it is almost like they are in Piaget's stage of concrete operations. Another participant made an analogy to the Peter Principle, "where you get promoted to your level of incompetence":

> They can cruise along with the course papers, the second-year paper, the 25-page comp[rehensive] exams . . . and suddenly, "OK, let's produce something that's 250 pages." Then, suddenly, [at] that level of specificity and detail and rigor, [they] may suddenly come crunch-up against their abilities.

In addition, these students' writing skills are often poor. Faculty, who are willing, find that they have to "spend hours" copyediting students' writing.

Less common but not unheard of is the "brilliant but totally eccentric" student. One participant talked about such a student who had "been around forever" and produced a 1,200-page dissertation.

> Eleven-hundred pages of this dissertation was [*sic*] really brilliant, really astonishingly good work in doing a review of the topic from the dawn of humanity until yesterday, and beautifully . . . and then petering out at the end with no significance. Just couldn't pull anything out of it. . . . He just couldn't make it work at the end. . . . With all of the brilliance, with all of the innovation, with all of the thoroughness, [the] incredibly comprehensive review about previous thinking . . . a critical analysis of what had gone on before, [he] couldn't answer the "So what?" [question].

Sometimes circumstances affect whether what should have been a good or very good dissertation ends up being just acceptable. Sometimes students are rushed and have to finish quickly because they have a job or a postdoc. Sometimes students "run out of gas" or they are "just so sick of the dissertation by the time they defend it that if they have to rewrite a page or two they'll spit up all over the table."

There was some disagreement among the faculty on whether they judged the student or the work. Some felt that they "should be judging products not people." Though others noted that "judgment of the person is always floating around in there a little bit." Ultimately, passing an acceptable dissertation is a "grudging," "painful judgment" for faculty because it is difficult to let a person go away "empty handed." The focus group participants said they typically only have to make this decision when they are the "second, third [reader], or more likely the outside member [of a dissertation committee]," where they have less control over the dissertation. More often than not, they decide not to "kill" the dissertation because the other committee members in the student's field are more positive about the dissertation and are more "ready to get him [*sic*] on his way and send him on to his next failure."

Faculty do not expect students who produce acceptable dissertations to get tenure-track jobs at research universities. They noted that "there is almost a tracking system going on" between the quality of the dissertation and the type of job a student will get. Indeed, faculty often make a "side bet" by not recommending students who write acceptable dissertations for college-level jobs or by undermining them in their letters of recommendation:

> Sometimes there is a level of dishonesty that is involved. It's really tragic, where the faculty member says, "Yes, you are fine. Go ahead and apply [for a research position] and then they write a letter that makes sure that you

don't get the job," which is a kind of hypocrisy. . . . Other faculty, they go the other way. They're rude and say, "Oh, by the way, you are not good enough." It's better than writing the letter that's full of negatives, but it's still kind of rude.

## Unacceptable

Most sociology departments have processes in place that make it "very unlikely" that a dissertation will fail. If a dissertation fails, it is because "the process breaks down." Most unacceptable dissertations are caught and stopped before they go to defense. They usually get stopped because the dissertation proposal is unacceptable or because the research or the chapter drafts are not at a level that the chair finds acceptable. One department even has a "pre-oral defense" meeting with the committee where students receive critical comments and are given "specific orders" about what they have to do to make the dissertation acceptable. However, the main "mechanism" that prevents failure is the "principal advisor" or dissertation chair, who should not allow students to defend unacceptable dissertations.

Typically, the chair would have to be "pretty out of touch" and "so disconnected to colleagues to think something is really good" when others thought it was not. Indeed, the culture of the dissertation defense is such that faculty "trust" that when a chair has deemed a dissertation ready to defend, the dissertation is passable. In cases where it is not:

> You're in a situation where your critique is not really of the student's work—the fact that the chair is so defensively engaged—and you're often forced [to approve it] . . . you end up sick to your stomach. I have been in situations where I have passed dissertations that should never have passed only because the dynamics of these processes can get really out of whack.

Often what happens is that faculty "end up with disagreements about relative quality." And more likely than not, committee members will withhold their signatures and require the student to "go back and do really substantial work." Rarely do faculty say, "This is a failure. You are done. You are out."

One participant described a situation where the committee "hoped that [the dissertation] would slide by and [the student] would go away or that I would kill it." As the Graduate School's representative, this participant reminded himself that his role was to police the process and make sure that crap doesn't get through or that students are not ill treated in the process. I decided that this was crap. I couldn't sign it, and I wasn't going to sign it, and it was irresponsible of the other members of the committee to let it along that way.

In instances where it is "obvious" that a student is never going to generate a dissertation that is adequate," the advisor should "in as avuncular a manner as possible" say, "Don't go away mad, just go away." Yet, faculty seem to take a passive approach to these situations. Rather than terminate students who produce "something we don't think is adequate," they hope the students will get "discouraged" and leave. In fact, these students' failure to quit was described as an "error in the system."

> The error in the system is that you get some very, very persistent student who keeps offering something that is not adequate . . . and then eventually we are beaten down or people just drop their heads.

Because "we've made the students suffer enough and ourselves suffer enough," at a certain point faculty feel "an obligation to say . . . 'OK, let's defend.'" Even though the faculty typically agree that they should judge the work and not the student, in the end "there is a judgment of the student." And faculty may say, "I don't want this guy going out there and trying to do sociology because I don't think he can do it."

Sometimes students' work is inadequate because they have been "out of touch with the community" and have done the "whole thing without much consultation." They have often been "off campus for quite a while and obviously were not getting the kind of feedback and input [they needed], not only from the professors, but from peers as well." As one participant put it:

> Successful dissertation writing requires a socialization process. It is not just a Lone Ranger—head off and go into the sunset and try and get it done— which . . . often leads to really dangerous outcomes because people could get lost.

## The Components of a Sociology Dissertation

The sociology faculty's comments about the matrix of components of the dissertation (see Table 1.2) were relatively benign. They basically agreed that all the components are "required," but felt that the structure worked better for quantitative, hypothetical-deductive dissertations, which are "based on the structure of a journal article," than for qualitative ones, where the book is the model.

Faculty who were critical of the matrix thought that it was the wrong way to think about the dissertation. "The right way of thinking is about it is: Do they have interesting questions? Do they have a good question? Has the question not yet been answered? . . . Is there some research strategy that the person can follow in order to answer this question?" In addition, the faculty noted that when they read a dissertation they not only look at the quality of each component, but also look at how they relate to each other, how they "interweave together." Indeed, the introduction and the literature and the theory are often one chapter "because that's a coherent task."

Three focus groups did not discuss the components of the dissertation and no focus group discussed the very good theory cell. Below we explore the characteristics of the components of the sociology dissertation (see Table 13.A in the appendix to this chapter) and what the faculty said about them.

## Introduction

The sociology dissertation should not read like a "detective" story. It should not be a "whodunit" or "mystery novel" where the answer to the "puzzle" comes at the end. Rather, it should start with, "This is the question I posed. This is why I posed it. This how I approached it. And here's a preview of where I think this is all going." The question should be set within the context of a social problem or body of theory, and the importance of the problem should be justified. According to one participant, if all the basics about what, why, and how are answered in the introduction in a stellar way, it is outstanding. If it is logical and done well, it is very good. If it is "done" and there are no fatal flaws in the logic, it is acceptable.

Outstanding introductions often start with a hook. The hook can be a "great quote, a punch, something that is going to get your interest right away" and helps make the case for why the study is important, new, interesting, or significant. Outstanding introductions show "an awareness right off the bat the student knows what they are talking about." They bring in the key literature, lay out a thesis, and identify the methods they will use to address the problem. Outstanding introductions entice the reader and cause him or her to say, "Wow! This is a really important topic."

The very good introduction takes a well-established topic, poses a clear research question, and demonstrates "one or more theoretical approaches that one might use." "But [it] isn't going to be path breaking. It isn't going to be surprising. It's just going to be good and solid."

At minimum, an acceptable introduction has a problem that can be discussed in the rest of the dissertation. It does the things an introduction needs to do, but it is not very exciting. Unacceptable ones leave the reader with "no idea what they are really getting at." They may go off on tangents of detail that are "just not comprehensible at this point in the reading." They may pick up some theoretical point and "have a big debate about it." They may "pick a fight that my method is changing the world and everybody is killing me or persecuting me."

## *Literature Review*

Literature reviews are not just summaries of the literature. Rather, they take a body of literature and "lean" it in a particular direction, while at the same time not being "a major annual review article." Faculty's opinions of how good a literature review is depend on "how broad the coverage of the literature is, how well they [the works cited] are integrated, how cleverly they . . . can see connections between concepts." At the same time, faculty said that writing a good literature review is an "art," a "craft" that develops through an apprenticeship process.

Outstanding literature reviews have a rhetorical and an analytic aspect. The rhetorical aspect is the "craft of knowing what needs to be cited [and] what doesn't need to be cited." The analytical aspect is "being able to organize the literature [around themes], which then becomes rhetoric." Outstanding literature reviews show an awareness of the different levels at which the literature may be relevant to the topic and succinctly synthesize information from a broad body of sources. The students focus on concepts and ideas, not who said what. They align the literature with the material that is going to be presented in the dissertation and "set you up to understand the contribution" they are going to make. They bring it all together in the end in a "neat way that's tight" so that "you see the thread right through the whole thing." Students who write outstanding literature reviews are "very critical" and often "pick out something that's wrong with the literature that nobody else has ever been able to find."

Students who write very good literature reviews do not use the literature "in the way that they're really building up a case for what they're doing and what their hypotheses are." They frequently present a "review of a lot of things in the general area" and then say, "OK, now we hypothesize that . . . ," leaving the reader to wonder, "Now where are you getting these hypotheses?"

Students who write acceptable literature reviews "are not thinking analytically." They just "regurgitate the stuff." They may "rattle off" the literature without really understanding it. Sometimes they "jam literatures together that don't make any sense," causing the reader to wonder, "Why are we reading five pages on an offshoot of something about Aristotle?" Or they might say, "Like Jones and Smith, my study will do this," or "I'm going to follow this one. I'm not going to criticize it." Whereas faculty "are always looking" for sentences like "While the literature has done this, I plan on doing this," which distinguish the outstanding from the acceptable.

## *Theory*

In sociology, theory means different things to different people. There is "no reigning orthodoxy," no theory with a capital *T*. For some people, theory is conceptual ideas that are used to organize data. For others it is "conflict theory, symbolic interaction, or critical theory."

Just as there are different views on theory, there are different ways of approaching the relationship between theory and empirical method in the sociology dissertation. In many cases, "it is not a specific set of testable statements. It is just a statement of their more morphological organization, almost more [like], 'Here are my assumptions about how the world works.' And that, of course, is linked to theory." Regardless of their views on theory, most faculty felt that the sociology dissertation "has to have some theory in it" and that there has to be "theoretical consistency across the different parts of the dissertation."

The outstanding dissertation knows the place of theory and uses it to help tell the story. Indeed, theory shows up in the introduction, literature review, and substantive parts of the dissertation. While it is rare for students to create theory, outstanding dissertations often synthesize theories or use conceptual ideas in creative, nuanced ways. Students whose theoretical work is outstanding see multiple levels and multiple relationships. They see "this one's kind of right in this aspect and this one's kind of right [in another aspect]."

## Methods

Methods in a sociology dissertation have to have basic validity. One participant, a qualitative researcher, said that he always inspects the data to see if
they are consistent with what the student said he or she did. He also looks
to see if the data were collected with skill, sensitivity, and were well recorded.

In addition to having a logical connection between theory and method,
questions posed and answers found, outstanding methods involve an element
of novelty, "doing something that isn't ordinarily thought about," finding a
way "to grapple with a problem that we had not thought about before." Or
they may involve using multiple methods "to show the different approaches
in coherent stories." Students whose methods are outstanding really understand what they did and why, and can discuss them competently. They are
also thorough in their documentation: "I'm not reading something and
wondering how they know this, because they tell me."

Very good and acceptable methods are appropriate for the research question and have basic validity. Very good methods are less novel and less interesting than outstanding ones, whereas acceptable methods are textbook and
unimaginative. In both cases, using a different method or including more
people or more groups of people would have made the study stronger and
more interesting.

Unacceptable methods are fatally flawed, "they don't seem to really get
at what [students] are interested in studying." In quantitative studies, students may have measures that are not valid or reliable for the concepts or
variables they want to study. One participant remembered a study where the
student tried to measure social capital (human relationships) using census
data, which do not ask questions about social capital. In qualitative studies,
the reader "doesn't quite feel comfortable with it." For example, a student
may have a nonrandom sample of eight people and state, "You find that
60% of them felt something."

## Data Analysis/Results

The data analysis/results component is the "heart" of the dissertation. It is
the part where faculty said they "spend most of our time." One participant
talked about how he advised his students to think about and write these
chapters:

> I talk to them about those chapters in terms of shape or story line. I want
> each chapter to have within it a story line. . . . We talk about [a] certain

size, ideas you put into a simple chapter, a section of a chapter. I also talk about, as a chapter is beginning to develop without the necessary overall shape of the dissertation, what order of the chapters is going to be and [how they] fit together.

Although the faculty highlighted issues related to qualitative and quantitative data across quality levels, the issues typically "transcend whether it is a qualitative or quantitative [study]." At the outstanding level, students have a data set that "speaks to the larger issues." In their analyses, they go "beyond what would normally be expected." They "draw out the best of the data," and ask "iterative" questions of them, about which one participant remarked, "I think it reflects a degree of both competence and confidence."

Students who function at the outstanding level make "links between the conceptual apparatus and what they found." Regardless of whether the data are qualitative or quantitative, these students see "complex patterns," "interrelationships," and "interesting things" in the data. They may provide an "extra, added measure of impact" by using their data to "disprove common theories instead of just supporting a person's argument." Students who do really outstanding work often do "some really clever stuff" in the way they graphically display their data.

Very good data analysis/results sections are data rich and show "a deeper level of understanding than the basic question." The findings are "staged" or put together in a coherent way, usually starting with descriptions and becoming more analytic and more theoretical as the analysis proceeds. They also use the data to address counterarguments or provide counteranalyses.

At the acceptable level, students use appropriate analytical methods, and their analyses "hold water." However, their chapters lack a clear story, argument, or point. They may suffer from too much or too little data. In the case of too much data,

> They'll include every regression equation, including ones that have no pertinence to the topic at hand, or inconclusive results, or no significance. . . . Sometimes it'll be a statistical table, and then it'll just describe exactly what's shown statistically verbally, so [it's] kind of information overkill; losing the significant and important findings in the midst of endless discussions of insignificant findings.

In the case of too little data, students are sent "back to put more data in." Sometime this component is considered acceptable when students "competently execute" their analytical tests, but come up with "null" findings. One participant discussed how he trained students who do quantitative research in how to come up with "something interesting regardless of which way the findings go." He has them set up columns for their analyses so that "if it turns out this way you can talk about this, or if it turns out this way or if it turns out that way, we can talk about it that way."

Both qualitative and quantitative dissertations can be unacceptable for a variety of reasons. Students may have "way too much data" that are not analyzed and do not answer their question. Alternatively, their analyses may be "reasonable"—"in part because I told him what analysis to do"—but they cannot interpret the results; they do not know how to "relate certain findings, especially quantitative findings, to the substantive meaning that they convey."

Additionally, students may use the wrong technique, misinterpret numbers, or use graphic displays to create totally misleading perceptions: "For example, [in] situations where one group has a mean of 9 and another group has a mean of 8.8, but you have the graph [that] started at 8.0 . . . one group is twice as high [as] the other."

Another common problem is overgeneralizing results. For example, in a quantitative study, a student might have a result that explains 5% of the variance and makes the "very solid statement" that "This clearly shows." In a qualitative study, even though their data do not support it, students might try to generalize what they found "to the whole, the rest of the world." Students also sometimes try to impute things that "just aren't in the data one way or the other." For example, they show that people have a certain degree of economic mobility and then generalize about their happiness when they were not asked about happiness.

### Discussion and Conclusion

By the time they get to the discussion and conclusion, students are "usually pooped out. They're tired. They want to be done." As a result, first drafts of the discussion and conclusion are often just summaries "of what they already told you," and thus otherwise good dissertations may initially "fall flat at the end."

One participant distinguished between the conclusion and the discussion. He said that the conclusion is basically a repetition of the findings, whereas the discussion, which is "more crucial than the conclusion," is the classic "Where do we go from here?" It is where students say, "We've done this. We've gone through all this. We've got this. What the hell is the importance of all this?" The discussion is also the place where students should point out some of the weaknesses in their research; though some students "can go overboard or underboard." Thus it is important for students to find the right balance, "not invalidating everything [they] did, but not ignoring the fact that there are weaknesses."

It is also important that the discussion connects the study to the "larger picture." Indeed, sociologists "are most often interested in structural relations and how is this a microcosm of that or how is it not, or what makes this finding counterintuitive and why." Some faculty encourage students to do some speculating. Said one participant, "I tell them to take some leaps at the end, take some chances and let the reader know that you're speculating."

The outstanding discussion and conclusion (hereafter "conclusion") briefly summarizes what was done, then "zeros in on the meaning" and draws something out of it. Indeed, one participant said that, at least for quantitative dissertations (he was not sure this was the case for qualitative dissertations), the best conclusions are in dissertations where the substantive chapters focus on the data and what they mean, and the concluding chapter makes the argument. The outstanding conclusion also connects the study to the larger literature, has a "fairly astute" discussion of the study's strengths and limitations and how it leads into new areas of inquiry. Students whose conclusions have policy implications "talk knowledgeably" about them.

Writing something that is "better than average or excellent" takes "a little second wind. . . . It means removing some of the shackles that graduate school has put on you in terms of keeping it within a little box" and stepping "outside the box of your last chapter and really go[ing] for it." "You tell what you think about this in relation to your values, in relation to the kind of society you think [should be]. It is the time you editorialize." At the same time, the conclusion "sticks to the substance of what was brought up. It doesn't just go off on a tangent." Writing an outstanding conclusion is "very hard to do and very rare. You also have to be brave to take it to that level."

At the acceptable level, the conclusion provides a brief, clear summary of the research, makes some connections, and acknowledges some of the study's limitations. Students who write acceptable conclusions "may not be very adept at looking at policy implications or thinking through what the next steps will be . . . but they have to have elements of linking it up and acknowledging limitations." Conclusions may fall in the acceptable category when students are "so immersed in the details of what they've done that they can't back up and see the bigger picture." Or they may be acceptable because students "don't have anything to say because the whole thing is overwritten in the first place; they've said everything." Indeed, one participant said, "You might even read their dissertation and [say] 'Wow! This is really exciting.' And then they say hardly anything [in the conclusion]."

The unacceptable conclusion is missing entirely, restates a section from the introduction, or is just a summary of "what I did." Unacceptable is also when "the student has no idea what they are talking about." They "don't get it." They are not able to say, "This is what this means or this is what I've done and this is what I think it means." This inability to see what it means often happens "because they're so bogged down with having worked the individual chapters."

## Notes

1. For information on the source of these data, see chapter 1, note 5. Some data came from the American Sociological Association's (ASA) Web site, http://www .asanet.org/research (accessed May 25, 2005), ASA (2003), and from Carla Howrey, ASA deputy executive director (personal communication, May 26, 2005).

# Appendix

## TABLE 13.A.
### The Components of a Sociology Dissertation and Their Characteristics at Different Quality Levels

| Components | Quality levels | | | |
| --- | --- | --- | --- | --- |
| | Outstanding | Very good | Acceptable | Unacceptable |
| Introduction | Short, focused, creative, and very synthetic; has a hook; states the problem and shows why it is interesting and important; explains the significance of the study; introduces the literature review; sets the context; locates the project in what has been done before; lays out a thesis and an organizational structure; provides a preview and a road map of where the research is going and what is in the coming chapters | Well written, but less eloquent; poses a clear research question; expresses clarity of purpose; focuses on the key issues; is good, solid but not surprising | Workmanlike; reasonably clear and focused; has a marginal hook but is not exciting; conveys what the research is about; shows understanding of the topic; provides an inkling of the theoretical and methodological approach; may leave something out but does not say anything absolutely wrong | Not grounded in anything; very defensive; tone is very politicized; takes inappropriate stances; goes off on incomprehensible tangents |

(continues)

**TABLE 13.A.**
**Continued**

| Components | Quality levels | | | |
| --- | --- | --- | --- | --- |
| | Outstanding | Very good | Acceptable | Unacceptable |
| **Literature review** | Demonstrates a grounded understanding of the literature; provides reasons for looking at the literature differently; draws on literature in a convincing and supple way; brings together and summarizes a broad body of material and makes meaningful distinctions without being exhaustive; knows what needs to be cited and what does not; analysis is organized around themes; is succinct; indicates the significance of the research | Provides a meaningful summary of the literature; includes both classic and recent citations; is not a laundry list of "Smith said this" and "Jones said that"; demonstrates a nuanced understanding of the literature; takes a body of material and leans it toward a particular direction; brings various intellectual resources to bear on the topic; builds a case for the research and for the hypotheses | Is ill conceived or seems wrong; not analytical, integrated, or synthesized; a stacked annotation, "this person said this" and "this person said this"; just regurgitates material; confusing; not clear why some literature is being cited and other literature is not | Omits people who have done the same thing the student is doing; has not looked at commonly understood bodies of relevant literature; cites articles that are out of date; misinterprets the literature; misquotes major theorists; shows lack of understanding of the literature and where their research fits in the field |

| Components | Quality levels | | | |
| --- | --- | --- | --- | --- |
| | Outstanding | Very good | Acceptable | Unacceptable |
| Theory | Provides a good, logical, sensible, coherent argument; clearly indicates understanding of the major perspective; shows up in the introduction, literature review, and in the substantive parts of the dissertation; is in student's own language; relates to other traditions and other ideas; evaluates a specific problem through a theoretical lens; evaluates different theories; sees multiple levels and multiple relationships; links observations to theory; uses conceptual ideas in a creative way; synthesizes theories; develops or creates theory | — | Is weakly understood; does not specify assumptions; shows slippage between the conceptual apparatus and the problem | No theory; completely unclear; ideas, theory, and material are not aligned |

*(continues)*

**TABLE 13.A.**
Continued

| Components | Quality levels | | | |
| | Outstanding | Very good | Acceptable | Unacceptable |
|---|---|---|---|---|
| **Methods** | Appropriate, clever, original, thorough; very well done; has basic validity; exhibits good judgment about what needs to be said and what can go in an appendix; connects questions and theory with methods; does something that ordinarily cannot be done; uses a novel method or multiple methods (triangulation); uses cutting-edge statistical techniques | More workmanlike; does not provide lengthy definitions of techniques already in the literature; use of a different technique might have been more appropriate or made it more interesting | Appropriate, competent; no fatal flaws; a rubber-stamped use of a textbook method; appropriate for the problem; has basic validity; sample is large enough but barely; uses a very unusual group that does not represent the average; yields a reasonably accurate answer; a different method might have been better | Fatally flawed; mismatch between method and problem; does not seem to understand the method; uses method improperly; the operationalization is inappropriate; no clear relationship between hypotheses and variables; variables do not capture the concept; no variance in one of the major variables; measures are not valid or reliable; statistical techniques are inappropriate or poorly explained |

| Components | Quality levels | | | |
|---|---|---|---|---|
| | Outstanding | Very good | Acceptable | Unacceptable |
| **Results/data analysis** | Appropriate; uses advanced techniques; interprets data properly; sees complex patterns in the data; does a high-level, iterative analysis of the data; uses tables, figures, charts, and maps to display the data cleverly; makes clear links between the conceptual apparatus and results; highlights the most important, original, and significant contributions; goes beyond supporting the argument and disproves common theories | Data rich; provides plausible arguments; sees interrelations that are not obvious; has rich illustrations | Analyses are well executed but not sophisticated or substantial; data are not rich; does not have enough substance; is not clear that the data are really evidence of the concepts; findings are null; provides too much information; loses significant and important findings in the midst of endless discussions of insignificant ones; includes every regression equation | Marginal analysis of the data; student does not know why he or she is using the technique; uses advanced techniques but sees nothing in the data; has obvious misinterpretations of the data; shows every iteration of the model, but cannot discern what is important; mindless presentation of data without interpretation; uses graphic displays to create misleading perceptions; evidence does not support the argument; results do not follow from the analysis and are interpreted incorrectly; oversells or overgeneralizes the results |

(continues)

**TABLE 13.A.**
Continued

| Components | Quality levels | | | |
| --- | --- | --- | --- | --- |
| | Outstanding | Very good | Acceptable | Unacceptable |
| **Discussion and conclusion** | Briefly summarizes what was done and reaches into new areas and different ways of seeing things; ties the whole study together; shows that the questions, methods, analyses, and findings are consistent; connects to the theoretical puzzles or debates they started with and takes them to another level; underscores the findings; discusses what is interesting and surprising about the results; recognizes the study's strengths, weaknesses, and limitations; sees the big picture significance of the work; speculates on and provides an astute discussion of future directions; has implications for the subfield, sociology, or social science | Discusses what is now known that was not known before; shows the limits of the research; indicates where future research might improve upon what was done; proposes logical follow-on research; focuses on very specific findings and neglects to bring out the general implications | Restates what has already been said; summarizes rather than analyzes; overstates the results; does not see or generalize the big picture; indicates that further research is necessary but does not provide specifics | Just a summary; no conclusion; takes a section out of the introduction and puts it in the conclusion; oversells the results |

# 14

# THE ENGLISH DISSERTATION

There are more than 145 Ph.D. programs in English (and literature) in the United States. The Modern Language Association's (MLA) Web site[1] lists 11 overarching scholarly areas comprising 80 divisions, some of which fall outside the purview of English departments. Graduate English programs enroll roughly 9,000 students (master's and doctoral) and graduate about 900 new Ph.D.s annually. The median time to degree is 9.7 years. About 6% of new English Ph.D.s go on to postdoctoral positions.[2]

Twenty-four faculty at seven universities participated in the focus groups. Overall, these faculty had 499 years of experience, had chaired an estimated 419 dissertations, and had sat on an estimated 829 dissertation committees. The average English focus group participant had been a professor for 21 years, had chaired 17 dissertations, and had sat on 35 dissertation committees. Below is a summary of the English focus groups' discussions. Their performance expectations for the dissertation are displayed in the tables. Their supporting discussion is recounted in the text.

## The Purpose of an English Dissertation

The English faculty saw the dissertation as serving many purposes (see Table 14.1). The "first purpose" of the dissertation is "to be written," "to be done," "to show that you can finish it." That said, the English faculty saw the dissertation more as means to an end than an end in itself, more as a process than a product:

> It is . . . a process that results in a product. . . . It's almost never a finished product. . . . This thing is not a thing. It's an idea that is in process and will often continue to be in process after they've graduated. . . . What's

### TABLE 14.1.
### The Purpose of an English Dissertation

To learn about research—how to figure out and ask interesting questions, and what it takes to do a long-term project and be professional in the field; to develop a richness, thickness, historical context, and the ability to compare different genres, set text against other text, and critic against critic; to demonstrate that the student can join and contribute to a conversation—knows what the questions are and the discussion is, knows how to use the terms and participate in the discussion; to show prima facie competence in the field—that the student has the capacity for extended, original research, the ability to write a booklike document that articulates the research, makes an argument about it, and is capable of making a significant contribution; to ensure the student has a firm grasp of the discipline; to get a job; is an apprenticeship; an important proving ground; a structural device to put students in the process of doing a sustained engagement; for practice at the labor of thinking something through seriously and carefully; preparation for publishing and teaching in the field; a tool for the field to assess the quality of its members; a writing sample and a calling card for a job; the point where the student crosses from being a student to being a scholar

valuable about it is not the product, but the process that they've undergone. . . . It has a lot to do with just stating an argument, then engaging in conversations and organizing time and gaining confidence and wielding authority and being familiar, and all kinds of things that are processes and verbs rather than products.

Along these lines, the English faculty saw the dissertation as a "structural device" for putting students in the process of "doing sustained engagement." "It's an important proving ground. . . . You have to be able to stay with the project through thick and thin, boring and interesting, [and] discouraging. It's a manic-depressive process."

The faculty also saw the dissertation as a "psychological institution," for getting the credential, about which one participant said, "I find the student can't actually get the perspective they need to complete it until they have actually done it." Another said, "One often discovers the point, the thesis statement of the dissertation only upon finishing it. So finishing it usually means that you understand what it's about." Indeed, the dissertation is the process of producing disciplinary knowledge. "It's not like there is some knowledge out there and you are going to go look for it and find it and put a frame around it."

The dissertation is also a "calling card" or "union card" for getting a job. It is something done to "to earn your entrance into the community of scholars," "to show that you have what it takes to be a member of the community," and which the community uses as a "litmus test," a "tool" to assess "the quality of its members." Several faculty used the metaphor of "apprenticeship" and talked about the apprentice producing "a masterpiece to enter a guild." Though one participant always tells students, "Think of it as a driver's license not a magnum opus, not your life's work, but something you're doing to prove your competence in a certain form of research and get on with it."

The English faculty noted that there are "different purposes" or "different levels" or "different grades of expectation" for the dissertation for different students. "Not all students have the same career objective," thus, according to one participant, "I tend to increasingly think of what kind of dissertation can I really expect this student to write." Ideally, the purpose of the dissertation, from the faculty's perspective, is to show whether the student is capable of making a significant contribution and to show "that mind at work over a long stretch of [time]." Though the faculty acknowledged, from the student's perspective, there are some "for whom [the dissertation] is simply a review of research or a union card." However, if students are hoping to spend a career "in a place like this," then they need to think about their dissertation as their first book and engage with it differently.

Just as the dissertation serves many purposes, its chapters also "have to serve a bunch of different purposes." Indeed, many faculty do not look at the dissertation as a "unified masterpiece" but rather as "something you can take apart and use in this pragmatic way to get yourself established." Thus, "you really only need two good chapters in a dissertation. One is your writing sample that you send out with your applications, and one is your job talk, and the rest, who cares? because nobody's going to read it. You just have to make your committee happy."

## Original Contribution

While the English faculty identified many ways to make an original contribution (see Table 14.2), many rejected the notion of originality. They said that it was a "suspect term," "a romantic concept," "an illusion," "meaningless." They indicated that "at one time originality . . . meant finding materials that had been lost, undiscovered, or more commonly unedited," but the

## TABLE 14.2.
### The Nature of an Original Contribution in English

Something no one else has done before; a fresh contribution that builds on or revises present knowledge about some text, movement, or author, and advances a scholarly discussion; a new look at an old subject, a new look at a new subject; looking at materials no one else has looked at; doing archival research; recovering materials that have been lost, uncollected, undiscovered, or previously unedited; improving someone else's idea; taking new text or unexpected materials and putting them in new combinations; synthesizing or recombining things that have already been said; putting canonical or semicanonical texts into new theoretical frameworks; taking models of inquiry or theoretical constructs from another field and connecting them with more traditional literary questions; joining a conversation; producing a surprising result; opening up new questions

field has since moved "away from thinking of originality at all." The faculty explained that English is a "collective discipline" that builds on what has come before. Consequently, "people don't make original contributions, they join conversations." "It's about collective change of the discourse that we all do together." One participant illustrated the difficulty the field had with the concept of originality by contrasting English with the sciences:

> I think one thing that makes some of these questions difficult for our field is that we're not science. We're not really . . . a progressive discipline in the sense that we can point to the knowledge of an element that did not exist before. . . . A lot of our work is recursive. We go over the same texts over and over again. There's a curious way in which scholarly work matches what's in the classroom. If you go to an eighth grade science class and you go to a [college] senior physics class, there's a real difference between the kind of physics that they're doing in there. Whereas in an eighth grade English class and a [college] senior seminar, the English major may be talking about the same book and may be, in fact, dealing with some of the same questions. You'll just be talking about it in a very different way. I think some of that comes into why it's difficult to define originality in our field. If someone discovers a new star, a new galaxy—the closest we have is a new text.

Other faculty felt that "it's almost impossible not to make an original contribution." They conceived originality as "putting together different things differently." Indeed, these faculty "defined" originality as "unforeseen recombinations," "the revision of received opinion," "relationships no one expected." Thus, for them originality is when "you actually learned something from the dissertation that you didn't know before."

Arbitrating between opposing camps, one participant said, "It seems like we're saying that we want originality, but not too much of it." Indeed, English faculty want students to "display confidence" that they "know the state of the field as it is," that they can situate themselves in "this ongoing conversation," and "say something different." According to one participant, "what I'm looking for in a dissertation" is:

> Here're X, Y, Z, and here's how they're arguing about this. I don't think they're talking about Q and here's why. That's important. Here's why saying this about that element makes the whole conversation different.

Indeed, what contemporary English faculty "pay most attention to" are "models of inquiry, theoretical constructs, paradigms, which often come from other disciplines." Thus originality is saying something like:

> These texts have never been thought of in terms of feminism. These texts have never been thought of in terms of the history of the book that's involved and the material production of the text," [even though the] framework in which it's being turned up is not original.

English faculty also "listen for a voice." "When you hear a voice in the dissertation, a presence or a distinctive perspective . . . it's just a harbinger of originality, real originality, genuine originality."

In contrast to the view that it is impossible not to make an original contribution, one participant noted that he had "been in dissertations" where he found "it was possible not to have made an original contribution in any way." He hastened to add that "those were not many." He described those dissertations as ones where "essentially what the students did was just go over what other scholars had already done. In some cases they have not read the scholars previously, so they haven't done their homework." He further characterized the kind of dissertation he did not find original as one

> that adopts the "puff-maker" approach to literature. Where you take whatever theoretical blade you want. You shove at the end of the machine and

push that dough through so that the text becomes formed in the shape of that blade but without any input of your own. Where it's more a disciplined theoretical template without adding anything of your own there.

One participant pointed out "the dark side" of originality, which is achieving "newness for the sake of originality." In these cases, the "newness is organizing the product through the articulation of ideas in a way that it is meant to sound different," which he thought was "false originality," but nevertheless an originality "that can succeed in the market despite its falsity, because it simply sounds new."

## Significant Contribution

A significant contribution in English is subjective—it is "in the eye of the beholder"—and bound to some measure of time. "You don't know when something is significant until ten years later when you say, 'Oh, this was the book that changed the way this bibliography is read.'" (See Table 14.3 for characteristics of a significant contribution.)

As in other disciplines, the concepts of original and significant were linked in many English faculty's minds. Most felt that in order for something to be significant, it had to be original, though others noted that something could be original but not be very significant. That said, the English faculty typically did not think that dissertations were significant "in the real sense of the word"; that is, in answering the "So what?" question, taking the argument and "making it go beyond the particulars of the field you're looking

### TABLE 14.3.
#### The Nature of a Significant Contribution in English

Not trivial; involves a conversation with the field; looks at material that has not been looked at before; a new way of reading something; an intervention in a central problem; argues that a noncentral argument needs to be more central in order to understand the field or the world beyond the field; makes an argument go beyond the particulars of the field being looked at; contributes something that others could use to talk about authors or the field; changes the way the history of a particular subject is viewed; opens things up for other fields and periods; alters the self-understanding of the field; provides a new way to look at the bigger picture at." Rather, the faculty felt that significance is something that "comes into humanistic work after more maturity than anyone [has] just finishing a Ph.D." However, during the course of the dissertation defense, if someone asks, "Have you thought of publishing part or all of this?" that person is implying that "there is significance that should be shared beyond this committee." They see the work as "something that, if read by colleagues in the field, their own work would profit from it." Thus while the English faculty typically do think of "dissertations themselves as significant," some faculty consider the "books that often emerge from them as significant."

## The Dissertation as a Whole

One of the slowest things to change in academe is the form of the dissertation. It "hasn't changed much since the 13th century" and is "a hallmark of the extraordinary conservatism of academic practices." However, in the "last 30 years," there have been "periods" when English departments have proclaimed that dissertations ought to be different for a variety of reasons. For instance, departments have said that they need to encourage students to write dissertations that are a series of essays rather than a book because that will be more useful to them in their careers "at certain kinds of schools." However, the traditional, book-style dissertation still is predominant in English, although, because of changes in the economics of publishing, most English faculty no longer tell students to "write a dissertation as if it's going to be a book," because most presses do not publish dissertations.[3] A dissertation now has to be "thoroughly revised before it's a book." Below we explore the characteristics of different quality English dissertations (see Table 14.4) and what the faculty said about them.

### *Outstanding*

Outstanding dissertations are original and significant and "break all the rules." They are strong in both analysis and syntheses. They open things up and create lots of connections, possibilities, and questions as opposed to flattening things out and closing them down. They make contributions that cannot be ignored and, as a result, "the field is no longer the way it was" before. According to one participant, one of the "break points" between the outstanding, very good, acceptable, and not acceptable dissertation is the

## TABLE 14.4.
## The Characteristics of Different Quality Dissertations in English

| Quality | Characteristics |
|---|---|
| **Outstanding** | Brilliant; accessible, adventurous, compelling, coherent, counter-intuitive, energetic, engaging, insightful, interesting, original, rich, sensitive, significant, surprising, unpredictable; very well written; has an original prose style; style has spark and elegance; well constructed; carefully and efficiently executed; intellectually solid yet creative; has a strong, confident, authoritative individual voice; voice has an affective dimension; is modest not arrogant; displays a fullness of exposition; startlingly lucid and thoughtful; the student has a wholly unexpected range of reading; shows a profound reading of the topic and a genuine sense of sources; very interdisciplinary; breaks all the rules; a new piece of research or insight; accesses sources not previously accessed; shows incredibly intense archival research on things that have not been committed to manuscript; asks new questions; makes original combinations of texts and ideas; synthesizes a number of texts; synthesizes from various fields; shows a progression of thought; has an enabling model or a very deep theoretical formula; synthesizes the critical tradition; brings in analytical paradigms that have not been deployed before in the treatment of a particular subject; thinks outside the existing framework; changes the existing framework; presents a very scrupulous analysis; reflects on its own methods of inquiry; comes up with interesting results and conclusions; sees the meaning within a broader context; opens up, branches out, and creates a lot of connections and possibilities; anticipates the questions that the field is going to be interested in; is filled with implications; very clearly makes a contribution to the field |
| **Very good** | Good, strong, intellectually mature, and engaging; not as well or as beautifully written; has less of an imaginative reach; has some fairly localized original points and some unfamiliar insights; significance is not quite as great; is well executed; has subtle turns and nuanced points but author is not quite in control of all the elements; is an efficient synthesis of existing knowledge; is better at synthesis than analysis; deploys knowledge in a natural, convincing, logical, and edifying manner; problem or concept is relatively predictable or redundant; poses more traditional questions; uses a new archive; the setup is somewhat familiar; uses a new theoretical framework; provides a new application of a theoretical |

| Quality | Characteristics |
|---|---|
| **Very good** | framework; works a paradigm or mode of inquiry very well; uses advanced methods; takes methods for granted; does not question its methods; does not always express its own knowledge of what it is about; the student goes into new territory without really knowing it; explores implications; makes a contribution to how a text or a few texts are read |
| **Acceptable** | Mediocre; workpersonlike; competent; is misconceived or conceived sloppily; muddled, plodding, inelegant; not quite worked through; not very interesting or persuasive; decent not dazzling or exciting; does not say anything particularly original or significant; is utterly predictable; knows the present knowledge on the topic or field; draws from present scholarship and uses it decently; the writing is fairly solid; has a flat treatment of things; sentences close down instead of opening out; applies one idea to five different texts; rehashes the critical tradition reasonably well; advances some arguments but is not very complex; presents the obvious as if it were a new discovery; demonstrates the ability to argue and sustain a discussion about a topic for 250 pages; may not contribute much to the conversation in the field |
| **Unacceptable** | Contains nothing new; thesis is unconvincing; writing and organization are incoherent or confused; has a lot of discrepancies; is not aware of basic conventions of the field; lacks basic research; engages irresponsibly with the secondary criticism; has not read what others have said on the topic; presents volumes of undigested, incoherent material; is presented as a chronology; cannot get away from repeating what others have said; is like a book report, a march through an author's work; lacks an argument; does not have a clear sense of its own argument; is unable to sustain an argument; lacks evidence; makes broad, unsupported statements |

"degree and the facility" the student has in answering the "So what?" question.

Outstanding dissertations are distinguished by the quality of the writing. They have an original prose style and a distinctive voice, one that is strong, confident, and displays a sense of control. Outstanding dissertations are engaging and thought provoking. They are "page-turners. You want to know what was going to happen next because you were confronted with ideas you hadn't seen before." "[With] every page, I'm learning something new." "They make connections that I haven't thought about, and they teach." They "turn you in directions that you would never have expected or that you would never have thought of yourself."

Students who write outstanding dissertations have learned to go beyond their mentor. They are adventurous, "willing to take a leap into some territory that hasn't been explored before." They are passionate about what they are doing and are committed to the idea that what they are saying is important and makes a difference. These students have a "quality of mind that shows a kind of flexibility and suppleness" and the "ability to think outside the existing framework," and, in doing so, they change the framework.

## Very Good

The difference between the outstanding and the very good English dissertation is a matter of degree. Very good dissertations have "those qualities," but they just do not have them "as strongly." One participant said that where all of the components of an outstanding dissertation are "calibrated at ten," the components of the very good dissertation are "calibrated at seven," often because the "author isn't quite in control of all the elements."

Very good dissertations tend to pose traditional questions; do a good, efficient synthesis of existing knowledge; and make localized original points. For instance, they may make a contribution to "how we read . . . a certain text or a couple of texts . . . , but it's not a big kind of original." At the same time, very good dissertations are "intellectually mature." The student has "digested the knowledge" and is able to "deploy it" in a manner that "feels natural and logical and convincing and edifying." Indeed, one of the criteria for very good is that the "piece has to teach something." "I want to feel that I have learned something." This learning often comes from archival material that the professor has not seen before, from a new theoretical framework, or from applying a theoretical framework differently. Very good dissertations also "give pleasure." They "speak to the part of us . . . that gets pleasure from intellectual engagement."

One participant identified two types of very good dissertations. One is "a diamond in the rough." It is not quite as polished as the outstanding dissertation, often because the student "didn't quite work hard enough." These are ones where faculty think "maybe you can work with them, inspire them, talk to them, get them to do something more"; ones where one more revision would make them outstanding. The other type is "very nice cubic zirconium." It will "simply never be a diamond." It is polished and "you can wear it out, but it's not the real thing." Regardless of type, the very good dissertation is apt to have two or three chapters that are worthy of publishing as articles.

## Acceptable

The acceptable dissertation is "like baking a cake." It goes through the "motions" and fulfills the "formula" for the "standard" English dissertation:

> It has an introduction that states the argument. [It has] three chapters . . . each one is a reading of a text, often a reading that comes out of a paper that was written in a seminar. Then there is a conclusion that puts it together.

The readings or analyses in the three chapters have some "intrinsic connection," but they are "not argued at a level that the world sees an earthshaking change in the argument," and the conclusion is usually "hasty."

To be acceptable, the English dissertation has to be book length. The "baseline" is a 200- to 250-page "term paper" that "shows the writer can sustain a discussion for 250 pages about a topic" in a way that is not "objectionable intellectually" or "disreputable" and shows that the student "knows what the present knowledge is in the field on this particular topic . . . and then uses the scholarship in a decent way."

Students who write acceptable dissertations often have not moved beyond being students. Indeed, faculty look for a "subtle distinction between someone who has followed what you said and someone who's thinking on their own." Faculty feel that the quality of the dissertation is an expression of the "writer's intelligence" and that "there is no way the acceptable student is going to . . . come up with fresh ideas." Ultimately, they realize that student has reached his or her limit, be it intellectual or psychological, and has "done as much as he or she is capable of." One participant, speaking for many, said, "I think we've all struggled to direct dissertations from students who we knew ultimately were limited and you just can't make those kinds of dissertations more interesting than the writer is him- or herself."

Acceptable dissertations are also written "by really good people who fucked up along the way."

If you look at them in the first semester and you think you know who's got the smarts, and maybe you do. [But] you don't know who has the patience and discipline to work on something for a really long time and stay with the project through all of its turns. . . . They don't have those skills as character traits.

At the acceptable level faculty take "criteria that are extraneous to the dissertation itself" into consideration. They often are "willing to adjust the standards to accommodate people who have more difficulties":

We're going to be a little bit more generous and take into account the more individual factors when we're looking at whether the dissertation is acceptable. . . . We also look at what you're going to do with this. Are you getting these qualifications so that you can go on into academia? Then the standard is different. . . . This is a really tricky issue because it addresses the issue that we do have a lot of subjectivity in what we consider acceptable. I don't think this is bad. I think this is part of being a humanist, taking the individual situations into account.

For instance, faculty view the dissertation as a "technical exercise" for students who plan to take jobs in community colleges or in a nonscholarly environment where they are not expected to publish. In addition to considering the career paths people are choosing, faculty recognize that what could have been a good dissertation may turn out to be an acceptable one because the student has a job waiting or a family to support, and if the dissertation is done by "X date" the student will get $3,000 more. Thus, because they know that "the Ph.D. has to work hand in hand with the market," faculty will pass a dissertation of "this status" and "let the market do the next step."

In short, while faculty really do "not want anybody else to read it," an acceptable dissertation is one that faculty look at and say, "This can do no harm. . . . Having my name attached to this text as an advisor will not damage my reputation. It will not enhance it, [but] it will probably not damage it."

### Unacceptable

The unacceptable dissertation does not meet faculty's understanding of "minimal standards": the research is insufficient, the thesis is unconvincing, or the writing is incoherent. The dissertation may also be too short (100 pages) or show a lack of awareness of the tools or conventions of the field. For instance, the student does not know "how to quote poetry or look up a 16th-century book in the microfilm," something the student should have learned long before getting to the dissertation.

Sometimes students are not capable of handling a big project. They have an area that they are interested in, but the work is not "well defined and clear in the head of the writer of the dissertation." For these students "it's like setting out to the ocean without a map or a compass. . . . It's just too much to deal with." Others "haven't been able to get up on the shoulders [of giants] to see anything new," they just keep "repeating what others have said."

Sometimes students cannot or will not listen to their advisors. They do not take comments and criticism into account and submit "revised" versions of their work that require exactly the same feedback. In these instances, faculty feel that "no learning" is happening and that "it's wasting my time and their time." Sometimes students may be overconfident or they may try to do too much. One participant talked about an "experimental" dissertation he refused to sign. In his opinion, "experiment" was "a substitute for argument, logic, clear writing, and several other things by someone who was trying to change the form of what a dissertation or a conventional book was" and the result was "unreadable."

The faculty said "if we do our jobs well," the student does not get to "that stage," and if the student does, it is "institutional failure," because the student should have been . . . alerted as to how far he or she was from meeting the standards that the institution demands." Indeed, even when faculty "have plenty of examples [of] somebody's writing, and know this is going to happen, . . . we don't step up and say . . ." (The participant did not complete the sentence, but presumably the word is "stop" or some close synonym.) Rather than be forthright with students, faculty send them a "signal" by disassociating themselves from them.

When a dissertation fails, faculty typically blame the advisor or the committee. For instance, the student may not have gotten enough help from the faculty in the preliminary stage of defining a really good, clear topic. One participant mentioned a dissertation that had been accepted by the director but then rejected by the department. He noted that most of the faculty "felt [that it] was much more . . . the dissertation director's fault than the student's." Another participant noted instances where the chair "really pushed it to defense" and the "outside member or somebody else said, 'I'm sorry.'"

## The Components of an English Dissertation

Most of the English focus group participants voiced strong objections to discussing the quality of individual components of the English dissertation (see Table 1.2). Indeed, the protocol for the focus group "blew up" at this point at one university. In general, the English faculty thought the matrix was "some kind of Germanic parody of Aristotle." They saw in it "a scientific background," "power imagery," "an external notion of what a dissertation in English looks like." Some thought that the matrix might work "for a literary dissertation" but said that that was a "very old-fashioned" view of the dissertation, given that "a lot of dissertations are not as textually bound." They pointed out that that the humanities were "very subjective" and that "there's contestation within the field over, not only values, but even the weight that's placed upon [different types of] dissertation[s]." They noted that different kinds of dissertations (e.g., drama, theory, early modern, contemporary fiction) would look very different from each other, that "there's a whole slew of things that are variable," and that comparing them would be like trying to compare "kumquats and grapes," thus making "it impossible to judge." However, one highly critical participant commented, "And yet, people do give prizes for things," meaning that judgments of quality are routinely made across different kinds of works.

The English faculty also felt that trying to develop a "quantitative assessment" with "hard and measurable terms and a list of criteria" "doesn't work," and that "trying to reduce [the dissertation] to a formula is killing the notion of ideas," because "ideas don't sit within well-defined categories." The faculty stressed the idea that pedagogy and the process of the dissertation were more important than the product, noting that the "boxes" in the matrix were lined up according to what seemed like a "sequential process" and that in English, the "elements" of a dissertation are not approached that way.

On the positive side, one participant said, "The things we have talked about [the component category labels] are generalizations of the kinds of things that probably cover 80 to 90% of the dissertation." Another thought that "in a certain way, this could be very useful as points about which the student should be very conscious."

Four focus groups did not formally discuss the components, though their participants did make an occasional comment about the quality of a component at other points during their focus group's discussion. As a group, the three focus groups that did discuss the matrix managed to say something about every cell. However, the amount of information in many cells is very thin. (See Table 14.A in the appendix to this chapter.) Below we explore the components of the English dissertation and what the faculty said about them.

### Introduction (of Problem or Concept)

The introduction to an English dissertation "is extraordinarily important." It presents the problem or concept that will be analyzed. As a chapter, it also contains the sources and the approach to analysis. The outstanding introduction "makes claims, articulates, and outlines the argument" and suggests to the reader that "this is a new model." The reader "sees right away" that the student is asking questions that are either new or are positioned in a different way, and this is "surprising." Regardless of the subject matter, the reader senses "immediately" that "this person has been thinking independently through what maybe is not a new problem, but they're into a new context or [they] slanted [their position] differently." Not only does the student show "much flare," but "he/she promises [that in] the remaining 250 pages, you're really going to know what I mean," and readers "will want to go to those additional locations to understand more of what [they] have already learned."

The acceptable introduction does the minimum and is "routine." It says, "Here's what the problem is I'm researching. Here's how I'm going to research it. Now let's go." It is "not awful, but it's not going to do anything but put you to sleep." The unacceptable introduction does not provide the reader with "much of a sense of what the problem is, what the dissertation is doing." It does not "let me know what I'm going to get."

### Review of Sources

The review of sources in an English dissertation is less a "review" and more a "use" of sources, because in English, "you don't just review sources, you position yourself in relation to sources, and then you continue to use them throughout." English discourages the separation of sources from the argument. Separating them "is not supposed to happen in our field"; they have to come into the argument in an "integral manner." Indeed, the idea of reviewing the "existing field" and then going on and doing your "thing" was considered a social science idea.

In an outstanding review, the sources are laid out and positioned in a way that explains why the project needs to be done, how these sources lead up to the question, or how they cover a question, but it still "leave[s] open and demand[s] a space that this other theoretical paradigm exposes . . . and you need to bring it to bear." In the outstanding review, the sources are subordinated to and integrated into the argument. "You don't get a sense that the sources are the authority, but [rather] that the author is the authority and is using these sources." Outstanding reviews also have fewer footnotes because the "materials are more digested."

Students who write outstanding reviews have not read "everything" in the field, rather they have read what is "pertinent," and "figuring out what that is, is really difficult." Their reading of selected sources is "efficient and astute." They do not simply review their sources; they interrogate them. They can perceive the "crux" of an argument or that part of an argument that is related to their topic and articulate it in one or two sentences. Indeed, their review is often "so good that it's clearer than the sources themselves," because the students "catch something and formulate it into something so that you actually are learning something about the source and having an ah-ha! moment."

Students who write outstanding reviews are also more likely to be "a little skeptical" about powerful figures in the field" but nonetheless use them generously. They are "not interested in making [their] point by playing off against other people, 'So-and-so's got it all wrong and I'm going to correct it.'" Rather, they say, "I'm using so-and-so," and "what I want to emphasize is this strain of his thinking to which little attention has been paid."

## Approach to Analysis

The approach to analysis is the theory or method behind the analysis. At the outstanding level, the approach is "inside the argument rather than external to it." Students present themselves as participants in the intellectual conversation "by paying the necessary tribute to the sacred cows without being submissive." They show a "sustaining" degree of "equality" that does not make them "appear arrogant." Students also display an "intellectual nimbleness"; they can write equally well about the "fine-grain stuff and the intellectually ambitious stuff." Outstanding approaches make the reader feel that "this was the perfect way to look at the material."

The very good approach to analysis is "strong on paper." Students who write them are "going to know it. They're going to understand it. But there's not going to be anything surprising there." While they "select some material in and some out," these students tend to take a subordinate position to the approach "Here, I'm following Foucault. Here, I'm following Freud." Further, while the student may have covered a certain domain and demonstrated what he or she knew and how the methodology was built, at the defense some committee members might say, "There are other ways you might have done this. You might have taken [other theories] into account or dismissed them or whatever. So you've affirmed what you are doing, but you may not be seeing it in terms of broad enough possibilities for the methodology."

## *Justification of Chosen Texts*

The justification of chosen texts is one of the most important parts of an English dissertation. It states "what's in and what's out." The process of making choices and justifying texts forces students to generate criteria, make judgments, and articulate why they have chosen the texts they did. As such, it is "already an evolution toward an argument." The justification also demonstrates students' understanding of the proper scope of the dissertation. In English faculty's assessment of quality, what "counts," is students' ability to convey to the reader that they know why this particular group of texts fits with the argument.

In the outstanding dissertation, "there are theoretical underpinnings to the choice." The presentation of the justification is often more implicit than explicit. In discussing the outstanding justification, one participant described what he liked to see:

> What I like the best is someone who will say the unknown or the less reputable author is the one who can change our perception of the canonical

authors. So the purpose of bringing in these forgotten texts is to reorient our entire notion of literary history or an idea of canonization around these literary texts. That's what I think is part of the project, at least in the dissertations I've directed. Part of the Americanist project is to say the cannon is always under revision. You always have to justify the text that you're choosing by saying why this is important and to whom and for what reason.

## Analysis of Texts

The analysis of text is "the most important" component of the English dissertation. Indeed, the "dissertation itself is the analysis of texts." Some faculty felt the term "analysis" was "way too limited:"

> Analysis is all about breaking something down into its component parts. In some sense, something additive, something connecting is more descriptive to me of the kind of work that students really do, which is connecting texts to each other, to themselves in different ways, and to other kinds of historical, social, scientific, et cetera, political [works].

Further, "right now" the field does not consider "the fairly close analysis or the application of a fairly small idea to a substantial number of texts . . . to be particularly interesting." It is "much more common these days" for a dissertation to treat culture as text than text on literary topics. For instance:

> We've had dissertations on the analysis of the discourse of the O. J. Simpson trial. . . . What [the dissertation] did was to try to read the trial and the newspaper coverage and the television coverage as if this were a massive text and to talk about how these texts worked, particularly if a person was trying to ask the question, Why was the white community not just outraged by the verdict but surprised? Why weren't they prepared? Because the black community was. It was talking about how these forms of discourse are very separate.

At the acceptable level, one participant noted that in talking about important figures, students will give you "potted notions of what they are." At the unacceptable level, one participant described how students may misuse knowledge and textual data:

> When you say Shakespeare's idea of society was that, "as Julius Caesar says," [and the student provides] a line from *Julius Caesar* from the character of Julius Caesar [which] is taken directly to mean almost as it were

taken out of Shakespeare's personal letters. The combination, the words coming out of a character in a play by Shakespeare are given the same valance in terms of historical persons' opinions as a person's testimony before a judge during the Elizabethan period or his own personal letters. That is simply bad. You should not do that. You also do not take a literary text to scavenge historical data straight out of it without letting your reader know that literary texts do not behave in the same way as other kinds of texts, as say journalistic reports, as some other statement of some truth. So that then when you're going to use evidence, that evidence from literary text . . . do[es] not communicate in the same way that . . . other texts do. That is extremely important. If I see a student doing that I know that the student has not matured.

## Conclusion

The conclusion needs to tell the reader "what you said." It should identify what was significant and why, and how the work might have implications for other things. The conclusion provides the student with the opportunity "to admit areas of inquiry in which he/she could not enter" and "to promise or to predict." One participant said he pushes students to make explicit the "operating principles they have been using throughout."

Some participants had slightly differing opinions on the importance and scope of the conclusion. One tells his students "don't waste your time with conclusions. Nobody reads a book through to that necessarily anyway. You need to put up front the actual . . . conclusions that you've drawn. You . . . have to rewrite your introduction; don't stick it all at the end of the manuscript." While one of his colleagues agreed that "you can't put the major findings in there," he also felt that students had to put in "a little something at the end." If they do not, then the reader gets to the end of the last chapter, "and it's like, and so? . . . What have they discovered?" The conclusion thus allows students "to connect what they've done."

Rather than "wrap things up," outstanding conclusions "open things up." Students who write outstanding conclusions see the significance of what they have done as well as the possibilities entailed in their argument. Outstanding dissertations are also generous. Instead of defensively trying to make things as tight and polished as possible, they raise new questions. They say, "Far from being concluded, look at what we can do now."

Unlike the outstanding conclusion that opens things up, very good, acceptable, and unacceptable conclusions "try to close things up." The acceptable conclusion "simply summarizes what went on in the preceding 220 pages." It repeats what it is "that I've found," about which one participant commented, "That isn't even a good conclusion for a three-page freshman English paper."

## Notes

1. See http://www.mla.org (Accessed February 23, 2006).

2. For information on the source of these data, see chapter 1, note 5. Some data came from the MLA Web site, http://www.mla.org (accessed January 2006), and from Doug Steward at the MLA (personal communication, June 2, 2006, and July 18, 2006).

3. At the 2005 annual meeting of the MLA, a special panel revealed a plan to overhaul the expectation of publishing a monograph as a condition of tenure. Although the plan does not address the graduate education, panel members agreed that the plan had "clear implications" for graduate education and the dissertation, and indicated that these issues would be tackled by another MLA panel at some point in the future (Jaschik, 2005).

# Appendix

## TABLE 14.A.
### The Components of an English Dissertation and Their Characteristics at Different Quality Levels

| Components | Quality levels | | | |
| --- | --- | --- | --- | --- |
| | Outstanding | Very good | Acceptable | Unacceptable |
| **Introduction (to problem or concept)** | Has an interesting idea and shows independent thinking about a problem, concept, or position; asks questions that are new or different; introduces the problem and positions it in relationship to contemporary scholarship on two levels: one, the criticism, and two, the theoretical paradigms that are going to be used to approach the problem; provides a very clear statement of the thesis; starts to introduce the justification of the chosen texts; articulates and outlines the argument; provides a road map of what will be covered in the dissertation | A very good problem or concept; has a convincing premise; provides a good statement of the thesis and purpose; indicates where it is going | A routine introduction of the problem and methods | Confused; is not clear what the topic is; introduces a lot of topics that are not clearly coordinated; does not provide enough justification for the project; does not define the problem or the approach; does not give a road map for the argument; talks about criticism without discussing the problem or the argument; talks about the theoretical approach or some of the theories that are going to be used without explaining how they are going to be used or why they are relevant to the problem and texts; lacks a sharply thought, thorough center |

*(continues)*

**TABLE 14.A.**
Continued

| Components | Quality levels | | | |
| --- | --- | --- | --- | --- |
| | Outstanding | Very good | Acceptable | Unacceptable |
| **Review of sources** | Provides a thorough, comprehensive review of capably chosen texts; presents an efficient and astute reading of the sources; shows command and authority over the sources; lays out and positions the sources to lead up to the question; interrogates rather than reviews sources; perceives the relevant crux of an argument and articulates it in one or two sentences; sources are subordinated to and integrated into the argument; shows how disparate combinations are part of the body; is more likely to be skeptical about powerful figures in the field but treats them respectfully | Knows what sources are pertinent; sources are a little less digested; exhibits less confidence in positioning the voice of the dissertation | Demonstrates the student has read the material; is subservient and regurgative; too long and dull | Inadequate; undigested; has big holes; student has not read enough; student does not understand the sources; sources are used awkwardly |

| Components | Quality levels | | | |
|---|---|---|---|---|
| | Outstanding | Very good | Acceptable | Unacceptable |
| **Approach to analysis** | Very clear, interesting; edifying; participates in a conversation; defines the questions clearly; has a well-defined, well-justified approach to answering the question; the perspective is clear and is sustained by existing paradigms; the perspective and material are harmoniously linked; firms out its methodologies against alternatives; discovers implications about a particular paradigm that were not intended or foreseen by the original author; accomplishes something that others have not accomplished | Selective; analysis is new but not surprising; takes a subordinate position; follows others' approaches; shows how the approach to the analysis is suited to demonstrating the thesis; affirms what student is doing but may not see enough possibilities for the methodology | States the method; method may be assumed rather than stated | Misreads the sources; states that the student is using a particular approach but it is no one else's understanding of that approach |

*(continues)*

**TABLE 14.A.**
Continued

| Components | Quality levels | | | |
|---|---|---|---|---|
| | Outstanding | Very good | Acceptable | Unacceptable |
| **Justification of chosen texts** | Is at a broad intellectual level; is often implicit; choice of texts is theoretically motivated; articulates why texts were chosen; uses a wide range of texts; brings in forgotten texts to reorient readers' notion of literary history; displays an interesting and creative reading of texts; talks sensibly about complicated issues; makes several points simultaneously; deals well with detail; does not range too far from source material | Justifies the texts being used; is reflexive | Uses readings to support a thesis; belabors the justification; assumes the text proves the argument | Confused, unclear, or inadequate; fails to offer justification for chosen texts; omits key texts; does not articulate the connection between texts; does not make sense with respect to the argument |
| **Analysis of texts** | Intellectually creative; a deft handling of textuality; makes connections between texts and other kinds of phenomena | Knows the texts; proves points; uses old-fashioned ways of supporting an argument with text; needs to be more open and creative | Routine; superficial; common knowledge | Misuses knowledge in reference texts |

| Components | Quality levels | | | |
|---|---|---|---|---|
| | Outstanding | Very good | Acceptable | Unacceptable |
| **Conclusion** | Interesting; unexpected; has a surprise ending; summarizes what has been said; recognizes gaps in the argument; identifies areas of inquiry where student did not venture; states the implications; raises new questions; shows possible lines of inquiry; pushes into new territory; opens things up; allows others to do more work | States what has been done; identifies the significance but not the full significance; does not state what it means for the field; does not indicate how others might follow up on it | Summarizes and repeats what has been found; celebrates itself for demonstrating what the introduction said it would demonstrate | Inadequate; student does not know what he or she is doing or has done |

# 15

# THE HISTORY DISSERTATION

There are more than 150 Ph.D. programs in history in the United States. These programs enroll over 10,000 students (master's and doctoral) and graduate roughly 900 new Ph.D.s annually. Although there are no formally tracked subfields, the American Historical Association's Web site[1] lists 12 of the largest geographic, temporal, and topical categories. These categories were reduced from more than 126 specializations comprising 352 specific fields reported by individual history departments. The median time to degree in history is 9.7 years. Roughly 5% of new history Ph.D.s go on to postdoctoral positions.[2]

Thirty-three faculty at nine universities participated in the focus groups. Overall, these faculty had 694[3] years of experience, had chaired an estimated 364 dissertations, and had sat on an estimated 1,045 dissertation committees. The average history focus group participant had been a professor for 22 years, had chaired 12 dissertations, and had sat on 34 dissertation committees. One side of one focus group's tape did not record. The facilitator took detailed notes that were used in the analysis. Below is a summary of the history focus groups' discussions. Their performance expectations for the dissertation are displayed in the tables. Their supporting discussion is recounted in the text.

## The Purpose of a History Dissertation

The history faculty saw the dissertation as having many purposes (see Table 15.1). Among these purposes, the faculty identified a community purpose and a personal-professional purpose. The community purpose is "to contribute to knowledge." The personal-professional purpose is "to get a job." The dissertation thus functions as a "calling card" that shows what the student is capable of as a scholar. Although they did not label it as such, the history

## TABLE 15.1.
### The Purpose of a History Dissertation

To train the students to be historians; to teach them to practice history on their own—how to do research, deal with blind alleys, and organize data into a coherent narrative; to learn how to do research on their own—how to ask questions of material, draw the evidence together, and write a long, coherent narrative that is original, significant, and interesting; to develop their skills to the level where they can be mentors; to demonstrate their mastery of the craft—show that they know how to do historical research, can pull together a sustained, coherent piece of work, and are capable of being scholars and do ongoing significant original research; to show that they have met the requirements and should be accepted to journeymen status or into the guild; to make an original and significant contribution; to add to the body of knowledge and set of interpretive theories and methods for producing historical knowledge; to use their research to turn out articles and a book that will establish them as experts in their field; to get a job and keep the job by turning the dissertation into a book

faculty also identified an individual purpose, which is "to show the Ph.D. candidate that she or he can do it," where "it" was defined as "follow the rules of the discipline." Faculty hope that "having done it once, [students] can do it again and again and again."

Doing a big project like a dissertation takes the student to "a whole new level." Indeed, the faculty asserted that the only way to "know what history is," and the only way to learn how to do research and reach the level where "you can be the mentor" is by "doing it" (doing history). And that involves the student struggling at length, "largely on his or her own with a lot of mentoring," with an enormous variety of sources and using his or her research, archival, contextual reading, hypothesis development, and interpretation skills, and pulling together a sustained, coherent piece of work. The history faculty made it clear that "there's no way to become a historian who can practice on a daily basis as a historian" until you have demonstrated that you can "produce this first masterwork." The dissertation is thus "a crucial part of the process of educating someone to be a historian—and there's no shortcut."

While faculty want students to produce something that is of publishable quality that will eventually become a book, they noted that a dissertation is not a book. A book is "a little more professional." It does not allow you to show "quite as much of your knowledge on your sleeve" and "you have to be more concise and perhaps even a little more daring with some of your formulations." To turn a dissertation into a book requires "some revision and refocus. Maybe additional material [and] maybe additional conceptualization."

## Original Contribution

The history faculty identified many ways to make an original contribution (see Table 15.2). In trying to "operationalize" what it means, the "simplest" thing faculty felt they could say was that "the dissertation has within it a preponderance of . . . information that the reader shouldn't know before." It causes the reader to say, "I never thought about that before. It never occurred to me." This originality can be achieved in a variety of ways, ranging from presenting new information to presenting of new interpretations.

At the new information end of the range, one participant, who commented that his was a "conservative view," emphasized new sources. He felt historical sources were always teaching you "things you didn't expect to learn" and that the "crucial" thing for a history Ph.D. was to get out a "fresh batch of sources." In a similar vein, another participant commented that the

### TABLE 15.2.
### The Nature of an Original Contribution in History

Something new; new questions, topics, sources, evidence, archives, approaches, methods, perspectives, analytical frameworks, interpretations, answers, conclusions; giving a new and true account of change over time in the past; adding something to knowledge; discovering, defining, or working with sources that were not used or were inadequately analyzed before; establishing linkages; putting sources together in fresh ways; rereading and reinterpreting sources; asking new questions of old material; a new twist, insight, perspective, or focus on primary or secondary literature; rethinking concepts and structures; involving empirical and theoretical comments; a conceptual framework or a compelling model that changes the way people think about history; fresh, new, and useful ways to interpret data; an interpretive insight or intervention; contradicting or overturning current historiography; drawing new conclusions from old material; breaking new ground by relating conclusions to larger issues of concern to the field; advancing a debate or conversation in a persuasive way kinds of dissertations he was used to reading depended "for the most part, but yet not entirely" on "archival work, that is, [on] unpublished material." Another participant noted that "there are some people who find unexplored mounds of information." He also said, "that's not typical."

At the other end of the range were faculty who emphasized interpretation. For them original has less to do with the subject matter than it does with the interpretation, methodology, or framework in which the information is analyzed. One participant viewed interpretation as "the middle level of abstraction above the data but . . . below some kind of a formal model" like those that social scientists use. According to these faculty, "history is interpretive," whereas "data just sit there" until someone applies interpretive theories and interpretive methods to them. Thus, for them, an original contribution is judged on its interpretive merits. These faculty also noted that "not all interpretations are created equal." Whereas one participant felt that the interpretive contribution should be persuasive, that is, provide "a new and compelling answer to a question that has never been addressed that way before" and establish "linkages that otherwise have not been created or seen before," another participant noted that it was "possible for a history dissertation to be accepted and be recognized by people working in the same field as a real contribution that other people are going to be building on when it is interpretively flat."

The faculty acknowledged that students could meet the originality criterion by filling a gap. However, most have a strong dislike for the gap-based dissertation. As a participant at Public University said, "Filling a gap implies that the field is going to remain stationary and you're just filling holes," whereas the goal of research is to "change the shape of a field, not to fill a gap." When his students do not have "any idea of what they are going to do" and say "they are going to fill a gap in the literature," one participant tells them:

> There are usually good reasons why there is a gap. Either it's not very important or nobody has been able to find any evidence that can really fill the gap. You're asking for trouble unless you have some inside knowledge that filling that gap is going to make a difference. Just filling a gap doesn't do anything.

Indeed, what faculty "love to see, but rarely do" are topics that are "grounded in and build upon the historiography, and also advance it, contribute to it, give it a new twist."

The "genius of history" is finding a perfectly obvious concept or even one that no one has recognized. In reading a dissertation with this "rare" type of original contribution the reader thinks, "This is completely self-evident." According to one participant:

> Yet the reason it's self-evident is because they've made such a strong case for what they're presenting that it must be something that I've known all along, and only after looking back at it, I say, "Wait a minute! This is entirely different." But they've done such a good job of making it evident and making it persuasive, that I assume I must have known this forever.

In addition to characterizing what an original contribution is, the history faculty also discussed what it is not. It is not "just doing something in a new way" or saying, "Oh, here is a new theory. I'll apply it to this particular subject." You have to show the connection between the source and the evidence and how it fits the theory. One participant described instances where students' work ends up being "unoriginal" because of deficiencies in their language skills:

> For example, people who we'll say are from the United States, whose native language is English, and they're writing about groups whose native language is something else, but they don't have the capacity to read the original sources or to interview people directly. So they're basing an awful lot of what they end up writing on hearsay and on what people want them to know. So, oftentimes, that work is not only unoriginal, but it's extremely problematic, and they don't even know how problematic it is.

In sum, the historians noted that an original contribution is "the minimum requirement for a Ph.D." In most dissertations, it is a "fresh view of a more or less familiar subject." And while "true originality" is a "rare quality," the contribution "can't be trivial." There also "has to be a standard of research in any dissertation." "No matter how brilliant the person's ideas might be, if he or she doesn't meet the minimum standards in the research, we are not going to approve it."

## Significant Contribution

Among other things, a significant contribution in history (see Table 15.3) is something that faculty have not seen before. Like faculty in other disciplines,

## TABLE 15.3.
### The Nature of a Significant Contribution in History

An original contribution; something not seen before that is novel, refreshing, and illuminating; is useful and of real consequence to others both inside and outside the field; something that people will notice and take into consideration in their teaching and research; changes or overturns a particular set of assumptions or the way people look at a problem; engages current conceptual and theoretical concerns; addresses hotly debated issues; makes new connections; refocuses an interpretation; is important to the field or subfield; reconceptualizes a field; engages in a wider conversation; generalizes and makes connections on a broader scale; says something about the human condition; opens up more areas of work; pushes disciplinary boundaries

the history faculty had a hard time distinguishing between "original" and "significant." While they thought that "you can be original without being significant," they were not sure about "the other away around." Indeed, one participant said, "significant is original."

When they read something that makes a significant contribution, historians feel they have learned new facts about history and/or learned new ways to interpret facts of history. However, one participant noted that novelty is insufficient without evidence. He said, "If you're going to talk about significance here, merely being fresh and original will get you nowhere in a historical discourse unless there are clear appearances sufficient to convince a reasonably neutral observer that there is substance behind your claim." Another participant tried to quantify how much new material had to be in the dissertation to make it significant.

> It has to be significantly new rather than just—I don't want to talk percentages—but something that reaches 95% familiar does not make for a good dissertation. Does it have to be 70% new? Or 80%? I don't know that that's really expected either, because sometimes it's a distinction between the areas, which are different and new, and the ones that are not, really make the best dissertations.

The history faculty distinguished among different levels of significance. Dissertations at a low level of significance make modest, solid contributions to the field. They "manifest confidence in research and writing, in exposition, and in thought of historical materials" but make only minor refinements on an interpretation. An example of a dissertation with a low level of significance would be a study of urban workers in Cleveland from 1820 to 1840 that has already been done and somebody does Cincinnati in the same period. "It's not likely to be a very significant study unless there's something about the profile of the two cities that turns out to be different." Although faculty pass dissertations with low levels of significance, they do not think that they are the basis of a major career, and they assume that students who write them will not become "fabulous contributors to the field."

Dissertations at higher levels of significance are "novel," "fresh," "illuminating." They may refocus an interpretation and change the way the historians view a particular set of data or a particular topic. At the highest level are dissertations that say something about the human condition. They pay closer attention to how the past sheds light "not maybe on how people are today, but on the same sorts of issues that occupy people today," and "give a sense of what the varieties of human experience can be" or provide "practical insight into what we are as people, why we behave in the way that we do." Faculty do not expect graduate students to make highly significant contributions and noted that the higher levels of significance are "very seldom seen." Rather, what most students do in their dissertations is "lay some groundwork" for making a significant contribution later in their career.

A significant contribution in history also "has a lot to do with audience." In the "most narrow, academically defined sense" it is something "other scholars find interesting" and useful. It starts by engaging the interest of the five readers (the dissertation committee) who are "proxies" for the larger scholarly world. It also engages broader issues—questions, problems, and topics—that others are interested in and care about, and it will affect how others think about or look at a problem. Indeed, one participant noted that the first and probably central question in a dissertation defense is, "How does this change the way somebody looks at this problem?"

Another participant noted that students often have trouble coming up with a topic that will be of interest to people outside the "immediate little area they are interested in" and commented that she still had trouble with it, too:

> because, on the one hand, you think about significance as your premium research project. It gets harder and harder [to come up with] such an important question that . . . I'd like to try to help answer. . . . Then you do your research . . . and then it gets relived up to the broader issues. . . . The next step in writing . . . is then to say, "All right now, what are the big

issues that led me into this in the first place? Now that I've got this information, what does that say about these bigger issues?" So it's the process of going back and forth between a dialogue with people outside your own area—and that might be outside the discipline as well—and yet, at the same time, maintaining a fairly close command of the materials you're working with. It seems to me that . . . this is a particular problem for graduate students because they get so immersed in their topics that it's very hard for them to pull back from it and say what are these figurations?

A participant in a different focus group said he tries to help students think about significance by telling them to "think in terms of the number of discussions and debates that are going on that are of current interest." Another participant asks students to think of significance in terms of teaching, "How will I now teach this differently, having read your dissertation?"

## The Dissertation as a Whole

The history dissertation is typically conceived of as a prospective book, mainly because it takes a book-size body of work to present something that is new empirically and theoretically, and to show that the student can write. But it is also because the standards for academic employment and tenure in the field require that faculty coming up for tenure have a published book or they are "out the door." However, not all history dissertations come in the same form and "the reality is that it may well be a series of articles." Below we explore the characteristics of different quality history dissertations (see Table 15.4) and what the faculty said about them.

### Outstanding

Outstanding dissertations are "fully realized." They are "incredibly well conceived," "treat the question fully," are "astonishingly documented" in terms of finding and using every possible form of information—interviews, archival materials, and so forth—and present an "extraordinary conclusion." They "turn things upside down" and push the discipline's boundaries. One participant used one word to describe outstanding—conceptualization—which he defined by example: "The student has taken what has seemed like a good topic and by the time they come to you with a draft, they've rethought the whole field and explained it to you in a way that you had never seen before, and then you always see it that way."

## TABLE 15.4.
### The Characteristics of Different Quality Dissertations in History

| Quality | Characteristics |
|---|---|
| **Outstanding** | Brilliant, one of a kind; well-conceived and fully realized; original, imaginative, interesting, surprising, compelling, and persuasive; very well written; written with transparency, grace, elegance, and literary skill; the student has a great gift for metaphors or a richness of language; uses telling quotes and anecdotes properly; makes minimum use of jargon; shows confidence and independence of mind; has a strong authorial voice; coherent; flows beautifully; has a controlling concept and a good, nonchronological organizational structure; asks new questions and uses information in very different ways; conveys the richness of the subject and issues involved; arguments are logical, rigorous, and sustained; each chapter has its own arguments and a very convincing way of dealing with part of the overall problem; has great transitions between chapters; written as a big symphony; tied together beautifully; very clearly and quickly states the historiographical problem being addressed and how other historians have dealt with it; positions the dissertation in a niche of some sort of problematic; the student has read and mastered a massive amount of material and thought about the problem in a new way; uses knowledge from other disciplines to address the problem in a way that it has not been addressed before; is theorized; has new methods and new evidence; does spectacular archival research; uncovers some very interesting archival material; is well documented; brings an impressive set of resources to bear on the problem; uses all the evidence to develop and tell an important and compelling story; builds a new model; synthesizes the data in an extraordinarily succinct way; journeys into the realm of analysis and interpretation and discusses what the sources say about the particular issue or time period; draws extraordinary conclusions; is influential; engages in a conversation with the field and guides the conversation in a new direction; pushes the discipline's boundaries |
| **Very good** | Well written; coherent; readable but not exciting; less original and ambitious; topics are rather small but may be important in a narrow sense; well grounded in the field but not fully realized; has great potential but has not followed through on everything completely; argument is not as strong as it could be; the student has done exceptional research, but it has a note card quality to |

*(continues)*

## TABLE 15.4.
### Continued

| Quality | Characteristics |
| --- | --- |
| **Very good** | it; less analytically sophisticated and not pulled together as well; displays a conception or an understanding of what historians do; the student is struggling to find his or her voice; chapters make sense; states the originality and significance of the contribution; the student has read some new sources; displays a good but not great use of sources; theory is interesting but will not make people want to go out and reinterpret their data; methods are rigorous, interesting, but not hugely path breaking; uses a limited body of material; contains extraneous material; takes a new look at evidence; exhausting use of evidence—every analytical or theoretical possibility is covered or pursued; explanation is conceptually tight and persuasive; interpretation is less imaginative and often beholden to earlier theoretical perspectives; is part of a conversation; adds some new wrinkles; makes a contribution in a few areas |
| **Acceptable** | Competent but not elegant; not particularly original; tends to be unimaginative and unsurprising; writing is pedestrian; lacks confidence; organization is weak and stodgy; is a gap filler; takes a conversation as given; finds a piece of information that is missing and supplies it; descriptive rather than analytical; tells a story that has not been told before but is not interpretive; does not have an integrated, central, sustained argument; argument falters, some part is left out or is not convincing; the student cannot figure out how to make a significant argument or make the argument match the sources better; rambles and covers a number of different points that have slightly different arguments; the student shows understanding of theoretical or interpretive issues at a simple-minded level; has done original archival research but does not know what to do with it; looks at a different data set but analysis and interpretation are not original; is based exclusively on secondary sources; the student is unable to see how other people may perceive the evidence; provides a lot of detail but no analysis; lacks or has a limited interpretation; does not participate in the conversation as an equal; makes a small contribution in some area |
| **Unacceptable** | Historiographically wrong or not grounded in solid and deep historiography; research is insufficient or inaccurate; makes up or steals data; plagiarizes a little-known source; is not significant or interesting; poorly written; pretentious; inarticulate; sloppy; |

| Quality | Characteristics |
|---|---|
| **Unacceptable** | ungrammatical; has spelling errors; lacks coherent narrative structure; narrator cannot find voice or overwhelms the analysis; cannot organize paragraphs and chapters; topic or problem is poorly defined; questions are biased in their conception; lacks an organizing, effective thesis; argument is weak, inconsistent, self-contradictory, or unconvincing; fails to engage theoretical or conceptual issues; the student did not use primary sources; is based exclusively on secondary sources or primary sources in translation; the student deliberately misreads sources; sources are not properly annotated in the footnotes; describes rather than interprets sources; the evidence is wrong; is analytically incoherent or confused in some way; lacks cogent interpretation; fails to address criticisms; does not make an empirical contribution |

The quality of the writing or prose also distinguishes the "exceptional" dissertation. Indeed, the quality of the writing is "perhaps more a concern to historians than it is to other disciplines." It matters a great deal to them that "academic writing meet a stylistic standard." In the outstanding dissertation, there is something about the language that makes it "edible," "quite tasty," and "compels" you to read it. The writing is elegant. "Like Goldilocks, there [are]n't too many words. There [are]n't too few words. It [is] just right." One participant described the writing in the best dissertation he had read in over 30 years as "moving." "There's no other word for it, it was moving. It told me . . . things that I cared about. It got me emotional about it. Those are the best."

Outstanding dissertations surprise and edify the reader. The surprise can be about the research findings. It can be about the ways in which familiar things are combined to result in an unfamiliar surprising synthesis. And it can be about the originality of a dissertation.

Outstanding dissertations also "teach you something that you didn't already know." When they read outstanding dissertations, faculty think: "I'm really learning from this." "I couldn't have written [this] [my]self." "I could see this as a book." "Wow, I can't wait until this is published." One participant described the experience of reading an outstanding dissertation as "humbling" and "wonderful" and added, "It doesn't happen very often, but when it does, it's spectacular." Outstanding dissertations also make faculty feel like they have to "go out and do something," about which another one remarked, "Like go rewrite your lecture."

Students who write outstanding dissertations see the dissertation not as "just an exercise or a hurdle, but [as] a passionate enterprise." They display "an independence from the educational process that they've just been through." Indeed, the faculty said that they have little to "total noninvolvement" with outstanding students' dissertations because these students devise their dissertations on their own. The topic, the questions posed, the research agenda come from the student. As a result, the work is "really theirs, not their advisor's, not their committee's, not the university's." "It's of the person. There's no 'you' in there at all." One participant, who keeps a list of all the graduate students he has had "by best and downward," thus described his interactions with one student on his list:

> It was almost embarrassing. He came to me with a draft of the dissertation. When I first read the draft I thought it was just spectacular. I said, "Put your cover page on it and let's go." He said, "I want to talk to you because I'm not really happy with it." I thought, "This is supposed to be my role. I'm supposed to be advising him." He told me what he wanted to do and I said, "You don't have to do that. This is a dissertation." But he said he would feel more comfortable. So I said, "All right." And in the end it was twice as good. He didn't need me at all. I wasn't contributing anything except reading.

Faculty in one focus group discussed the relationship between the topic and the quality of a dissertation. They said that it is harder to write a dissertation that "people are going to care about" when the dissertation is on a topic that "everybody thinks is hot right now." They noted that some advisors may be "deluded" into thinking that a dissertation is outstanding merely because it is on a fashionable or "hot" topic, when, in fact, an outstanding dissertation is really one that has enduring characteristics that "transcend its fashionableness." Dissertations that endure are ones that "you would really like to read 20 years from now," whereas, with hindsight, the others were only interesting because they were "hitting on the fashionable topic." The ability—"either through intuition, or luck, or clever advising"—to figure that out, "what the next thing is going to be," and be "ahead of the curve" can also be an "enormous benefit" in writing a dissertation that people will think is original and interesting and deem outstanding.

## Very Good

The "vast majority" of history dissertations are in the very good range. When they read very good dissertations, history faculty "realize there is a conversation there." They see that the students have moved beyond "trying to please their professor" and have established "their own independent voice," which, according to one participant is, "on some fundamental level," the "originality." Indeed, he noted that establishing an independent voice "may be the single most important thing a good dissertation accomplishes" and that is "the hardest thing to convey to a student."

Very good dissertations lack some of the qualities of the outstanding dissertation. They are often on smaller topics and are less original, less ambitious, and less convincing. One participant tried to explain the difference between an outstanding and a very good dissertation quantitatively:

> If the outstanding dissertation . . . scores outstanding on four characteristics—empirical, theoretical and methodological, and style—. . . it's simple, we can say that a dissertation [that] is very good but not outstanding either scores high on only three out of those four, that one of those is just not up to the standards of the rest, or simply is not outstanding on all four of them at the same time.

Many very good dissertations have the potential to be outstanding but fall short, primarily because of the quality of the writing. The students do not "write as well as the top-tier people." One participant described such a dissertation:

> He had gone and done two years of marvelous research and found material . . . an enormous amount of material, conceptualized it brilliantly, conceptualized how to think about the terminology. . . . He just doesn't write as well. It's a very rich dissertation. A very good dissertation. An original contribution. . . . So, it's mostly in the presentation [which is deficient], and it's depressing [that it did not live up to its potential].

Another participant in that focus group noted that the "opposite" could cause a potentially outstanding dissertation to end up being very good. In these types of very good dissertations, "The research is fine. The writing is fine, but they don't quite understand what they've got yet." He went on to note that "that happens a lot" with the "more ambitious dissertations" where students are "trying to work with newer categories."

Very good dissertations were also described as when "there is something not quite as it should be." For instance, in some dissertations the faculty know that there is other material that the student might have brought into the analysis, "yet, for a variety of reasons, usually money or time, the student wasn't able to do that." Very good dissertations are also ones where the "pieces are there," but they "haven't followed through completely on everything" And there are those with a lot of extraneous material: "450 good pages straining to get out of this 800-page tome." In short, the very good dissertation is often the one in which "the whole is much less than the sum of its parts."

## *Acceptable*

Acceptable dissertations are "gap fillers" rather than "door openers." At minimum, the student who writes one has a "basic competence at the apparatus," which means the student "know[s] how to do acceptable research and know[s] how to write an acceptable sentence and do[es] it in paragraph form and say[s] something which no one has said before." However, the student usually cannot take the work "into an alley where we call it an interpretive, deliberate dissertation."

Acceptable dissertations often have multiple problems. Sometimes they are missing evidence, but, more commonly, the argument is missing. Sometimes the students lack the "ability to see how other people may perceive [their] evidence."

Some students may produce acceptable dissertations because they have taken jobs and have to finish more quickly than they want to. Others produce acceptable dissertations because they are "not very bright," or are missing a certain "quality of mind." These students often have to be spoon-fed "every step of the way," for example, by being told:

> "Here's a good way of dealing with this evidence. Here's what we'll do with that evidence." They get it once you tell them, but they don't have any sense of confidence about it and they can't build on it. They can't see new things. It's [the dissertation] a pass because of my original thinking.

Others never "get it."

> You can explain and explain and explain. It's like leading the horse to
> water, they just don't get it. . . . They can't figure out how to do it—how
> to make it a more significant argument or how to make the argument
> match the sources better, or whatever.

A dissertation may wind up being acceptable because the advisor "decided to let go before it was really done." However, good dissertation advisors will make students "go home and do more." One participant said that
he has asked the "occasional" doctoral student "to do nine or ten drafts." In
these cases, "the student stays with it and then [it] is deemed to be acceptable, or the student gives up, or I give up for the student." Because faculty
(high producers anyway) want students to succeed, they often end up "fixing
bad dissertations." One participant talked about the "hours" he "put into
not just the argument but the writing and copyediting. In other words, do
I find myself wondering whether I can take the damn thing and write it
myself."

As in other disciplines, the historians acknowledged that acceptable dissertations ranged in quality from competent to marginal. Most of their comments about the "low end," "absolute bottom" dissertation focused on their,
and/or the dissertation committee's, decision to pass it. In almost all the cases
where the focus group participants were "caused to accept" or passed "a marginal product," they were the outside or the second reader. The faculty described a "kind of academic courtesy" where "if it passes the mentor's
muster" and is not "utterly atrocious" they will "let it though." "That's literally what they're doing, just letting it through."

In talking about the "just barely passing" dissertation, faculty in one
department noted that less competitive departments like theirs "develop a
sense of loyalty to their students." They said these types of departments "try
to build up a sense in general that we appear to help students get through
their program." The focus group participants also indicated that they will
"give a pass" to a marginal dissertation for "mechanical skills" and the
"hard-work factor." In these cases, the students have "fulfilled [their] side of
the bargain"—"They worked very hard. They did travel here and they did
find this, they did find that."—and passing the students is "our side of the
bargain."

Faculty will also often pass marginal dissertations because the students have a job waiting—and "you don't want to be responsible for them losing their job." They know that many of these students will go off and do something other than research and college-level teaching.

## Unacceptable

According to the focus group participants, an unacceptable dissertation should never come to defense. It should be stopped before it gets to that stage. If an unacceptable dissertation makes it that far, it is "a failure of the advisor" or an "institutional failure of mentoring," and "a very painful situation." It can also indicate a breakdown between the advisor and the student. "They are not communicating and the advisor does not know what to do anymore."

Unacceptable dissertations are "a mess." They suffer from one or more of the deficiencies outlined in Table 15.4. Alluding to the concept of implicit criteria, one participant said:

> We have a picture in our mind of what an acceptable dissertation is and we can see that that person wasn't going to get there. . . . I think I'm realizing that we can use these magic four categories [empirical, theoretical, and methodological, and style] for [the unacceptable dissertation] as well, because . . . if something between those four categories is horribly wrong, just one thing, it's not acceptable.

A dissertation could have some very good ideas but is unacceptable because it is poorly written, "because, as Orwell said, 'It's not possible to say good things in bad English.'" At the nuts-and-bolts level, the poorly written dissertation is "inarticulate." The grammar is so bad that faculty cannot understand it. Indeed, one participant commented, "Bad grammar is actually more common than I'd like to admit in our department." Other students have trouble writing organized paragraphs and chapters.

The faculty in one focus group noted that the "architecture" of a dissertation is something that students have not had practice with. "The first time you do it is the first time you do it." When they sit down to write a dissertation, students "have all this material, and they have not had training on how to manage the data, how to organize that much material." The good students "figure it out." The "bad ones write note cards." The "bad ones" may also do "scissors-and-paste history," where they pile up one quotation after another in an (unsuccessful or unconvincing) attempt to support an argument.

Some students cannot find their voices as historians. They provide a "voice-over" of what happened. They can narrate what the evidence says but are incapable of analyzing it on their own. They never gain control over the problem of "Why am I doing this?" One participant thought this derived "partly from graduate training and writing essays about [what other scholars say]," and noted that when they get to the dissertation, some students find it hard "to finally speak for themselves."

Similarly, some students cannot make the transition from course taker (consumers of knowledge) to independent scholar (producers of knowledge). One participant described such a student, his "worst student ever," as follows:

> He was this walking encyclopedia who could not organize a thought in his mind. His mind worked like an encyclopedia. Mention a word, and he'd go to that word and he could cite you all kinds of things, but he couldn't explain the relationship between any two words. He came with these marvelous recommendations because he was a spectacular undergraduate, because he did well on tests. In a certain amount of undergraduate history stuff, if your memory is good enough, you can look very good. But the further you go, the more you have to conceptualize, and more of his weaknesses became manifest.

This student ultimately passed because his committee members "closed [their] eyes and signed." However, his advisor felt as though he had constructed the dissertation for him.

Sometimes dissertations are unacceptable because students fail to address their advisor's and committee members' criticisms and continue "in the wrong way." These students either do not want to make the requested changes or "can't quite grasp what we're looking for." Sometimes students' dissertations are unacceptable because they have left the university for a number of years, often because they have taken a job, and fail to keep up with the research that has been done in their area in the intervening years. As a result, their dissertation is no longer an original contribution. In one such case that was mentioned, the committee passed it "out of courtesy." They "grandfathered" it, reasoning that "by the standard under [which] it was composed, it was probably acceptable."

In the worst case, the student gets caught in the ideological conditions or problems within a department or between committee members. The student is asked to do "incompatible things" and is really caught "betwixt and between." The result is "invariably failure" or the dissertation is at least "only minimally acceptable" because the student has "to carve out a position between two incompatible positions" and produces "an ideological dissertation, which is trying to serve more than one master."

## The Components of a History Dissertation

Although the history faculty did not necessarily like having to discuss the components of the history dissertation (see Table 1.2), only one history focus group had strong objections to it. The participants felt that the matrix was an attempt to strip the reasonably textured discussion they had just had about the dissertation into something that could be fed into a computer, which resulted in the following amusing exchange among the participants:

> *Participant 1* (referring to his colleague): When she saw this matrix she started suspecting that a computer was lying behind this exercise. I see you've got some army coders off there listening to our tape and decoding our responses.

> *Participant 2*: We should say hello to them.

> *Participant 3*: Hi coders!

At one point, the faculty in this department said, "We're dicking your categories," and "We boycott," though in the same set of comments the latter participant said, "I like the broad framework."

Faculty in other focus groups felt that the categories were "too neat and discrete." They said that in a good dissertation "everything is integrated," they are not separate components. They also felt that the categories were "kind of apples and oranges," because the middle three (historiographic review, sources/methods, and exposition/analysis) had to do with the characteristics of the study, whereas the first and last (introduction and conclusion) were really sections of the dissertation. However, like the dissenting faculty above, they agreed that every piece of historical writing "would have all of these characteristics."

With respect to the individual components, the historians noted that the first three—introduction, historiographic review, and sources/methods—should be in the introduction. They felt that "interpretive and conceptual frame or narrative" was a better term than "methods" and should be its own column. One participant felt that "argument" should be included somewhere, perhaps under "exposition and analysis." Another participant felt that argument, exposition, and analysis were three separate components.

Two focus groups did not discuss most of the components. Below we explore the characteristics of the components of a history dissertation (see Table 15.A in the appendix to this chapter) and what the faculty said about them.

## Introduction

The introduction to a history dissertation has to characterize the whole work. It has to very succinctly articulate the topic and thesis. It has to present the argument and provide some insight into the sources and methodology. And it should situate the work in the historiography.

History introductions come in a variety of forms. Some are narrative, some analytical. Some are short, some long. The introduction is the place where the "student learns to show his or her own voice or style." Introductions are hard to write, and students often have a lot of trouble with them. Indeed, this is the part of the dissertation that is most often sent back for revision.

The outstanding introduction makes people want to read the dissertation. It often starts with a hook—a situation, a paradox, or a surprise. One participant tells students that "at most, you've got three pages to grab someone who doesn't have to read this." The outstanding introduction provides a "dramatic and crisp" statement of the problem, addresses the importance, originality, and significance of the topic and the distinctiveness of the approach, and it teases out some of the broader implications that bear on theoretical questions that are of interest to a larger interdisciplinary group of scholars. The outstanding introduction is also a self-marketing tool. It has to sell the author, because the introduction might be the only thing that a search committee reads. "If they don't win that inning, nobody's going to look at the other stuff. So, this has to be enticing, exciting, and communicate its purpose."

Very good introductions are engaging. They have "some significance," but they do not "have to have a lot." The exposition is good "but might take a while to get there."

Acceptable introductions are "just repetitions of our gap fillers." The question and the argument are simplistic and turgid. They say, "This is a study of the governorship of the planning process in the San Gabriel Valley from 1920 to 1980. . . . In chapter 2 I will do Y in a certain way." Or they say, "There is a model out there and we used to think because of Jones and Smith's primary work on Illinois and California, we can now look at Delaware from this perspective and on, and on, and on."

After reading an unacceptable introduction, the reader does "not know or care what the dissertation will do," because the introduction does not do what an introduction is supposed to do. One participant noted that it is not just an organizational issue, "it's an intellectual issue. It's a matter of intellectual drive, of having focus." In response to the facilitator's question about whether historians wrote the introduction first or last, one participant responded, "You write the bad one first."

## Historiographic Review

A historiographic review is a review of other interpretations of history. Although one participant felt that there was a growing trend for history dissertations to have elaborate historiographic reviews, several of the focus group participants said they did not like them; many discouraged them. One participant said that he tells students "the word 'historiographic' is a synonym for boring." Others said, "They bore you to tears. I don't like to read them." "Some of the more tedious dissertations . . . have a chapter on the historiography." One historian opined that students who write them are seeking an "imprimatur" of people in the field: "Professor so-and-so and so-and-so has done this outstanding work, and mine will fit just right in this way." He went on to note that people in the field "will normally know if you know the historiography or not and so will the dissertation director." Another participant felt that historiography makes students more conservative, whereas "theoretical concerns, or interdisciplinary interests, or . . . political and social concerns make them more daring." To the extent that there is historiography in the dissertation, the focus group participants said it should be in the beginning of the substantive chapters. They want to see students state the argument (the interpretation), indicate where it is going, and, in the process, engage in a conversation with the leading scholars. They want students to "keep the historian in the footnotes."

Outstanding dissertations often have "surprisingly little historiography" because it is embedded in the analysis. To the extent that history dissertations have a historiographic review, the outstanding one is "brief and it shows the student's ability to concisely and fairly summarize a large body of literature." It shows empathy for and appreciation of the earlier works. It indicates what the significant issues are and "how what you're saying contends with or advances it." One participant said that reading a "good review" is like "listening to a good conversation. You see the debate. You see that developing collective train of thought and struggle."

The acceptable historiographic review was characterized in two ways. One is a 50-page chapter that "discusses every single book and article that has come out in that field." The other would "simply say there are five books on this subject. Number one says this, and number two says that, number three says the other thing." Students who write them are "paying homage to whatever," but not really engaging the problem in a significant way—and "That is a boring and stupid historiographic review." One participant noted that it takes intellectual ability to be selective and focus the review "toward your particular interest."

## Sources/Methods

The historians typically separated sources from methods or methodology in their discussions and spent more time talking about sources than methods. Although they felt that methods needed to be laid out explicitly in the dissertation proposal, they did not feel that they had to explained in detail in the dissertation itself, because they become "obvious from the exposition or the scholarly apparatus" and can be addressed in footnotes, endnotes, or the bibliography. With respect to sources, faculty are interested in seeing how students use them; that they are using them in an interesting, original, and significant way. For both sources and methods the "most important things" are

> Is the author imaginative? . . . Is he or she thinking, "This question of mine, where would the best possible evidence be? Is there some evidence that people haven't thought about applying to this problem? And does it exist? And can I find it? Will it work?"

One presumably more senior participant contrasted how sources were treated when he was a graduate student with how they are treated now, and noted that historians are paying more attention to "sources as texts within history":

> When I was a graduate student you had documents and they told you what was true. [Students] simply reported what had happened. All you had to do was find a document and then you wrote an account, "This is what happened." I think that that kind of simple certainty about our sources was an advantage to a large extent. We're much more conscious [now] of who wrote this source and why, and for what purpose, and how do we read that particular source in a fashion that is appropriate. Then, for those who are more postmodern, we can say [in] the multiple readings of that source for different interpretations of it, what are the subtexts? I think that we're more self-conscious.

The outstanding use of sources and methods is when students identify new approaches that relate directly to the problem they identified in their introduction. One participant said that outstanding is when there is a synergy between new sources and new methods and new questions. "If you hit all those, you are in great shape." However, outstanding is "very often not new sources as much as it is a new way of looking at old sources or known sources."

Outstanding students were described as resourceful, energetic, and a little bit gutsy. They employ "backbreaking" methodology, leave "no stone unturned," and "milk" their sources. They "show you sources you didn't know existed and show you ways to use them that you didn't think of." Because old sources are "never complete" and someone can never know whether he or she is "reading them correctly," outstanding students show a "strange mix of real confidence about [their] sources but also a humility before them."

For the historians, very good sources/methods had to do with what students did when they discovered that their sources told them "something very different than what they started out thinking." The question becomes, "Can they then deal with that? And what do they do? Can they say, 'Oh, I didn't find what I thought I was going to find, instead I found [X], now what is this telling me? And what am I going to do?'" One participant said that this is exactly what happened to her when she started writing her dissertation:

> I expected the ruling class to have affected the Minneapolis Public Schools
> in such a way. I went to do the research and it was the opposite. I felt like
> an idiot. I went to my advisor and said, "I must have done something
> wrong. It didn't work out that way." He said, "No, you absolutely did
> something right. And now you are going to figure out what to do with it."

While there are a lot of "nervous breakdowns" when this happens, very good
students "embrace the challenge" and "just move on." Indeed, dealing with
it was described as a "transforming" process:

> You are not the same as when you started. . . . Your sophistication isn't the
> same . . . because of these kinds of experiences. There is nothing you can
> do in a classroom that can replicate that. They have to do it themselves.

An acceptable use of sources and methods at the solid end of the acceptable scale involves doing predictable things with sources, competently and
thoroughly. At the lower end of the scale, students may not use the right
sources and methods for their particular problem. Their approach is, "Well,
I'm doing this problem. I know that the major archives are empty, so I'm
going to go do my time there and say I've covered that work." Their treatment of their sources is also undifferentiated. According to one participant,
they say, "This is what I looked at. This is what it is. This is what it looks
like. This is what it does. And this is what it says."

In the unacceptable category, the worst students are the ones who "go
somewhere" and "like a vacuum cleaner, they suck it up and come back with
mounds and mounds" of material that they have not read. They end up
sitting in front of "all this completely undigested material," material that
they should have read and digested in the course of doing their research, and
"they are totally freaked." This failure to read and engage with documents
early on was described as a "huge problem," one that leads to "a lot of un-
finished dissertations or unformulated ideas," and one that has gotten worse
because of the proliferation of photocopying machines.

### Exposition/Analysis

Exposition/analysis is the "heart" or "meat" of the dissertation. It is where
"you prove what you said you were going to explore," where "you substanti-
ate what you have exposed," and where "your interpretation answers the

question you posed." Faculty look for consistency in the exposition and analysis, for the ability to "sustain ways of analyzing and giving exposition to the field." Although some students do outstanding analyses "no matter who you put them with," most students "don't come to us . . . ready formed and ready for historical research." Thus, the quality of the exposition and analysis is often a function of mentoring, the advisor's ability to push students to ask larger questions about the data and to push them in the analysis.

Outstanding analyses make the reader feel like they are in the company of a good guide, "like you've got a good bus driver on this trip." They anticipate and answer readers' questions about the argument and explain the importance of anecdotes. Students' whose expositions and analyses are outstanding have both the confidence and flexibility to "change the topic with the sources without completely panicking." They often do not "come back [from the field] with exactly the same question they left with," which would make faculty suspect "there is kind of a round-peg-in-a-square-hole thing going on." When they encounter problems, they can regroup and write their write-ups as if they understood their question all along.

The acceptable exposition/analysis "isn't a read that fires you [up]. As you're reading it, it's like, 'Oh, OK, well there is another kind of brick that we [didn't need to know.]' When they read an unacceptable one, readers think, 'Oh, I am going to die. Tell me why this makes a difference? Why should we care?'"

### Conclusion

The function of the conclusion is to return to the broader issues, to take the ideas and information that have been presented throughout the bulk of the dissertation and put them in a wider context. Ideally, the conclusion should pull the dissertation together, say something interesting, emphasize what the reader generally did not know before, and point the way toward new and interesting future research. For many "young scholars" the conclusion is the most difficult part to write because "they are so close to the material that they don't know what to say."

Several participants said that the conclusion was the "least important" part of the dissertation. One stated, "You don't need a conclusion. By that time, I'm exhausted, and if you haven't persuaded me by now, I don't care how many pages it is." Others felt that the conclusion was important. According to a participant, faculty in one department often tell [their] students that hiring committees are only going to read the introduction and conclusion, so the introduction has to say what they are going to do, and how they are going to do it. The conclusion has to say what they did and what it means. If they can do that, then people won't have to read the middle to know they are a good job candidate.

One participant remarked that he "always" finds conclusions "so disappointing." He did not think it was "fair to judge what was otherwise a worthwhile work by my disappointment. So I pretty much do discount my disappointment in terms of an individual dissertation. But over time I have become more distraught over the empty bite of the conclusion." In a similar vein, another historian who had "very strong feelings" about conclusions observed:

> Systemwide conclusions are often very anemic and underdeveloped. . . . It just seems that even in very good dissertations you get to the conclusion and you're thinking, "Now knock it home!" or "Here we go!" and it's three pages. Sometimes it's not even called a conclusion, it's called an epilogue or a final thought or something like that. So I don't know what happened to the conclusion. . . . All of this work and there are two or three pages of that. I really do have quite a thing about it. I don't know where it happened, because it happens in all kinds of institutions. . . . Maybe it's just fatigue and exhaustion. . . . Maybe it's just collapsing as you cross the finish line. But you can collapse and then you can get up again.

Outstanding conclusions are "very, very hard to write." They go beyond summarizing the work. They are ones where "you get to the conclusion and you think you've learned all this stuff and then they draw out some more implications . . . that you hadn't thought of." They talk about the work's meaning to the bigger world and invite reflection on the topic. They may have a comparative or a cross-temporal dimension. They suggest ways in which the field can now move forward, about which one participant remarked, "that kind of boldness is really rare."

Conclusions are often viewed as acceptable because the body of the dissertation was "richer and smarter" than portrayed in the conclusion. They fail to develop a sense of "how exciting this was and where it might lead." One participant remarked that "not every student has the confidence in their analytical abilities to say, 'This is what it means.'"

## Notes

1. See http://www.historians.org/projects/cge/PhD/Specializations.cfm (accessed February 23, 2006).

2. Data on the number of Ph.D. programs, graduate enrollment, and new Ph.D.s come from Bender et al. (2004) as well as from Paul Katz, former research director of the Committee on Graduate Education of the American Historical Association, who also provided some data and information (personal communication, August 16, 2005, and August 21, 2005). For information on the sources of data on time to degree and postdocs, see chapter 1, note 5.

3. The totals and averages are based on the 31 focus group participants who provided data.

# Appendix

## TABLE 15.A.

### The Components of a History Dissertation and Their Characteristics at Different Quality Levels

| Components | Quality levels | | | |
| --- | --- | --- | --- | --- |
| | Outstanding | Very good | Acceptable | Unacceptable |
| Introduction | Beautifully written; concise, thoughtful, succinct, persuasive; has a motivational hook; asks a question that grabs, entices, and excites the reader; sets up and defines the problem clearly and forcefully; provides a clear statement of the thesis; grounds it in the broader historiographic fields; explains why it is important and significant; maps out the procedures, approaches, and methodology; introduces the sources, difficulties, and challenges confronted; provides a road map for the ensuing chapters and tells the reader what to expect | Provides a good exposition of the problem but is less graceful; explains why it is important and significant; situates the work in the historiography; speaks only to student's own subfield | Writing is pedestrian, uninteresting, and awkward; merely orients the reader to the problem but not as precisely, thoughtfully, or intriguingly as it could; itemizes the chapters and their content; does not conceptualize the train of thought | Very pedestrian; either too long or too short; does not provide a sense that it is an introduction or does not do the things an introduction is supposed to do; does not grab the reader; is just a summary; has no point; raises issues that are not developed or ignores issues that are developed; is not coherent; moves backward and forward on a variety of scales of argument, time, or method; makes an excessive claim of significance |

(continues)

TABLE 15.A.
Continued

| Components | Quality levels | | | |
|---|---|---|---|---|
| | Outstanding | Very good | Acceptable | Unacceptable |
| **Historiographic review** | Brief; concisely and fairly summarizes a large body of literature; identifies salient works and themes; uses rather than lists prior works; avoids, "so and so wrote"; demonstrates mastery of relevant secondary sources; treats secondary sources with empathy and respect when demonstrating their shortcomings; situates the problem in the historiography and theory; historicizes the historiography; engages in the conversation; provides a sense of what the turning points in the literature are and where the literature might be going; shows why the student is coming at the problem from a different direction | Command of the historiography is more limited; selective; picks out those parts of the historiography that are specifically relevant to the problem being addressed; is thin with respect to the problem the student is looking at; exhibits some tendency to oversimplify historical trends or be overly critical of prior literature; shows the debates in the literature; states what issues will be addressed and identifies the gaps; indicates how the student plans to fill in the gaps; takes a defensive stance that exaggerates the extent to which the dissertation and its interpretation are novel or better | Tends to be an undifferentiated list; an annotated bibliography; hits all the major works; is not selective; does not distinguish between more and less relevant works; range consulted is too constrained by the self-definition of the topic; uncritically accepts what has been written as true; does not place the work in a historiographic context | Mechanical; too thin; shows no awareness of what has been written on the topic; student did not look at enough secondary sources; student misinterprets or does not understand the literature; student is intellectually confused; jumps around; does not fit problem into the historiography; student focuses entire argument against a recent book or article |

| Components | Quality levels | | | |
|---|---|---|---|---|
| | Outstanding | Very good | Acceptable | Unacceptable |
| **Sources/methods** | Brief, thorough, clear; innovative; sources are exciting, reliable, has a high degree of integrity; integrates sources; squeezes sources unexpected, interesting information from sources; has a synergy among new questions, methods, and sources; figures out a new way to understand the problem, theory, methodology, or sources; approaches sources with a completely different understanding; takes traditional sources and looks at them in a new way; opens up new sources; generates new kinds of evidence; shows why method used is superior; uses cutting-edge methodology; successfully defends method and analysis; shows that its theory and method is more valuable, subject to fewer criticisms, and has fewer flaws than previous theories and methods; recognizes biases and limitations of sources and their interpretation; argument is well documented | Uses a more limited range of sources; relies on printed primary sources; rises to the challenge when sources contradict original position; tends to accept what sources say as true | Undeveloped; undifferentiated; out of fashion; has a very limited range of sources, sometimes uses only one source or one genre of sources; makes unsupportable assumptions; student has a dim awareness of the limitations of the sources; does not explain much | Incoherent; undigested; insufficient research; does not have a method; does not have enough data; student does not know what to read or how to read it; student does not understand the sources; student does not actually read the material and engage with it; relies solely on secondary sources; material is taken off a Web site; makes sources fit the question; imposes a pattern on the sources; sources are not documented; methods are not described |

*(continues)*

**TABLE 15.A.**
Continued

| Components | Quality levels | | | |
| --- | --- | --- | --- | --- |
| | Outstanding | Very good | Acceptable | Unacceptable |
| **Exposition/ analysis** | Elegant, everything is there for a reason; consistent; argument or exposition is rich and appropriate; has proper balance between original; new ideas and detailed, close analysis; analysis is sophisticated; keeps big picture in mind; analytical presentation has a distinct voice; asks larger questions; pursues questions to appropriate conclusions; sources and interpretation are mutually supportive; interpretation answers the question; almost every paragraph has a telling quote or anecdote; answers the "So what?" question | Data are not as clearly tied to the question; interprets the raw material within the context of the conversation; makes some leaps between data and interpretation | Coherent; writing is acceptable, but the style is not very interesting or exciting; very heavily jargoned; covers enough material; uses chronology as an organizer; has no real analysis; has a decent descriptive narrative; gets the story straight, explains the story sequentially with cause and effect relationships; does not see the story in all of its complexity; shows awareness of the theoretical issues underpinning the research; the relationship between the sources and the interpretation of evidence is not spelled out clearly; interpretation is too simplistic | Fails to convey the argument; argument does not have a sense of hierarchy; interpretation of data is not cogent; sources contradict the interpretation; is not clear how the chapters differ; does not answer the "So what?" question |

| Components | Quality levels | | | |
|---|---|---|---|---|
| | Outstanding | Very good | Acceptable | Unacceptable |
| **Conclusion** | Is full of surprises; recapitulates the work in a more precise and different way; presents the primary problem, shows how the evidence was presented to answer the original question; pulls the work together and says something interesting; has an epilogue, which may bring some theme forward in time and show how its implications change with time; puts the work in a wider context; shows the broader implications; explains the significance of the work for the field, history, and/or humanity; points out new, interesting, and exciting possibilities for future research | Short; sums up the work well but does not go beyond summary; student is afraid to insert his or her own voice | Underdeveloped; provides a very bald and brief restatement of the problem; summarizes what happened in the chapters; states what the major points are; ties it all together but does not deliver the goods that have been withheld; answers the "So what?" question; shows its relevance; makes platitudes about the history of the world | Is missing; appalling; too brief; trails off into nothingness; does not tie things up; introduces new thoughts or information; student is still struggling to figure out what is being argued; says that it has implications for the present |

# 16

# THE PHILOSOPHY
# DISSERTATION

There are more than 100 Ph.D. programs in philosophy in the United States. Graduate philosophy programs graduate roughly 300 new Ph.D.s annually. The median time to degree is 9.2 years.[1]

Thirty-two faculty at nine universities participated in the focus groups. There were technical problems with one university's tape and, consequently, it was not transcribed. Fortunately, the facilitator took detailed notes and they were included in the analysis. Overall, the focus group faculty had 863 years of experience, had chaired an estimated 325 dissertations, and had sat on an estimated 908 dissertation committees.[2] The average focus group participant had been a professor for 28 years, had chaired 10 dissertations, and had sat on 29 dissertation committees. Below is a summary of the philosophy focus groups' discussions. Their performance expectations for the dissertation are displayed in the tables. Their supporting discussion is recounted in the text.

## The Purpose of a Philosophy Dissertation

The philosophy faculty saw the dissertation as serving many purposes (see Table 16.1). Most viewed the dissertation as a learning process, an exercise through which students acquire competencies and demonstrate that they can engage in a very long, sustained examination of a single subject; meet minimum professional standards; and contribute to the philosophical conversation. One participant noted that there are "certain skills" that are developed in "undertaking a project of that sort" that are not developed very well in course work:

## TABLE 16.1.
### The Purpose of a Philosophy Dissertation

To educate the person in how to do philosophy well and independently; to learn how to do sustained, decent, independent philosophical research and how to write close to professional standards; to demonstrate research capacity and competence and the skills necessary for a successful career; to show the student can identify an important issue and deal with it in a sustained, somewhat original way, is capable of writing really well, has the capacity for engaging in the state of the art; can contribute to and participate in a sophisticated philosophical discussion at a professional level; to force students to write with rigor, clarity, and systematicity; to provide experience working in an extended way on some narrowly focused issue; to gain fluency and competence in a certain kind of relative thinking; to become an independent practitioner; to get a job; is the last stage in the student's philosophical education; a training document; an exercise that prepares students to do research; certifies them as someone who is capable of doing research in the field; is a foundation for further work; a jumping-off point for the student's career

Just writing a paper at a time for 10 weeks or 15 weeks . . . brings out certain skills. Dissertations bring out a different kind of skill by requiring a higher level of complexity. . . . There is a difference in what it takes to do a good course paper, and some students falter. [Some students have] done fairly well or rather well in course papers, [but] when they undertake . . . doing something of [dissertation] scope. . . . they find that they can't [do as well].

In response, one of his colleagues said that there "could be a reasonable debate or a reasonable disagreement among people in our field" about whether the dissertation is a "necessary stage in philosophers' development, because much of what the profession does is journal-length articles, and that is the sort of thing that is done in normal course work." Thus, he said, there may not be "sufficient purpose" for a dissertation that is a "lengthy, systematic treatment of a single topic." Meanwhile, a participant in a different focus group noted that although students could demonstrate their ability to participate in the philosophical conversation by writing articles, "the thing about a dissertation is that it is supposed to demonstrate that you could eventually write books." Along these lines, more than one participant noted that writing a long, sustained piece of scholarly work is a "stumbling block" for many students and is the reason for the high rate of attrition at the dissertation stage.

At the same time, the philosophers criticized some students' "obsession" with trying to write a "magnum opus." They felt that writing a dissertation that is "likely to have a lasting impact upon the discipline" was an "unrealistic expectation" and is "paralyzing for the student." Rather, they asserted that the dissertation is "the last stage in your philosophical education, not the capstone of your career." It is a "first statement," a "protobook" that demonstrates students' ability "to contribute to and participate in a sophisticated philosophical discussion." The magnum opus is something that "should come in the middle or end of your career."

Faculty in one focus group had a debate about whether the purpose of the dissertation was to help students get a job. One participant saw students' dissertations "prospectively" as "a jumping-off point for their career." Some participants thought that view was "crass," others did not, noting that the dissertation is very important in students' search for a position, "because the first question they're going to be asked at any interview is, 'What was your dissertation on?' It defines an area of specialization when they're searching for jobs. It's going to be what generated the job talk they give." "You've got to prove to the people who are going to hire you that you have something you can work on." "And most letters that your referees are going to write are going to be about the dissertation." One participant tried to resolve the debate by stating, "You have to ask, 'The purpose for whom?' " She went on to say:

> It seems to me . . . that the purpose of the dissertation is to educate the person in how to do philosophy well and independently. That's the purpose of the dissertation. Whether it leads to a job talk is important . . . , but it's not, from my perspective, the purpose of the dissertation. . . . It seems to me that one has to separate these questions. So, the purpose of the dissertation from the professor's point of view is that the person gain fluency and competence in a certain kind of relative thinking and now be an independent practitioner in the world. Whether he or she gets a job is a different . . . question, which the dissertation ought not to be essentially aimed at or compromised for the sake of.

## Original Contribution

The philosophy faculty identified many ways to make an original contribution (see Table 16.2). They noted that these ways were, in part, a function of

## TABLE 16.2.
### The Nature of an Original Contribution in Philosophy

Something no one else has said before that goes beyond simply reporting on what other people have said; assembling the literature in an interesting way; connecting things that have not been connected before; making comparisons that have not been made before; producing a thoughtful, critical assessment of certain major philosophers or commentators upon major philosophers; coming up with a new, distinctive way to think about or understand a great thinker or an existing problem; providing a new organization of or context for thought or arguments; articulating an existing view that has not been articulated very well; providing an exegesis of a philosophical position; adding a consideration, set of considerations, or line of argument; finding gaps in an argument that shed light on the argument; challenging orthodoxy; showing that a widely held view is subject to a counter-example; showing that a counterexample can be gotten around; framing a theory in a plausible way that evades or gets around difficulties; devising a system that formalizes some concepts; backing up or supporting a conclusion; answering a question differently or coming up with an entirely new conclusion; redefining a problem in ways pertinent to the ongoing conversation; making a breakthrough on an established interpretation; coming up with a new argument or new support for a contested premise; discovering a conceptual distinction, connection, or some novel line of argument that has a significant bearing on the truth or falsity of a major philosophical issue or problem; making an independent, authentic discovery of something interesting; positing something and putting it forth as a set of views about a philosophical issue; has the potential to change the way people think about the question; contributes to or changes the direction of an ongoing discussion; reforms or enlarges the boundaries of the discipline

the type of philosophy the student was doing, for instance, historical, comparative, or analytical. Because philosophy has been around for 2,500 years, it is much harder to come up with an original contribution "in the sense you might find in other disciplines," that is, something "completely new and different," the way Spinoza or Nietzsche did, about which one participant remarked, "You can't ask our students to do what we ourselves can't do." Indeed, an original contribution in a dissertation is "very rare." Yet, one participant felt that there was room for independent, authentic discovery, though it may be rooted in something that "might have been noted before but is now thought of in a new way by the person." He commented that in the 19th century John Stuart Mill argued that "genius can be authentic even if it rediscovers, so long as it does it on its own grounds and for its own argument authentically."

The philosophers also noted that original contributions do not have "one look," that originality is "elastic." One focus group discussed the "range" in terms of "weak" and "strong" contributions. Weak is something that is philosophically interesting and "as far as anybody can tell, it hasn't been written before." Strong is "when no one has done this before and it's interesting and important." In addition, something that is "strikingly original" is when somebody "takes something from outside philosophy, from some other discipline . . . and then uses it to throw new and interesting light on other things."

In general, the philosophy faculty do not expect students to make an original contribution in their dissertations, though they do expect the dissertation to have "some component of originality," something along of the lines of having the "potential to change the way people think about the question." However, the dissertation does not have to be successful in doing that. Rather, the philosophers want to see "signs of originality" in the formulation of the problem, in the critical assessment of major philosophers or commentators upon a major philosopher, in the organization of arguments, or in the examples chosen. But what is most important to the faculty is that the dissertation shows a high level of philosophical sophistication, a capacity to contribute to the ongoing discussion of the topic, and do more than simply report on what other people have said.

The philosophers also discussed the standard of originality, both in terms of the community and the department, though they did not use those terms. According to one participant, the community standard is, "Is he or she saying something that's new and different enough to justify publication?" about which his colleague remarked, "That still leaves the question, 'What justifies publication?'" A participant at a different university said that "what gets published is something that contributes to an ongoing debate and which is recognized as a contribution to that [debate]" and noted that "its originality may actually make it unpublishable sometimes, depending on how well it connects." Her colleague explained that "a journal has an idea that it's going to support a particular intellectual inquiry . . . and something too wild is not going to engage them." The participant who said that a dissertation's originality might make it unpublishable remarked, "I don't think that pure originality is actually rewarded in this profession, either in publications or in dissertations."

Faculty in a department they themselves described as "not first rate" noted that different departments or universities hold students to different standards of originality. They felt that their department's standards were lower than that of "first-rate" programs and wondered whether this was "in part a function of the kinds of students we get here."

In addition to identifying what an original contribution is, the philosophers also identified what it is not. A dissertation that "merely surveyed the existing secondary literature" does not count as a contribution, nor does one that "provided a new interpretation of some important central text of a great philosopher . . . unless it connected with the current state of philosophical argument of some one of the large issues."

## Significant Contribution

What counts as a significant contribution in philosophy is "extremely subjective." It is a "value judgment" about impact and influence on people's philosophical views that is recognized in retrospect. However, one participant noted that for reasons unconnected to its value, a contribution may not have a wide influence. Indeed, contributions can be very original, but for "better or worse" if they "don't happen to take off, they will be like the prophet who's not heard." (See Table 16.3 for characteristics of a significant contribution in philosophy.)

### TABLE 16.3.
#### The Nature of a Significant Contribution in Philosophy

A very original, groundbreaking contribution that is publishable, has an impact on readers' philosophical views, and motivates them to think about the views the student advanced and contemplate writing about those new views; says something interesting that is different from what others have said; provides an updated look at enduring questions; gives an interesting, unprecedented, persuasive resolution to a long-standing problem; affects the conversation; sets the agenda for other people; redirects or transforms the subject; will change the field and make all philosophy go in a different direction

Significant contributions move the literature and play a role in the ongoing philosophical discussion. Most dissertations do not meet "that standard." The standard was further defined as

> having something interesting to say that's different than what other people have said, enough just to think that editors of a reputable journal would think that it would be worth giving journal pages [to]. . . . Significant in the sense that people in the discipline start responding in large numbers and thinking that they should take this into account.

Not only is it very rare for a graduate student to make a significant contribution, but the philosophy faculty do not expect graduate students to do so. According to one participant,

> To come out with really significant results in philosophy you have to think about things for a really long time. Most graduate students haven't been thinking about things long enough for that. You have to keep putting things together in different ways and different ways until something happens. I think what I'm really looking for in a graduate student . . . is some signs of the ability to do that. I'm making a prediction about future success. It's not necessarily going to be based on the originality of the contribution.

For one participant, significant was not about the contribution, but was rather about the topic. He felt that the terms "original" and "significant" were "overblown" and explained that "most peoples' dissertations are contributions to them becoming . . . professional philosophers, which may mean being able to be teachers rather than researchers." Indeed, the dissertation is where "you are first practicing being a philosopher." And "unless you are a freaking genius or something," it is highly unlikely that a dissertation will be so significant that it will set a research agenda for others.

One participant discussed what a significant contribution was not. He felt that a "relatively insignificant" dissertation was one that was "way too cautious." It is one that is "so busy defending itself against every conceivable little objection that it just can't cut loose and say anything that would surprise you."

## The Dissertation as a Whole

Some universities no longer require philosophy graduate students to submit the traditional book-style dissertation. Rather students may submit a series of connected essays or papers because article publishing rather than book publishing is increasingly what most philosophers do, and articles are where most important contributions in philosophy appear. The argument for the essay-style dissertation was characterized as, "If X who's a well-known philosopher hasn't written a book, why should a graduate student? Is it really necessary in order to prepare one for the discipline? . . . Wouldn't they be better served writing three very good articles that they can publish right off, rather than a book that probably won't get published . . . in its original form? Below we explore the characteristics of different quality philosophy dissertations (see Table 16.4) and what the faculty said about them.

### *Outstanding*

Although the philosophy faculty identified many characteristics of outstanding dissertations, a number thought that outstanding "resists explication," that there are "indefinitely many ways" in which a dissertation can be outstanding, and that there was "no essence, . . . no single feature or set of features that all exceptionally good dissertations have to have." One participant wanted to "make clear" that he would not say, "Does this dissertation fit these particular criteria well? . . . Therefore I judge it to be an excellent dissertation." Rather, "It's always the reverse."

Despite the foregoing, one participant noted that outstanding dissertations are "good philosophy"—"the arguments are well developed, they are pertinent, they are clear, they lead to a nice conclusion . . . they are original, they are significant, and [they are] well written." Another said that the "one thing" that distinguished the "very best" from the others is "creativity or imagination":

> The student is not simply going to the literature and figuring out mistakes that have been made and . . . coming up with criticisms. . . . There is a transformation of the material, coming up with ideas and a way of looking at a problem that has not been seen before. It is very hard to do at the dissertation-writing level. So that is fairly rare, but I've seen a few of them. That is what it takes to do really outstanding work in philosophy.

## TABLE 16.4.
### The Characteristics of Different Quality Dissertations in Philosophy

| Quality | Characteristics |
|---|---|
| **Outstanding** | Well written; the writing is stylistic, artistic, clear, and transparent; language is used appropriately and with accuracy and precision; is original and significant; shows vision, creativity, imagination, insight, and sophistication; well organized; very focused and to the point; has ingenuity, depth, fire, action, enthusiasm; the argument is brilliant, smashingly interesting, well developed; shows good judgment and philosophical sophistication; has an independent and authoritative voice; gives own views and argues for them; shows real mastery of complicated literature and sensitivity to the history of the tradition; each part is motivated by a significant function within the overall argument; is seamless and carefully argued; painstakingly sets up the problem; phrases or sets a problem in a new light; has a bright idea and attempts to work it out in various ways and trace its implications; has elaborate arguments or subarguments; does a fine-grained analysis; provides a new argument for an old issue; discovers a new problem; introduces a new category that illuminates the problem and generates new insights; reinterprets or does something interestingly different with other philosophers' thought that shows that it needs to be taken more seriously; handles lots of subtle distinctions and keeps them all going without getting confused; is synthetic or interdisciplinary; ties together a lot of material in a new way; student has thought about the objections and navigates through anticipated criticism; arguments lead to a nice conclusion; has lots of interesting future directions; alters the trajectory of the field; opens up a whole new field of inquiry |
| **Very good** | Short; well written; rigorous, competent, fully informed; interesting, but not compelling; has less originality and less long-range significance; has an interesting topic and some original insights and observations; exhibits mastery of the important literature on the topic; shows a good grasp of the problem and how to do philosophy; may have brilliant ideas, but they are inadequately worked out or not expressed cleanly and clearly; may have an idea that is well worked out and confidently put but is not groundbreaking; articulates and gives shape to a vague idea; raises a number of interesting issues but does not get much traction on them; takes a vision and carefully and methodically demonstrates that a point has validity and purpose; is argued well, but the argument has an obvious flaw; some avenues are not explored adequately; |

*(continues)*

## TABLE 16.4.
### Continued

| Quality | Characteristics |
|---|---|
| **Very good** | has a lot of free statement of the standard positions; could move the discussion forward in a useful way |
| **Acceptable** | Journeymanlike; a good local treatment of local issues; complete, good enough; not very interesting, original, or significant; exhibits immaturity of scholarship; not as clear as it should be; overly cautious; meandering, plodding; the student has sufficient grasp of the problem; shows a clear understanding of the issues and takes them a little further; the student has read a lot of the literature and can expound on it satisfactorily and make some points that have not already been made; strings together what others have said; is very much within the established pattern of argumentation but adds another wrinkle; is on the right track, but does not make a good case for it; the student can make a good case for his or her position even if it seems wrongheaded; lines or argument are not particularly imaginative, insightful, or likely to go anywhere; issues of equal importance are handled unevenly; makes a few distinctions of interest; fails to draw distinctions; has covered all the bases and has tried to respond to objections; presents some criticisms or defenses of the things being discussed that go beyond basic reporting; is constricted in its truthfulness; is not terribly persuasive or does not persuade; adds a little step to the conversation, but the contribution is not impressive |
| **Unacceptable** | Badly written; not interesting; rambling, sloppy, paltry, under-argued, full of gaps; argument lacks clarity and coherence; lacks understanding of how to treat a philosophical issue; the student is unable to master basic professional standards; the student has a good idea but cannot handle it; the student has not looked at enough aspects of the problem; the student does not really understand the issue or existing arguments; the student is incapable of getting a clear understanding of something he or she was confused about; the student does not attend to or is unable to get a handle on the literature on the subject; missed some literature; misrepresents other people's views; the student is unable to organize his or her approach to the subject adequately; chapters are not well done; puts forth really bad arguments; advances patently invalid arguments from premises that are false or unwarranted; overlooks things that make what the student says uninteresting; the student thinks that a certain objection is good when it is not; has weak objections; the student does not recognize that there are objections; the student is incapable of taking criticism into account; barely adds an iota to the discussion |

The quality of the interactions faculty have with students also helps to define outstanding:

> It's when we meet, it's productive and they're heading in the right direction, and they're gaining control of the material, and by the time they are done, I feel we are colleagues about this rather than me pulling them along and making sure we finally survive the oral so we can get the degree. . . . If you really feel like this written product is now the embodiment of a whole set of intellectual and independent thinking and intellectual skills, those are the ones I've gotten the most satisfaction out of.

When they read an outstanding dissertation, faculty say, "Ah!" It is the "aha, factor." "You knew it. It's so obvious. Look at that. I should have known." Outstanding dissertations also have a lot of the "virtues" of a good book in terms of balance and coverage. They are more or less publishable as they stand. According to one participant, "A dissertation like that shows me what I think a dissertation needs to show—that the person is ready to enter philosophical discussion at the highest level."

## Very Good

Very good philosophy dissertations show that the student "knows how to do this work." They show that the student has a good grasp of the problem, knows the literature, can argue and discuss various positions, and can make his or her own point. However, compared to the outstanding dissertation, the very good one is less original and less significant. Rather than having an "ambitious vision," the very good one takes "a kernel of that vision and really methodologically, carefully demonstrat[es] that a point has validity and purpose."

Very good dissertations were also characterized as "incomplete," as not being finished contributions. In some cases this is because the student is "under an external gun." The student "ha[s] to have the dissertation done." Thus the "director" will allow such a dissertation to "come forward" rather than say, "Well, you're not ready to defend yet." Had the student had more time he or she might have "had more to say" on "some of the questions that were left hanging."

Sometimes dissertations are very good rather than outstanding because students set their "sights very high, but they don't realize their aim as well as one would wish." However, these students show that "they can get in the ring with some pretty good people and hold their own." Sometimes the student's idea "just doesn't work." However, the student does a "masterful job" of "showing why it doesn't work" and, in the process, shows the ability to do philosophy and turn out "some good things in the way of scholarship." Indeed, very good dissertations are "useful." They point out something that is worth pointing out to people working in that field, but they do not start a "big discussion."

## Acceptable

Acceptable dissertations are correct and competent. They show a "sufficient" grasp of the problem. The treatment of the literature is "reasonably good." There is "some" criticism of the issues being discussed that goes beyond "just reporting." But they are not particularly imaginative, insightful, or "likely to go anywhere." They are "OK." "They're good enough." They are often "boring."

Many dissertations in the acceptable category are "usually things that probably shouldn't be accepted" but get accepted because of the context surrounding it and other "personal considerations." Sometimes the student already has a job and "you don't want to be the obstacle to their career." Sometimes the student is leaving philosophy or thinking about leaving, "so you might want to pass a dissertation." Sometimes "you really like the writer." The student is "someone you can't bear to say no to." One participant described one such student:

> It was a situation about a student who'd been in the program for a very long time. [The student] had been passed from advisor to advisor, from committee to committee over a number of years, and it got to be to the point where—I was on the last committee who worked on this—and . . . everybody felt very badly personally for this student. They knew this was an intelligent student, but every time we would make suggestions on how to fix something, the student would fix it and other things would get worse. The overall coherence of the thing would just get worse and worse and worse until we just said we've got to stop it here. . . . I am quite sure that no one on this committee would have, even for a moment, thought of accepting it unless they knew very well the candidate, knew the explanations worked, . . . had a strong sense of what came before the dissertation, and so forth.

Sometimes acceptable is the "best that some people are really up to" These students lack "intellectual power" and require "much hand-holding." They have to be pulled "every step along the way." What they produce on paper "meets the criteria," but faculty do not think these students could "turn around and do it again without you doing all that work with them again." Indeed,

> It is often the case that in the oral you still feel [that] if you hadn't worked with them so intensively this would never have happened. . . . Some are so not really clear about things you thought we were clear about. . . . You get text which is acceptable, but then, [in] the oral, they are still fumbling.

One participant commented, "I had to defend [one] yesterday." By that he meant, "I had to tell him what each chapter [was] about."

The philosophers also classified as acceptable dissertations that they thought were "flat out wrong" in the way they dealt with some figure or problem. However, because faculty are "more interested in whether the student is able to make a good case for a position," than whether "it agrees with me or agrees with the consensus in the literature," they will pass it. Indeed, one participant mentioned a dissertation that was passed with "disclaimers." The student "had a hard time persuading anyone that his theory was plausible, although no one was able to persuade him that it wasn't."

Finally, in discussing the acceptable dissertation, one focus group facilitator asked the participating faculty whether there were some dissertations they were "embarrassed to have passed." The participants responded, "Of course, yes." They let the facilitator in on a "dirty little secret" about things that affect faculty's decision to pass a dissertation—and that is "knowing what is going to happen afterwards."

> For example, if a student is going to go back to another country, say Nigeria, and has a teaching position there . . . and they won't be expected to publish . . . at least in the journals in the Western world, I think people . . . are more lax in a situation like that. That makes me feel a little embarrassed. I've got mixed feelings about it in terms of my integrity. . . . Yeah, standards are low, but, on the other hand, this is a person who is going back to a job at a certain place. Do I think he or she would be able to contribute to the literature? No. But is that really a big deal in their case?

## Unacceptable

Unacceptable is "not a real category." Unacceptable dissertations "typically don't get done" and (supposedly) "never come up for defense." The dissertation director is "not supposed to let it get to that stage." If the director does, "that means the director has failed."

Unacceptable dissertations were described as ones that "fall down in column three [development/defense of the thesis] and column four [recognition and response to possible objections]" of the matrix of components of a philosophy dissertation (see Table 1.2). Among other things, it's possible that an unacceptable dissertation "completely misrepresents the views of people, advances patently invalid arguments from premises that are false and unwarranted," about which one participant said, "Just one of those features is enough to screw up a dissertation." Another participant added, "When you combine them all, it's hell." A dissertation with these problems is typically

> advanced by a student who should never have been accepted into the program, who has been allowed to reach the dissertation stage through the cowardice of members of the faculty or the ability of the student to use the regulations of the university to his or her advantage. . . . It reaches the point where one is concerned about potential litigation if you don't get rid of this student. . . . These are students who, through the cowardice of the department or the bureaucratic nature of the university, have been enabled to remain in the program.

One member of this focus group commented, "We knew that they couldn't write a dissertation in their first semester." These remarks raise the questions about why faculty give students who do poor quality work *As* in the first place and why they passively "hope they will go away," rather than proactively counseling them out when they first recognize their inadequacies.

A participant in another focus group talked about the "signs of unacceptability" in students' work and behavior. These students

> don't seem to be able to get sufficiently sophisticated to have a good take on the subject, to be able to handle the other literature on the subject, to be able even to organize their approach to the subject adequately. They have a big idea that they can't handle. Or they seem to be incapable of taking criticism into account, so that they aren't getting any better at what they are doing with it. You sit there and talk to them for a couple of hours

about a draft. They go back and produce another draft that has all the faults of the first draft on the very topic. After a while you say, "This isn't working." . . . It is an inability to get their engagement with their topic or their thinking up to the level of interest and sophistication that I would regard as necessary for me to be prepared to go through with the dissertation on that topic.

Another participant in a different focus group characterized students who write unacceptable dissertations as ones who are "unable to master basic professional standards in the area."

A few of the focus group faculty indicated that they have "wanted to vote against passage" of a dissertation but have made "a hard decision to decide to go ahead and sign that piece of paper anyhow." They have "not been happy signing the thing" but have done so because as one participant said, "I'm so peripheral to the person's work that I feel I shouldn't stand in the way," or because (the "dirty little secret") the students are "going to be teaching and never publishing in their whole life." Their decisions are "tailor[ed] a little bit to the individual." "Almost like making excuses sometimes."

One participant was on a committee where the oral defense was "aborted."

I guess the director had not really seen what was going to be submitted until it was too late to abort. Actually the candidate was living in another state and arrived to defend something that was just very gappy, very sloppy. He thought he could just fill in all these references and fill in some arguments that just had lots of ellipses. When he came in, the committee told him he was not ready to defend the dissertation. He said, "You've got to be kidding, right?" The committee told him they weren't kidding. . . . He eventually wrote a dissertation that was accepted.

Another participant talked about committees he had been on where one or two members refused to approve the dissertation.

What happened was that the committee got reformulated and we were off it. . . . The thesis was revised and was accepted at that point. . . . But it's almost impossible to flunk a student at the oral Ph.D. exam. It's much better to resign from the committee earlier if you see that coming.

Finally, one participant summed up the situation in which an unacceptable dissertation is allowed to advance. He said, "We know what a bad defense is. It's false premises."

## The Components of a Philosophy Dissertation

The philosophy faculty had mixed feelings about the matrix of components of the dissertation (see Table 1.2), and one focus group did not discuss it. In general, the philosophers agreed that the categories were "reasonable," that they were "sound in terms of functions that dissertations have to meet." Some noted that there are many different ways of doing a dissertation, that philosophy dissertations are not "structured like this," and that the tasks that the components describe do not all necessarily get done in individual sections. The philosophers were more troubled by the "criteria" (the quality levels), and some noted that "judgments that are made are often more holistic than [the matrix] implies." Participants in one focus group felt there should be a category between "not very good" (acceptable) and "very good," because most of the dissertations they see are "OK to good." One participant in another focus group said that "in one sense our criteria are minimally acceptable performance in all these categories and probably better than minimally acceptable in some." Another participant wanted to "just say 'less of the same' for the second [very good], and 'even less' for the third [acceptable], and 'almost none' for the fourth [unacceptable/failing]." The philosophers also felt that things like structure and clear writing were missing from the matrix. Below we explore the characteristics of the components of a philosophy dissertation (see Table 16.A in the appendix to this chapter) and what the faculty said about them.

### Introduction/Statement and Clarification of the Problem

Although there was some minor disagreement among the philosophers as to whether a philosophy dissertation has to have an introduction, they agreed that a dissertation has to state the general problem, specify the points that are going to be advanced, and position the dissertation in relation to other work that has been done on the topic. Ideally the introduction/statement and clarification of the problem (hereafter "introduction") should be set up in a way that would be clear even to a nonspecialist, provide some indication of the strategy that is going to be used, and some guidance as to the structure of what is to come. "The more coherent and clear a person can be about that, the more likely it's going to be a successful dissertation." One participant noted that he has been at "oral exams where it still isn't made clear what the problem is."

Faculty in more than one focus group said that "clarity is not enough" to make an introduction outstanding or even very good. To be outstanding, the introduction has to show that the problem is compelling, that something "really motivates the problem." It should state "why it's important in this world right now," though the motivation could be "purely intellectual" rather than "real world." The problem should be laid out in an original, imaginative, and interesting way. As one participant said, "It's outstanding when it's fun to read. It's really well written. It's very clear, and it, just even by stating what the problem is, is already interesting."

A very good introduction is interesting to those working in the field. It is "not unpleasant to read," but it "maybe isn't, 'Gee, that's really different. I haven't thought about that or looked at it that way before.'" Unacceptable is when the student thinks there is a problem "when there isn't one." The student "really doesn't get it," or "They don't know what they're talking about."

## *Demonstration of Knowledge of the Literature*

Demonstration of knowledge of the literature is "not just showing off a knowledge of the literature," it is knowing the relevant literature and picking "the things that are appropriate for what is really at stake in your dissertation," because "there is no such thing as just covering all of it." Demonstrating knowledge of the literature involves dealing with the selected works in a way that shows that "you understand them" and can "do something [with them] either critically or by way of appropriating lines of argument."

Outstanding literature reviews show a "sweeping grasp" of the relevant literature. They include things that "might not be obviously relevant at first, but which the student has tracked down on his or her own and seen as potentially relevant, and grabbed, understood, and effectively integrated into the work" in an original and imaginative way. Indeed, the literature is incorporated into the argument throughout the entire discussion and is used to "really move the field forward." When they read an outstanding discussion of the literature, the committee members feel they "learned something about the literature."

In their discussion of outstanding, the philosophers also stated what outstanding is not. Outstanding is not "overtaking the terminology of each author and repeating how the authors' view is within their own terminology without showing how they're all talking about the same thing." "It isn't book[ish] or quirkish. There isn't a section of 'Here's what others say. Here's what I say.'"

Acceptable is when students try to talk about everything in the literature on their topic, discuss things that are not worth talking about, fail to address relevant parts of the literature, or when they do not "quite get the most interesting insight or perspective on why that particular part of the literature is relevant." In this latter instance, faculty want to say, "Yeah, but, if you really thought harder about what Clark is up to. . . . Yeah, some people take it this way, but there are other more interesting interpretations of what he's up to and you probably ought to have really looked at those." By contrast, unacceptable is when students "haven't done enough background reading to know what out of the background reading to select. . . . that's directly relevant to the dissertation." It is also when students do not understand the literature or handle it properly.

### Development/Defense of the Thesis(es)

The development and defense of the thesis involves presenting and developing the argument, showing how it differs from the standard view, and stating what is new about it. It also involves anticipating the problems the argument might spark "in the minds of those who pay attention to these matters," and dealing with those objections.

Students who do an extraordinary job of developing and defending their thesis "have seen all the problems and they've got a solution or a plausible solution to every one of them." Indeed, when reading such a dissertation, faculty think up objections, and then they "turn the page and there's the objection and there's a really good answer to it." In outstanding dissertations, the thesis may initially seem implausible, but the student demonstrates "that it really is right."

Very good ones are not quite as clear and leave a "couple of questions" for the committee. Students who write acceptable ones "have a clear plan." Faculty can "see where they're going" and what the arguments are supposed to be. However, the arguments are less convincing than faculty would like them to be or students fail to take certain objections into account. In the case of the unacceptable development and defense of the thesis, one participant said, "It wouldn't just be a poor philosophy dissertation, it wouldn't be a philosophy dissertation."

### Recognition and Response to Possible Objections

Recognition and response to possible objections is part of the defense of the thesis. It involves anticipating and raising real or theoretical objections to arguments against the thesis and showing how and why they misconstrue the problem, make false assumptions, or other philosophical moves that one can legitimately raise questions about.

A student who does an outstanding job of recognizing and responding to possible objections is a "worthy adversary." The student not only raises and responds to every objection the reader can think of, the student also raises some that "you never even would have thought of yourself and . . . answers those as well." The arguments are valid, sound, and cannot be overcome easily.

The very good recognition and response to possible objections is not quite as clear and "doesn't progress with the same kind of clarity and rigor." Students may say something that "seems . . . like it's a response, but you're not convinced that they really answered the objection." They may have "nailed" the first one, but they do not necessarily nail all the others.

Students whose recognition and response to possible objections are unacceptable "don't really consider objections or answers to them." They "can't think in any way except their own way and can't imagine anybody disagreeing with them" because their position is "so right." "If you disagree with them, you are an idiot."

### Conclusion

The conclusion or conclusions of a philosophy dissertation may be stated in the last chapter or they may be incorporated along the way in the main body of the dissertation. While some philosophers said that the conclusion should "sum up what you have done" and "what it means," others noted that they "don't care that much about it." "Rarely" is the student required or expected to do "anymore than state what he or she has accomplished." Indeed, a conclusion can be as simple as "none of these things work and I think we understand a little better now why." Little was said about any of the quality levels that is not contained in Table 16.A.

## Notes

1. For information on the source of these data, see chapter 1, note 5.

2. The totals and averages are based on the 31 focus group participants who provided data.

# Appendix

## TABLE 16.A.

### The Components of a Philosophy Dissertation and Their Characteristics at Different Quality Levels

| Components | Quality levels | | | |
|---|---|---|---|---|
| | Outstanding | Very good | Acceptable | Unacceptable |
| **Introduction/ statement and clarification of the problem** | Clear, crisp, focused, interesting; well written and well organized; motivates the problem; explains and clarifies the problem very effectively; lays the problem out quickly in an original, interesting, and imaginative way; shows that it is compelling; sums up a grand, important position in couchable terms; positions the dissertation in relation to other work that has been done on the topic; specifies what points are going to be advanced; provides an indication of the strategy; talks about choices and philosophical methods and why they are going to be employed; provides guidance on the structure of what is to come; discusses how the different parts of the dissertation contribute to the treatment of the problem; provides a complete answer to the "So what?" question | Comprehensive but not exhaustive; reasonably succinct; reasonably well written; very clear; provides a novel and original statement of the problem; does a good job of laying out the problem; covers all the bases; provides a good sense of where it is going; has a good road map of the problem space and of the major components | Provides an off-the-shelf characterization of an established, usually small problem; is a little turgid; is unable to clearly distinguish between a couple of different problems; gives the reader a sense of where it is going; shows appreciation for the issues; makes a small point that is vague or imprecise | Not clear or succinct; question is ambiguous or not understandable; misunderstands or misrepresents the problem; does not clarify the problem |

*(continues)*

**TABLE 16.A.**
Continued

| Components | Quality levels | | | |
| --- | --- | --- | --- | --- |
| | Outstanding | Very good | Acceptable | Unacceptable |
| **Demonstration of knowledge of the literature** | Clear, crisp, lucid; original, imaginative, and thorough coverage and review of the literature; runs through the entire dissertation; shows sweeping grasp of the literature, including things that might not be obviously relevant at first; shows good judgment; is not comprehensive, rather identifies the most appropriate, interesting, and important works, critics, and points; identifies conceptual categories and uses them to classify the literature; pulls things together; sees relationships between two philosophers or works; knows when distinctions matter, when not to go after an idea, and when to back up and fill in; anticipates objections and deals with them effectively; uses the literature to advance the field | Comprehensive but not exhaustive; reasonably succinct; laid out for easy comprehension; literature is selected wisely and judiciously; shows command of most of the relevant literature; may have missed an important argument in an article; may not have taken into account other things that people have been saying | Workmanlike; lacks original insight; reads and basically understands the right texts; omits some important literature; includes literature that is not particularly interesting or worthwhile; does not quite get the most interesting insight or perspective on a particular part of the relevant literature; treats the literature uncharitably; has problems with arguments and interpretations throughout; critiques are easy or pointless | Student reads the right literature but does not understand it very well; does not understand or address something important; gets the literature wrong; ignores some literatures; deliberately misinterprets some literature; provides caricature versions of important philosophers or texts; does not call upon primary sources completely or adequately; relies on secondary sources |

| | Quality levels | | | |
|---|---|---|---|---|
| **Components** | **Outstanding** | **Very good** | **Acceptable** | **Unacceptable** |
| **Development/ defense of the thesis(es)** | Very well done; has a developed, mature, distinct voice and point of view; student has arrived at his or her own positions; develops the arguments in defense of the thesis; presents effective, convincing arguments that have not been made before; shows where student's position differs from the standard and what is new; makes interesting points; demonstrates that seemingly implausible points are plausible; presents a serious new argument as a dialectic | Not quite as clear; the whole structure does not progress with the same kind of clarity, rigor, and fullness | Well developed but not interesting; does not make all the arguments needed to deal with the problem effectively; arguments are less convincing; provides some arguments for the thesis and then does not consider some of the plausible objections | Unclear; not well articulated; has mistakes in logic; is not clear what is being argued or how the pieces fit together; makes claims that are not particularly plausible and does not provide adequate support for them; leaves claims hanging; examples are not relevant; the conclusion does not follow from the argument |

*(continues)*

**TABLE 16.A.**
Continued

| Components | Quality levels | | | |
| --- | --- | --- | --- | --- |
| | Outstanding | Very good | Acceptable | Unacceptable |
| **Recognition and response to possible objections** | Exhibits a degree of sophistication in dealing with particular objections and in understanding what it is to object and respond appropriately; shows a good sense of how to weigh objections and responses; raises potential objections, responds to them and sets parameters for what is reasonable to consider; takes on really big objections and gives plausible responses to them; is alert to the objections in the literature and makes them stronger; impressively answers seemingly unanswerable objections; turns up something deep and important | Gets most of the objections; has something reasonable to say about most of them; says something that balances the scales against the objection | Workmanlike; misses some objections that the student should have seen; does not fully answer the objections; answers are not convincing | Student is unaware of obvious objections; does not see potential objections; does not understand the objections; response to objections raises additional objections; student thinks he or she has answered an objection but has not; has nothing to say about objections; student cannot see what another position would argue or what anyone could possibly say against his or her position; student cannot imagine anyone disagreeing with him or her |

| Components | Quality levels | | | |
|---|---|---|---|---|
| | Outstanding | Very good | Acceptable | Unacceptable |
| **Conclusion** | Sums up what has been done and what it means; proves the point; arrives at some interesting, novel, and important conclusions; the conclusions are clear; identifies what has been accomplished or settled and what has not been; identifies the contribution; identifies questions that need to be raised; discusses next steps; opens up a whole new set of issues | Interesting, but is not quite as interesting or important; well stated; well developed, shows how it relates to the argument; is not going to change the literature or affect the field significantly | Mildly interesting; follows from the argument; restates what has been accomplished, but is a little muddy; does not place the summary into a larger context or meaning; does not identify the next steps | Uninteresting; very short; not well done or well articulated; just a summary; claims it accomplished all kinds of things it did not |

## List of Participating Universities, Deans, Coordinators, and Facilitators

**Duke University**
Lewis Siegel, *dean*
Leigh de Neef, *coordinator*
Douglas James, *facilitator*

**Michigan State University**
Karen Klomparens, *dean*
Shelby Berkowitz, *coordinator and facilitator*

**Northwestern University**
Jan Allen, *associate dean*
Bernhard Streitwieser, *lead coordinator and facilitator*
Melissa Quinby, *coordinator and facilitator*

**State University of New York at Stony Brook**
Lawrence Martin, *dean*
Rita Nolan, *coordinator*
Matthew DeTemple, *facilitator*

**Syracuse University**
John Mercer, *dean*
Stacey Lane Tice, *coordinator and facilitator*

**University of Colorado**
Carol B. Lynch, *dean*
Candice L. Miller, *coordinator*
Thomas A. Cyr, *facilitator*

**University of Illinois**
Richard Wheeler, *dean*
Karen Carney, *coordinator*
John C. Ory, *facilitator*

**University of Kansas**
Diana B. Carlin, *dean*
Lisa Wolf-Wendel, *coordinator and lead facilitator*
Susan B. Twombly, *facilitator*

**University of Southern California**
Joseph Hellige, *dean*
Dean Campbell, *coordinator and facilitator*

## Details on the Study's Methodology

During the summer and early fall of 2003, deans of graduate schools at Doctoral/Research Universities-Extensive that awarded the Ph.D. in 10 targeted departments (*sciences*: biology, electrical and computer engineering, physics/physics and astronomy, mathematics; *social sciences*: economics, psychology, sociology; *humanities*: English, history, philosophy) were invited to participate in the study until a sample of 10 relatively diverse universities was achieved. The deans were asked to ensure the commitment and participation of the 10 selected departments and hire someone experienced in conducting focus groups to serve as a facilitator. The facilitators were paid with grant funds. Once the facilitators were identified, they were sent electronic copies of all the background materials needed to understand and implement the study.[1] Each facilitator participated in about a one-hour-long telephone training session. Some universities appointed a coordinator, usually an administrator, to assist the facilitator in scheduling and coordinating, and sometimes conducting, the focus group sessions.

The deans were provided with tailored E-mails that introduced the study and the university's facilitator to the participating department chairs and requested their cooperation. Depending on the university, the dean, the coordinator, or the facilitator asked the department chairs to identify four to six high-Ph.D.-productive faculty, that is, faculty who had advised many doctoral students and had served on many dissertation committees. The facilitator or the coordinator invited these faculty to participate in a two-hour-long, tape-recorded focus group and scheduled a time and place for the focus group meeting.

Once the focus group was scheduled, the facilitator sent the faculty a confirmatory E-mail and requested the following background information: how many years they had been a faculty member; how many dissertations they had advised; and how many dissertations committees they had sat on, both inside and outside the department. (See Table 1.3 for summary information.)

One to three days before the focus group session, the facilitator or co-ordinator sent each participating faculty member a reminder along with a discipline-specific version of the focus group protocol or "worksheet." The protocol was sent to the faculty in advance as a way of priming their thoughts about the issues, and, hopefully, stimulating a deeper, more interesting and more focused discussion of them. The faculty were asked to think about the issues and jot down their thoughts.

At each focus group session, the facilitator provided an overview of the purpose of the focus group, obtained the faculty's informed consent, and implemented the protocol (below), and passed out copies of that discipline's matrix (see Table 1.2 for a matrix that lists the components faculty in each discipline were asked to discuss). Each focus group session was tape-recorded. Worksheets with comments that were brought to the focus group were collected at the end of the focus group session.

### Protocol

#### *Original and Significant Contribution*

The most common and sometimes only requirement departments and universities have for the award of the Ph.D. is that the dissertation makes an original and/or significant contribution.

1. Tell me what it means to make an original contribution in _____ *(field)?* What does it look like?

2. Tell me what it means to make a significant contribution in _____ *(field)?* What does it look like?

#### *The Dissertation*

Now I'd like to talk about the dissertation.

3. What is the purpose of the dissertation?

4. I'd like you to think about the most outstanding dissertation or dissertations you have read. Tell me what made those dissertations so outstanding. What are the characteristics of an outstanding dissertation?

5. Now think about a dissertation that was very good but not outstanding. What made it very good and what is the difference between a very good and an outstanding dissertation?

6. Now think about a dissertation that was acceptable but not very good.

What made it acceptable and what is the difference between an acceptable and a very good dissertation?

7. Now think about a dissertation that was unacceptable or that you didn't pass. What made it unacceptable and what is the difference between an unacceptable and acceptable dissertation?

### The Components of a Dissertation

8. Now I'd like to repeat this exercise focusing on the major components of a dissertation. I have a matrix that will help guide our discussion. (Pass out the matrix.)

(Go down each column): What are the characteristics of a _____ (*quality*) _____ (*component*)?

The matrix (Table 1.2) contains the essential components of a dissertation and was designed to best match the structure or intellectual tasks required of the dissertation in the different disciplines. The essential components initially derived from my experiences as a doctoral student in three different disciplines (psychology, history of science, and sociology), my familiarity with the basic requirements of science and social science dissertations, and my sense that all dissertations had introductions/problem statements, included some sort of literature review, were set within a theoretical context, had some sort of methodology for approaching and analyzing the data or material, and had a conclusion. The study was already under way when one of the facilitators told me about a 1997 Council of Graduate Schools (CGS) publication, *The Role and Nature of the Doctoral Dissertation: A Policy Statement*. This publication describes a 1990 CGS study that was conducted in 50 universities in the United States and Canada on why universities require the dissertation and what it should be. The report recommends that the dissertation, regardless of field, should do five things that correspond closely with the components of a dissertation identified for this study. They are:

- reveal the student's ability to analyze, interpret, and synthesize information
- demonstrate the student's knowledge of the literature relating to the project or at least acknowledge prior scholarship on which the dissertation is built

- describe the methods and procedures used
- present results in a sequential and logical manner
- display the student's ability to discuss fully and coherently the meaning of the results. In the sciences the work must be described in sufficient detail to permit an independent investigator to replicate the results.

As mentioned in chapter 1, the protocol was initially implemented in seven departments at two universities (referred to as Public University and Private University) as part of another study. The matrix was dropped because of time constraints. However, based on initial attempts to implement it, it became clear that the original structure (introduction, literature review, theory, methods, analysis/results, discussion/conclusion) would not work for mathematics and the humanities disciplines. Thus, the structure for the mathematics and humanities matrices used in this study were developed in consultation with the director of graduate studies or a high-Ph.D.-productive faculty member in those disciplines at the University of Maryland, and then "confirmed" with the director of graduate studies at Michigan State University via the dean of the graduate school. Initial attempts to implement the matrix also indicated that faculty were likely to raise challenges to it. This was discussed with this study's facilitators during the telephone training. In addition, because it was unclear how long it would take focus groups to work though the protocol and the matrix, facilitators were told that if they had trouble implementing the matrix they should focus on "outstanding"—the level most students are aiming for, and "acceptable"—the level no graduate student wants to fall below.

## The Sample and the Data

The study was ultimately implemented in 74 departments in nine universities[2] (see chapter 1, note 4, or Appendix A for a list of universities) between October 2003 and March 2004. Two hundred and seventy-six (276) faculty participated in the focus group sessions, which typically lasted roughly 90 minutes. Most focus groups had three or four participants, a few ran with only two, and one had eight. As mentioned above and in chapter 1, the faculty were asked to provide background data on their years of service and experience with dissertations both as an advisor and as a committee member (see Table 1.3).

With very few exceptions, all focus groups covered each protocol item. However, not every focus group addressed each cell in its discipline's matrix, and a few did not address the matrix at all. The degree to which the matrix was covered appears to be a function of time constraints, faculty resistance to the matrix, and the facilitator's confidence in implementing it. Some facilitators were hesitant about it, others approached it matter-of-factly and got through all or most cells with most focus groups. Thus, although the data presented for the protocol items come from almost every focus group in each discipline, the data presented for most matrix cells come from one to a few focus groups in that discipline.

## Data Handling and Analysis

The facilitators sent the focus group tapes directly to a business services company for transcription.[3] When the tapes were transcribed, no effort was made to link participants individually with their responses. Thus although each participant's utterances were recorded separately as "R" (for respondent) and are presented in the text as "Participant," the identity of the speaker is not recoverable from the transcript, neither in most cases is the speaker's gender. (Data on participants' gender and race/ethnicity were not collected.) Consequently, given the national demographics of senior faculty, and my experience conducting focus groups with senior, high-Ph.D.-productive faculty, the overwhelming majority of whom were male, the participants have been referred to as "he," unless I listened to that passage and heard a female voice, there is evidence in the transcript that the respondent is female or the respondent was referred to by name by another participant. The facilitator's (interviewer's) questions and comments were linked to the interviewer. In most instances where a focus group dialogue is presented in the text, the speakers are referred to as Participant 1, Participant 2, and so on.

As noted in chapter 1, transcripts of the focus group discussions were edited so that all potentially identifying information, such as names, locations, dates, specialty areas, and the like, was altered, taken to a higher level of generality, or deleted entirely. For readability, common but distracting components of speech such as "ah," "um," "you know," "I mean," "I think," and "sort of" were deleted from the quotations that appear in the text unless they were particularly meaningful. False sentence starts were also frequently deleted, as was the word "and" when it linked sentences, as it often does in spoken language. In most instances, ellipses (. . .) are not used to indicate these deletions. However, discrepancies in grammar such as subject/pronoun disagreement ("he" followed by "they") were not corrected.

The transcripts were coded by protocol item and matrix cell, as well as for critical comments about the matrix itself, general comments about the project or focus group, comments related to advising, and comments about variability among graduate students. General remarks about the dissertation as a whole or a component often provided useful contextual information and were coded to the relevant "outstanding" category so they would appear early in the analysis of that component.

It should be noted that because spoken language is often imprecise and because discussions tend to digress and jump around, the coding was not always straightforward and judgments had to be made based on where the focus group was or seemed to be in the protocol and/or the context surrounding the response. For instance, the word "good" was variously used to mean "outstanding," "very good," and "acceptable." Similarly, "excellent" could mean "outstanding" or "very good." Sometimes faculty jumped from component to component or quality to quality in their response to an item; consequently it was not always clear what component and what quality level was being discussed.

Also as noted in chapter 1, the coded transcripts were entered into N6 (QSR, 2002), a qualitative data analysis software program, by discipline. Each discipline's data were then sorted by protocol item and matrix cell, and indexed to corresponding nodes. After each node report was printed, each discipline's data were further reduced through a four-stage winnowing process. In stage one, each node report was read and relevant information was highlighted. The highlighted information was then cut and pasted into summary tables by university (see Table B.1), though no overall summary was written. In stage two, each initial summary table was read and characteristics for that item were extracted and placed in a reduced summary table identical to Table B.1. In stage three, the characteristics were synthesized across universities into a summary. Finally, in stage four, characteristics that appeared in many of the discipline-based summary tables were extracted and synthesized into an overall summary for that item. Characteristics that were idiosyncratic to a discipline were noted.

**TABLE B.1.**
**Shell for Analyzing the Data**

| Discipline: | | | | |
|---|---|---|---|---|
| Component: | | | | |
| Quality: | | | | |
| University A | University B | University C | University D | University E |
|  |  |  |  |  |
| University F | University G | University H | University I | Summary |
|  |  |  |  |  |

The summaries in the tables typically start with general indeterminate qualities, followed by technical qualities, followed by expected impact. The technical qualities were ordered as best as possible by their generally expected sequential appearance in the dissertation. For "original" and "significant," they were ordered as best as possible by degree of originality or significance. The summaries for "purpose" were ordered by "to train," "to learn," "to demonstrate," "to show," by other "to" objectives, and then by concrete statements of what a dissertation is.

The disciplinary summary tables were sent back to each participating university. The dean was asked to send each discipline's summary tables, along with a note from me, to the focus group participants. The note from me clarified the purpose of the study and what the results would be used for (there was some confusion on this in some focus groups). Participants were asked to review and comment on their discipline's results, and provide additional characteristics for thin or empty cells.

Six faculty sent comments or minor edits to the tables directly to me, though none provided additional characteristics for thin or empty cells. The coordinators at two universities sent E-mails saying that the few faculty who responded to them indicated the tables were fine and represented their discussions.

Finally, while the focus group faculty were reviewing the preliminary tables, my graduate research assistant, Jeannie Brown Leonard, conducted focus groups with graduate students who were at the dissertation stage of their education in eight of the disciplines in this study at a Doctoral/Research University—Extensive. The purpose of these focus groups was to add the graduate student's perspective. The participating students were asked questions about their understanding of the dissertation and its evaluation, and about their concerns about their dissertation and how it would be judged. They were then told about this study and asked to read through the performance expectations that had been created for their discipline and give their reactions. They were probed about whether they found the expectations helpful and whether they thought having such expectations would help them with their dissertations and make them less concerned about how their dissertation would be judged by their committees. This study's results can be found in Brown Leonard (2006).

## Notes

1. These materials include the grant proposal, a checklist of tasks, an invitee tracking sheet, a department tracking sheet, a draft E-mail to department chairs, a draft faculty invitation letter, a draft nonresponse follow-up, a confirmation and request for background information E-mail, a background information data sheet, a reminder E-mail, discipline-specific worksheets, discipline-specific protocols, and draft thank-you E-mails.

2. One university was dismissed for failing to take the actions necessary to implement the project in a timely fashion.

3. Regrettably, many of the tapes were poorly transcribed. Although my research assistant and I I listened to quite a few tapes and corrected many passages in this volume, it was not possible to go back and review and correct every direct quote in this book. I am, however, confident that the essential meanings of the quotes are correct, even if the exact words are not.

# REFERENCES

Adams, G. B., & White, J. D. (1994). Dissertation research in public administration and cognate fields: An assessment of methods and quality. *Public Administration Review, 54*(6), 565–576.

Amabile, T. M. (1988). A model of creativity and innovation in organizations. *Research in Organizational Behavior, 10*, 123–167.

Amabile, T. M. (1996). *Creativity in context.* Boulder, CO: Westview Press.

American Productivity and Quality Center. (1998). *Assessing learning outcomes.* Houston, TX: Author.

American Sociological Association. (2003). *How does your department compare? A peer analysis from the 2000–2001 survey of baccalaureate and graduate programs in sociology.* Washington, DC: Author.

Anderson, L. (2002. April). *The underlying structure of examiners' reports.* Paper presented at the American Education Research Association Conference, New Orleans, LA.

Association of American Universities. (1998). *Committee on Graduate Education report and recommendations.* Washington, DC: Author.

Austin, A. (2002, November). *Assessing doctoral student's progress along developmental dimensions.* Paper presented at the annual meeting of the Association for the Study of Higher Education, Sacramento, CA. Retrieved May 20, 2005, from www.carnegiefoundation.org/CID/ashe?austin.pdf

Bargar, R. R., & Duncan, J. K. (1982). Cultivating creative endeavor in doctoral research. *Journal of Higher Education, 52*(1), 1–31.

Becher, T. (1989). *Academic tribes and territories: Intellectual enquiry and the cultures of disciplines.* Bristol, PA: Open University Press.

Becher, T., & Trowler, P. R. (2001). *Academic tribes and territories: Intellectual enquiry and the cultures of disciplines* (2nd ed.). Philadelphia: Open University Press.

Bender, T., Katz, P. M., Palmer, C., and the Committee on Graduate Education of the American Historical Association. (2004). *The education of historians for the twenty-first century.* Chicago: University of Illinois Press.

Benkin, E. M. (1984). *Where have all the doctoral students gone? A study of doctoral student attrition at UCLA.* Unpublished doctoral dissertation, University of California, Los Angeles.

Berelson, B. (1960). *Graduate education in the United States.* New York: McGraw-Hill.

Biglan, A. (1973a). The characteristics of subject matter in different academic areas. *Journal of Applied Psychology, 57*(3), 195–203.

Biglan, A. (1973b). Relationships between subject matter characteristics and the structure and output of university departments. *Journal of Applied Psychology, 57*(3), 204–218.

Boote, D. N., & Beile, P. (2004, April). *The quality of dissertation literature reviews: A missing link research preparation.* Paper presented at the annual meeting of the American Educational Research Association, San Diego, CA.

Boote, D. N., & Beile, P. M. (2005). Scholars before researchers: On the centrality of the dissertation literature review in research preparation. *Educational Researcher, 34*(6), 3–15.

Borkwoski, N. A. (2006). Changing our thinking about assessment at the doctoral level. In P. L. Maki & N. Borkowski (Eds.), *The assessment of doctoral education: Emerging criteria and new models for improving outcomes* (pp. 11–51). Sterling, VA: Stylus.

Bourke, S. (2002, April). *Links between PhD candidate background, aspects of candidature, examiner information, and the examiner reports.* Paper presented at the American Education Research Association Conference, New Orleans, LA.

Bowen, C. C. (1971). The historical context of the university press in America. *Scholarly Publishing, 2,* 329–349.

Bowen, W. G., & Rudenstine, N. L. (1992). *In pursuit of the Ph.D.* Princeton, NJ: Princeton University Press.

Brown Leonard, J. (2006). Doctoral students' perspectives on the dissertation. In P. L. Maki & N. Borkowski (Eds.), *The assessment of doctoral education: Emerging criteria and new models for improving outcomes* (pp. 197–214 ). Sterling, VA: Stylus.

Bruce, C. (1994). Research students' early experiences of the dissertation literature review. *Studies in Higher Education, 19*(2), 217–229.

Bruce, C. (2001). Interpreting the scope of their literature reviews: Significant differences in research students' concerns. *New World Library, 102*(1163/1164), 158–165.

Choy, S. P., & Cataldi, E. F. (2006). *Student financing of graduate and first-professional education, 2003–04* (NCES 2006-185). U.S. Department of Education. Washington, DC: National Center for Education Statistics. Retrieved May 31, 2006, from http://nces.ed.gov/pubs2006/2006185a.pdf

Committee on Science, Engineering, and Public Policy. (1995). *Reshaping the graduate education of scientists and engineers.* Washington, DC: National Academy Press.

Committee on Science, Engineering, and Public Policy. (2000). *Enhancing the postdoctoral experience for scientists and engineers.* Washington, DC: National Academy Press.

Council of Graduate Schools. (1997). *The role and nature of the doctoral dissertation: A policy statement.* Washington, DC: Author.

Council of Graduate Schools. (2004). *The doctor of philosophy degree: A policy statement.* Washington, DC: Author.

Cude, W. (2001). *The Ph.D. trap revisited.* Toronto, Ontario, Canada: Dundurn Group.

Cyr, T., & Muth, R. (2006). Portfolios in doctoral education. In P. L. Maki & N. Borkowski (Eds.), *The assessment of doctoral education: Emerging criteria and new models for improving outcomes* (pp. 215–237 ). Sterling, VA: Stylus.

Delamont, S., Atkinson, P., & Parry, O. (2002). *The doctoral experience: Success and failure in graduate school.* London: Falmer Press.

Geiger, R. L. (1986). *To advance knowledge: The growth of American research universities, 1900–1940.* New York: Oxford University Press.

Geiger, R. L. (1993). *Research and relevant knowledge: American research universities since World War II.* New York: Oxford University Press.

Golde, C. M., & Dore, T. M. (2001). *At cross purposes: What the experiences of today's doctoral students reveal about doctoral education.* Philadelphia, PA: The Pew Charitable Trusts.

Golde, C. M., Jones, L., Conklin Bueschel, A., & Walker, G. E. (2006). In P. L. Maki & N. Borkowski (Eds.), *The assessment of doctoral education: Emerging criteria and new models for improving outcomes* (pp. 53–82). Sterling, VA: Stylus.

Golde, C. M., Walker, G. E., & Associates. (2006). *Envisioning the future of doctoral education: Preparing stewards of the discipline. Carnegie essays on the doctorate.* San Francisco: Jossey-Bass.

Goodchild, L. F., & Miller, M. M. (1997). The American doctorate and dissertation: Six developmental stages. In L. F. Goodchild, K. E. Green, E. L. Katz, & R. C. Kluever (Eds.), *Rethinking the dissertation process: Tackling personal and institutional obstacles. New Directions for Higher Education, No. 99, 25*(3), 17–32. San Francisco: Jossey-Bass.

Hart, C. (1999). *Doing a literature review: Releasing the social science research imagination.* Thousand Oaks, CA: Sage.

Hill, S. T., Hoffer, T. B., & Golladay, M. J. (2004). *Plans for postdoctoral research appointments among recent U.S. doctorate recipients* (NSF 04-308). Arlington, VA: National Science Foundation.

Holbrook, A. (2002a, April). *Examining the quality of doctoral research.* Symposium presented at the American Education Research Association Conference, New Orleans, LA.

Holbrook, A. (2002b, April). *How examiners of doctoral theses utilize the written report.* Paper presented at the American Education Research Association Conference, New Orleans, LA.

Holbrook, A., & Bourke, S. (2002, April). *PhD assessment: Design of the study, qualities of examiner reports and candidature information.* Paper presented at the American Education Research Association Conference, New Orleans, LA.

Huba, M. E., & Freed, J. E. (2000). *Learner-centered assessment on college campuses: Shifting the focus from teaching to learning.* Boston: Allyn & Bacon.

Huba, M. E., Schuh, J., & Shelly, M. (2006). Recasting doctoral education: Applying principles of authentic assessment to the preliminary examination. In P. L. Maki & N. Borkowski (Eds.), *The assessment of doctoral education: Emerging criteria and new models for improving outcomes* (pp. 239–272 ). Sterling, VA: Stylus.

Ibarra, R. A. (2001). *Beyond affirmative action: Reframing the context of higher education.* Madison: University of Wisconsin Press.

Isaac, P. D., Quinlan, S. V., & Walker, M. M. (1992). Faculty perceptions of the doctoral dissertation. *Journal of Higher Education, 63*(3), 241–268.

Jaschik, S. (2005, December). Radical change for tenure. *Inside Higher Ed.* Retrieved December 30, 2005, from http://insiderhighered.com/news/2005/12/30/tenure.

Johnston, S. (1997). Examining the examiners: An analysis of examiners' reports on doctoral theses. *Studies in Higher Education, 22*(3), 333–347.

Katz, E. L. (1997). Key players in the dissertation process. In L. F. Goodchild, K. E. Green, E. L. Katz, & R. C. Kluever (Eds.), *Rethinking the dissertation process: Tackling personal and institutional obstacles. New Directions for Higher Education, No. 99, 25*(3), 5–16. San Francisco: Jossey-Bass.

Katz, J. (1976). Development of mind. In J. Katz & R. T. Hartnett (Eds.), *Scholars in the making: The development of graduate and professional students* (pp. 107–126). Cambridge, MA: Ballinger.

Katz, J., & Hartnett, R. T. (1976). Recommendations for training better scholars. In J. Katz & R. T. Hartnett (Eds.), *Scholars in the making: The development of graduate and professional students* (pp. 261–280). Cambridge, MA: Ballinger.

Kuhn, T. S. (1962). *The structure of scientific revolutions.* Chicago: University of Chicago Press.

Linkon, S. L. (2005, July/August). How can assessment work for us? *Academe: The Bulletin of the American Association of University Professors.* Retrieved June 2, 2006, from http://www.aaup.org/publications/Academe/2005/05ja/05jalink.htm

Lovat, T. (2002, April). *"Ways of knowing": How examiners position themselves in relation to the doctoral.* Paper presented at the American Education Research Association Conference, New Orleans, LA.

Lovitts, B. E. (2001). *Leaving the ivory tower: The causes and consequences of departure from doctoral study.* Lanham, MD: Rowman & Littlefield.

Lovitts, B. E. (2002, November). *Making the implicit explicit: A conceptual approach for assessing the outcomes of doctoral education.* Paper presented at the annual meeting of the Association for the Study of Higher Education, Sacramento, CA. Retrieved from www.carnegiefoundation.org/CID/ashe?lovitts.pdf

Lovitts, B. E. (2004). *Faculty perspectives on issues related to the transition to independent research.* Unpublished manuscript.

Lovitts, B. E. (2005). Being a good course-taker is not enough. A theoretical perspective on the transition to independent research. *Studies in Higher Education, 30*(2), 137–154.

Magner, D. K. (1989, November). Minority grad students: Path to the professoriate can be rocky. *Chronicle of Higher Education,* pp. 19, 22.

Maki, P. L. (1998, October). *Developing an initial student outcomes assessment plan.* New England Association of Schools and Colleges Commission on Institutions of Higher Education Fall Workshop, Storrs, CT.

Maki, P. L.(2004). *Assessing for learning: Building a sustainable commitment across the institution.* Sterling, VA: Stylus.

Maki, P. L., & Borkowski, N. (Eds.). (2006). *The assessment of doctoral education: Emerging criteria and new models for improving outcomes.* Sterling, VA: Stylus.

Miller, C. (2006). Case study for Making the Implicit Explicit Research Project conducted at the University of Colorado at Boulder: An administrator's experiences and perspectives. In P. L. Maki & N. Borkowski (Eds.), *The assessment of doctoral education: Emerging criteria and new models for improving outcomes* (pp. 188–195). Sterling, VA: Stylus.

Moore, R. W. (1985). *Winning the Ph.D. game.* New York: Dodd, Mead.

Moskal, B. M. (2000). Scoring rubrics: what, when and how? *Practical Assessment: Research & Evaluation, 7*(3). Retrieved August 28, 2003, from http://edresearch.org/pare/getvn.asp?v = 7&n = 3

Moskal, B. M., & Leydens, J. A. (2000). Scoring rubric development: validity and reliability. *Practical Assessment: Research & Evaluation, 7*(10). Retrieved August 28, 2003, from http://edresearch.org/pare/getvn.asp?v = 7&n = 10.

Mullins, G., & Kiley, M. (2002). "It's a PhD, not a Nobel Prize": How experienced examiners assess research theses. *Studies in Higher Education, 27*(4), 369–386.

Murphy, P. D., & Gerst, J. (1996, May). *Assessment of student learning in graduate programs.* Paper presented at the Association of Institutional Research Annual Forum, Albuquerque, NM.

National Association of Graduate-Professional Students. (2001). *The 2000 national doctoral program survey.* Retrieved from http://survey.nagps.org

National Center for Education Statistics. (n.d.). *Digest of education statistics tables and figures, 2003.* Table 216. Washington, DC: Author. Retrieved May 27, 2005, from http://nces.ed.gov/programs/digest/d03/tables/dt216.asp

National Opinion Research Center. (2004). *Doctorate recipients from United States universities: Summary report 2003*. Chicago: Author. Retrieved from http://www.norc.uchicago.edu/issues/sed-2003.pdf

Nerad, M., & Cerny, J. (1991, May). From facts to action: Expanding the educational role of the graduate division. *Communicator*.

Nerad, M., & Miller, D. S. (1997). The institution cares: Berkeley's efforts to support dissertation writing in the humanities and social sciences. In L. F. Goodchild, K. E. Green, E. L. Katz, & R. C. Kluever (Eds.), *Rethinking the dissertation process: Tackling personal and institutional obstacles. New Directions for Higher Education, No. 99, 25(3)*75–90. San Francisco: Jossey-Bass.

Nickerson, R. S. (1999). Enhancing creativity. In R. J. Sternberg (Ed.), *Handbook of creativity* (pp. 392–430). Cambridge, U.K.: Cambridge University Press.

Nyquist, J. (2002, November/December). The PhD: A tapestry of change for the 21st century. *Change, 34*(6), pp. 12–20.

Nyquist, J., & Woodford, B. (2000). *Re-envisioning the PhD: What concerns do we have?* Seattle: Center for Instructional Development and Research, University of Washington.

O'Brien, P. K. (1995). The reform of doctoral dissertations in the humanities and social sciences. *Higher Education Review, 28*(1), 3–19.

Ostriker, J. P., & Kuh, C. V. (2003). *Assessing research-doctorate programs: A methodology study*. Washington, DC: National Academies Press.

Paltridge, B. (2002). Thesis and dissertation writing: An examination of published advice and actual practice. *English for Specific Purposes, 21*, 125–143.

Perlmutter, D. D. (2006, February). Betrayed by your adviser. *Chronicle of Higher Education*. Retrieved February 20, 2006, from http://chronicle.com/jobs/news/2006/02/2006022001c/careers.html

QSR International Pty Ltd. (2002). N6 (Version 6 of NUD*IST) [computer software]. Doncaster, Victoria, Australia: Author.

Runco, M. A., & Sakamoto, S. O. (1999). Experimental studies of creativity. In R. J. Sternberg (Ed.), *Handbook of creativity* (pp. 62–92). Cambridge, U.K.: Cambridge University Press.

Sabar, N. (2002). Toward principled practice in evaluation: Learning from instructors' dilemmas in evaluating graduate students. *Studies in Educational Evaluation, 28*, 329–345.

Schmidt, J. (2000). *Disciplined minds: A critical look at salaried professionals and the soul-battering system that shapes their lives*. Lanham, MD: Rowman & Littlefield.

Simon, M., & Forgette-Giroux, R. (2001). A rubric for scoring postsecondary academic skills. *Practical Assessment: Research & Evaluation, 7*(3): Retrieved August 28, 2003, from http://edresearch.org/pare/getvn.asp?v=7&n=18

Simpkins, W. S. (1987). The way examiners assess critical thinking in educational administration theses. *Journal of Educational Administration, 25*(2), 248–268.

Southern Association of Colleges and Schools. (2001). *Principles of accreditation: Foundation for Quality Enhancement.* Decatur, GA: Author.

Sternberg, R. J. (1988). *The triarchic mind: A new theory of human intelligence.* New York: Viking.

Sternberg, R. J. (2003). The development of creativity as a decision-making process. In R. K. Sawyer, V. John-Steiner, S. Moran, R. J. Sternberg, D. H. Feldman, J. Nakamura, et al., (Eds.), *Creativity and development* (pp. 91–138). New York: Oxford University Press.

Sternberg, R. J., & Lubart, T. I. (1995). *Defying the crowd: Cultivating creativity in a culture of conformity.* New York: Free Press.

Sternberg, R. J., & Lubart, T. I. (1999). The concept of creativity: Prospects and paradigms. In R. J. Sternberg (Ed.), *Handbook of creativity* (pp. 3–15). Cambridge, U.K.: Cambridge University Press.

Stevens, D. D., & Levi, A. (2004). *Introduction to rubrics: An assessment tool to save grading time, convey effective feedback, and promote student learning.* Sterling, VA: Stylus.

Stock, W. A., & Siegfried, J. J. (2006). Time-to-degree for the economics Ph.D. class of 2001–02. *American Economic Review, 96*(2), 467–474.

Storr, R. J. (1953). *The beginnings of graduate education in America.* Chicago: University of Chicago Press.

Storr, R. J. (1973). *The beginning of the future: A historical approach to graduate education in the arts and sciences.* New York: McGraw-Hill.

Swales, J., & Najjar, H. (1987). The writing of research article introductions. *Written Communication, 4*(2), 175–191.

Syverson, P. D. (n.d.). *Graduate enrollment and degrees: 1986 to 2001.* Washington, DC: Council of Graduate Schools. Retrieved from http://www.cgsnet.org/pdf/ged2001.pdf

Tebbel, J. (1987). *Between covers: The rise and transformation of book publishing in America.* New York: Oxford University Press.

Thurgood, L., Golladay, M., & Hill, S. T. (2006). *Doctorates in the 20th century.* Arlington, VA: National Science Foundation.

Tinkler, P., & Jackson, C. (2000). Examining the doctorate: Institutional policy and the PhD examination process in Britain. *Studies in Higher Education, 25*(2), 167–180.

Veysey, L. R. (1965). *The emergence of the American university.* Chicago: University of Chicago Press.

Weisberg, R. W. (1999). Creativity and knowledge: A challenge to theories. In R. J.

Sternberg (Ed.), *Handbook of creativity* (pp. 226–250). Cambridge, U.K.: Cambridge University Press.

Whitehead, A. N. (1929). *The aims of education and other essays*. New York: MacMillan.

Wiggins. G. (1989). A true test: Toward more authentic and equitable assessment. *Phi Delta Kappan, 70*(9), 703–713.

Williams, W. M., & Yang, L. T. (1999). Organizational creativity. In R. J. Sternberg (Ed.), *Handbook of creativity* (pp. 373–391). Cambridge, U.K.: Cambridge University Press

Winter, R., Griffiths, M., & Green, K. (2000). The "academic" qualities of practice: What are the criteria for a practiced-based PhD? *Studies in Higher Education, 25*(1), 25–37.

Zuckerman, H. (1978). Theory choice and problem choice in science. In J. Gaston (Ed.), *Sociology of science: Problems, approaches, and research* (pp. 65–95). San Francisco: Jossey-Bass.

*Page numbers with *t* indicate tables.

acceptable dissertations
  in biology, 127t, 129–30
  characteristics of, 37t, 40–41
  in economics, 226–27t, 229–30
  in electrical and computer engineering, 175t,
    178–79
  in English, 309t, 311–12
  in history, 336t, 340–42
  in mathematics, 200–208, 203t
  in philosophy, 368t, 370–71
  in physics, 151t, 152–53
  in psychology, 253–54t, 255–56
  in sociology, 279–80t, 282–85
alumni surveys in assessing quality, 109–10
American Historical Association
  concern of, on focus of comprehension exam,
    65
  historical categories of, 327
American Sociological Association, sections and
    interest areas in, 271
analytical approach
  in English dissertations, 316–17, 323t
  in philosophy dissertation, 86
applied disciplines, 60–61
applied mathematics, 197
apprenticeship, psychological dissertations as out-
    growth of, 249–50
archival research, 85
assessments
  authentic, 23
  of doctoral education, xiv–xv
  formative, 22
  outcomes, 21–24, 26
  relationship between excellence and, 20–26
  summative, 22
authentic assessments, 23

biology, Ph.D. programs in, 121
biology dissertations, 121–44
  components of, 132–38
    data analysis/results, 136–37
    discussion and conclusion, 137–38, 144t
    introduction, 132–33, 139t
    literature review, 133–34, 140t
    methods, 135–36, 142t

results/data analysis, 143t
    theory, 134–35, 141t
  original contribution in, 123–24, 123t
  purpose of, 121–22, 122t, 123
  research in, 75–76
  significant contribution in, 124–25, 124t
  topic selection in, 70
  as a whole, 125–26, 127–28t, 128–32
    acceptable, 127t, 129–30
    outstanding, 126, 127t, 128–29
    unacceptable, 127t, 130–32
    very good, 127t, 129
biopsychology, 251
book-style dissertations in English, 307

career paths
  influence of dissertation on new, 92–93
  role of publication in, 91–92
coherence, 7
community purpose of history dissertations, 327
comparative dissertation in philosophy, 86
compilation-of-publishable-research-articles dis-
    sertation, 35
complex-traditional dissertation, 35
comprehensive exams, 64–66
conceptualization in history dissertations, 334
conclusion. *See also* discussion and conclusion
  in English dissertations, 319–20, 325t
  in history dissertations, 350–51, 357t
  in mathematics dissertations, 214–15, 218t
  in philosophy dissertations, 377–78, 383t
consequence, significant contribution and, 33
continental philosophy, 86
Council of Graduate Schools' Ph.D. Completion
    Project Workshop, xvi
course assignments, four-stage process for develop-
    ing rubrics for, 105
course evaluations in assessing quality, 109–10
course work, 62–64
  in mathematics dissertations, 196
creativity, concept of, 51n
critical thinking, 7
  originality as component in, 10
cultural studies dissertation, research in, 85

data, 390–91
  handling and analysis of, 391–94, 393t

data analysis/results
  in biology dissertations, 136–37
  in economics dissertations, 238, 245*t*
  in electrical and computer engineering disserta-
    tions, 186–88, 193*t*
  in physics dissertations, 160–61
  in psychology dissertations, 262–63, 269*t*
  in sociology dissertations, 290–92, 299*t*
dead-end dissertation, 74
defense of thesis in philosophy dissertations, 376–
  77, 381*t*
dependent course-work-to-candidacy stage, 62
disciplinary approaches
  comprehensive exams in, 64–66
  course work in, 62–64
  dissertation proposals and, 66–68
  dissertation research in, 74–87
  publication of dissertation in, 89–92
  research on, 60–62
  topic selection and, 68–74
  writing dissertation in, 87–89
discussion and conclusion, 6. *See also* conclusion
  in biology dissertations, 137–38, 144*t*
  in economics dissertations, 239–46*t*
  in electrical and computer engineering disserta-
    tions, 188, 194*t*
  in generic dissertations, 100*t*
  in physics dissertations, 161, 165*t*
  in psychology dissertations, 263–64, 270*t*
  quality of, in dissertation, 47–48, 58*t*
  in sociology dissertations, 292–94, 300*t*
dissertation(s). *See also* acceptable dissertations;
    outstanding dissertations; unacceptable dis-
    sertations; very good dissertations
  acceptable, 37*t*, 40–41
  book-style, 307
  characteristics of good/passing and poor/failing,
    9*t*
  compilation-of-publishable-research-articles, 35
  complex-traditional, 35
  components of, 6
  criteria for success or failure of, 7–8
  dead-end, 74
  dimensions of different components of generic,
    100*t*
  disciplinary approaches to doctoral training and
    development of, 59–96
  essay-style, 240*n*
  faculty's standards for judging, 8–10
  focus groups on judging quality of, 12–16
  hidden criteria for passing, 117
  importance of characteristics, 5
  influence of, on new Ph.D.'s career path, 92–93
  matrix of components of, 13*t*
  nature of original contribution as purpose of,
    31–33, 31*t*
  outstanding, 35, 36*t*, 38–39
  passage of poor-quality, 4

proposal for, 66–68
provision of feedback on, 24–25
publication of, 26*n*, 89–92
purposes of, 4–5, 29–31, 29*t*
  establishing performance expectations for, 114
  original contribution in, 31–33, 31*t*
  significant contribution in, 33–34, 34*t*
quality of, 34–35, 36–38*t*, 38–42
quality of components of, 43–48, 53–68
  discussion and conclusion, 47–48, 58*t*
  introduction, 43–44, 53*t*
  literature review, 44–45, 54*t*
  methods/approach, 45–46, 56*t*
  results/data analysis, 46–47, 57*t*
  theory, 45, 55*t*
quality of foreign in, 6–7
reflections of, 3
research on standards and criteria for judging,
  4–10
as rite of passage, 30
role of, in doctoral education, xiv
significant contribution as purpose of, 33–34,
  34*t*
simple-traditional, 35
standards for evaluating, 3
stipulations in passing, 3–4
successful completion of, 3
technical and indeterminate qualities in evaluating, 7–8
topic-based, 35
as true test of doctoral education, 23
types of, 35
unacceptable, 37–38*t*, 41–42
universal qualities of, 27–58
very good, 36–37*t*, 39–40
view of, as extended argument, 114
writing, 87–89
writing quality in, 48–49
dissertation abstracts, review of, 5
dissertation committee
  recommendations of, 3–4
  sitting on, that failed a dissertation, 41–42
dissertation research, 74–87
  in biology, 75–76
  in cultural studies, 85
  in economics, 80–81
  in engineering, 78
  in English, 83–84
  in history, 84–86
  in humanities, 82–87
  in mathematics, 79–80
  in philosophy, 86–87
  in physics, 76–77
  in psychology, 81–82
  in sciences, 75–80
  in social sciences, 80–82
  in sociology, 82
dissertation topic

areas of specialization in selection of, 63
  ranking of importance, 5–6
doctoral education
  assessment of, 20
  assessments of, xiv–xv
  disciplinary approaches to, and development of
    dissertation, 59–96
  dissertation as true test of, 23
  dissertation in, xiv
  excellence in, 20–21
  role of dissertation in, xiv

econometrics, 235–36, 237
economics, course requirements of programs in, 63
economics dissertations, 219–46
  components of, 231–32
    data analysis/results, 238, 245t
    discussion and conclusion in, 239–46t
    introduction, 232–33, 241t
    literature review, 234–35, 242t
    methods, 237–38, 244t
    theory, 235–36, 243t
  dissertation proposals in, 67
  dissertation research in, 80–81
  purpose of, 219–21, 220t
    original contribution, 221–22, 221t
    significant contribution, 222–25, 223t
  topic choice in, 71
  as a whole, 225
    acceptable, 226–27t, 229–30
    outstanding, 225, 226t, 227–28
    unacceptable, 227t, 231
    very good, 226t, 228–29
economics theory, 235–36
education
  as function of psychological dissertations, 247
  national discussion on reform, xiii–xiv
  success in, xiii
elective courses, 62–63
electrical and computer engineering dissertations,
    167–94
  components of, 180–81
    data analysis/results, 186–88, 193t
    discussion and conclusion, 188, 194t
    introduction, 181–82, 190t
    literature review, 182–83, 191t
    methods, 185–86, 192t
    theory, 184–85, 192t
  purpose of, 168–69, 168t
    original contribution, 169–72, 170t
    significant contribution in, 172–74, 172t
  as a whole, 174
    acceptable, 178–79
    outstanding, 174, 175t, 176–77
    unacceptable, 179–80
    very good, 175t, 177–78
engineering. *See also* electrical and computer engi-
    neering dissertations
  dissertation proposals in, 67

dissertation research in, 78
  topic selection for dissertation in, 69–70
English
  contrasting, with sciences, 304
  course requirements of, 63–64
  number of Ph.D. programs in, 301
English dissertations, 301–25
  book-style, 307
  components of, 314–15
    analysis of texts, 318–19, 324t
    approach to analysis, 316–17, 323t
    conclusion, 319–20, 325t
    introduction, 315, 321t
    justification of chosen texts, 317–18, 324t
    review of sources, 315–16, 322t
  proposal for, 68
  purpose of, 301–3, 302t
    original contribution, 303–6, 304t
    significant contribution, 306–7, 306t
  research in, 83–84
  topic selection for, 72–73
  as a whole, 307
    acceptable, 309t, 311–12
    outstanding, 307, 308t, 309–10
    unacceptable, 309t, 312–14
    very good, 308–9t, 310–11
essay-style dissertations
  in economics, 240n
  in psychology, 251
ethics, evaluation, 24–25
ethnic minorities, topic selection for, 74
evaluation ethics, 24–25
evaluative function of psychological dissertations,
    247
excellence
  achieving, 19–26
  relationship between assessment and, 20–26
executive summary, function of introduction as,
    43
exit interviews in assessing quality, 109–10
exposition/analysis in history dissertations, 349–
    50, 356t
external examiners' reports, 7

faculty, standards for judging dissertations, 8–10
feedback, dissertation provision of, on, 24–25
fill-the-gap dissertation, 73
focus groups
  background information on faculty who partici-
    pated in, by discipline, 15t
  on judging dissertation quality, 12–16
  transcripts of discussions, 14, 16
formative assessment, 22
future directions in mathematics dissertations,
    214–15, 218t

gap-based dissertations in history dissertations, 330
Grade Point Averages (GPAs) scores, 21
graduate education, stages of, 62

graduate faculty, views of, on role and function of dissertation, 4–5
Graduate Record Examination (GRE) scores, 21, 23
graduate students
  decline in reading and writing skills of, 48–49
  number of, 27–28
group discussions, tape-recording, 111*n*
guess my rule, xiii

hard disciplines, 60, 61
  research in, 61
  topic selection for dissertation in, 69
hidden criteria for passing dissertations, 117
historical dissertation in philosophy, 86
historiographic review, 44
  in history dissertations, 346–47, 354*t*
history
  comprehensive exam in, 65
  number of Ph.D. programs in, 327
history dissertations, 327–57
  components of, 344–45
    conclusion, 350–51, 357*t*
    exposition/analysis, 349–50, 356*t*
    historiographic review, 346–47, 354*t*
    introduction, 345–46, 353*t*
    sources/methods, 347–49, 355*t*
  proposal of, 68
  purpose of, 327–29, 328*t*
    original contribution, 329–31, 329*t*
    significant contribution, 331–34, 332*t*
  research in, 84–86
  topic selection for, 73
  as a whole, 334
    acceptable, 336*t*, 340–42
    outstanding, 334, 335*t*, 337–38
    unacceptable, 336–37*t*, 342–44
    very good, 335–36*t*, 339–40
humanities, 387
  terms of appraisal in, 62
humanities dissertations, 87–89
  influence of, on career path in, 92–93
  proposal in, 68
  publication of, 91–92
  research in, 82–87

imaginative approach, 11
independence, 5, 10–11, 19
independent research
  exhibition of, in dissertation, 50–51*n*
  transition to, 75
indeterminate qualities, 7–8
indirect measures of student satisfaction in assessing quality, 109–10
intellectual grasp, 7
intellectual rigor, 19
interpretation, emphasis of, in history dissertations, 330
introduction

in biology dissertations, 132–33, 139*t*
in economics dissertations, 232–33, 241*t*
in electrical and computer engineering dissertations, 181–82, 190*t*
in English dissertations, 315, 321*t*
in generic dissertations, 100*t*
in history dissertations, 345–46, 353*t*
in mathematics dissertations, 210–11, 216*t*
in philosophy dissertations, 374–75, 379*t*
in physics dissertations, 155–56, 162*t*
in psychology dissertations, 258–59, 265*t*
quality of, in dissertation, 43–44, 53*t*
sample rubrics for, 101–2*t*
in sociology dissertations, 287–88, 295*t*

justification of chosen texts in English dissertations, 317–18, 324*t*

knowledge
  original contribution to, 10–12
  significant contribution to, 10–12
knowledge growth
  in hard disciplines, 61
  in soft disciplines, 61
knowledge of literature, demonstration of, in philosophy dissertations, 375–76, 381*t*

learning outcomes, development of informed measures of, 3
length of documents, 5
literature, discussion of, in mathematics dissertations, 211–12, 217*t*
literature review, 6
  in biology dissertations, 133–34, 140*t*
  in economics dissertations, 234–35, 242*t*
  in electrical and computer engineering dissertations, 182–83, 191*t*
  in generic dissertations, 100*t*
  objectives of, 51–52*n*
  in philosophy dissertations, 375–76, 381*t*
  in physics dissertations, 156–57, 163*t*
  in psychology dissertations, 259–60, 266*t*
  quality of, in dissertations, 44–45, 54*t*
  rubrics on, 6
  in sociology dissertations, 288–89, 296*t*
literature review scoring rubric, 103–4*t*

macroeconomic theory, 237
Making the Implicit Explicit (MIE) study, xv
  origins of, xv–xvii
  scale descriptions in, 98–99
mathematical economics, 237
mathematics
  applied, 197
  classical model of graduate education in, 79
  comprehension exam in, 65
  course requirements of doctoral programs in, 63
  pure, 197
mathematics dissertations, 195–218

components of, 209–10
    approach to problem (techniques), 212–13,
        218*t*
    conclusions/future directions, 214–15, 218*t*
    discussion of literature, 211–12, 217*t*
    introduction/problem statement, 210–11, 216*t*
    proof of results, 213–14, 218*t*
    statement of results/theorems, 212, 217*t*
    purpose of, 195–98, 196*t*
        original contribution, 198–200, 198*t*
        significant contribution, 200–202, 201*t*
    research in, 79–80
    topic selection in, 70–71
    as a whole, 202
        acceptable, 203*t*, 206–8
        outstanding, 202, 203–4*t*, 204–5
        unacceptable, 204*t*, 208–9
        very good, 203*t*, 206
metarubric in assessing quality of rubrics, 106,
    107–8*t*
methodological expertise, 19
methods, 6
    in biology dissertations, 135–36, 142*t*
    in economics dissertations, 237–38, 244*t*
    in electrical and computer engineering disserta-
        tions, 185–86, 192*t*
    in generic dissertation, 100*t*
    in physics dissertations, 159–60, 164*t*
    in psychology dissertations, 261–62, 268*t*
    quality of, in dissertation, 56*t*
    quality of, in dissertations, 45–46, 56*t*
    in sociology dissertations, 290, 298*t*
Michigan State University, graduate handbooks
    project at, 26*n*
microeconomic theory, 237
Mill, John Stuart, 362–63
Modern Language Association (MLA), 301
monograph, publishing, as condition of Tenure of
    Office Act (1867), 320*n*

National Research Council (NRC), xiv
New England Education Association of Schools
    and Colleges' Commission on Institutions of
    Higher Education, Student Outcomes As-
    sessment Plan, 21
Nietzsche, 362
normal science, 114

original contribution, 3, 10–12
    in biological dissertations, 123–24, 123*t*
    in economics dissertations, 221–22, 221*t*
    in electrical and computer engineering disserta-
        tions, 169–72, 170*t*
    in English dissertations, 303–6, 304*t*
    in history dissertations, 329–31, 329*t*
    in mathematics dissertations, 198–200, 198*t*
    nature of, as purpose of dissertation, 31–33, 31*t*
    in philosophy dissertations, 361–64, 362*t*
    in physics dissertations, 147

    in psychology dissertations, 249–50, 249*t*
    as purpose of dissertation, 30
    in sociology dissertations, 273–75, 274*t*
originality, 5, 17*n*, 19
    as component of critical thinking, 10
    concept of, 51*n*
    indeterminate qualities of, 11
    levels or degrees of, 32–33
    relationship between significance and, 34
outcomes assessment, 21–22, 26
    benefits of, 23–24
outstanding dissertations, 35, 36*t*, 38–39
    in biology, 126, 127*t*, 128–29
    characteristics of, 35, 36*t*, 38–39
    in economics, 225, 226*t*, 227–28
    in electrical and computer engineering, 174,
        175*t*, 176–77
    in English, 307, 308*t*, 309–10
    in history, 334, 335*t*, 337–38
    in mathematics, 202, 203–4*t*, 204–5
    in philosophy, 366, 367*t*, 369
    in physics, 150, 151*t*, 152
    in psychology, 252, 253*t*
    in sociology, 278, 279*t*, 280–82

performance expectations, xiii
    purpose of establishing, for dissertations, 114
    recommendations for developing, 115–16
personal-professional purpose of history disserta-
    tions, 327
Ph.D.s, primary markets for new, 92
philosophy dissertations, 359–84
    analytical, 86
    comparative*n*, 86
    components of, 374
        conclusion, 377–78, 383*t*
        demonstration of knowledge of literature,
            375–76, 381*t*
        development/defense of thesis, 376–77, 381*t*
        introduction/statement and clarification of
            problem, 374–75, 379*t*
        recognition and response to possible objec-
            tions, 377, 382*t*
    historical, 86
    proposal in, 68
    purpose of, 359–61, 360*t*
        original contribution, 361–64, 362*t*
    research in, 86–87
    significant contribution, 364–65, 364*t*
    as a whole, 366
        acceptable, 368*t*, 370–71
        outstanding, 366, 367*t*, 369
        unacceptable, 368*t*, 372–74
        very good, 367–68*t*, 369
physics dissertations
    components of, 154–55
        data analysis/results for, 160–61
        discussion and conclusion of, 161, 165*t*
        introduction to, 155–56, 162*t*

literature review to, 156–57, 163*t*
    methods for, 159–60, 164*t*
    results/data analysis for, 165*t*
    theory for, 157–58, 163*t*
original contribution in, 147–48, 147*t*
research in, 76–77
significant contribution in, 148–50, 148*t*
topic selection for, 69–70
as a whole, 150
    acceptable, 151*t*, 152–53
    outstanding, 150, 151*t*.152
    unacceptable, 153–54
    very good, 151*t*, 152
writing, 88
problem statement
    in mathematics dissertations, 210–13, 216*t*, 218*t*
    in philosophy dissertations, 374–75, 379*t*
process, dissertation as, 29–30
product, dissertation as, 30
proof of results in mathematics dissertations, 213–14, 218*t*
*Psychological Bulletin,* reviews in, 259–60
psychology dissertations, 247–70
    components of, 258
        data analysis/results, 262–63, 269*t*
        discussion and conclusion, 263–64, 270*t*
        introduction, 258–59, 265*t*
        literature review, 259–60, 266*t*
        methods, 261–62, 268*t*
        theory, 260–61, 267*t*
    influence of, on career path, 92
    proposal in, 67
    purpose of, 247–49, 248*t*
        original contribution, 249–50, 249*t*
        significant contribution, 250–51, 250*t*
    research in, 81–82
    topic selection for, 71–72
    as a whole, 251–52
        acceptable, 253–54*t*, 255–56
        outstanding, 252, 253*t*
        unacceptable, 254*t*, 256–58
        very good, 252, 253*t*, 254–55
psychology doctoral programs, course-work phase of, 63
publication of dissertation, 19, 89–92
publishability, 5
pure discipline, 60, 61
pure mathematicians, 197

quality, indicators in assessing, 5

racial minorities, topic selection for, 74
recognition and response to possible objections in philosophy dissertations, 377, 382*t*
regional accrediting agencies, xiv
research
    archival, 85
    dissertation, 74–87
    students' interest in and enthusiasm for, 73–74

research-doctoral programs, National Research Council (NRC) survey of, xv
results/data analysis, 6
    in biology dissertations, 143*t*
    in electrical and computer engineering dissertations, 193*t*
    in generic dissertation, 100*t*
    in physics dissertations, 165*t*
    quality of, in dissertations, 46–47, 57*t*
review of sources in English dissertations, 315–16, 322*t*
*The Role and Nature of the Doctoral Dissertation: A Policy Statement,* 389
rubrics, 97–111
    basic components of, 98–99, 98*t*
    defined, 97–99
    developing, 99, 105–6
    dimensions of, 99
    early provision of, 108–9
    four-stage process for developing for course assignments, 105
    on literature reviews, 6
    literature review scoring, 103–4*t*
    metarubrics in assessing quality of, 106, 107–8*t*
    as not appropriate for summative assessment, 114–15
    as not appropriate in rating dissertations, 113–14
    programs and, 109–11
    sample for introduction to dissertation, 101–2*t*
    scale of, 98
    students and, 106, 108–9
rural specialties, 62

sample, 390–91
scale of rubric, 98
sciences, 387
    comprehensive exam in, 65
    contrasting English with, 304
    dissertation proposals in, 67
    dissertation research in, 75–80
    influence of dissertation on career path in, 92
    publication of dissertation in, 89–90
    writing dissertation in, 87–88
scissors-and-paste history, 343
significance, 5, 17*n*
    relationship between originality and, 34
significant contribution, 3, 51*n*
    in biological dissertations, 124–25, 124*t*
    in economics dissertations, 222–25, 223*t*
    in electrical and computer engineering dissertations, 172–74, 172*t*
    in English dissertations, 306–7, 306*t*
    in history dissertations, 331–34, 332*t*
    to knowledge, 10–12
    in mathematics dissertations, 200–202, 201*t*
    in philosophy dissertations, 364–65, 364*t*
    in physics dissertations, 148–50, 149*t*
    in psychology dissertations, 250–51, 250*t*

as purpose of dissertation, 30, 33–34, 34*t*
in sociology dissertations, 275–77, 275*t*
simple-traditional dissertation, 35
social sciences, 387
  dissertation proposals in, 67
  dissertation research in, 80–82
  publication of dissertation in, 90–91
  terms of appraisal in, 61–62
societal function of psychological dissertations, 247
sociology dissertations, 271–300
  components of, 286–87
    data analysis/results, 290–92, 299*t*
    discussion and conclusion, 292–94, 300*t*
    introduction, 287–88, 295*t*
    literature review, 288–89, 296*t*
    methods, 290, 298*t*
    theory, 289, 297*t*
  purpose of, 271–73, 272*t*
    original contribution, 273–75, 274*t*
    significant contribution, 275–77, 275*t*
  research in, 82
  topic selection for, 72
  as a whole, 277–78
    acceptable, 279–80*t*, 282–85
    outstanding, 278, 279*t*, 280–82
    unacceptable, 280*t*, 285–86
    very good, 279*t*, 282
sociology doctoral programs, course-work phase of, 63
soft disciplines, 60, 61
sources/methods in history dissertations, 347–49, 355*t*
Spinoza, 362
statement of results/theorems in mathematics dissertations, 212, 217*t*
students, rubrics and, 106, 108–9
study, methodology of, 387–90
substantial time commitment, 5
substantive contribution, 19
summative assessment, 22
  rubrics as not appropriate for, 114–15

tape-recording, group discussions, 111*n*
task description in rubrics, 98
teaching assistantship as source of financial support, 82–83
technical qualities, 7
tenure, publishing monograph as condition of, 320*n*
text analysis in English dissertations, 318–19, 324*t*
textual clarity, 19
theory, 6
  in biology dissertations, 134–35, 141*t*
  in economics dissertations, 235–36, 243*t*

in electrical and computer engineering dissertations, 184–85, 192*t*
in generic dissertation, 100*t*
in physics dissertations, 157–58, 163*t*
in psychology dissertations, 260–61, 267*t*
quality of, in dissertations, 45, 55*t*
in sociology dissertations, 289, 297*t*
theory-driven dissertations in biology, 134
thesis development in philosophy dissertations, 376–77, 381*t*
timescale in assessment of significance, 149
tome-style dissertations in psychology, 252
topic-based dissertations, 35
topic selection for dissertations, 68–74
transcripts of focus discussions, 14, 16
typographical errors, correcting, 4

unacceptable dissertations
  in biology, 127*t*, 130–32
  characteristics of, 37–38*t*, 41–42
  in economics, 227*t*, 231
  in electrical and computer engineering, 175–76*t*, 179–80
  in English, 309*t*, 312–14
  in history, 336–37*t*, 342–44
  in mathematics, 204*t*, 208–9
  in philosophy, 368*t*, 372–74
  in physics, 153–54
  in psychology, 254*t*, 256–58
  in sociology, 280*t*, 285–86
urban/rural dimension, 62
urban specialties, 62

very good dissertations
  in biology, 127*t*, 129
  characteristics of, 36–37*t*, 39–40
  in economics, 226*t*, 228–29
  in electrical and computer engineering, 174, 175*t*, 176–77
  in English, 308–9*t*, 310–11
  in history, 335–36*t*, 339–40
  in mathematics, 203*t*, 206
  in philosophy, 367–68*t*, 369
  in physics, 151*t*, 152
  in psychology, 252, 253*t*, 254–55
  in sociology, 279*t*, 282
voice-over, 343

women, topic selection for, 74
wow factor in introductions, 44
writing
  correcting typographical errors and, 4
  of dissertation, 87–89
  quality of, in dissertations, 48–49, 337

# Resources for students that apply the insights of *Making the Implicit Explicit* to improving the quality of their dissertations

**Developing Quality Dissertations in the Sciences**
A Graduate Student's Guide
978-1-57922-259-8

**Developing Quality Dissertations in the Humanities**
A Graduate Student's Guide
978-1-57922-260-4

**Developing Quality Dissertations in the Social Sciences**
A Graduate Student's Guide
978-1-57922-261-1

These short booklets are designed to be given to graduate students as they begin their studies.

They explain the purposes of the dissertation and the criteria by which it will be assessed. They help students understand the context of their course work, the need to take an active role in shaping their studies, and the importance of thinking ahead about the components of the dissertation and the quality of scholarship they will need to demonstrate.

These booklets are intended to support the dissertation research and writing process by providing faculty and advisors with guidelines for setting clear expectations for student performance, and with a model for helping students produce the desired quality of work.

They encourage dialog between faculty and students about the quality of the components of their dissertation project. They include rubrics that students can use to self-assess their work and that can aid faculty in providing focused feedback.

Setting explicit targets and benchmarks of excellence of the sort advocated in these booklets will enable departments and universities to respond to demands for accountability with clear criteria for, and evidence of, success; and will raise the overall quality of student performance.

Each booklet, $7.95

**Quantity discounts available. Call Stylus toll free, 1-800-232-0223 or email StylusMail@PressWarehouse.com.**